Samuel Johnson
as Book Reviewer

Samuel Johnson as Book Reviewer

A Duty to Examine the Labors of the Learned

Brian Hanley

DELAWARE

Newark: University of Delaware Press
London: Associated University Presses

Associated University Presses
440 Forsgate Drive
Cranbury, NJ 08512

Associated University Presses
16 Barter Street
London WC1A 2AH, England

Associated University Presses
P.O. Box 338, Port Credit
Mississauga, Ontario
Canada L5G 4L8

The paper used in this publication meets the requirements of the American National Standard for Permanence of Paper for Printed Library Materials Z39.48-1984.

Library of Congress Cataloging-in-Publication Data

Hanley, Brian J., 1961–
    Samuel Johnson as book reviewer : a duty to examine the labors of the learned / Brian J. Hanley.
        p.   cm.
    Includes bibliographical references (p.   ) and index.
    ISBN 0-87413-736-5 (alk. paper)
    1. Samuel Johnson, 1709 1784   Knowledge   Literature. 2. Johnson, Samuel, 1709–1784—Knowledge and learning. 3. Book reviewing—Great Britain—History—18th century. 4. Criticism—Great Britain—History—18th century. 5. Great Britain—Intellectual life—18th century. I. Title.

PR3537.L5 H36 2001
828'.609—dc21

                                                                        00-031654

PRINTED IN THE UNITED STATES OF AMERICA

*No one has been more supportive of my work on Johnson
than my wife, Terry.
It is with great pleasure
that I dedicate this work to her,
and to my son, Bryce*

Contents

Foreword

With Samuel Johnson's reputation secure for his writings on morality, philology, criticism, and biography, particularly the *Rambler*, *A Dictionary of the English Language*, *Rasselas*, and the *Lives of the Poets*, it has been tempting for students of Johnson to focus on these works and largely ignore the fact that he also demands attention as a first-rate journalist. Johnson is, in fact, the first professional author of importance in English. Perhaps these less known works have been ignored because consciously or subconsciously, in the minds of some students of Johnson, there is a feeling of embarrassment that one of the greatest writers in English literature had to write to eat and thereby became tainted by the world of trade. That a writer was degraded by writing for money was a truism long before Johnson became an author, and in the middle years of the eighteenth century writing for hire, becoming a hackney or hack writer, was inextricably associated with Grub Street and, thanks to Pope's *Dunciad*, with the world of the dunces. But, as Johnson realized, it was not merely writing for hire that made one a hack or a dunce, but a lack of integrity and a failure of moral sense. Just how a professional writer maintains a sense of integrity is neatly summed up by an exchange between Johnson and Boswell on 14 September 1777. Boswell reports that Johnson "was somewhat disappointed in finding that the edition of *The English Poets*, for which he was to write Prefaces and Lives, was not an undertaking directed by him: but that he was to furnish a Preface and Life to any poet the booksellers pleased. I asked him if he would do this for any dunce's works, if they should ask him." Johnson replied, "Yes, sir, and say he was a dunce."

As early as January 1739, in an anonymous letter to the *Gentleman's Magazine,* Johnson observes: "The character of an author must be allowed to imply in itself something amiable and great; it conveys at once the idea of ability and good-nature, of knowledge, and a disposition to communicate it. To instruct ignorance, reclaim error, and reform vice, are designs highly worthy of applause and imitation." He adds that it is important for an author to engage in "discovering the truth, and recommending it, by the ornaments of eloquence, to the favour of mankind." Allegiance to this personal

9

credo, expressed by Johnson throughout his career, is pertinent to the book reviews he contributed to the *Literary Magazine*, the *Gentleman's Magazine*, and the *Critical Review*, for even though the anonymous reviews belonged to the world of the journalist, published in what Johnson described as "the *Ephemerae* of learning," he managed to "carefully enquire after truth, and diligently impart it."

While these reviews merit careful study, they have received little attention. In 1979 Donald D. Eddy published his groundbreaking study, *Samuel Johnson: Book Reviewer in the Literary Magazine*. Although there continues to be debate about the attribution of one review or another to Johnson, Eddy has in large measure determined the canon of the reviews— no small contribution to Johnson studies, given the confusion of the canon that then existed because of the numerous attributions of reviews to Johnson that were actually written by his imitator John Hawkesworth. Eddy comments on the characteristics of Johnson's reviews, but the major thrust of his work is bibliographical, providing a descriptive bibliography that identifies and describes the editions of the works Johnson reviewed. Brian J. Hanley's study, although in a sense the successor to Eddy's work, is an original work of scholarship, answering many questions about the reviews. What has seemed, for example, even to the most ardent Johnsonian, a random selection of books to be reviewed is here explained and justified. Just where the reviews fit into the literary, social, and economic context of the middle third of the eighteenth century is also explained. The *Literary Magazine*, for which Johnson wrote forty reviews, is usefully placed in the context of its two most important rivals, the *Monthly Review* and the *Critical Review*. In fact, several of the reviews for the *Literary Magazine*, Hanley argues, were written in response to those in the two rival periodicals, although this does not appear ever to be the sole criterion for Johnson in selecting a book for review. As a professional author Johnson was usually shrewd in identifying his potential readership. Nevertheless, even at the risk of failing to compete successfully in the marketplace, Johnson never wavered from the standard he set for himself as a reviewer. This examination of all of Johnson's reviews enables us to better understand his techniques as a reviewer, which in turn illuminates why he reviewed the books that he did. For more than forty years, Donald Greene argued that Johnson could only be understood to his fullest by reading *all* of his writings. The truth of this proposition is demonstrated by this study, which provides numerous valuable insights into Johnson's thought and his life as a professional author. Book reviewing, however, is only a small portion of Johnson's output as a professional author; much remains to be examined. Hanley provides a model, setting a high standard for all such future studies.

O M Brack Jr.

Acknowledgments

I could not have completed this project without the help of several people. I have benefited immensely from the discerning and genial advice of Professor O M Brack Jr. I am grateful also to the late Dr. David Fleeman, the late Professor Robert L. Haig, and Professor Albrecht B. Strauss, the three of whom, by counsel and by example, encouraged my interest in Johnson. A word of thanks is due to Mr. Mike Jackson, Arizona State University, for his insights on the eighteenth-century book trade. I would like to thank also the staff of the United States Air Force Academy Cadet Library, in particular Noel Defosset and Kelly Merriam, for their courteousness and efficiency. Finally, I am very much indebted to Brigadier General Jack M. Shuttleworth, Colonel Thomas G. Bowie Jr., Professor Donald Anderson, Lieutenant Colonel James H. Meredith, and other colleagues, past and present, in the Department of English, United States Air Force Academy, who collectively sustain an intellectually nurturing environment that deserves to be recorded.

Introduction

The rapid development of book reviewing during the eighteenth century—the "revolution that was to change the literary marketplace forever"—has attracted a great deal of scholarly attention over the past decade, which makes the neglect of the forty-seven reviews that Samuel Johnson contributed to the *Gentleman's Magazine* (three reviews), the *Literary Magazine* (forty reviews), and the *Critical Review* (four reviews) all the more difficult to understand.[1] The present volume addresses what is in fact a significant gap in Johnsonian studies by providing a comprehensive critical analysis of Johnson's sporadic but prolific career as a book reviewer.[2] Though the emphasis in this volume is on Johnson's reviewing technique and the theory behind it, considerable attention is also given to Johnson's practices as they relate to competing reviews published in other journals. It is worth noting, for instance, that roughly half of Johnson's *Literary Magazine* reviews are of titles reviewed previously in the *Monthly Review* and the *Critical Review*, thus suggesting that Johnson routinely consulted these journals before deciding on what to review. Significantly, many of Johnson's reviews were written as allusive responses to reviews published earlier in the *Monthly* or the *Critical*. As we shall see, Johnson's reviews—far from being on the whole nothing more than indifferent hackwork, as some scholars have contended—often surpass those published elsewhere in terms of evenhandedness and intellectual rigor.[3]

It must be said straightaway that in one sense Samuel Johnson necessarily occupies a modest place overall amongst eighteenth-century reviewers if only because unlike, say, Tobias Smollett, Johnson allocated little of his professional life to reviewing, and his occasional activity as a reviewer could not possibly have had the impact on contemporary letters that the widely read and long-lived *Monthly* and *Critical* did. Johnson reviewed regularly for a mere fourteen months in a literary career that began in 1732 and ended only a few days before his death in December 1784, and he did so for a relatively obscure and short-lived periodical, the *Literary Magazine*.[4] Nevertheless, Johnson's career as a reviewer yielded a fairly substantial volume of literary criticism. Indeed, the forty reviews Johnson wrote

13

in the *Literary Magazine*, along with the seven others he contributed to the *Gentleman's* and the *Critical*, total some 180,000 words. By comparison, Johnson's *Idler* and *Adventurer* essays together total some 130,000 words, his *Rambler* essays some 260,000 words.

Johnson's reviews reward study for a number of reasons. To begin with, the reviews embody Johnson's broader critical outlook, in particular his well-known conviction that all literary activity should promote individual or social welfare and his understanding of the worthy but subordinate role of the critic in the world of professional letters. In his reviews, Johnson almost always emphasizes the beneficent intentions of the authors under consideration while assigning relatively less weight to the literary or scientific value of their work. What Johnson's reviews offer us, essentially, are evaluations of writers who exemplify the altruistic habits of mind that Johnson celebrates in the *Rambler* papers on authorship and elsewhere. Johnson's declaration in *Rambler* 3 that the "task of an author is, either to teach what is not known, or to recommend known truths, by his manner of adorning them," neatly describes the quality that Johnson evidently looked for as he considered which authors to review. Indeed, the litmus test of Johnson's decision whether to review a given title seems to be the author's commitment to the rule spelled out in the *Preface to Shakespeare:* "[I]t is always a writer's duty to make the world better."[5] The authors Johnson reviews achieve this objective with varying degrees of success; what seems to catch Johnson's eye is clear evidence of their beneficent impulse.

As for the critic's place, Johnson steadfastly refuses to tell the reading public what to think of a given title, because he realizes that the critical intelligence is vulnerable to various prejudices, particularly when the subject is the work of a contemporary author.[6] Johnson sets before the reading public a judicious introduction to meritorious titles, thus allowing prospective book buyers to make up their own minds as to whether a given title is worth buying. There are a handful of exceptions to Johnson's refusal to make dogmatic pronouncements. As we shall see, however, in these few instances Johnson seems to have had very good reasons for going beyond what is in fact his telltale restraint as a reviewer. Put another way, Johnson's relation to the authors under review is best understood as that of defense attorney and client. Johnson often dwells upon a favorable feature of a given work that otherwise might go unnoticed or misunderstood, or he will point out extenuating circumstances when discussing an author's shortcomings. Whatever the specifics, as a rule Johnson pleads a case for the authors he has chosen to review and then turns the matter over to the jury— readers, that is—for the final decision.

Johnson's reviews also command attention because, contrary to what some scholars have contended, they reflect his keen concern with the state of contemporary letters.[7] Johnson's reputation today rests chiefly on literary projects that transcend their historical moment—the *Dictionary*, the *Lives of the Poets*, the edition of *Shakespeare Plays*. Even so, as a reviewer Johnson can be said to contribute his fair share to reforming what he and many of his contemporaries viewed as an increasingly disordered literary marketplace by reviewing only authors who have something worthwhile to say—leaving the incorrigibly foolish and the dull to the obscurity they deserve. Finally, Johnson's reviews illustrate the vastness of his learning in ways that no other work from his pen does apart from the *Dictionary*. Johnson's book reviews offer contemporary readers discerning and in many instances quite lengthy surveys of titles bearing on such subjects as electrical engineering, the conversion of salt water into fresh, experiments in biology, pathology, military science, beekeeping, moral philosophy, zoology, history, the translation of ancient texts, poetry, drama, journalism, controversial political issues, and so on. Indeed, thanks in large measure to Johnson's resourcefulness in selecting and presenting material extracted from the volumes under review, many of Johnson's reviews stand alone as moral, political, philosophical, scientific, or literary essays in their own right. Thus, we can read Johnson's reviews not only as specific expressions of his general critical views and his encyclopedic interests but also as thoughtful studies of the intellectual landscape of mid-eighteenth-century England.

Chapter 1 provides context for the discussion of Johnson's reviews by surveying the contemporaneous state of the literary marketplace and Johnson's understanding of the chief literary issues of the day as expressed in his *Rambler*, *Adventurer*, and *Idler* essays. The second, third, and fourth chapters discuss Johnson's work in the *Literary Magazine* (1756–57), where Johnson reviewed most intensely and most frequently. Chapter 2 covers Johnson's reviews of historical, literary, and philosophical titles (a total of twelve reviews are discussed here). Chapter 3 surveys Johnson's work as a reviewer of journalistic publications and books dealing with current affairs (seventeen titles). Chapter 4 discusses Johnson's reviews of books in the physical, practical, and natural sciences (eleven titles). Chapter 5, entitled "Samuel Johnson: Occasional Reviewer in the *Gentleman's Magazine* and the *Critical Review*," examines the seven reviews Johnson contributed to these two journals. The chapter also includes a discussion of the authenticity issues surrounding the many reviews attributed to Johnson but not widely accepted as his that appeared in the *Gentleman's Magazine*. Chapter 6, entitled "Book Reviewing in the Moral Essays," examines Johnson's allusive commentary on recently published works in nine *Rambler*, *Adventurer*, and *Idler* essays. The appendix evaluates the authenticity of seven *Literary Magazine* reviews attributed to Johnson by Donald Greene. Overall, this volume demonstrates that Johnson's reviews occupy an important place in Johnson's canon of literary criticism and should be of special interest to students of Johnson's interaction with the late Augustan literary world.

Samuel Johnson
as Book Reviewer

1

Samuel Johnson and the Mid-Eighteenth-Century Literary World

As CRITICAL ESSAYS ON CONTEMPORARY WORKS, JOHNSON'S REVIEWS CAN BE FULLY appreciated only when they are placed in the context of Johnson's broader understanding of the mid-eighteenth-century literary marketplace. It is thus necessary briefly to survey the state of professional letters in Johnson's day and Johnson's attitude to the contemporary literary world as expressed in the *Rambler* (1750–52), *Adventurer* (1753–54), and *Idler* (1758–60) papers. Several prominent controversies were developing in 1733, when the twenty-four-year-old Johnson earned his first paycheck as a writer,[1] and had engulfed professional letters by 1756, when Johnson took over the editorship of the *Literary Magazine*, the journal that published all but seven of his four-dozen book reviews.

As several scholars have pointed out, the literary marketplace during the middle-third of the eighteenth century was widely perceived by contemporaries to be disordered, or at least in a state of turbulent transition.[2] One prominent complaint of the period centered on the belief that an increasing number of inept authors, underwritten by venal booksellers and trafficking in depraved and foolish material, were infecting public taste, debasing the language, and crowding out meritorious authors.[3] The operative idea here is "perceived," because there had always been an element in the book trade eager to produce sordid or slapdash material for a public willing to pay for it. Indeed, the book trade had been retailing frivolity, inanity, and low voluptuousness right up until the lapse of the Licensing Act in 1694, as a perusal of Robert Clavell's *A Catalogue of Books Printed in England Since the Dreadful Fire of London in 1666 to the End of Michaelmas Term, 1695* bears out.[4] Even so, publications bemoaning the literary marketplace's appetite for coarseness and vacuity continue to grow in number and intensity during the first half of the eighteenth century.

Criticism of the unregulated book trade's chaotic character is given particularly forceful expression in 1728 with the publication of Alexander Pope's *The Dunciad*, which appeared five months or so before Johnson entered Oxford.[5] The tumultuousness of the maturing literary marketplace is also reflected in the founding of the *Grub-Street Journal* in 1730, "perhaps the most widely read weekly essay-journal of the 1730s" according to Bertrand Goldgar. Of interest is the preface to the *Memoirs of the Society of Grub-Street*, a compilation of previous numbers, published in 1737, where the lapse of the Licensing Act is singled out as the wellspring of the recent— and unprecedented—proliferation of incompetent and vulgar writers: "[M]any, who could never have distinguished themselves by their writings, had they shewed a due regard to religion, morality, truth, or even common decency," declares the editor Richard Russel, "have become very infamously eminent, by composing or translating false *Histories*, lewd or immoral *Treatises*, *Novels*, *Plays*, or *Poems*." The *Grub-Street Journal* owed its existence to the rising tide of such material, Russel points out, its chief objective being "to repress, in some degree at least, the exorbitances of Authors, Booksellers, Printers, and Publishers." Also noteworthy is Russel's willingness to assign some of the blame for the marketplace's outrageousness to the public. A collateral goal of the journal, Russel states in the twelfth number, is "to reform the taste of the generality of readers, which is very much depraved; insomuch that for one person who writes ill, there are at least twenty who judge amiss." If only the book-buying public could be persuaded to insist on something better, Russel adds, then "the retailers of lewd and vicious nonsense would be soon obliged to take up some other employment, if not useful, yet however less prejudicial, to the public."[6] Just at the moment when Johnson was struggling to gain a foothold in professional letters—that is, during the mid-1730s—the prospects of authorship as a commercial enterprise had aroused passionate debate in prominent critical circles.

The viewpoint embodied in the *Grub-Street Journal* would continue to ripen in the public mind over the next decade, calling forth the immediately popular *Monthly Review* in 1749. We should not overlook the fact that the *Monthly Review* was at the core a commercial rather than a scholarly venture. A bookseller and former watchmaker, Ralph Griffiths took the lead in exploiting fully the broadly felt need for a journal that would offer discerning yet impartial advice on the mass of material flowing from the commercial press. Like all successful entrepreneurial efforts, the *Monthly Review* came into being in order to meet an existing marketplace demand. There was nothing of a technical nature prohibiting such a journal from existing any earlier, nor was the *Monthly*'s extract/summary/brief comment format much of a departure from what one found in the learned review journals of the previous century. As its initial "Advertisement" makes clear, however, the *Monthly*'s prospects hinge on the supposition that within the marketplace at the current moment exists a critical mass of nonspecialist book buyers who, fed up with the profusion of inferior books and deceptive advertisements, are ready to support a regular review journal. "When the abuse of title pages is obviously come to such a pass, that few readers care to take in a book, any more than a servant, without a recommendation," the "Advertisement" reads, "to acquaint the public that a summary review of the productions of the press, as they occur to notice, was perhaps never more necessary than now, would be superfluous and vain."[7] The problems alluded to in the *Monthly Review*'s "Advertisement" had been brewing for many years, but the demand for what can aptly be described as modern book reviewing would not crystallize until 1749.

The *Monthly*'s pledge to survey all newly published works—not strictly scholarly titles, but mass-market literature in particular, such as novels, petty poetry, conduct books, volumes dealing with the practical arts, political and religious pamphlets, compilations of well–known material, and so forth—proved to be a revolutionary concept that both reflected and further encouraged the growth of the literary marketplace. Hardly less significant is that the traditional reviewing format of extract and summary strung together with tersely neutral remarks, which the *Monthly* had inherited from the scholarly review journals that proliferated during the first half of the century, soon gave way to an emphasis on straightforward evaluative commentary. In fact, by the mid-1750s both the *Monthly Review* and its chief rival, the *Critical Review*, which began publication in March 1756, had come to think of themselves as much-needed arbiters of literary merit rather than as mere providers of material extracted from newly published works, a view evidently accepted not only by the public, who were buying these journals in increasing numbers, but by authors as well. In fact, one prominent characteristic of both journals—and perhaps a reason for their enduring popularity—is that they never ceased reminding readers of their importance as distributors of fame and as agents of literary reform.[8]

During the years preceding and following the historic publication of the *Monthly*'s inaugural issue, Samuel Johnson was gradually making his way in the world of professional letters, earning his living chiefly by contributing to Edward Cave's *Gentleman's Magazine* between 1738 and the mid-1740s and, from 1746 until 1755, compiling his *Dictionary of the English Language*.[9] Challenging though the *Dictionary* project was, in March 1750 Johnson began the twice-weekly *Rambler* series. Johnson took on the duties of "Mr. Rambler" because he had to supplement his income, a circumstance that almost certainly provided the inspiration to write a number of essays that explore the aims and hazards of authorship in its contemporary context. The reputation of the *Rambler* today rests largely on Johnson's searching analysis of timeless moral concepts, rendered in magnificent prose. Even so, we should remember that roughly one-quarter of Johnson's *Rambler* essays deal in some significant way with literary matters, and many of these pieces carry a distinct contemporaneous element.[10] Much the same can be said for the two other essay serials that Johnson contributed to during the 1750s, though it must be admitted that the *Adventurer* (1753–54) and *Idler* (1758–60) papers rarely rise to the intellectual level one routinely finds in the *Rambler* series.[11]

It is important to acknowledge that Johnson wrote frequently and intensely about authorship during the 1750s, exhibiting in his journalistic commentary an interest in contemporary literary issues that has not yet been fully apprehended by scholars. Johnson may not have been a crusader for high literary standards in the same manner as, say, Tobias Smollett.[12] And much of what Johnson says in regards to the aims and hazards of authorship is essentially conventional. In fact, a genre of criticism devoted to evaluating the state of professional letters had been developing since the age of Dryden and had matured by the time Johnson's literary career began in the late 1730s.[13] Nevertheless, Johnson's many *Rambler*, *Adventurer*, and *Idler* essays on literary subjects offer perceptive observations on the exalted purposes of authorship and the hazards of writing for the literary marketplace during a particularly turbulent moment in the history of English letters. It is in this context that Johnson's reviews should be studied, as they illustrate and extend Johnson's broader views on the contemporary literary world as expressed in the *Rambler*, *Adventurer*, and *Idler* papers.

The contemporary aspect of Johnson's *Rambler*, *Adventurer*, and *Idler* papers on authorship divides naturally, it seems, into four broad categories: the beneficent aims of authorship; the internal hazard of authorial self-delusion; the external hazards of the traditional patronage culture and the emergence of regular book reviewing. These categories are important because, as we shall see, they provide a framework for understanding Johnson's manner of proceeding as a book reviewer—most especially in the *Literary Magazine*, where the vast majority of Johnson's reviews appeared between May 1756 and July 1757.

JOHNSON ON THE AIMS OF AUTHORSHIP

In the course of a literary career that spanned more than half a century, Johnson often found occasion to remark on authorship—a profession he unfailingly invested with high moral and civic seriousness. Almost every scholarly investigation of Johnson's thought has called attention to, or at least touched upon, Johnson's numerous and spirited affirmations of the socially and morally uplifting purposes of authorship. Indeed, so artfully expressed and well known are Johnson's views on this matter that his writings are often characterized as a pure distillation of the classical and Renaissance humanist traditions in which the profession of letters is understood to be a pragmatic and persuasive enterprise, the foundational premise being that a given work of literature has no value apart from its capacity to impart socially and morally uplifting truths in a manner that attracts and keeps reader interest. In Johnson's view, essentially, authors serve as agents of civilization and their works as catalysts for self-reformation, irrespective of the genre they choose to write in.[14]

Johnson's outlook on the lofty purposes of authorship in a contemporary context finds particularly forceful expression in *Rambler* 4, where Johnson allusively attacks the novels of Smollett and Fielding and praises those by Samuel Richardson.[15] The novel in 1750 was widely considered by critics as one of the least worthy of literary forms despite its great popularity with the reading public.[16] Yet Johnson in *Rambler* 4 praises the genre in theory even though he objects to the practices of Smollett, Fielding, and most other novelists. Indeed, Johnson departs sharply from the dominant contemporary view of the novel as a mere trifling diversion and sets forth a solid case for its aesthetic and social worthiness. Because most of today's familiar histories are written "to the young, the ignorant, and the idle," Johnson observes, it is important to examine the extent of their influence. Though widely thought of as a form of light "entertainment," realistic novels actually serve as "lectures of conduct, and introductions into life" for young people, Johnson argues, the quotidian element being particularly attractive to the naive or poorly tutored reader.[17] Far from being a contemptible literary form, Johnson would have us believe here, novels theoretically may work as an extraordinarily effective vehicle for moral instruction, because they appeal to sections of the reading public least capable of resisting vice. We should keep Johnson's basic position in mind when we consider his refusal to review novels in the *Literary Magazine*. Johnson's decision to refrain from reviewing novels clearly reflects his belief that contemporary novelists have failed to measure up to the great responsibilities of authorship Johnson identifies in *Rambler* 4.

Another instance of Johnson arguing for the beneficent aims of authorship in a contemporary context is *Rambler* 145. Essentially, Johnson's essay emphasizes the civic and moral importance of journalism at a historical moment when news-writing was generally accepted as among the meanest sorts of literary activity. Significantly, in his closing remarks Johnson broadens his apologetic commentary to include the humbler categories of authors—"the abridger, the compiler and translator."[18] Johnson goes on to assert that, as "every writer has his use, every writer ought to have his patrons; and since no man, however high he may now stand, can be certain that he shall not be soon thrown down from his elevation by criticism or caprice." Johnson adds that the "common interest of learning requires that her sons should cease from intestine hostilities, and instead of sacrificing each other to malice and contempt, endeavour to avert persecution from the meanest of their fraternity."[19] Not only does Johnson in *Rambler* 145 unite journalists, translators, compilers, abridgers, and members of the most exalted of authorial occupations under the same professional standard—an innovative assertion in itself—but he also makes a point of arguing that today's poet or tragedian might easily be forced to make tomorrow's living by filling newspaper columns or abridging well-known works—a widely known truth, Johnson argues, but one that dare not speak its own name in polite literary circles.[20]

What thus makes *Rambler* 145 and *Rambler* 4 remarkable is that Johnson uses the forum of the moral essay to exalt in particular the least respected of authorial activities—doubtless because, as Johnson must have known firsthand from his own Grub Street days of the 1730s and early 1740s, it was just these sorts of literary occupations that were attracting the largest share of aspiring writers at midcentury. As we shall see, Johnson's work as a reviewer embodies the viewpoint expressed in both of these essays: worthy compilers, abridgers, translators, and journalists are given a sympathetic reception in the *Literary Magazine*, while the many incompetent writers—which, as far as Johnson was concerned, included the vast majority of novelists writing in the mid-1750s—are ignored.

A handful of other essays on the aims of authorship can also be tied to the immediate historical moment. *Rambler* 154, for instance, offers a rousing defense of the beneficent aims of professional letters as a part of an allusive attack on a recently published translation of J.-J. Rousseau's first book, *An Essay on the Arts and Sciences*, a subject discussed at length in chapter 6. *Adventurer* 115 (1753), "Reflections on the Present State of Literature" (*Universal Visiter,* 1756), and *Idler*s 85 and 94 (1759/60) resemble *Rambler* 154 insofar as they can be read as complaints about the contemporary turmoil of the literary marketplace that reflect Johnson's exalted view of the authorial calling and, collaterally, provide important background for a study of Johnson's choice of books for review and his manner of proceeding as a reviewer.

As mentioned previously, the proliferation of valueless works by avocational authors was something of a commonplace in critical circles during the middle third of the eighteenth century. Indeed, the widely held perception that the book trade was obsessed with profits and was indifferent to literary merit in some measure led to the creation and subsequent popularity of regular reviewing. It scarcely needs mentioning that Johnson's four essays on the subject—*Adventurer* 115, "Reflections on the Present State of Literature," *Idler* 85, and *Idler* 94—are deftly expressed but late and rather conventional examples of the age's ceaseless complaining about the degradation of professional letters. If one browses through the first few annual volumes of the *Monthly Review* and the *Critical Review*—or even issues of the *Grub-Street Journal* (1730–37)—one will encounter no shortage of ululations on the ascendancy of inanity, vulgarity, and ineptitude afflicting professional letters. Even so, these four essays are important to our understanding of how Johnson viewed his own duties as a cultural critic—not only as a writer of essays but also as a reviewer. Johnson in these essays is an accurate and at times savagely witty observer of the contemporary literary scene, certainly. But we also find Johnson here exemplifying his own conception of the author as teacher and benefactor. Rather than merely adding his mite to the massive critical weight already pitted against the rising tide of literary incompetence, Johnson works to stimulate self-reform amongst aspiring writers.

Adventurer 115 begins by taking up a subject that had been in play at least since the 1730s: the upsurge in avocational authorship made possible by the emergence of a robust literary marketplace. We live in "The Age of Authors," Johnson declares, "though it may, perhaps, be true, that at all times more have been willing than have been able to write, yet there is no reason for believing, that the dogmatical legions of the present race were ever equalled in number by any former period."[21] Previously, authorship was "left to those, who by study, or appearance of study, were supposed to have gained knowledge unattainable by the busy part of mankind," yet over the last several years legions of incompetent novices—artisans, mechanics, merchants, sailors, farmers, and the like—have burdened the literary world with trifling material.[22]

From here, Johnson goes on to offer a lecture on the prerequisites of authorship, properly understood. "Let it be deeply impressed and frequently recollected, that he who has not obtained the proper qualifications of an author, can have no excuse for the arrogance of writing, but the power of imparting something necessary to be known," Johnson declares. Johnson then advances a principle that can be said to explain his later denunciations of Soame Jenyns. "No man is a rhetorician or philosopher by chance," Johnson declares. "He who knows that he undertakes to write on questions which he has never studied, may without hesitation determine, that he is about to waste his own time and that of his reader, and expose himself to the derision of those whom he aspires to instruct."[23] For Johnson, all of this is a matter of common sense. But as he himself admits in *Rambler* 3, *Adventurer* 85, *Adventurer* 137, and elsewhere, it frequently falls upon authors to remind, to inculcate, to impress, and to help readers to achieve a rational appreciation of what has always been taken for granted. The recent proliferation of incompetent novices demonstrates that the time-proven means of literary excellence possess no inherent prescriptive authority. By way of example and carefully constructed argument, *Adventurer* 115 thus offers a rousing affirmation of the proper aims of authorship at a historically troubled moment for professional letters.

Johnson would again consider authorship in relation to its contemporary ills twenty-eight months later in his essay, "Reflections on the Present State of Literature," published in the April 1756 number of the *Universal Visiter*.[24] For readers used to the carefully measured analysis and scholarly disposition of the earlier *Rambler* and the *Adventurer* essays, the bitter and rather graceless reproaches of incompetent writers here might come as something of a shock. The recent swelling of the authorial ranks, for instance, is described as that of a pestilential "swarm." Women writers in particular are ridiculed for their supposed aversion to "clean linen." One may certainly argue that Johnson's modest proposal—an expendable frontline combat force staffed by the literary inept—is unduly spiteful and, perhaps, unbecoming of his considerable polemical powers.[25] Nevertheless, "Reflections on the Present State of Literature" is very much an apt companion to *Adventurer* 115. For instance, we find here, as we do in the earlier piece, the implicit suggestion that the contemporary plight of letters is a legacy of the lapse of the Licensing Act. In fact, Johnson borrows freely from the earlier essay in developing this point. "It is not now, as in former times, when men studied long, and past through the severities of discipline, and the probation of public trials, before they presumed to think themselves qualified for instructors of their countrymen," Johnson argues. Nowadays, however, "the inclosures of literature are thrown open to every man whom idleness disposes to loiter, or whom pride inclines to set himself to view." From here Johnson goes on to list the sorts of banal and foolish titles— "The sailor publishes his journal, the farmer writes the process of his annual labour; he that succeeds in his trade thinks his wealth a proof of his understanding, and boldly tutors the public"—that clutter contemporary bookstalls.[26] The profusion of untutored, occasional authors is a lingering source of vexation for Johnson, clearly, but the broader point here is that the unprecedented opportunities for publication created by an unregulated literary marketplace have obscured the high obligations of authorship taken for granted by previous generations of aspiring writers.

A more significant similarity between *Adventurer* 115 and "Reflections" is Johnson's stalwart defense of the high social and moral aims of authorship. It is perhaps easy to miss on account of the essay's prevailing malevolence, but Johnson's underlying objective is to rescue the reputation of professional authorship from present-day aberrations. "There is no gift of nature, or effect of art, however beneficial to mankind, which either by casual deviations, or foolish perversions, is not sometimes mischievous," Johnson declares in the essay's opening sentence. "The medicine, which rightly applied, has power to cure, has, when rashness or ignorance prescribes it, the same power to destroy." A few sentences later, Johnson attempts to place the recent upsurge in patently unworthy literature in perspective by calling attention to authorship's civilizing heritage:

> If letters were considered only as a means of pleasure, it might well be doubted in what degree of estimation they should be held; but when they are referred to necessity, the controversy is at an end: it soon appears, that they may sometimes incommode us, yet human life would scarcely rise, without them, above the common existence of animal nature: we might indeed breathe and eat in universal ignorance, but must want all that gives pleasure or security, all the embellishments and delights, and most of the conveniences and comforts of our present condition.[27]

The theme of Johnson's essay crystallizes here: authorship remains a beneficent profession. Much literary criticism of the period decried the degenerate state of letters and, certainly, the "Reflections on the State of Literature" contributes something to the contemporary chorus of complaints. But in its own irascible and hyperbolic way, the essay is meant to work as a timely reminder of the altruistic ends of authorship.

Idler 85 addresses, as do *Adventurer* 115 and the "Reflections," the profusion in recent years of unworthy titles and the corresponding confusion in the public mind regarding the proper ends of literary activity. "One of the peculiarities which distinguish the present age is the multiplication of books," Johnson declares. "Every day brings new advertisements of literary undertakings, and we are flattered with repeated promises of growing wise on easier terms than our progenitors." Johnson then goes on to discuss the compilation format, which in his view is in itself unexceptionable and, if deftly executed, can be of great use to a variety of reading tastes. Even so, the recent popularity of slapdash compilations signifies an underlying dry rot in professional letters. Booksellers and authors are entitled to some of the blame for the overall raffish condition of contemporary letters, Johnson suggests, but so too are contemporary readers. "When the treasures of ancient knowledge lye unexamined, and original authors are neglected and forgotten, compilers and plagiaries are encouraged, who give us again what we had known before, and grow great by setting before us what our own sloth had hidden from our view." Johnson closes the essay on a note of intense exasperation: "[S]uch is the present state of our literature, that the ancient sage who thought 'a great book a great evil,' would now consider a bulky writer who engrossed a year, and a swarm of pamphleteers who stole each an hour, as equal wasters of human life, and would make no other difference between them, than between a beast of prey, and a flight of locusts."[28] What commands attention here is Johnson's sternly moralistic language: undemanding readers are slothful; the age is corrupt; a bulky compilation wastes human life; a carefully assembled compilation is beneficent and its author honestly employed; and so forth. By framing his argument in this way, Johnson emphatically reminds readers that authorship is not merely one of many modern commercial occupations but a profession devoted to sustaining civilization.

Idler 94 employs similar language in making basically the same point. There are some "who claim the name of authors merely to disgrace it, and fill the world with volumes only to bury letters in their own rubbish," Johnson observes. "The traveller who tells, in a pompous folio, that he saw the Pantheon at Rome, and the Medicean Venus at Florence; the natural historian who, describing the productions of a narrow island, recounts all that it has in common with every other part of the world," Johnson declares as he surveys the wretched state of the book trade,

> the collector of antiquities, that accounts every thing a curiosity which the ruins of Herculaneum happen to emit, though an instrument already shewn in a thousand repositories, or a cup common to the ancients, the moderns, and all mankind, may be justly censured as the persecutors of students, and the thieves of that time which never can be restored.[29]

The topicality of Johnson's commentary is obvious enough: the sorts of titles referred to—travel narratives, natural histories, antiquarian volumes centering on Greece and Rome—enjoyed great popularity during the middle third of the eighteenth century.[30] Of greater importance here are the revelations of Johnson's understanding of the contemporary literary scene. As we saw in *Adventurer* 115, "Reflections," and *Idler* 85, Johnson is careful to portray the recent overgrowth of literary mediocrity not as a mere annoyance, but as a serious moral and social problem. The unimaginative compilation, the insipid travel narrative, and other forms of worthless literature ultimately undermine the progress of knowledge not only because they crowd out meritorious titles but also because they feed the public's growing skepticism toward the value of books.

To summarize: the outlook expressed in the handful of essays discussed in this section helps to contextualize Johnson's assertion in the *Literary Magazine*'s inaugural number that "a few only" of "all the writings which this age of writers may offer" shall be awarded the status of a review. The essentially appreciative character of Johnson's reviewing in the *Literary Magazine* can be said to reflect both Johnson's belief in the lofty purposes of authorship and his perceptive grasp of some of the destabilizing trends in the book trade. As subsequent chapters shall bear out, the *Literary Magazine* functions as a showcase of what Johnson considers to be examples of worthy authors and meritorious titles in an age that, increasingly, demonstrated what Johnson clearly believed was a retarded or debauched understanding of the proper aims of authorship.

INTERNAL HAZARDS: AUTHORIAL SELF-DELUSION

The previous discussion proves well enough that Johnson was troubled by the vast scale of literary knavery and tomfoolery afflicting the contemporary literary world. In the essays discussed in this section, Johnson avoids the sort of sweeping denunciations of contemporary literary ineptitude that characterize, for instance, *Adventurer* 115, and instead probes the psychology of modern authorship—particularly incompetent or unjustified authorship. In Johnson's view, the disappearance of heavy-handed state control over professional letters in the early part of the eighteenth century and the attendant growth in the printing and advertising industries, the emergence of regular reviewing, and the occasional award of spectacular copyright payments to authors such as Henry Fielding and Alexander Pope combined to entice unprecedented numbers of people to try their hand at writing for the public during the middle third of the eighteenth century.[31] In *Ramblers* 2, 16, and 146, *Idler* 55, and the "Weekly Correspondent" essay in the *Public Ledger*, Johnson works to temper the inflated ambitions of many aspiring authors by calling attention to the scarcity of literary glory and by illuminating the distinctively modern aspects of authorial self-deception.

In themselves, these five essays are worth studying as revelations of Johnson's outlook on professional letters at midcentury, but they are important also for what they tell us about Johnson's manner of proceeding as a book reviewer. Johnson's apologetic treatment in the *Literary Magazine* of works that had received unfavorable reviews elsewhere, and his abridgment of extracted material in ways that make many of the works under review appear more attractive than they actually are, can be said to embody Johnson's perceptive understanding, as expressed in *Rambler* 2, *Rambler* 146, and the "Weekly Correspondent" essay, of the hostility and indifference of the literary marketplace that confront the talented and the incompetent author alike. Johnson knows well the difficulties of establishing a literary reputation, in other words, so we see him as a reviewer going to some lengths to help worthy authors receive a sympathetic hearing by the public. Johnson's parody of authorial self-delusion in *Rambler* 16 and *Idler* 55, meanwhile, works as a fit introduction both to Johnson's dismissive

reviews of Thomas Blackwell and Soame Jenyns, and his decision to ignore the multitude of trashy books and pamphlets produced by the great
numbers of incompetent writers who sought easy fame and fortune through
the unregulated book trade.

Rambler 2 (March 1750) offers a deeply pessimistic evaluation of the
contemporaneous literary scene. Johnson's own professional trials probably inform the gloomy temperament of the essay, but the chief purpose of
Rambler 2 is to inculcate in aspiring authors a sober understanding of the
difficulties of gaining literary reputation. In typical *Rambler* fashion,
Johnson approaches a timely issue by way of a universal commonplace.[32]
As satirists and moralists have been telling us for ages, Johnson observes,
an obsessive concern with future happiness is a natural but ultimately futile habit of mind. While it is true that without the capacity to imagine
grand schemes "few enterprises of great labour or hazard would be undertaken," the time-proven maxim that warns "against keeping our view too
intent upon remote advantages" remains particularly relevant to the modern literary world. "Perhaps no class of human species requires more to be
cautioned against" excessively sanguine expectations of future happiness
and glory "than those that aspire to the name of authors," Johnson asserts.

> A man of lively fancy no sooner finds a hint moving in his mind, than he
> makes momentaneous excursions to the press, and to the world, and, with
> a little encouragement from flattery, pushes forward into future ages, and
> prognosticates the honours to be paid him, when envy is extinct, and fac-
> tion forgotten, and those, whom partiality now suffers to obscure him, shall
> have given way to other triflers of as short duration as themselves.[33]

Here Johnson addresses what was for him and his contemporaries a distinctively modern problem. Before the lapse of the Licensing Act in 1694
and the astounding growth of the English book trade that followed, aspiring authors simply did not make "momentaneous excursions to the press."
There was the matter of securing a patron, perhaps, and of getting one's
subject matter vetted by the licenser. And even if such obstacles were sur-
mounted, the aspiring literary celebrity had to contend with a primitive
publishing and advertising apparatus—not to mention a much smaller reading public and the absence of firm copyright protections.[34] The planted
axiom in the passage quoted here is that the culture of commercial letters—regular reviewing, widespread advertising, increasing demand brought
about by the growth of the reading public—encourages aspiring authors to
embrace the alluring but false notion that only a reluctance to contract with
a printer stands in the way of fame and fortune.

Having taken note of the unprecedented ease with which anyone nowadays can translate passing fancy into actual publication, Johnson moves on

to examine the temptation to indulge unreasonable expectations of literary glory—the "writer's malady," as Johnson puts the matter. "It may not be unfit for him who makes a new entrance into the lettered world, so far to suspect his own powers as to believe that he possibly may deserve neglect." Browse through any library catalog, Johnson declares, and one will find no shortage of moldering, unread titles by long-forgotten writers who in their day felt assured of enduring fame. The situation is much worse nowadays, Johnson goes on to explain.

> [T]hough it should happen that an author is capable of excelling, yet his merit may pass without notice, huddled in the mass of things, and thrown into the general miscellany of life. He that endeavours after fame by writing solicits the regard of a multitude fluctuating in pleasures, or immersed in business, without time for intellectual amusements; he appeals to judges prepossessed by passions, or corrupted by prejudices, which preclude their approbation of any new performance. Some are too indolent to read any thing, till its reputation is established; others too envious to promote that fame, which gives them pain by its increase. What is new is opposed, because most are unwilling to be taught; and what is known is rejected, because it is not sufficiently considered, that men more frequently require to be reminded than informed. The learned are afraid to declare their opinion early, lest they should put their reputation in hazard; the ignorant always imagine themselves giving some proof of delicacy, when they refuse to be pleased: and he that finds his way to reputation, through all these obstructions, must acknowledge that he is indebted to other causes besides his industry, his learning, or his wit.[35]

The universality of Johnson's observations here is obvious enough—readers are loath to confront their own ignorance; envy is as troubling a vice in professional letters as it is anywhere else—but we should not overlook the well-defined contemporaneous element on display here. That many readers refuse to consider a given work "till its reputation is established" can be read as an allusion to the immediately successful *Monthly Review* (begun in May 1749), which retailed itself as a discriminating time-saver for readers bewildered by the profusion of dishonest title pages and extravagant advertisements.[36] A "multitude fluctuating in pleasures, immersed in business, without time for intellectual amusements" aptly describes the diverse reading public at midcentury, whose appetite for every kind of printed material propelled the growth of the marketplace: the very class of reader, in other words, that would prefer, say, the octavo abridgment of Johnson's *Dictionary* (1756)—created for the "greater number of readers, who, seldom intending to write or presuming to judge, turn over books only to amuse their leisure, and to gain degrees of knowledge suitable to lower characters"—instead of the more expensive and scholarly two-volume folio.[37] On the whole, *Rambler* 2 means to encourage authors to think rationally about the conditions of the marketplace, where too many variables are in play to allow for reliable predictions about the progress of reputation.

With its ruminations on the scarcity and impermanence of literary fame, *Rambler* 146 (August 1751) is an apt companion to *Rambler* 2. But perhaps more so than its predecessor, *Rambler* 146 emphasizes the inhospitality of the marketplace particularly to highly conscientious authors. The first half of the essay comprises a sketch of a fictional author who after years of effort has produced "a work intended to burst upon mankind with unexpected lustre, and withdraw the attention of the learned world." Bracing himself both for excessive praise and censure, Johnson's fictional author heads for the coffeehouses to take the full measure of his public standing—only to discover that his work has gone unnoticed. Exasperated, the author discreetly raises his own work as a topic and is promptly greeted by stock responses:

> [O]ne has seen the work advertised, but never met with any that had read it; another has been so often imposed upon by specious titles, that he never buys a book till its character is established; a third wonders what any man can hope to produce after so many writers of great eminence; the next has enquired after the author, but can hear no account of him, and therefore suspects the name to be fictitious; and another knows him to be a man condemned by indigence to write too frequently what he does not understand.[38]

In a manner that recalls the futile excuse-making of Richard Savage, the raffish author who befriended the then obscure Johnson in the late 1730s and whose tragic life Johnson recounted in his 1744 biography, Johnson's fictional author attributes his misfortunes to the ignorance of the public, the malice of rivals, and the prevailing intellectual degeneracy of the age—soothing his bruised pride in the meantime by imagining that future generations will venerate his work even while they decry the philistinism of his contemporaries.[39]

It would be tempting to interpret Johnson's fictional sketch as nothing more than a humdrum rebuke to authorial hubris, but details embedded in the narrative encourage a more nuanced reading. To begin with, we are told nothing about the topic of the fictional author's work, nor are we given any indication of its scholarly value—though we do know that the book was years in the making. This point is significant because Johnson wants us to pity the "author" not for thinking of his work as better than it actually is but for embracing an unjustified faith in the beneficence and evenhandedness of the literary marketplace. The fictional author's book may well be meritorious, but readers nowadays, being for the most part jaded or otherwise unambitious, often reject newly published works for arbitrary reasons. Illustrations of this point can be found in Johnson's reference to "specious titles" and the coffeehouse patron's assertion that he refuses to buy a book until "its character is established." Both of these comments evidently allude to the *Monthly Review* and the circumstances that gave rise to its popularity. The doubts raised about the authenticity of the name on the title page and the observation on the starveling author who grasps at any sort of literary work are additional reflections of growing popular skepticism concerning the value of literature produced for the marketplace. None of these speculations applies to Johnson's fictional author, but this is the very point Johnson tries to make in *Rambler* 146: aspiring writers are thus warned that they face unprecedented levels of public hostility and apathy.

In the second half of *Rambler* 146 Johnson goes on to illuminate the reasons behind the scarcity of literary fame. "It seems not to be sufficiently considered how little renown can be admitted in the world," Johnson states. "Mankind are kept perpetually busy by their fears or desires, and have not more leisure from their own affairs, than to acquaint themselves with the accidents of the current day." Hardly less important is that scholars, the traditional custodians of enduring literary celebrity, can be counted on to sustain the reputation of a relatively minute number of works and authors. Perhaps not surprisingly, *Rambler* 146 ends on a note of intense despair: "[S]ince it is so difficult to obtain the notice of contemporaries, how little is to be hoped from future time," Johnson states. "What can merit effect by its own force, when the help of art or friendship can scarcely support it?"[40] What might explain such a spirit-crushing outlook? The challenges of the *Dictionary* project may have weighed heavily on Johnson's mind at the moment when he composed number 146. Another plausible explanation is the persistently sluggish sales of the *Rambler*.[41] Whatever private motivations may be in play here, Johnson's main objective is to throw cold water on the widespread though largely unwarranted ardor for publication by highlighting the trials of modern authorship.

Another of Johnson's periodical essays that comments on the scarcity of literary fame remains to this day unjustifiably obscure. Immediately striking about Johnson's "Weekly Correspondent" essay, published in the *Public Ledger* on 2 December 1760, is that Johnson essentially avers nothing not declared earlier in *Rambler* 2, *Rambler* 146, and elsewhere. Even so, the first "Weekly Correspondent" essay deserves to reach a wider scholarly readership than it has done thus far, not only because it embodies the reflections of an author who was more mature and more experienced than the writer of the *Rambler* series but also because the substantial literary qualities of the essay and the occasion for its publication are emblematic of Johnson's achievement as an observer of the contemporaneous literary scene.

The 2 December 1760 "Weekly Correspondent" piece was the first of what was almost certainly intended to be another of Johnson's essay serials. Significantly, the essay takes for its theme the relation between the "Weekly Correspondent" and his prospective readership, thus bringing to mind the inaugural *Rambler* and *Idler* essays in which Johnson seeks to establish a distinctive authorial persona before embarking on the kinds of miscellaneous subjects covered in subsequent numbers. In keeping with the pattern established by the *Rambler* and *Idler*, the "Weekly Correspondent" papers of 9 December (the coronation of King George III) and 16 December (the recent demolition of some London buildings) discuss subjects of general public interest. A similarly topical fourth piece referred to at the end of Johnson's 16 December essay—"Having thus told you what I have already done; I shall proceed, in my next letter, to tell you what I design"—never materialized. E. L. McAdam surmises that the series ended abruptly because Johnson's edition of Shakespeare's plays—underway since 1756 and not completed until October 1765—demanded his full attention, but this surmise seems implausible.[42] Indeed, it is worth recalling that Johnson composed nearly 250 *Rambler* and *Adventurer* papers during the most intense stages of the much more demanding *Dictionary* project. Johnson especially enjoyed journalistic work of this kind, and so it is not hard to imagine him eagerly embracing a "Weekly Correspondent" program in late 1760, the *Idler* papers having come to a conclusion eight months earlier.[43]

Perhaps a more convincing explanation for the cessation of Johnson's "Weekly Correspondent" column is that Oliver Goldsmith's "Chinese Letters," which had been appearing in the *Public Ledger* since January 1760, proved to be sufficient literary material for what was in fact a paper designed to facilitate the buying and selling of everyday goods and services. The *Public Ledger* exists to permit "every Man to see at one View as he sits at Home in his Chair," Johnson states in the prefatory address (January 1760), "various Sollicitudes of the rest, and know where to avail himself of the Wants of others, or to supply those of his own."[44] Whatever the specific circumstances surrounding Johnson's "Weekly Correspondent" essays, in the first number we find Johnson ruminating on the trials of modern authorship before what must have been a fairly large and highly diversified readership.

In the opening paragraphs the "Weekly Correspondent" self-consciously defies tradition by withholding revelations about his private life. "Readers have been accustomed to expect some account of a New Author. And the Essayists seem to think that they are invested with some peculiar right to talk of themselves, inherited perhaps from their ancestor Montaigne," Johnson declares, taking up a theme—the difficulties the essayist faces when addressing the public for the first time—explored previously in *Rambler* 1 and *Idler* 1. "But since Experience always teaches us, that Expectation produces Disappointment, I shall not attempt to impress upon you, or your readers [the essay is addressed to the editor], any such particular character of myself, as may enable you to anticipate my performances." Johnson goes on to justify his reticence and in doing so sets before readers a trenchant consideration of modern authorship's trials:

> There is no reason why the series of my life and conversation should be entrusted to those who have given no promise of secrecy, and of whom I cannot guess whether they are gentle or severe, captious or candid, benevolent or malicious. A book is very seldom taken up with very kind intentions: few wish to be pleased, and much fewer wish to be taught. The general design of readers is to exert the acuteness of remark, or to display the superiority of contempt. He that undertakes to furnish literary amusements, must expect no tenderness but from the ignorant and the young, who are not too proud to own a master, and having never yet aspired to the reputation of thinking for themselves, have neither been made vain by praise, nor sullen by censure. A writer therefore does not engage his readers on equal terms: he may present himself to their notice, but they may neglect him without hazard. The most laboured performance of wit and learning is as easily thrown into the fire, as a taylor's bill. The demonstrator may try to convince the reason, and the man of fancy to move the passions; but when each has done all that he can, no man is obliged to have his passions moved, or his reason convinced: all may refuse to read; or all may read without attention, and refuse to understand. From such injurious treatment the poor author has no appeal, but to posterity; but posterity is too distant to help him, and however loudly he may call upon it, he is seldom in any real haste to be heard. It is much safer to lie concealed in nameless obscurity; and, instead of imploring posterity, to have this comfort in his disappointments, that none know them but himself.[45]

The stark alienation here of the "Weekly Correspondent" raises certain questions. Does Johnson mean to rebuke the commercial classes and less ambitious readers in general—the very readership whose needs the *Public Ledger* sought to address—for not approaching literature in the serious manner it deserves? Or does the essay merely register an eruption of the melancholy and self-doubt that plagued Johnson all of his life? Both of these themes are probably present to some degree. But when we recall that the "Weekly Correspondent" column was almost certainly intended to be a regular feature of the *Public Ledger*, the plainspokenness here can be seen as establishing a measure of credibility for Johnson's persona, which later papers might build on. We are given to understand that the "Weekly Correspondent" is no deluded novice but a wise and somewhat jaded observer of the literary world. Aspiring authors are thus well-advised to heed his un-adorned yet clear-headed counsel on literary matters, while the general reader is invited to sample the discerning, if at times blunt, commentary of the "Weekly Correspondent" on various other topics.

It certainly is a pity that the "Weekly Correspondent" column ended after three installments. The inaugural essay leads us to believe—as does the precedent set by the *Rambler* and *Idler* papers—that literary topics would have featured prominently in the series, just as they do in the *Rambler*, *Idler*, and *Adventurer* papers. Nevertheless, Johnson's first "Weekly Corre-spondent" essay remains a significant commentary in its own right, be-cause it demonstrates that the scarcity of literary fame was much on Johnson's mind at the close of 1760 even though the previous decade must be considered as his most successful: the *Dictionary*, the *Rambler*, and *Rasselas* spring immediately to mind, of course, but there were other note-worthy achievements as well, including the popularity of the *Adventurer* and *Idler* series, the award of the honorary M.A. from Oxford, and the revival of the Shakespeare edition, which Johnson was forced to abandon in 1745.

The gloominess of *Rambler* 2, *Rambler* 146, and the "Weekly Corre-spondent" essay derives at least in part from Johnson's keen understanding of marketplace capriciousness. The most talented of aspiring authors might easily "pass without notice," as Johnson puts the matter in *Rambler* 2, just as unworthy authors may find themselves exalted on account of an influen-tial patron or the trendiness of their writings. Indeed, not only in the essays discussed here but in incidental asides elsewhere in his canon of literary criticism Johnson is careful to portray writing for the marketplace as an intrinsically "hazardous" activity, a contest of sorts in which fame-hungry writers square off against the malignancy of critics and the sullen indiffer-ence of readers. Triumphant authors may acquire celebrity and their works immortality, while the losers—by far the greater portion of aspiring writ-ers—must come to terms with disgrace or oblivion.[46] In Johnson's view, nothing much can be done about this state of affairs apart from warning authors against expecting a sympathetic or even an impartial reception in the marketplace. *Rambler* 16 and *Idler* 55 examine a more tractable prob-lem: the tendency of contemporaneous authors to overlook their inadequa-cies and to estimate their prospects by the light of the marketplace's capac-ity to deliver fame and fortune to a select few.

Significantly, Johnson's touch in *Rambler* 16 and *Idler* 55 is much lighter, his means of persuasion being parody rather than despairing medi-tation. A critical mass of aspiring authors might be willing to risk the long odds or failures discussed in *Rambler*s 2 and 146 so long as the payoff in fame and fortune remained as generous as it was in the case of, say, Henry Fielding or Alexander Pope. But few can stand the prospect of looking ridiculous, especially in front of the very people they are trying to impress with their gravity and insight. *Rambler* 16 and *Idler* 55 seek to exploit just such an emotion by depicting a pair of characters who make fools of themselves because they refuse to reflect even momentarily on their worthiness as authors.

Rambler 16 (May 1750) takes the form of a "letter" from "Misellus," a fictional author whose capacity for rational self-assessment has been suborned by the trappings of the literary marketplace. Claiming to act on a previous *Rambler* observation that "a writer might easily find means of introducing his genius to the world, for the 'presses of England were open'"—an allusion to the brisk growth of the unlicensed book trade—Misellus has since confronted what he thinks of as the many burdens of literary celebrity but what are in truth the bitter fruits of his vainglory. A throng of coffeehouse regulars quickly discovers, for instance, that perfunctory or even transparently phony praise is enough to get Misellus to pay for round after round of food and drink. "I have now found that nothing is so expensive as great abilities, unless there is join'd with them an insatiable eagerness of praise," Misellus declares. Other coffeehouse patrons boisterously lampoon both Misellus and his inaugural work, a circumstance interpreted as the malice of less capable rivals. So besotted is Misellus with himself that even longtime friends find him insufferable—an inevitable consequence of literary eminence, Misellus concludes. "I live in the town like a lion in his desart, or an eagle on his rock, too great for friendship or society, and condemned to solitude, by unhappy elevation, and dreaded ascendency." Though supposedly a plea for help—"how to divest myself of the laurels which are so cumbersome to the wearer"—Misellus's remarks conform to the rest of his "letter," insofar as they express in the guise of a lament an underlying self-satisfaction.[47] To be sure, Johnson is careful to portray Misellus's failings as ultimately moral. His entrenched and exaggerated self-regard eventually becomes a source of amusement and exploitation for his acquaintances, a fate easily avoided by frequent self-examination. But Johnson also encourages us to read *Rambler* 16 as a satiric portrait of authorial self-delusion in a distinctly contemporaneous context.

To begin with, *Rambler* 16 would have us believe that the appearance of one's name on the title page of a mass-produced book is a transforming experience, the catalyst of Misellus's self-delusion clearly being the ease with which he publishes his work. Indeed, the extremity of Misellus's self-deception finds expression in the print run of his privately published volume.

He contracts for the printing of "several thousand" copies even though print runs in excess of two thousand during the eighteenth century were, from a financial standpoint, needlessly risky.[48]

Misellus's survey of the hazards of fame also reflects contemporaneous circumstances. We are told that Misellus frequently changes residences for fear of "piratical booksellers" who await the chance to steal his private papers—a certain allusion to the famous feud between Alexander Pope (d. 1744) and the controversial bookseller Edmund Curll (d. 1747). In a manner that brings to mind Pope's pioneering manipulation of his public image—particularly his penchant for commissioning portraits of himself for public sale—Misellus bemoans the invasion of his privacy by eighteenth-century predecessors of today's paparazzi. "Others may be persecuted but I am haunted," Misellus declares. "I have good reason to believe that eleven painters are now dogging me, for they know that he who can get my face first will make his fortune." Significantly, the portraiture itself does not bother Misellus so much as the unlicensed exploitation of his image: "[I]t is not fair to sell my face," Misellus declares, "without admitting me to share the profit."[49]

Rambler 16 thus satirizes authorial vanity in a distinctly modern setting. True, in the *Life of Savage*, *Rambler* 21, *Adventurer* 138, and elsewhere Johnson is careful to emphasize that the unruliness of the authorial imagination on the eve of publication is a universal and timeless hazard of professional writing. But *Rambler* 16 is intended to warn aspiring authors that the temptation to overestimate one's prospects and talents is greater nowadays than ever before, thanks to the rapid growth in recent years of the literary marketplace and the rise of the culture of literary celebrity embodied in aspects of Pope's career.

Johnson would again employ the fictional correspondent as a means of satirizing authorial self-delusion in *Idler* 55 (May 1759). The thwarted author whose "letter" constitutes *Idler* 55 travels to London from an unnamed distant county convinced that his natural history is destined to become a literary landmark. As must have been the case for countless aspiring authors who beat a path to London during the middle third of the eighteenth century, Johnson's fictional author soon discovers that the book trade is quite pleased to get along without him. Prospective patrons and the president of the Royal Society prove to be similarly dismissive. Where "must knowledge and industry find their recompence," the author asks as he tries to weave epochal significance into his quotidian experiences, "thus neglected by the high and cheated by the low?"[50] The earnest plea of Johnson's fictional author here might evoke pity in readers when considered in isolation, but details embedded in *Idler* 55 show that the fictional author's most formidable tormentor is his undisciplined imagination.

The most obvious measure of the fictional author's self-delusion is his massive ignorance of marketplace economics. Within "five years" thirty thousand copies of his book will be sold, the author muses to himself, generating a hefty fifteen thousand pounds sterling in profits. What Johnson's fictional author assumes here is that authors are entitled to at least a share of the copyright for subsequent editions, even though royalties of this kind did not exist in the 1750s. And only an author who enjoyed the status of, say, Alexander Pope could get away with leasing a copyright. The normal practice at midcentury was for booksellers to purchase copyrights outright. In the case of a work with a narrow appeal, such as the fictional author's natural history, the author was expected to support production costs through subscription or direct payment. This was so because a large work of uncertain value amounted to a considerable risk for a bookseller who, in paying for the copyright and in purchasing the paper—50 percent of publication costs in Johnson's day—tied up considerable capital that was not recovered unless the book sold well. Famous for his *Dictionary* and his *Rambler* series, even Johnson had to rely on private subscriptions to underwrite his edition of Shakespeare's plays.[51]

Johnson lets readers know that his fictional author's natural history is tumid enough to discourage all but the most incautious booksellers from purchasing the copyright. The entire range of local flora, fauna, and "subterranean treasures" is set forth; we are also told that one prospective printer refuses to subsidize publication on the grounds that "a book of that size 'would never do.'" Of greater significance is the fictional author's delusion when it comes to assessing his contribution to English letters:

> I considered that natural history is neither temporary nor local, and that tho' I limited my enquiries to my own county, yet every part of the earth has productions common to the rest. Civil history may be partially studied, the revolutions of one nation may be neglected by another, but after that in which all have an interest, all must be inquisitive. No man can have sunk so far into stupidity as not to consider the properties of the ground on which he walks, of the plants on which he feeds, or the animals that delight his ear or amuse his eye.[52]

Amusingly, Johnson's fictional author here confuses what we think of today as Augustan notions of "general nature" in the arts (the pursuit of representative rather than obscure or trivial truths) with "nature" as in "the natural world" (a recipe for failure, given contemporaneous expectations of natural histories). As Johnson himself had pointed out some two years earlier in his *Literary Magazine* review of Patrick Browne's *Natural History of Jamaica*, a proper natural history focuses on the exotic and ignores the ordinary. "Natural History is above most other kinds of compositions subject to repetition," Johnson writes in his review of Browne's volume. Thus authors should select items "that are distinguished by some permanent and natural difference from the same species in other places; or that are little known to those in whose language the book is written."[53] In a manner similar to Browne, Johnson's fictional author blunders by emphasizing the commonplace at the expense of the unfamiliar.

Were the natural history as worthy as Johnson's fictional author imagines, his anticipation of selling thirty thousand copies—to say nothing of attracting the interest of high society upon his arrival in London—would have struck Johnson's contemporaries as a risible fantasy. Not only was the demand for natural histories rather limited to begin with, but the market for such works had become saturated by the 1750s, if not earlier.[54] Aspects of Johnson's career highlight further the author's profound misunderstanding of the contemporaneous book trade. Perhaps a work of comparable size to that of his fictional author, Johnson's *Dictionary* (1755) came into being in response to a demand that had been brewing for nearly two hundred years. Johnson was offered the job of compiling the *Dictionary* because of his hard-earned reputation among booksellers as a diligent, capable scholar. Johnson's *Dictionary* turned a solid profit for the booksellers and, insofar as the bolstering of his reputation was concerned, for Johnson as well. Yet in five editions over a period of some thirty years, a mere seventy-three hundred copies were produced—perhaps two thousand of these (second edition) in the form of inexpensive weekly printings of sheets.[55] While it is true that the favors of the great materialized on the eve of the *Dictionary*'s publication in April 1755—Chesterfield's flattering commentaries in the *World* of the previous November; the Oxford M.A. in February 1755— Johnson's achievement by then was unquestioned. Even the least experienced of London's authors would have been aware of such basic truths about the book trade; they must have howled at the wildly impracticable expectations of Johnson's fictional natural historian.[56]

Confronted by the realities of the literary marketplace—booksellers demand hard evidence of profitability; the Royal Society and the nobility are loath to squander patronage on one of London's innumerable novice authors—Johnson's fictional author invokes what are portrayed in *Rambler* 16, *Rambler* 146, the *Life of Savage,* and elsewhere as nothing more than shopworn canards. Johnson's fictional author blames the degeneracy of the age, threatening "in emulation of Raleigh" to burn his work and so leave his contemporaries to "the curses of posterity." Perhaps friends have pirated his ideas, Johnson's fictional author muses to himself, selling their "treacherous intelligence at a higher price than the fraudulence of the trade will now allow me for my book." The venality and ignorance of the booksellers fit into the picture as well, he is convinced. Easily the most striking reflection of the fictional author's self-delusion is his belligerence in dealing with a sympathetic printer, who offers him 200 copies of his natural history if he manages to procure subscriptions for 500. The similarity between Johnson's contract with Jacob Tonson, the publisher of Johnson's edition of Shakespeare's plays (1756), and the deal rejected by Johnson's fictional author illuminates the printer's magnanimity. Out of a first edition print run of 1,000 copies Johnson was allowed to keep 250 for his property. Yet instead of embracing what is by any sensible person's reckoning a generous proposition Johnson's fictional author assaults the printer.[57]

At this point it would be tempting to categorize *Idler* 55 as just one more satirical attack on deluded novices—an essay-length version, in other words, of the sneering remarks one often finds in the review journals of the 1750s—but there is more to the essay than that. It is worth noting that Johnson endows his fictional author with a number of admirable traits. He studies widely before considering himself "qualified" "to become an author," and he rejects intellectual determinism and allows his own inclinations to wander a bit before settling on natural history. What is more, Johnson's fictional author spares no labor in researching his subject: eight years of intense study and experimentation pass before his manuscript is finished to his satisfaction. Friends knowledgeable about natural history are consulted, but Johnson's fictional author refuses to yield control of the work's underlying design.[58]

What Johnson wants us to believe is that the fictional author's unrealistic ambitions are at the root of his great disappointments. True enough, the dynamics of the literary marketplace account for a measure of the fictional author's distress. But we are also given to understand that nothing short of astounding wealth and celebrity would have satisfied Johnson's fictional author, a point dramatized by the rejection of the subscription scheme—one any prudent author would have gladly accepted. What we find in *Idler* 55, as in *Rambler*s 2, 16, and 146 and the "Weekly Correspondent" essay, is Johnson striving to debunk some of the destructive myths that circulate amongst authors regarding the capacity of the literary marketplace to deliver fame and fortune.

The understanding of the scarcity of literary fame expressed in these five essays accounts in some measure for Johnson's sympathetic treatment of imperfect but essentially meritorious books in the *Literary Magazine*. The reviewer's duty as Johnson conceived it in the preface to the *Literary Magazine*'s first number is to "influence the public voice, and hasten the popularity of a valuable Work," a statement that implicitly acknowledges what *Rambler*s 2 and 146 state explicitly—that worthy publications may flounder, given the turbulence of the contemporary literary marketplace and the cynicism it has bred amongst readers and critics alike. *Rambler* 16 and *Idler* 55 provide further insight into Johnson's stern rejection of Thomas Blackwell's *Memoirs of the Court of Augustus* and Soame Jenyns's *A Free Inquiry into the Nature and Origin of Evil* (works that, in Johnson's view, reveal more about the vaingloriousness of their authors than about the subjects they profess to treat) and Johnson's decision to ignore the countless titles produced by patently incompetent authors.

EXTERNAL HAZARDS: TRADITIONAL PATRONAGE

Johnson's *Dictionary* offers four definitions of "Patron," two of which are relevant to Johnson's work as a book reviewer and as an observer of the contemporary literary scene (the others center on religious and ecclesiastical meanings). Sense one reads, "One who countenances, supports or protects. Commonly a wretch who supports with insolence, and is paid with flattery." The third sense is defined as follows: "Advocate; defender; vindicator." Whether Johnson in the latter half of sense one means to allude to his experiences with Lord Chesterfield, or whether the commentary simply reflects his general disdain for the dependent state in which traditional patronage places authors is a matter for speculation. Whatever the case, we should not overlook the fact that Johnson's definitions of "Patron" are essentially favorable: a patron is an "Advocate," a "vindicator," one who "supports," "protects," and so on. These terms aptly describe Johnson's work as a book reviewer. Johnson's four reviews in the *Critical*, for instance, are concrete acts of support for literary friends or acquaintances; and certainly Johnson's many apologetic reviews in the *Literary Magazine*—that is, reviews crafted as rebuttals to unfavorable pieces on the same subject published elsewhere—can be characterized as advocatory or vindicatory.

The following discussion illuminates Johnson's vigorous opposition in the *Rambler* to traditional forms of patronage and, correspondingly, his faith in the marketplace as a nurturer of literary merit. Johnson's work as a book reviewer complements the general outlook expressed in the *Rambler* essays on patronage. As subsequent chapters shall bear out, Johnson's reviews are basically acts of patronage directed at meritorious authors whose worthy efforts might otherwise be obscured by the tumultuousness of the contemporary literary marketplace. Much as a literary patron might provide material and moral encouragement to a favored writer, Johnson as book reviewer "supports" and "protects" meritorious authors by making sure their books are given a sympathetic introduction to what Johnson presumes to be a literary marketplace that is hostile or indifferent to the worthy author.

What was Samuel Johnson's underlying attitude to the culture of literary patronage as it existed in his day? There remains considerable disagreement among scholars on this matter. One popular school of thought holds that Johnson's outspoken criticism of patronage in the *Rambler* papers (1750–52) and elsewhere derives chiefly from his humiliation at the hands of Philip Dormer Stanhope, fourth earl of Chesterfield, who failed to deliver on his alleged promises to support Johnson as he was compiling his *Dictionary of the English Language* (1746-55). A competing view discerns an evolution in Johnson's outlook from the scorn expressed in the *Rambler* and the *Dictionary* to mild approval by the time the *Lives of the Poets* was composed in the late 1770s. Each of these positions is plausible, but neither takes into account the full context of Johnson's published commentary on patronage—particularly in the *Rambler* essay serial. There is plenty of evidence to suggest that Johnson's attitude was more complicated than either of these interpretations allows for. In the *Lives of the Poets* Johnson readily acknowledged the primacy of patronage in previous literary eras, but in his *Rambler* essays he encourages contemporaneous authors to place their faith in the literary marketplace rather than in the professed good intentions of any prospective patron. What makes Johnson's commentary distinctive is that his outlook contrasts sharply with the prevailing habits of his age, in which patronage and the literary marketplace complemented each other as sources of sustenance for aspiring authors.

"Is not a Patron, My Lord, one who looks with unconcern on a Man struggling for Life in the water and when he has reached ground encumbers him with help?" writes Samuel Johnson in his famous letter to Lord Chesterfield, dated 7 February 1755. "The notice which you have been pleased to take of my Labours, had it been early, had been kind; but it has been delayed till I am indifferent and cannot enjoy it, till I am solitary and cannot impart it, till I am known and do not want it."[59] Johnson's epistolary rebuke to Lord Chesterfield and the unsatisfying relationship that the letter recalls stand together as one of the more mythogenic episodes in English literary history, but the actual impact of the Chesterfield affair on Johnson's underlying attitude to patronage is easily exaggerated. Johnson was plainly offended by Chesterfield's self-serving, opportunistic endorsement of the *Dictionary* on the eve of publication, but it strains credulity to argue, as some scholars have, that Johnson saw himself as forcing a turning point in history when he wrote the famous letter, or to claim that the *Rambler* essays on patronage are suffused with autobiographical detail.[60] To begin with, it is worth recalling that Johnson decided to address the *Plan of a Dictionary of the English Language* (1747) to Chesterfield not because he craved aristocratic approval but because he needed an alibi for what at the time was his tardy execution of the project. Nor should we forget that the

Plan itself avoids the conventional fulsomeness that Johnson rails against in the *Rambler* papers on patronage. Given the traditional grandiloquence of dedicatory addresses, one might easily interpret Johnson's rhetorical restraint as mildly ironical at the very least.[61] Boswell's record of Johnson's conversation tells us that the unpleasantness between him and Lord Chesterfield amounted to nothing more than a private affair, and one of no particular consequence as far as Johnson was concerned.[62]

Additional evidence leads us to believe that Johnson's attitude to patronage was more sophisticated than interpretations based on the famous "Letter to Lord Chesterfield" would have us believe. To begin with, *Rambler* 136 (1751)—composed, we might imagine, when Chesterfield's empty promises were foremost in Johnson's mind—acknowledges the capacity of traditional patronage for good. "An author may with great propriety inscribe his work to him by whose encouragement it was undertaken," Johnson states, "or by whose liberality he has been enabled to prosecute it, and he may justly rejoice in his own fortitude that dares to rescue merit from obscurity." The twenty or so ghostwritten dedications that Johnson wrote in the years following the publication of the *Dictionary* suggest further that he did not find patronage itself to be a morally objectionable enterprise. And as O M Brack and Gae Holladay have demonstrated, Johnson was himself a literary patron in the broader senses of the term. Also worth noting is that the *Life of Savage* (1744) and the *Lives of the Poets* (1779-81) presented Johnson with ample opportunity to speak out against traditional forms of patronage, yet his commentary is dispassionate and even-handed.[63]

A recent attempt to ascertain Johnson's attitude to traditional forms of literary patronage is made by Dustin Griffin in *Literary Patronage in England, 1650–1800*. Griffin argues that the outlook embodied in the *Rambler* series and the Chesterfield letter mellowed to the point of approval by the time Johnson composed the *Lives of the Poets* (1779–81). "The full record shows that Johnson was much less critical of the private patron than we have heard," Griffin declares, and "that his attitude changed significantly from the 1740s to the late 1770s." Johnson ultimately viewed patronage as "no bad way to encourage and sustain genius"—if only because Johnson was himself "a participant in the traditional patronage system." Though "easily corrupted and often corrupt," Griffin adds, patronage occupied "a proper place" in the republic of letters as far as Johnson was concerned.[64]

Griffin's analysis of the eighteenth-century patronage culture in England is indispensable to students of the period, certainly, but his interpretation of Johnson's thought is seriously flawed. To begin with, Griffin's assertion that Johnson approved of traditional patronage because he was himself a beneficiary rests on a faulty premise. Griffin cites Johnson's prospects of obtaining a church living and his acceptance of the royal pension as evidence of his participation in traditional patronage, but these circumstances need further clarification. In 1756 the father of Johnson's friend Bennet Langton offered Johnson a parish living in Lincolnshire on the condition that he accept holy orders. Boswell tells us that Johnson refused, partly because he felt morally unworthy of the position, but also because he did not want to leave London. It is thus difficult to interpret this episode as demonstrating even a slight attraction in Johnson to traditional forms of patronage. We should also note that Johnson does not seem to have envied Thomas Birch (1705–66), a literary man whose livelihood was largely secured by the intercession of "appreciative and loyal patrons." Johnson's acceptance of the royal pension in 1763 was based on the understanding that it was strictly "honorary" and free from any political expectations whatsoever.[65]

Griffin sets forth Johnson's three subscription schemes—*The Poems of Politian* (1734), the *Harleian Catalogue* (1742), and the edition of Shakespeare's plays (1756–65)—as additional examples of his involvement with the patronage culture, but this argument also amounts to a misreading of Johnson's career. The three subscription schemes were based on contracts with booksellers, thus making the relation between subscriber and Johnson strictly one of buyer/seller. If anything, Johnson's subscription projects reflect an unwillingness to seek traditional forms of patronage as a means of publishing financially risky works. Griffin also claims that Johnson's numerous dedications reflect an underlying approval of traditional patronage. But Johnson looked upon such tasks as honest but humdrum work, as minor efforts written in the name of the author and dashed off as a way of helping friends or of earning a bit of money.[66]

A much more crippling weakness in Griffin's argument is his attempt to prove an evolution in Johnson's attitude by comparing the treatment of patronage in the *Rambler*, a journal that contains a great deal of commentary on contemporaneous issues even though the series ostensibly dwells on the universal and the timeless, with that of the *Lives of the Poets*, a work of literary history.[67] This is not to suggest that these texts must be studied in isolation from each other, or that no coherent body of thought emerges from Johnson's consideration of patronage in its historical or contemporaneous aspects. Rather, the *Lives* and the *Rambler* collectively express a more nuanced understanding of patronage than Griffin would have us believe. As a highly conscientious scholar Johnson would never misrepresent the primacy of patronage in previous eras—no matter how frustrating his own personal experiences with Lord Chesterfield may have been. Nor would Johnson raise doubts about the suitability of patronage for a handful of highly talented and well-connected contemporary poets such as James

Thomson (d. 1748). Even so, Johnson believed that as far as the general run of modern aspiring authors was concerned, the marketplace was a much more reliable and generous promoter of literary merit.

Before exploring this point further it is necessary briefly to consider the standing of patronage in Johnson's day. Dustin Griffin has successfully shown that patronage was alive and well throughout the eighteenth century, though it was no longer the dominant force in professional letters that it had been in previous centuries. Equally significant is that patronage during the age of Johnson divides neatly into two categories: political and social. Political patronage, the more frequently practiced of the two, normally took the form of an appointment to a church living or an award of a sinecure in government service. In an arrangement of this kind the author was expected to write on behalf of the patron's interests whenever called upon to do so. By contrast, social patronage as practiced by Lord Chesterfield and other members of the nobility "always provided not primary but supplementary income," Griffin points out. The author who benefited from social patronage would also garner a measure of prestige from having his work endorsed by the social elite. As a reward for encouraging and protecting an author in this way, the social patron would receive the copyright of the work and whatever entertainment it may have provided. If the work sold well the social patron would also benefit from the association of his name with a significant literary achievement.[68]

Johnson's *Life of Savage* provides a case study of the supplemental and occasional nature of both social and political patronage in the eighteenth century. Lord Tyrconnel, Mrs. Oldfield, and Queen Caroline all provided the poet Richard Savage with stipends or other kinds of material support—though except for Oldfield none of these were as generous as Savage had hoped. These social patrons viewed Savage not as a complete dependent but as a talented author whose work entitled him to recognition and encouragement. Savage also stood as a candidate for political patronage, as he was told at one point that the Walpole Administration intended to award him a sinecure as a means of "setting him at length free from that indigence by which he had hitherto been oppressed." This promise was made in the same spirit as were the other activities of his patrons: all parties worked under the assumption that Savage would earn the better part of his living and all of his fame from the staging of his plays, the copyright sales of his poetry, subscription schemes, and so forth.[69]

Savage's essentially favorable experiences with patronage were not enough to convince his biographer of its enduring worthiness. Indeed, Johnson's *Rambler* essays invariably depict patronage and the marketplace not as complementary or interconnected means of providing a livelihood for authors—which is precisely how things worked in Johnson's day—but as starkly contrasting moral options. When considered in relation to each other patronage is always portrayed as corrupting and stifling, while the marketplace is cast as evenhanded and welcoming. That this is Johnson's underlying position is illustrated further by his letters and conversation. Writing to his friend Giuseppi Baretti in 1762, Johnson recommends that Baretti, whose patron had failed to deliver on promised support, "quit" his dreams of "greatness" and "preferment," and instead "try once more the fortune of literature and industry."[70] Johnson makes the same point during his visit to the Hebrides in 1773. In response to a complaint from Boswell regarding the contemporaneous dearth of munificent patrons, Johnson makes a case for the obsolescence of traditional patronage and, collaterally, asserts that the marketplace more effectively promotes literary merit:

> If learning cannot support a man, if he must sit with his hands across till somebody feeds him, it [patronage] is as to him a bad thing, and it is better as it is. With patronage, what flattery! what falsehood! While a man is in equilibrio, he throws truth among the multitude, and lets them take it as they please: in patronage, he must say what pleases his patron, and it is an equal chance whether that be truth or falsehood.[71]

Particularly noteworthy here is the complete absence of ambiguity or reservation. Johnson associates the marketplace with authorial independence and dignity, patronage with sloth, toadyism, and uncertainty. Johnson uncompromisingly rejects traditional patronage because as far as he was concerned the possibility of exploitation far outweighed the doubtful and often trifling advantages of political or social patronage.

Published expressions of Johnson's outlook on political patronage and the marketplace can be found as early as 1739. Appearing in the January issue of the *Gentleman's Magazine*, Johnson's "Letter to Mr. Urban" bemoans the newspaper industry's reliance on what is best described as political propaganda—much of it written, as Johnson surely knew, by writers working for political patrons. To "single out any Man for a perpetual Mark of Reproach, or Theme of Panegyrick, to praise or libel by the Week, is a Conduct to the last Degree shameless and profligate," Johnson declares. Elsewhere in the essay Johnson characterizes partisan writers as "Prostitutes of the Pen, who poison the Principles of Nations."[72] In his role as a disgruntled "correspondent" who speaks on behalf of the reading public, Johnson asserts that a commitment to truth will attract and keep readers, while a reliance on political propaganda will drive down the circulation of newspapers. Political patronage and the marketplace are thus cast as employers competing for the services of news writers. To accept political patronage, in other words, is to tie one's fate to that of a minister or government that may fall out of favor tomorrow, while a reputation for reliable reporting will never fail to draw a robust, loyal readership. The emphatic contrast Johnson draws here between the marketplace and political patronage anticipates his treatment of the subject in the *Rambler* series eleven years later.

*Rambler*s 26 and 27 (June 1750) together offer a fictional account of a talented but improvident modern writer whose lofty expectations of political patronage soon give way to what Johnson would have us believe is the manner in which most authors are treated by their supposed benefactors. *Rambler* 26 begins as many of Johnson's "letters" from "correspondents" do, with "Eubulus" calling attention to the didactic value of his experiences. "My narrative will not exhibit any great variety of events, or extraordinary revolutions," Eubulus declares, "but may, perhaps, be not less useful, because I shall relate nothing which is not likely to happen to a thousand others." Eubulus's troubles begin during his time as an undergraduate, when acquaintances encourage him to believe that his appetite for high living and disdain for hard study betoken a brilliant career in public service. Eubulus eventually leaves the university without taking a degree, alienating along the way an uncle who sponsored Eubulus on the condition that he pursue a career in law. "[I] was often so much elated with my superiority to the youths with whom I conversed, that I began to listen, with great attention, to those that recommended to me a wider and more conspicuous theatre," Eubulus recalls, adding that he was "particularly touched with an observation, made by one of my friends: That it was not by lingering in the university, that Prior became ambassador, or Addison secretary of state."[73] Interestingly enough, it is the invocation of Matthew Prior (1664–1721) and Joseph Addison (1672–1719) here that inspires Eubulus to repudiate a promising arrangement and so allows him eventually to be drawn into the degrading world of political patronage.

The references to Prior and Addison underscore Eubulus's deeply flawed understanding of the culture of political patronage. As Johnson almost certainly knew, Addison and Prior did indeed "linger" at university long enough, at least, for each to complete his undergraduate studies (Addison attended Queen's College, Oxford; Prior, St. John's College, Cambridge). More significantly, Addison and Prior attracted influential patrons on account of their literary talent, which was acquired and honed as part of their formal education. Prominent diplomatic appointments were offered to Addison and Prior, moreover, because they were demonstrably capable of handling the immense responsibilities such positions entailed. Details of this sort remain invisible to Eubulus, who looks upon patronage—as perhaps many aspiring authors did in the wake of the reign of Queen Anne (d. 1714), the golden age of patronage—as a kind of beauty contest, the chief prerequisites being glibness and a yearning for the trappings of high social position.[74]

As Johnson's narrative develops, both the unreliability of the patron-age culture and the foolhardiness of Eubulus's rejection of a proper university education become increasingly apparent. Eubulus's first few patrons are fickle and frivolous but hardly malicious. "Charinus" warmly promises to find a "place" for Eubulus but is soon distracted by a procession of social commitments. No direct harm comes to Eubulus here, but we are given to understand that he is frittering away his time. The most reliable patron turns out to be the most nefarious. The "favour" of "Eutyches the states-man" was "more permanent than that of the others," Eubulus recalls in *Rambler* 27, but his "demands were, indeed, very often such as virtue could not easily consent to gratify." At one point Eutyches is censured publicly for a grave but unspecified wrongdoing. Eubulus is asked to write propaganda exonerating his patron, which he does successfully enough—but at the price of a clean conscience. Soon afterward Eubulus comes into a small inheritance that allows him to escape the morally repugnant duties that political patronage inevitably requires. "I am now endeavouring to recover the dignity, and hope to make some reparation for my crime and follies," states Eubulus in the final sentence of number 27, "by informing others, who may be led after the same pageants, that they are about to engage in a course of life, in which they are to purchase, by a thousand miseries, the privilege of repentance."[75] It is worth emphasizing here that Eubulus gets everything that he dreamed of during his heady youth: a well-known political figure as a patron and a guaranteed forum for his writings, not to mention the other usufructs that accompany high political appointments. Even so, these emoluments—alluring though they may be at first glance—ultimately prove to be the evanescent part of a Faustian bargain.

Social patronage is treated with equal severity in the *Rambler* series. An example of this is *Rambler* 91, which allegorically characterizes the marketplace and social patronage as stark moral opposites. A judicious and generous friend to the "Sciences" (i.e., learning) in its pristine state, "Patronage" in Johnson's narrative is eventually suborned by "Pride," "Caprice," and "Flattery"—with predictable results:

> It frequently happened that Science, unwilling to lose the antient prerogative of recommending to Patronage, would lead her followers into the Hall of Expectation; but they were soon discouraged from attending, for not only Envy and Suspicion incessantly tormented them, but Impudence considered them as intruders, and incited Infamy to blacken them.[76]

We can detect a biographical element here—in Johnson's famous letter we are given to understand that he was treated in a similar way when he visited Lord Chesterfield—but Johnson's chief message is that the culture of social patronage is not merely obtuse on occasion but temperamentally antagonistic to genuine literary merit.[77]

Countless other indignities are suffered at the hands of "Patronage" before the "Sciences" are driven into exile. They eventually find refuge in the "cottage of Independence, the daughter of Fortitude," where they are instructed by "Prudence and Parsimony to support themselves in dignity and quiet."[78] Johnson's stern rejection of social patronage is obvious enough here, but the unvarnished portrayal of the literary marketplace—the "Sciences" end up in a remote cottage rather than in a shining city on a hill—is equally significant, because it reveals a good deal about the contemporaneous context of the essay. Johnson in *Rambler* 91 speaks to aspiring writers who may have been striving after social patronage as a way of buffering or escaping from what was widely thought of as the cramping and stressful circumstances of commercial authorship. The literary marketplace remains a stalwart ally of literary merit, Johnson encourages readers to believe, no matter how modest its financial rewards may seem.

Rambler 163 offers a similarly sharp contrast between social patronage and writing for the general public. The myth of Tantalus "was perhaps originally suggested to some poet by the conduct of his patron, by the daily contemplation of splendor which he never must partake, by fruitless attempts to catch at interdicted happiness, and by the sudden evanescence of his reward, when he thought his labours almost at an end," Johnson states as he introduces a "letter" from "Liberalis," a name that, significantly enough, means "freeborn."[79] Johnson's opening observations here are rather time-worn. For the moment at least, we are encouraged to expect another morality tale of the deluded aspiring author who becomes the easy prey of an unscrupulous patron. Indeed, a regular reader of the *Rambler* might well have sensed a trace of staleness here, concluding perhaps that "Mr. Rambler" in number 163 is merely recycling commonplaces from numbers 21, 26, 27, 91, and 104.[80] But what makes number 163 distinctive is that Johnson's protagonist is not a helpless or naive author who, in the manner of Eubulus, is lured into the patronage culture. Rather, in "Liberalis" Johnson presents us with a demonstrably successful modern author who has rejected the marketplace in favor of patronage and who writes to "Mr. Rambler" explaining why he has come to regret his choice.

As his "correspondence" makes clear, Liberalis is talented, diligent, and remarkably aware of the workings of the literary marketplace. We learn of Liberalis's numerous first-place finishes in several undergraduate literary competitions, for instance. We are also told that, having labored for years on what was to become his inaugural publication, Liberalis delays his departure from university until the necessary finishing touches are completed—thus demonstrating a commendable fastidiousness. Though confident of his prospects Liberalis chooses to remain anonymous when it comes time to publish, knowing as he does "that no performance is so favourably read as that of a writer who suppresses his name." The literary marketplace responds exactly as Liberalis had anticipated. His book sells briskly, its reputation enhanced by Liberalis's shrewd self-promotion. "I wandered from one place of concourse to another," Liberalis recalls, "feasted from morning to night on the repetition of my own praises, and enjoyed the various conjectures of criticks, the mistaken candour of my friends, and the impotent malice of my enemies." Liberalis thus stimulates interest in his work with carefully planted praises. Because no name is attached to the title page, rivals have no choice but to collaborate in the work's success by making self-aggrandizing claims about their supposed relation to the anonymous author. Keenly aware of the necessity of writing to a high standard yet also sufficiently cunning to make even the marketplace's most daunting menaces work for him, Liberalis is clearly at home in the world of commercial letters.[81]

What dooms Liberalis is a hedonistic streak that leaves him vulnerable to the blandishments of social patronage. It is important to note that Liberalis chooses authorship over other professions not for the lofty purposes that motivated Johnson, but because of its superior capacity to gratify his overweening vanity: "[N]othing entered my imagination, but honours, caresses, and rewards, riches without labour, and luxury without expense," Liberalis recalls himself thinking as his literary project neared completion. Not surprisingly, Liberalis eagerly parlays his initial literary success into a place in the retinue of "Aurantius, the standing patron of merit." What follows is a fictional rendition of Johnson's understanding of the pathology of social patronage.

At first, Aurantius merely tantalizes Liberalis with vague praise that "included no particular promise, and therefore conferred no claim." Aurantius's breezy, insincere encouragement of Liberalis soon descends into cruelty. Convinced that Aurantius means well, Liberalis with pleasure and in good conscience exhausts his meager savings as he waits for an appointment to a position "of dignity and profit" that Aurantius has no serious intention of offering him. In the meantime, Aurantius treats Liberalis with increasing scorn. Asked to write on particular subjects, Liberalis invariably finds his compositions belittled and then rewritten by his patron. The final straw comes in the form of a particularly seedy quid pro quo. "[I]n the eighth year of my servitude, when the clamour of creditors was vehement, and my necessity known to be extreme," Liberalis recalls, Aurantius "offered me a small office, but hinted his expectations that I should marry a young woman with whom he had been acquainted." Liberalis is thus impelled to repudiate the social patronage he once desperately craved.

"I turned away with that contempt with which I shall never want spirit to treat the wretch," Liberalis declares, "who lures the credulous and thoughtless to maintain the show of his levee, and the mirth of his table, at the expence of honour, happiness, and life."[82]

The story of Liberalis exemplifies nicely Johnson's treatment of traditional forms of patronage in the *Rambler* series. Of course, Johnson's outlook departs significantly from the actual relation between traditional patronage and the literary marketplace during the mid-eighteenth century, as Dustin Griffin has shown, but clearly Johnson believed, and wanted his contemporaries to believe, that traditional forms of patronage had outlived their usefulness and that the literary marketplace had proved itself to be a much more reliable friend to meritorious authors. Johnson's work as a book reviewer extends the attack on traditional patronage found in the *Rambler* papers. Johnson's book reviews in at least a minor way seek to accelerate the decline of traditional patronage by helping deserving authors make their way in the literary world. What Johnson's practices as a reviewer suggest is that book reviewing, properly understood, can and should replace traditional forms of patronage as a means of supporting and protecting literary merit.

EXTERNAL HAZARDS: THE EMERGENCE OF
THE *MONTHLY REVIEW* AND *CRITICAL REVIEW*

The rise of book reviewing during the mid-eighteenth century was briefly touched upon earlier in this chapter as part a broader discussion of major trends in the literary marketplace. Johnson was both a writer and the subject of reviews, so it is not much of a surprise to find that he held strong opinions on this emerging branch of literary criticism.[83] Essentially, Johnson looked upon the normative practices and immediate success of the two leading review journals as a menace to the general run of aspiring authors. However, Johnson also makes clear in a number of essays and in his own practices as a reviewer that criticism directed at the work of living writers is a necessary and beneficial activity, if conducted with an awareness of the various limitations of critical intelligence.[84]

Particularly distressing to Johnson is that the carefully cultivated identity of the *Monthly* and the *Critical*, who retailed themselves as supreme judges of merit and dispensers of reputation, in fact contributed to the wretchedness of contemporary letters.[85] In the "Reflections on the Present State of Literature" (*Universal Visiter,* April 1756), for instance, Johnson portrays the *Monthly*, the *Critical*, and their imitators as predators who specialize in exploiting the vulnerability of fellow authors. "The *Reviewers* and *Critical Reviewers*, the *Remarkers* and *Examiners*, can satisfy their hunger only by devouring their brethren," Johnson says as part of a broader commentary on the desperate conditions of present-day authorship. "I am far from imagining that they are naturally more ravenous or blood-thirsty than those on whom they fall with so much violence and fury," Johnson adds, "but they are hungry, and hunger must be satisfied; and these savages, when their bellies are full, will fawn on those whom they now bite." The implication here, clearly, is that the leading review journals place their own survival in the marketplace ahead of critical integrity.[86]

Equally strident in its outlook on the major review journals is Johnson's "Preliminary Discourse" to the *London Chronicle* (1 January 1757). Johnson ultimately contributed little to the only newspaper he is reported to have read regularly. And it is worth noting that the *London Chronicle* preface was almost certainly based on a prospectus provided by the owners rather than being a completely original piece. No evidence exists, moreover, to suggest that Johnson was expected to write regularly for the *London Chronicle;* he was paid one guinea for the work and that, it seems, was the end of the matter.[87] Even so, the "Preliminary Discourse" illuminates further Johnson's underlying attitude to book reviewing. "That Part of our Work by which it is distinguished from all others, is the *Literary Journal*, or Account of the Labours of the *Learned*," Johnson declares. "This was, for a long Time, among the Deficiencies of English Literature, but as the Caprice of Man is always starting from too little to too much, we have now, amongst other Disturbers of human Quiet, a numerous body of *Reviewers* and *Remarkers*."[88] Significantly, Johnson here acknowledges the potential worthiness of reviewing even as he criticizes the prevailing practices of contemporary reviewers. Johnson goes on to highlight the characteristics of the *Monthly* and the *Critical* against what he sees as legitimate objectives of book reviewing. "We shall endeavour to avoid that Petulance which treats with Contempt whatever has hitherto been reputed sacred," Johnson declares, in a thinly veiled rebuke to the *Monthly*'s alleged nonconformism. "We shall repress that Elation of Malignity, which wantons in the Cruelties of Criticism, and not only murders Reputation, but Murders it by Torture," Johnson adds, allusively attacking the *Critical* for its telltale imperiousness and acerbity:[89]

> Whenever we feel ourselves ignorant, we shall, at least, be modest. Our Intention is not to preoccupy Judgment by Praise or Censure, but to gratify Curiosity by early Intelligence, and to tell rather what our Authors have attempted, than what they have performed. The Titles of Books are necessarily short, and therefore disclose but imperfectly the Contents; they are sometimes fraudulent, and intended to raise false Expectations. In our

Account this Brevity will be extended, and these Frauds, whenever they are detected, will be exposed; for though we write without Intention to injure, we shall not suffer ourselves to be made Parties to Deceit.[90]

Here and in the "Reflections on the Present State of Literature," Johnson speaks not as a victim of savage reviewing—after all, the only work by Johnson that had been reviewed at the time was the *Dictionary*, and it was generally well received—but as a member of the reviewing fraternity himself. Indeed, the reviewing policy set forth here neatly summarizes Johnson's own practices as a reviewer in the *Literary Magazine*, where thirty-two of his forty reviews had already appeared. Of greater significance is that in both the "Reflections" and the "Preliminary Discourse" Johnson attempts to unmask what he believes are the major review journals' false but widely accepted claims to critical authority. Far from being discerning and impartial adjudicators of literary merit, Johnson would have us believe, the *Monthly* and *Critical* are perhaps best thought of as purveyors of malice and pettifoggery.[91]

Additional anecdotal evidence of Johnson's impatience with the imperiousness of the major review journals can be found in his rejection in 1759 of a suggestion by Goldsmith, by then a frequent contributor to both the *Critical Review* and *Monthly Review*, that he and Johnson review each other's recent publications *(Rasselas, The Present State of Polite Learning)*. "'[S]et Reviewers at defiance!'" Johnson claims to have said at the time.[92] But perhaps the most interesting of Johnson's rebukes to reviewers is his earliest. In the third number of the *Rambler* we find Johnson offering allusive criticism of the *Monthly Review* ten months after its commencement in May 1749.

To understand fully *Rambler* 3 (March 1750) we must begin by considering the objectives of the *Monthly Review* as expressed in its initial "Advertisement":

> When the abuse of title-pages is obviously come to such a pass, that few readers care to take in a book, any more than a servant, without a recommendation; to acquaint the public that a summary review of the productions of the press, as they occur to notice, was perhaps never more necessary than now, would be superfluous and vain. The cure then for this general complaint is evidently, and only, to be found in a periodical work, whose sole object should be to give a compendious account of those productions of the press, as they come out, that are worth notice; an account, in short, which should, in virtue of its candour, and justness of distinction, obtain authority enough for its representations to be serviceable to such as would choose to have some idea of a book before they lay out their money or time on it.[93]

To these aims one must add the promise made in the *Monthly*'s third number to "register all the new Things in general, without exception to any, on account of their lowness of rank, or price." The marketplace immediately validated the *Monthly Review*'s self-appointed role as a civilizing force in a chaotic book trade. The print quantity of the *Monthly* began at 1,000 copies for each of its first three issues. After dipping to 750 in August and then to 500 in November 1749, the number of issues printed each month climbed to 1,000 for 1750 and continued to rise after that. By the time *Rambler* 3 appeared on 27 March 1750, ten numbers of the *Monthly* had already been published, with the eleventh issue due within a few days. Johnson likely would have acquired a solid idea of the *Monthly*'s popularity through his frequent meetings with the printer of the *Monthly,* William Strahan, who served not only as the printer for the *Dictionary* project but also as a liaison between Johnson and the sponsoring booksellers. Johnson, in fact, began renting the now-famous house at 17 Gough Square in 1747 chiefly because of its proximity to Strahan's printing house.[94]

Rambler 3 begins with a survey of the hazards that confront contemporary authors. The prejudices of readers are noted—"men must not only be persuaded of their errors, but reconciled to their guide; they must not only confess their ignorance, but what is still less pleasing, must allow that he from whom they are to learn is more knowing than themselves"—but the most daunting menace in the view of "Mr. Rambler" is the domineering impulse of "modern criticks." There "is a certain race of men, that either imagine it their duty, or make it their amusement, to hinder the reception of every work of learning or genius," Johnson observes, "who stand as centinels in the avenues of fame, and value themselves upon giving Ignorance and Envy the first notice of prey." Significantly, Johnson points out that these "modern criticks" have the "watchfulness" but not the "eyes" of "Argus"; in other words, they might very well live up to claims of surveying every new work, but readers are advised not to expect anything in the way of discerning or trustworthy analysis.[95]

Thus, we can see that the *Monthly*'s claims to comprehensiveness and impartiality—much heralded in its advertisements—are singled out in the essay ("every work" is scrutinized; the "Argus" reference), as is the review journal's equally prominent pledge to examine new works as soon as they appear ("centinels in the avenues of fame"). The corrosive impact of heavy-handed reviewing on public opinion, which Johnson would decry years later in his prefatory essay to the *London Chronicle*, is also addressed here— "modern criticks" who give "first notice" to ignorance and envy, and generally "hinder the reception" of works—and so is the *Monthly*'s emphasis on the anonymity of its staff writers, the early title pages mentioning that each volume was the work of "several hands" ("a certain race of men,"

Johnson notes in the essay).[96] The allegorical history of criticism that fills out *Rambler* 3, meanwhile, is intended to give historical perspective to Johnson's observations on the vanity of attempting authoritative judgments on contemporaneous works.

To be sure, the characterization of the *Monthly* in *Rambler* 3 is heavily exaggerated. Most reviews in the first dozen issues of the *Monthly* comprise extract and summary strung together with blandly critical remarks, though pronounced criticism does appear occasionally. Nevertheless, the book-buying public's eagerness to rely on the *Monthly* almost certainly gave the journal a menacing aspect in the eyes of some aspiring writers. Johnson speaks on behalf of such authors in *Rambler* 3, as he attempts to illuminate the potential abuses of a monthly journal that promises an impartial yet judicious survey of all newly published works. Johnson does not attack book reviewing as a concept here, but rather the folly of a review journal that arrogates the authority to arbitrate between readers and authors. On this point *Rambler* 3 anticipates Johnson's later attacks on regular reviewing in the "Reflections on the Present State of Literature" and in the *London Chronicle* prefatory essay and, collaterally, sheds light on Johnson's reluctance as a reviewer himself to make dogmatic pronouncements.

Johnson clearly despised reviewing as practiced by the most influential journals of the period, but it is equally clear, as Johnson's preface to the *London Chronicle* demonstrates, that he accepted in theory the basic legitimacy of book reviewing. Several *Rambler* papers provide further evidence of Johnson's underlying position that book reviewing, if practiced judiciously, might benefit the contemporary literary world. One of the major literary themes of the *Rambler* series is the vulnerability of meritorious authors in particular to the indifference and cynicism of the contemporary reading public.[97] Johnson repeatedly argues in the *Rambler* series and elsewhere that genuine literary merit is normally not enough to guarantee literary reputation, thus implying that the critic's job is to help readers see beyond their prejudices and received opinion on literary matters, and to make sound judgments of newly published books: "to improve opinion into knowledge," as Johnson put the matter in *Rambler* 92.[98] Indeed, Johnson's many commentaries on authorship would lead us to believe that a warrantable place in professional letters exists for a temperate strain of contemporaneous criticism, one that avoids all the obvious pitfalls—making dogmatic judgments that are inevitably infected by the critic's innate biases; assuming that one's judgments embody the critical clarity that only comes with the passage of time—but which offers book buyers an intelligent survey of new works that by any sensible person's reckoning add to the stock of human knowledge or innocent amusement.

Put another way, Johnson's general outlook on the art of criticism allows for book reviewing of the kind Johnson actually practiced, even as it also allusively rejects the sort of dogmatic approach embraced by the leading review journals. Unlike his counterparts at the leading review journals, who thought of themselves as supreme arbiters of literary merit, Johnson looked upon reviewing as a worthy but subordinate activity. As subsequent chapters shall bear out, Johnson's reviews exemplify the idea that the benefits of reviewing were limited to advancing the prospects of worthy authors and helping the general run of readers make informed choices about which titles were worth buying at a historical moment when the book trade was producing a vast amount of literature—much of it, as Johnson observes in *Rambler* 16, *Adventurer* 115, the "Reflections on the Present State of Literature," and *Idler* 2, of questionable value.

2

Johnson as a Reviewer of Historical, Literary, and Philosophical Titles in the *Literary Magazine*

IN THE SPRING OF 1755, SHORTLY BEFORE THE PUBLICATION OF THE *DICTIONARY*, Samuel Johnson began investigating the possibility of establishing a review journal devoted to serious works of scholarship. The following entry appears in his diary for March/early April 1755:

> *The Annals of Literature, foreign as well as domestick.* Imitate Le Clerk—Bayle—Barbeyrac. Infelicity of Journals in England. Works of the Learned. We cannot take in all. Sometimes copy from foreign Journalists. Always tell.[1]

Johnson's plan to start a review journal that would cater to the tastes of scholars and the academically minded among the leisured classes would surface again in a letter to Thomas Warton, written at about the time of the diary entry. "I intend in the winter to open a Bibliotheque, and remember that you have subscribed a Sheet a year," Johnson declares; "let us try likewise if we cannot persuade your Brother [Joseph Warton] to subscribe another."[2] The scholarly periodical envisioned here never materialized, but these private statements suggest strongly that Johnson looked upon regular reviewing not strictly as a means of earning a living when no congenial literary work was available, as some Johnson scholars have claimed, but as a consequential and dignified critical occupation.[3]

Also worth noting about the diary entry is Johnson's remark on the "Infelicity" of contemporary review journals. The *Dictionary* tersely defines "Infelicity" as "Unhappiness; misery; calamity," which would lead us to conclude that the state of book reviewing in Johnson's opinion was not merely imperfect or flawed but positively wretched. Should we read Johnson's remarks on this point as conveying contempt for the practices of the *Monthly Review* and the handful of less successful imitators? Or does Johnson here mean to say that important works of scholarship are regularly crowded out of the marketplace, thanks to the sheer volume of less worthy material and the current absence of a journal devoted to reviewing scholarly titles? Whatever is specifically meant here, at some point within the next twelve months Johnson accepted the editorship of the *Literary Magazine*, the only time in his career when he would write book reviews with some regularity.

The editorship of the *Literary Magazine* initially must have struck Johnson as a severe compromise, if the journals given as models in his diary entry are anything to go by. Jean Le Clerc's *Bibliotheque Universelle et Historique* (1686–93), Pierre Bayle's *Nouvelles de la Republique des Lettres* (1684–87), and Jean Barbeyrac's *Bibliotheque raisonnée des Ouvrages des Scavans* (1728–53) differed fundamentally from review periodicals exemplified by the *Monthly Review* and its many imitators, which included to a limited extent the *Literary Magazine*, even though both categories of journals relied heavily on abstracted material.[4] The French journals listed by Johnson were international in scope, publishing abstracts of books written in Latin and other foreign languages and addressed specifically to a learned group of readers. By contrast, the *Literary Magazine* was "designed for general perusal," as Johnson put the matter in the prefatory essay of the first issue.[5] What is more, the *Literary Magazine*'s review section competed for space with news accounts, the reprinting of governmental documents, the publication of obituary notices, lists of marriages, births, and ministerial appointments, and the like. Needless to say, had Johnson reviewed nothing but learned works, the *Literary Magazine* would have taken on a split personality—half populist and half scholarly—thus appealing convincingly to neither a middlebrow nor an erudite readership. Johnson ultimately would make the best of the circumstances by giving priority to what were in his view worthier sorts of material and avoiding the detritus cast about by the unregulated book trade. The *Monthly Review*'s aim of comprehensiveness required its staff writers to review, for instance, *Bumfodder for the Ladies: A Poem on Soft Paper* (1753) and *A Letter from a Cobler to the People of England, on Affairs of Importance* (1755), but Johnson gave himself license to ignore plainly unworthy publications and he focuses instead on books representing the higher echelons of popular literature, such as works in the physical and natural sciences, translations of ancient texts, histories, significant political pamphlets, and so on.[6]

The *Literary Magazine* was not designed to compete directly with the *Monthly Review* or its chief rival, the *Critical Review*. In matters of form, the *Literary Magazine* is best thought of as an imitator of the *Gentleman's Magazine*—both periodicals averaged about fifty-five octavo pages per monthly issue—and, in terms of content, as a journal of opinion that persistently and at times obstreperously opposed the war with France (the Seven Years' War, 1756–63). The review section of the *Literary Magazine* varied in size from issue to issue and was superintended by Johnson from May 1756 until July 1757—though Johnson ceased contributing regularly to the *Literary Magazine* by November 1756. It seems that future Vinerian Professor of Law Robert Chambers, who was at the time an Oxford undergraduate, and Griffith Jones, who would eventually serve as editor of the *London Chronicle* and the *Public Ledger*, contributed material to the *Literary Magazine*, as did *Gray's-Inn Journal* author and playwright Arthur Murphy.[7]

As literary editor, Johnson presumably selected the books he reviewed.[8] Johnson also wrote the bulk of the journal's reviews during this period, along with what would prove to be the *Literary Magazine*'s most controversial editorial pieces, such as the "Introduction to the Political State of Great-Britain" and the "Reflections on the Present State of Affairs, 1756." Indeed, Johnson's frequent criticisms of England's war effort almost certainly inhibited sales of the journal and, perhaps, hastened his departure. The circulation of the *Literary Magazine* hovered around five hundred per issue during Johnson's tenure—less than one-fourth that of the *Monthly Review* and about one-seventh the circulation of the *Gentleman's Magazine*. The eagerness of the *Literary Magazine*'s proprietors to bring about improvements in its fortunes—apart from accepting Johnson's resignation— is also marked by the journal's name change and the much greater emphasis on politics at the expense of literary material that followed Johnson's departure. As Donald Greene has pointed out, the *Literary Magazine* from 1757 onward became "violently patriotic," going so far as to modify its name in January 1758 to the *Literary and Antigallican Magazine*. Such actions ultimately proved fruitless, as the *Literary Magazine* folded in July 1758 after the publication of its twenty-seventh number.[9]

The seriousness and intelligence that Johnson would bring to his only stint as a regular reviewer is foreshadowed in his essay "To the Public," which prefaced the *Literary Magazine*'s inaugural issue. "The literary History necessarily contains an account of the Labours of the Learned, in which whether we shall shew much judgment or sagacity, must be left to our Readers to determine," Johnson states as he sets forth the journal's reviewing policy; "we can promise only justness and candour."

> It is not to be expected that we can insert extensive extracts or critical Examinations of all the writings which this age of writers may offer to our notice. A few only will deserve the distinction of criticism, and a few only will obtain it. We shall try to select the best and most important pieces, and

are not without hope, that we may sometimes influence the public voice, and hasten the popularity of a valuable Work.[10]

Fully to appreciate the significance of these remarks one must be familiar not only with the practices of the two major review journals at the time but also with Johnson's understanding of the contemporary literary landscape as expressed in his essay serials and occasional journalistic commentary. By characterizing his reviewing as an account of "the Labours of the Learned," for instance, Johnson essentially pledges to focus attention on aspiring writers who have met the traditional prerequisites of authorship spelled out in *Rambler* 154 and *Adventurer* 115. That comparatively few authors will receive the "distinction of criticism," meanwhile, is a way of conferring justified neglect on the multitude of worthless productions turned out by the legions of inept dabblers, hacks, and novices discussed in the "Reflections on the Present State of Literature," *Rambler* 16, *Idler* 2, and elsewhere. Such a policy also spares Johnson the necessity of writing captious reviews—a practice that, as Johnson makes clear in his prefatory essay to the *London Chronicle*, did so much to demean the worthy estate of criticism. The explicit intention to "influence the public voice, and hasten the popularity of a valuable Work" addresses the difficulties worthy authors face in gaining a fair hearing from the public, points explored fully in *Rambler*s 1, 2, 146, and elsewhere. A favorable review would encourage the sale of a meritorious book that might otherwise go unnoticed in the sea of new works flowing from the popular presses, or perhaps rescue a deserving work from an incompetent review. Indeed, Johnson here can be said to look upon reviewing as the literary marketplace's answer to traditional forms of literary patronage.[11] We can interpret Johnson's reviewing policy in the *Literary Magazine*, in other words, as an extension of his generally dismissive attitude to social and political patronage as expressed in *Rambler*s 21, 26, 27, 91, 104, 163, and elsewhere.[12]

Also worth noting about the *Literary Magazine* prefatory essay is its conformity to Johnson's well-known views on the primacy of popular judgment.[13] In the prefatory essay Johnson pledges to set forth, to the extent that time and space allow, works that have met basic scholarly and aesthetic standards. It is then up to the public to adjudicate between the competing but essentially legitimate claims to literary honors made by the authors under review. Of equal importance is Johnson's promise to screen out patently unsuitable works—the very kinds of books, as he points out in *Idler* 85, that "distract choice without supplying any real want"—so that readers can choose from among worthwhile books rather than a bewildering array of deceptive advertisements and bombastic titles churned out by the book trade.[14]

How do Johnson's actual practices compare to the ambitious aims suggested by the *Literary Magazine*'s prefatory essay? To begin with, almost all of the works reviewed by Johnson are also given notice in the *Monthly Review*, the *Critical Review*, or both. Many of the titles Johnson reviewed were given notice earlier by the *Monthly* or *Critical*, thus suggesting the possibility that Johnson routinely consulted the two leading review journals before deciding on what books to review in the *Literary Magazine*.[15] In fact, as this and subsequent chapters bear out, several of Johnson's reviews appear to rebut or in some way comment on competing reviews published in the *Monthly* or the *Critical*. We can safely say, then, that Johnson did not intend to use the *Literary Magazine* to advance any sort of eccentric canon of works, or as a matter of principle to celebrate authors who were otherwise ignored by the reviewing press.

Perusing a bibliography of Johnson's known contributions to the *Literary Magazine* demonstrates clearly enough that Johnson reviewed a remarkably diverse collection of books, as we find him giving notice to works on subjects ranging from apiculture and bleaching to moral philosophy and public affairs. Of the thirty-eight books that Johnson reviewed in the *Literary Magazine*, twelve fall into the category of literature of the humanities; fifteen titles can be described as journalistic works and public policy pamphlets and treatises (discussed in chapter 3); and eleven belong under the heading of practical arts and the physical sciences (discussed in chapter 4).

In regard to the literature of the humanities, Johnson's choice of books to review in the *Literary Magazine* can fairly be described as at least mildly idiosyncratic—especially when we bear in mind trends in the mid-eighteenth-century book trade. Johnson gives scant attention to religious and philosophical works, for instance, and he evidently chose to review neither novels nor drama. Poetic works and travel narratives are also underrepresented among the books Johnson reviewed.

Johnson's reluctance to review works of theology or speculative philosophy in the *Literary Magazine*—Soame Jenyns's *Free Inquiry* and Isaac Newton's *Four Letters to Bentley* are the notable exceptions—may be a reflection of what Pat Rogers characterizes as Johnson's "sceptical and even dry intellect," that is, his evident indifference to broad, abstract issues that bear little obvious relation to everyday human experience. It is also possible that Johnson's religious sensibility—the nagging self-doubt about his moral fitness and his fear of dissolution after death—made such topics particularly uncongenial for extended analysis. "The Christian religion was with him such a certain and established truth," Joshua Reynolds observes in his biographical account of Johnson, "that he considered it as a kind of profanation to hold any argument about its truth."[16] Certainly there was no shortage of theological and philosophical books available for review. The March and April 1756 issues of the *Monthly*, which appeared just before the inaugural issue of the *Literary Magazine*, give us a rough idea of the sorts of material being produced by English presses. The "Main Articles" section of the March issue, for instance, features reviews of Richard Parry's *The Scripture-Account of the Lord's Supper*, Thomas Sharp's *Three Discourses on Mr. Hutchinson's Exposition of Cherubim*, and J. Strong's *Observations on Important Points of Faith*. The "Monthly Catalogue" section, meanwhile, gives notice to *A Vindication of the Quakers, Deism Refuted, The Case of the Jews Considered, The Wonderful Signs of Christ's Second Coming, A Dissertation Proving the Light of the Gospel is the Light of Nature*, and *A Letter to the Reverend Mr. Law*. The April number carries reviews of *A New Method of demonstrating from Reason and Philosophy, the Four Fundamental Points of Religion* and *The Folly and Danger of Enthusiasm; or, The Wickedness of Attempting to Know the Secret Councils of God*. A fair number of published sermons is given notice in these two issues as well.[17] Any of the titles noted here would have served as a fit subject for review, yet Johnson chose to ignore these and countless other similar works.

The near-complete absence of prose fiction in Johnson's choice of books for review—the one exception being Elizabeth Harrison's *Miscellanies*, which he subscribed to—is easier to pin down. As *Rambler* 4 makes clear, Johnson held a low opinion of the contemporary run of realistic novels, even though he acknowledged the theoretical worthiness of the genre itself.[18] Not surprisingly, when Johnson assumed the editorship of the *Literary Magazine* he not only refused to review novels himself but evidently kept his staff from reviewing them as well. True, four or five novels are listed in the *Literary Magazine*'s "Books Published" section under "Entertainment"; but none are given substantive notice during Johnson's tenure. What makes this policy significant is that marketplace demand for novels rose sharply during the mid-1750s, and the appearance of new titles spiked upward from roughly thirty-two in 1754 to more than fifty in 1756. In "one form or another the novel was the most popular genre of the period, reaching the widest audience," writes W. A. Speck in *Society and Literature in England, 1700–1760*. "It transcended the barriers between the gentle reader and the middling sort, and even made contact with some of the masses."[19] Evidence of the novel's popularity—and its dubious status in the eyes of opinion-makers—at the moment when Johnson superintended the *Literary Magazine* can be found in book reviews of the period. "The season for novels is now set in," writes the reviewer of the *History of Lavinia Rawlins Monthly* (November 1755), "and the press is likely to produce a plenteous harvest; but, if those that shall hereafter be brought to the market, prove no

better than the first crop, we shall have no great appetite for more of 'em."
Similar observations are made in the review of the *Adventures of Jack Smart
Monthly* (April 1756). "It is amazing, that notwithstanding the vast knowledge of human nature, strength of genius, fecundity of wit, and happiness
of expression, which are required in a novel-writer, so many vile romances
should, almost daily, crawl from the press."[20] In their unsparing criticisms
of badly written novels, the reviewers in the *Monthly* and, later, in the *Critical*
clearly share common ground with Johnson's pronouncements on prose
fiction in *Rambler* 4. Nevertheless, the *Critical* and the *Monthly* awarded
novels a measure of status by reviewing even the worst examples of the
genre—if only because the public insisted on buying novels in great numbers and so looked to the review journals for information on new titles. As
far as Johnson was concerned, editing a review journal—even one directed
to a general, as opposed to a scholarly, readership—meant honoring a basic threshold of merit when it came to selecting material for review, irrespective of marketplace trends.[21]

That Johnson chose to ignore drama and poetry can be accounted for
on similar grounds. Writing for the *Critical Review* in December 1764,
Johnson characterized Goldsmith's *The Traveller* as the best example of
poetry "since the death of Pope" (1744). Five years later Johnson suggested that the post-Pope literary scene generally came up short on imaginative genius. "'It was worth while being a dunce then,'" Johnson declares
while talking about the *Dunciad*. "'It is not worth while being a dunce
now, when there are no wits.'" Johnson harbored similar opinions of the
English stage. "There is scarce a tragedy of the last century which has not
debased its most important incidents, and polluted its most serious
interlocutions with buffoonery and meanness," Johnson declares in *Rambler* 125 (1751). Contemporaneous comedies are equally disappointing in
Johnson's view. Goldsmith's *The Good-Natured Man* (1768), Johnson is
reported to have observed, "was the best comedy that had appeared since
'The Provoked Husband' [1728]." While discussing Goldsmith's *She Stoops
to Conquer* (1773), Johnson claims not to know of any other contemporary
comedy "that has so much exhilarated an audience, that has answered the
great end of comedy—making an audience merry."[22]

Of the twelve books in the humanities that Johnson does review in the
Literary Magazine, seven are either historical accounts (Blackwell's *Memoirs
of the Court of Augustus,* Birch's *History of the Royal Society,* Keith's *Catalogue of Scottish Bishops,* Parkin's *Account of the Invasion under William
Duke of Normandy*) or modern editions of previously published material
(Browne's *Christian Morals,* Hampton's *Polybius,* Lennox's *Memoirs of
the Duke of Sully*). As mentioned previously, Johnson reviews two philosophical titles (Jenyns's *A Free Inquiry* and Newton's *Four Letters*) and

only one work of imaginative literature (Harrison's *Moral Miscellanies*). Joseph Warton's *Essay on the Writing and Genius of Pope* is the only work of literary criticism that Johnson reviewed. Johnson also chose to review a travel narrative, Keyssler's *Travels through Germany*. Travel narratives were immensely popular during the eighteenth century, as Thomas Curley and Percy G. Adams have pointed out. [23] That Johnson did not review more of them may perhaps reflect his view, expressed a few years later in *Idler*s 94 and 97 (1760), that recent examples in the genre were on the whole poorly conceived and haphazardly written.

What generalizations can we make about Johnson's manner of proceeding as a reviewer of works in the humanities? Johnson's reviews of such titles, as is the case for his reviews of other types of works in the *Literary Magazine*, at first glance appear wholly conventional; that is, generally speaking Johnson's reviews comprise extracted material introduced by brief critical observations and strung together with terse and often neutral connective remarks. Nevertheless, we can see at work in these reviews— as we can in the others by Johnson in the *Literary Magazine*—a coherent theoretical outlook on reviewing.

First, Johnson almost always hedges his literary judgments—the Jenyns and Blackwell reviews are the notable exceptions, as we shall see—a feature that gives his reviewing in the *Literary Magazine* a tentativeness very much at odds with the studied critical aggressiveness of the *Monthly* and the *Critical* from the mid-1750s onward.[24] Hampton's *Polybius*, Johnson declares, "*appears* to be one of the books which will long do honour to the present age"; Warton's dismissive view of formal criticism is neither invalid nor praiseworthy, but instead "deserves great attention"; Robert Keith "*appears* to have studied" the history of Scottish bishops "with great diligence"; the contributors to Harrison's *Moral Miscellanies* "*have laboured*" to enliven their narratives and poetry with "brightness of imagery" and "purity of sentiment"; and so on (emphasis added). Clearly, Johnson's carefully qualified commentary reflects what he understood to be the inevitable unreliability of dogmatic or heavily assertive criticism directed at the work of living writers. Johnson's book reviews, in other words, can be said to complement his pronouncements on the fallibility of contemporaneous criticism as expressed in *Rambler*s 92, 93, 125, 176, and elsewhere.[25] As discussed earlier, Johnson's basic position is that posterity makes the final call regarding an author's literary achievement. The reviewer's charter is merely to call attention to evidently meritorious titles in ways that allow the reading public to make an intelligent decision as to whether a given book is worth buying or not.

A kindred characteristic of Johnson's reviewing is the relatively heavy weight Johnson assigns to authorial intent. We see this most clearly in

Johnson's withering attacks on Thomas Blackwell and Soame Jenyns, authors whose stubborn self-deception and unjustified self-satisfaction, Johnson would have us believe, led them to retail patently iniquitous or foolish ideas as high civic-mindedness. Contrasting examples can be found in the reviews of Elizabeth Harrison's *Moral Miscellanies* and Charles Parkin's *Impartial Account*, works that in Johnson's view deserve to be treated sympathetically on account of their authors' altruistic objectives— even if, in the case of Harrison's contributors, no definitive word can be said about their achievement or, in the case of Parkin, the author's observations amount to little more than political clichés. On a broader level, then, Johnson's reviews square nicely with his fixed outlook on the beneficent purposes of literature. All literary activity, as Johnson avers numerous times in the *Rambler* papers and elsewhere, should serve individual or social welfare. Those authors who exemplify what Johnson sees as the basic qualification of authorship, properly understood—a desire to communicate worthwhile knowledge—are thus entitled to a sympathetic review, even if their actual literary achievement may prove to be modest or negligible. By the same token, authors who betray the exalted aims of the profession of letters, as Johnson believed Blackwell and Jenyns did, deserve the severest censure.

A third generalization worth making is that not only does Johnson frequently revise the material he takes from books under review, as Donald Eddy has amply demonstrated, but he also chooses with great care his extracts, which often take up the majority part of his reviews not only of literary works but also of the scientific and journalistic/public policy titles as well.[26] Johnson uses extracted material to dramatize or to underscore his general observations, as is the case for the Harrison and Warton reviews, or to validate his private outlook on subjects touched upon by the author under review, which is what we find in the Hampton and Keyssler reviews. Of equal importance is that Johnson often employs extracts in ways that transform his reviews of largely humdrum or abstruse works into intellectually substantive yet broadly appealing essays in their own right. In the reviews of Parkin's *Impartial Account of the Invasion under William Duke of Normandy* and Cleeve's essay on the national debt, for instance, Johnson reprints material from these titles worthy of the general public's attention, even as he warns readers of the prevailing banality of the books under review. In his review of Home's *Experiments on Bleaching* and Keith's volume on Scottish bishops—books that transmit substantive knowledge to a discrete readership—Johnson chooses material that the common reader may find engrossing. As a rule, the extracts Johnson chooses are never mere page fillers but critically significant material that is artfully integrated into Johnson's overall evaluation. To understand Johnson's appraisal of any given work requires us to look closely at Johnson's choice of extracted material.

We can also make broad observations on Johnson's reviewing of works in the humanities written by friends. Johnson was on friendly terms with Thomas Birch, Charlotte Lennox, and Joseph Warton when he reviewed their books in the *Literary Magazine*, and he was a subscriber to Harrison's *Miscellanies;* he also reviews his own work on Thomas Browne. Yet, as we shall see, Johnson's reviews of these titles are temperamentally indistinguishable from Johnson's other reviews, and when compared with competing notices published elsewhere are not necessarily more favorable. It seems that Johnson looked upon reviewing a friend's work dispassionately as in itself a form of patronage—puffing works, in Johnson's view, being beyond the pale even when a friend's literary prospects were at the stake. [27] As Johnson points out in *Rambler* 93, the critical intelligence can be debauched just as easily when directed by "kindness" or "veneration" as when it is infected by "malevolence" or "contempt."[28] An apt way to characterize the matter, then, is that Johnson reviewed a handful of what were in his view essentially worthy titles that happened to be written by friends.

An important point is worth exploring here that is merely touched upon in the preceding paragraph. Johnson's work as a reviewer embodies the robustness of his authorial integrity, particularly in the face of rather sensitive or straitened circumstances. Johnson's critical independence might easily have been compromised by a number of pressures. For instance, Johnson almost certainly needed the regular pay that the literary editorship promised; surely he must have been tempted to review books in a manner that advanced, or at least did not undermine, his professional prospects. Although Johnson completed or initiated a clutch of miscellaneous literary projects beginning in 1756—three contributions to Christopher Smart's *Universal Visiter;* an edition of Sir Thomas Browne's *Christian Morals*, accompanied by a biography; a half-dozen or so prefaces and dedications— his only significant source of income between mid-1756 and July 1757, apart from whatever he earned as editor of the *Literary Magazine*, appears to have been the subscription fees associated with the edition of Shakespeare's plays (the *Proposals* having been issued in June 1756). Thus, the *Literary Magazine*'s financial success must have taken on a particular urgency for Johnson—all the more so when we recall Johnson's brief imprisonment for indebtedness in March 1756, weeks before the publication of the magazine's inaugural issue.[29]

Nevertheless, Johnson's reviewing practices testify to his stalwart refusal to exchange critical integrity for financial advantage. Johnson's avoidance of novels in spite of the genre's immense popularity has already been mentioned, but we should also recall that he refrains from puffing titles published by booksellers with whom he routinely did business, most especially three prominent sponsors of Johnson's *Dictionary:* Andrew Millar (Birch's *History of the Royal Society,* Russell's *Natural History,* Lucas's *Essay, Sully's Memoirs*) and the Dodsley brothers (Hampton's *Polybius,* Newton's *Four Letters,* Evans's *Map,* Jenyns's *Free Inquiry*). True, Johnson wrote sympathetic reviews of many of the titles published by Millar and the Dodsleys, but Johnson did so based strictly on the merits of the works at hand, and we should not forget that he levels due criticism at some of these titles—the Jenyns volume in particular—as well. Certainly the following anecdote from Boswell's *Life* captures Johnson's outlook on this matter. "I was somewhat disappointed in finding that the edition of the English Poets, for which he [Johnson] was to write Prefaces and Lives, was not an undertaking directed by him: but that he was to furnish a Preface and Life to any poet the booksellers pleased," Boswell says as he recollects a conversation from September 1777. "I asked him if he would do this to any dunce's works, if they should ask him." Johnson replied: "'Yes, Sir; and *say* he was a dunce.'" Johnson's work as a reviewer gives concrete expression to his general outlook on the lofty responsibilities of the critic, as the passage from Boswell suggests. Friendship, the prospects of furthering ties with influential booksellers, prevailing (but in Johnson's view unsavory) trends in the book trade: none of these things could force Johnson to compromise what he saw as his duty to meritorious authors, the reading public, and the highest traditions of professional letters. "The difference between a hack and an author was not, in the long run, so great," writes Lawrence Lipking in his recent biography of Johnson. "It consisted of one main point: the hack serves anyone who hires him, the author serves his people as a whole."[30] Lipking here is referring to Johnson the lexicographer, but his comments apply equally as well to Samuel Johnson, book reviewer in the *Literary Magazine*.

A critical survey of Johnson's reviews of literary, philosophical, and historical titles in the *Literary Magazine* follows. What I hope to illumine in this and subsequent chapters is the resourcefulness that Johnson routinely brought to book reviewing. While Johnson's reviews cannot often stand comparison to his best critical writings, by the standards of the day— and by the standards he set for himself—Johnson's book reviews amount to a remarkable collection of critical essays that has been underappreciated thus far.

Thomas Birch (1705–66), *The History of the Royal Society of London***, vols. 1 and 2.** Reviewed by Tobias Smollett in the *Critical,* January/ February 1756; reviewed by Johnson, 15 May 1756; reviewed in the *Monthly* (reviewer unknown), May 1756.[31] Johnson's review of *The History of the Royal Society* is one of a half-dozen or so in the *Literary Magazine* that evaluates the work of a friend or acquaintance. As mentioned earlier, Johnson approaches this rather sensitive task with a commendable degree of disinterestedness. Even so, Johnson's mixed review of Birch's two-volume *History* may also reflect what Edward Ruhe has described as Johnson's "disordered" relationship with Birch. The friendship began soon after Edward Cave hired Johnson as a staff writer for the *Gentleman's Magazine* in 1738, Birch at the time being an occasional contributor to the monthly journal. Johnson came to admire Birch's great learning and his skills as a conversationalist, but Birch does not appear to have harbored a reciprocal measure of goodwill for Johnson. Indeed, Birch seems to have resented Johnson's friendship with fellow *GM* contributor Elizabeth Carter, for whom Birch held a romantic interest during the late 1730s. Birch's courtship of Carter was short-lived, but in subsequent years relations between Johnson and Birch never quite recovered from what Birch evidently perceived to be Johnson's obtrusiveness.[32] The two men maintained some sort of connection over the years that followed, but they were never to grow close despite initiatives by Johnson "to resume the friendship on its earlier footing."[33] The iciness of their relationship finds expression in the nine letters Johnson wrote to Birch between 1743 and 1756. The letters are invariably brief and rather formal; absent is the sort of warmth one finds in, say, Johnson's correspondences with Charlotte Lennox.[34] Put off perhaps by Birch's aloofness, Johnson may not have seen a virtue or necessity in writing a charitable review of a work he found essentially meritorious but wanting in some respects.

Johnson begins his review by criticizing Birch for casting his narrative more in the form of a "diary" than an astutely organized "history," though these remarks are offset somewhat by praise for the archival value of Birch's two-volume, 1,012-page account of the first eleven years of the Royal Society.

> This book might more properly have been intitled by the author a diary than a history, as it proceeds regularly from day to day so minutely as to number over the members present at each committee, and so slowly, that two large volumes contain only the transactions of the eleven first years from the institution of the Society. I am yet far from intending to represent this work as useless. Many particularities are of importance to one man, though they appear trifling to another, and it is always more safe to admit copiousness than to affect brevity.[35]

Johnson then briefly expands on the mildly appreciative commentary offered here.

Many informations will be afforded to the biographer. I know not where else it can be found, but here and in *Ward*, that *Cowley* was doctor in physic. And whenever any other institution of the same kind shall be attempted, the exact relation of the progress of the Royal Society may furnish precedents. These volumes consist of an exact journal of the Society; of some papers delivered to them, which tho' registered and preserved, had been never printed; and of short memoirs of the more eminent members, inserted at the end of the year in which each died.[36]

The *History of the Royal Society* may strike some as an impenetrable mass of undigested fact, Johnson suggests in his critical commentary, but diligent and patient readers will doubtless find a good supply of worthwhile knowledge between the covers of Birch's two volumes.

What makes Johnson's brief review—at roughly twenty-two hundred words the Birch piece is only slightly longer than Johnson's review of Bourchier Cleeve's sixteen-page *Scheme*—of further interest is the extracted material. Johnson might easily have selected any number of papers on speculative topics from Birch's *History*—astronomy, physics, mathematics, chemistry, and the like—but he instead chose to reprint a piece by the physician Walter Needham (1631–91) on china varnish and a report on the climate of Greenland by the founding publisher of the *Philosophical Transactions*, Henry Oldenburg (1615–77).[37] The selection of these two pieces can be said to reflect Johnson's interest in the practical arts and in exotic places. Students of the *Rambler* series doubtless will recall Johnson's appreciative evaluation of practical science (nos. 9, 83, 137), but we should also remember that Johnson was particularly interested in the manufacture of china. Indeed, Johnson is reported to have visited the Chelsea China Manufactory at least twice a week during the 1750s, each visit lasting the entire day.[38] Also relevant here are the two fictional *Rambler* narratives set in Greenland (nos. 186 and 187). Equally significant is that Johnson probably assumed that the middlebrow character of the two essays was more suitable to the readership of the *Literary Magazine*. Johnson eschews the more demanding of academic essays in Birch's *History* and instead focuses on material that can be read and enjoyed by the general reader. Johnson thus offers intelligent, evenhanded critical commentary for the prospective customer of Birch's work while using the extracts to educate the general public whether they buy the volume or not—much as he does in almost every other review that he contributes to the *Literary Magazine*.

Tobias Smollett's review in the inaugural number of the *Critical* agrees in the essentials with Johnson's *Literary Magazine* piece; like Johnson he too concludes that Birch's *History* assembles plenty of valuable scientific information, though Smollett does concede that the work may contain an excessive amount of detail for most readers' tastes. Smollett's mockery of some of the more speculative pieces, however, sets his review apart from Johnson's. The *History of the Royal Society* contains "some things that may appear trifling, and some that are fictitious and unphilosophical," Smollett observes, but such things are useful because "they are the *straws* and *feathers* with which crazy fellows tickle themselves, till they expose their own futility and ill-nature."[39] Lengthy extracts from Birch's introduction and experiments contained in the *History* follow. The commentary in the *Monthly* mirrors that of the *Literary Magazine* and the *Critical* in the essentials. The *Monthly* reviewer argues that Birch's *History* offers little of interest to the nonspecialist reader. Nevertheless, the work's historical worth cannot be questioned.[40] The *Monthly* piece stands out, however, by offering readers an impressive digest of the various subjects—experiments related to tanning, freezing, chemistry, geometry, horticulture, pathology, physics, and so on—discussed in Birch's *History*. Doubtless, the *Monthly* encouraged philosophically minded book buyers to consider Birch's *History*, though, as the reviewer suggests early on, ordinary readers will find little reason to purchase the set.

The sheer variety of subject matter previewed by the *Monthly* thus emphasizes the extent to which Johnson's review reflects his own personal intellectual interests and his resourceful approach to book reviewing. In particular, the *Literary Magazine* piece exemplifies Johnson's habit of using the book review not merely as an introduction to meritorious titles but as a means of transmitting worthwhile knowledge to a diverse reading public. Johnson's review functions, in effect, as a pair of independent essays on subjects that may appeal to the general run of readers. As reviews, the *Monthly* and *Critical* pieces are satisfactory in every way. Indeed, it is the comparison of these perfectly suitable reviews with their *Literary Magazine* counterpart that underscores Johnson's innovativeness as a reviewer.

Joseph Warton (1722–1800), *An Essay on the Writings and Genius of Pope*. Reviewed by Johnson, 15 May 1756; reviewed by Tobias Smollett in the *Critical,* April 1756; reviewed by James Grainger in the *Monthly,* June 1756. The poet and critic Joseph Warton was the elder son of Thomas Warton, professor of poetry at Oxford from 1718 until 1728. When the *Essay on the Writings and Genius of Pope* appeared in mid-1756, Warton already enjoyed a modest literary reputation, thanks to the success of his preromantic poem, *The Enthusiast; or, The Lover of Nature* (1744) and his *Odes on Various Subjects* (1746). Warton's poems no longer appear in the major literature anthologies, but his *Essay* remains important because it reflected and contributed to the emergence of romantic poetics during the 1740s.[41] In fact, Warton's revisionary approach to Pope's poetry led Robert Dodsley—who doubtless felt indebted to Pope for helping him get started in the book trade—to withdraw his offer to publish the work under his imprint, though Dodsley did "arrange for its publication by Mary Cooper," who often acted as Dodsley's agent.[42] In his dedicatory address to the poet Edward Young (1683–1765), Warton promises a complete rethinking of Pope's high literary standing. "I revere the memory of POPE, I respect and honour his abilities," Warton declares, "but I do not think him at the head of his profession." Warton acknowledges that Pope's poetry exhibits wit and sense but not sublimity or pathos—hence his middle ranking. Indeed, Warton's effort to depreciate Pope's reputation crystallizes in his ranking of the English poets. Warton situates Pope near Nathaniel Lee (1649–92) and Thomas Otway (1651–85), and well beneath Edmund Spenser, William Shakespeare, and John Milton—England's "only three sublime and pathetic poets." The reference here to the "sublime and pathetic" introduces Warton's collateral objective, which is to depreciate Augustan poetics in general. A "clear head, and acute understanding" do not a poet make, Warton argues. Rather "it is a creative and glowing IMAGINATION . . . and that alone, that can stamp a writer with this exalted and very uncommon character, which so few possess, and of which so few can properly judge."[43] Warton thus holds that the values of Augustan poetry—its reliance on wit, for instance, and its preference for prescribed forms (e.g., satire, pastoral)—undermine poetic genius.

One curious aspect of the *Essay*'s publication is that Warton mentioned nothing of it to his friend of nearly four years, Samuel Johnson, which comes as something of a surprise, given their apparently amiable relationship. Johnson's numerous letters to Warton suggest such friendliness, certainly, as does Warton's warm acknowledgment of Johnson's critical acumen in the preface to his edition of Virgil (1753).[44] In a letter to Warton dated 15 April 1756, Johnson recalls that he has "lately seen an octavo book which I suspect to be yours, though I have not yet read above ten pages. That way of publishing without acquainting your friends is a wicked trick." Johnson adds that he "will not so far depend upon a mere conjecture as to charge you with a fraud which I cannot prove you to have committed."[45] It remains unclear as to whether Warton immediately confirmed his authorship or whether Johnson merely assumed the *Essay* was Warton's when he wrote the review a few weeks after composing this letter. Whatever the case, Johnson ultimately wrote what was for him a remarkably indulgent review, praising aspects of Warton's scholarship while refraining from criticizing what Johnson almost certainly viewed as a dubious central argument.

Such a reading departs somewhat from conventional thinking on the Warton review. E. A. Bloom sees Johnson's review as a probing example of literary criticism. "Almost every point set forth by Warton is enlarged or criticized by Johnson, evidence of a greater display of interest in his subject than he shows in many of his other reviews." Bloom adds that Johnson generally "found himself in agreement with Warton's learned judgments," and the few courteously disputatious remarks only add to the review's aura of scholarly rigor and impartiality. Donald Eddy also claims that Johnson offers a "detailed and thorough" analysis of the *Essay on Pope*. "Its subject engages Johnson's attention and interest," Eddy adds, and Johnson "brings to it a wealth of information and mature opinion." O M Brack and Gae Holladay essentially agree with Bloom and Eddy, though they interpret Johnson's "general approval" of the *Essay* as an attempt to temper the review's occasional depreciative remarks.[46] Bloom and the others rightly call attention to the rigor of Johnson's evaluation of discrete arguments in the *Essay*, and their readings are on the whole perfectly satisfactory. Even so, scholars thus far have overlooked an important aspect of Johnson's review. What the Warton piece reveals is Johnson's perceptive grasp of the significance of book reviewing and the extremes of Johnson's benevolence when it came to helping literary friends. A harsh review might drive away readers, Johnson appears to have assumed, while an abstention might be equally as harmful, given the fact that increasing numbers of book buyers were relying on review journals to help them sort through the multitude of books being turned out by the commercial presses.

What evidence is there to suggest that Johnson is less than straightforward in his treatment of the *Essay*? To start with, Johnson's admiration of Pope should have generated a much more contentious survey of Warton's attempt to devalue Pope's literary reputation. In the *Lives of the Poets*— where as a rule Johnson seems to have assigned space proportionate to the significance of the author—Pope's biography is the largest by a substantial margin, longer than Milton's "Life" by half and dwarfing considerably the biography of Thomas Otway, who precedes Pope in Warton's ranking of English poets. In the "Life" Johnson celebrates the wit and elegance of Pope's poetry, the very aspects of Pope's reputation that the *Essay* seeks to depreciate.[47] As Jean Hagstrum has amply demonstrated, Johnson's "Life of Pope" emphasizes the extraordinary rhetorical qualities of Pope's poetry while downplaying the values that Warton claims are essential components of poetic genius: sublimity and pathos. It "is to rhetorical beauty that Johnson responded most strongly," Hagstrum argues, "and it is Pope who becomes for him its great exemplar."[48] A particularly illuminating example of this is Johnson's evaluation of Pope's translation of *The Iliad*. The "purpose of a writer is to be read, and the criticism which would destroy the power of pleasing must be blown aside," Johnson declares in commenting on Pope's work as a translator. "Pope wrote for his own age and his own nation: he knew that it was necessary to colour the images and point the sentiments of his author; he therefore made him graceful, but lost him some of his sublimity."[49] Here, Johnson praises Pope precisely because he subordinates sublimity to wit, sense, and beauty, a point he returns to at the close of the "Life." "It is remarked by Watts that there is scarcely a happy combination of words or phrase poetically elegant in the English language which Pope has not inserted into his version of Homer," Johnson asserts.

> New sentiments and new images others may produce, but to attempt any further improvement of versification will be dangerous. Art and diligence have now done their best, and what shall be added will be the effort of tedious toil and needless curiosity. After all this it is surely superfluous to answer the question that has once been asked, Whether Pope was a poet? otherwise than by asking in return, If Pope be not a poetry, where is poetry to be found?

The commentary here amounts to a rousing defense of Pope's reputation and works well enough as a conclusion to the "Life"—but such is Johnson's commitment to defending the aesthetics of Pope's poetry that he refuses to let matters rest and adds a historical perspective to his argument.

> Let us look round upon the present time, and back upon the past; let us enquire to whom the voice of mankind has decreed the wreath of poetry; let their productions be examined and their claims stated, and the pretensions of Pope will be no more disputed. Had he given the world only his version the name of poet must have been allowed him; if the writer of the *Iliad* were to class his successors he would assign a very high place to his translator, without requiring any other evidence of his genius.[50]

Johnson's analysis of Pope's poetry is thus marked by a strongly apologetic character. Of particular significance here is the weight Johnson assigns to Pope's *Iliad*, which in Johnson's view is a poetic masterpiece in its own right. Speaking on behalf of Homer—whose works exemplify sublimity and pathos, the very values Warton exalts—Johnson concludes the "Life of Pope" by celebrating the aesthetic values embodied in Pope's poetry and, on the whole, offers a spirited defense of Pope's lofty literary standing.

Also worth considering is the following anecdote from Boswell's *Life* (31 March 1772), which offers us a conversational echo of the *Literary Magazine* review:

> He [Johnson] praised Dr. Joseph Warton's Essay on Pope; but said, he supposed we should have no more of it, as the authour had not been able to persuade the world to think of Pope as he did. BOSWELL. "Why, Sir, should that prevent him from continuing his work? He is an ingenious Counsel,

who has made the most of his cause: he is not obliged to gain it." JOHNSON. "But, Sir, there is a difference when the cause is of a man's own making."[51]

Here we find Johnson expressing a fondness for Warton even as rejects, or at least withholds approval of, the thesis of the *Essay*—much as he had done sixteen years earlier in the *Literary Magazine* review.

As many scholars have pointed out, Johnson's review of Warton's *Essay* comes across as evenhanded, closely argued, and thorough. Most readers coming to Warton's volume for the first time might easily have been daunted by the 334-page *Essay*, which comprises one modestly sized "section" (the first is 19 pages) and five large sections. Making matters worse is the absence of any sort of concluding argument: Warton's volume simply comes to an abrupt end. Doubtless with common readers in mind, Johnson condenses the mass of material in Warton's thick and rather digressive book and reshapes it into a coherent, lucid survey of Pope's writings that blends seamlessly with Warton's particular criticisms and Johnson's corresponding rebuttals and endorsements. As in many of his other reviews, Johnson makes Warton's volume seem much more accessible to ordinary readers than it actually is. In fact, Johnson's review, which totals some three thousand words, functions as an independent critical essay that does not require a familiarity with Warton's volume. Johnson begins with Pope's pastorals, moves to *Windsor Forest*, Pope's lyric poetry, the *Essay on Criticism*, and the *Rape of the Lock*, and ends with Pope's translation of the epistle *Sappho to Phaon*—at each stage modifying, extending, refuting, or, perhaps most important, clarifying Warton's criticisms. Take for instance the following comment by Johnson, which not only summarizes pages 30 through 50 of the text but also catches Warton advancing an argument on page 42 of the *Essay* that contradicts a statement made on page 11:

> Mentioning *Thomson* and other descriptive poets, he [Warton] remarks that writers fail in their copies for want of acquaintance with originals, and justly ridicules those who think they can form just ideas of valleys, mountains, and rivers in a garret in the *Strand*. For this reason I cannot regret with this author, that *Pope* laid aside his design of writing *American* pastorals; for as he must have painted scenes which he never saw, and manners he never knew, his performance, though it might have been a pleasing amusement of fancy, would have exhibited no representation of nature or of life.[52]

On page thirty of the *Essay*, Warton begins a survey of the descriptive poetry of William Collins, John Denham, John Dyer, Thomas Gray, John Milton, and Virgil. Warton concludes his discussion of descriptive poetry with the following comment on James Thomson's *The Seasons:*

[Thomson] painted from his own actual observations: his descriptions have
therefore a distinctness and truth, which are utterly wanting to those, of
poets who have never looked abroad on the objects themselves. Thomson
was accustomed to wander away into the country for days and for weeks,
attentive to, 'each rural sight, each rural sound;' while many a poet who
has dwelt for years in the Strand, has attempted to describe fields and rivers and generally succeeded accordingly. Hence that nauseous repetition
of the same circumstances; hence that disgusting impropriety of introducing what may be called a set of hereditary images, without proper regard to
the age, or climate, or occasion, in which they were formerly used.[53]

Of course, this material is abridged masterfully in Johnson's review. Scarcely
less important is that Johnson in the passage quoted previously calls attention to Warton's earlier, contradictory claim that Pope might easily have
written a superior American pastoral. "The subject would have been fruitful of the most poetical imagery," Warton writes, "and, if properly executed,
would have rescued the author from the accusation here urged, of having
written Eclogues without invention."[54] Using a mere one hundred words,
Johnson thus conveys an argument that in Warton's volume requires thou-
sands of words and, at the same time, defends Pope by illuminating Warton's
lack of consistency on a significant matter. As an abstract of a rather thick
volume that lacks an easily discernible structure, Johnson's review of
Warton's *Essay* is itself a work of art—a point that will be developed further when Johnson's review is compared with Tobias Smollett's in the *Critical* and James Grainger's in the *Monthly*.

Nevertheless, a close reading of the *Literary Magazine* review reveals
that Johnson's treatment of Warton's central thesis is more aptly described
as diplomatic rather than impartial. Take the opening sentences, for instance, where Johnson manages to avoid even a mention of the *Essay*'s
attack on Pope's standing and Augustan poetics. This comes as surprise not
only because Johnson's reviews as a rule exhibit a keen understanding of
the volume at hand but also because Johnson's own poetry—the *Vanity of
Human Wishes* in particular (1749)—embodies the values Warton depreci-
ates.[55]

This is a very curious and entertaining miscellany of critical remarks and
literary history. Though the book promises nothing but observations on the
writings of *Pope*, yet no opportunity is neglected of introducing the character of any other writer, or the mention of any performance or event in
which learning is interested. From *Pope*, however, he always takes his hint,
and to *Pope* he returns again from his digressions. The facts which he mentions though they are seldom *anecdotes* in a rigorous sense, are often such
as are very little known, and such as will delight more readers than naked
criticism.[56]

Johnson normally devotes much attention to authorial intent in his reviewing, yet here we find him uncharacteristically obscure. Indeed, to portray Warton's sweeping reevaluation of Pope as a "miscellany" that "promises nothing but observations on the writings of *Pope*" borders on misrepresentation.

Over the next several columns the review takes on an evenhanded but ultimately reticent character. Though Johnson commends some of Warton's judgments and disputes others—Warton "with much justice" calls attention to the lack of originality of Pope's pastorals; in his evaluation of *Windsor Forest* Warton argues "without proof, that descriptive poetry was by no means the excellence of Pope"—an examination of the *Essay* shows that at his most contentious Johnson does little more than nibble at the edges. Take for instance Warton's depreciation of formal criticism:

> Whether or no, the natural powers be not confined and debilitated by that timidity and caution which is occasioned by a regard to the dictates of art: or whether, that philosophical, that geometrical, and systematical spirit so much in vogue, which has spread itself from the sciences even into polite literature, by consulting only REASON, has not diminished and destroyed SENTIMENT; and made our poets write from and to the HEAD rather than the HEART: or whether, lastly, when just models, from which the rules have necessarily been drawn, have once appeared, succeeding writers, by ambitiously endeavouring to surpass those models, and to be original and new, do not become distorted and unnatural, in their thoughts and diction.[57]

It would be easy to find in Johnson's critical writings assertions that contradict the things Warton argues for here: the proper uses and limits of rules as discussed in *Rambler*s 125, 156, and 158, for instance; the historical evolution of criticism (a subject that Johnson himself hoped to treat at length at some point); the nature of genius.[58] Of particular interest is Warton's choice of the word "sentiment" as a synonym for emotion or feeling. In the *Dictionary*, Johnson defines "sentiment" as "Thought; notion; opinion," or "The sense considered distinctly from the language or things; a striking sentence in a composition." Johnson's *Dictionary* would thus lead us to believe that "sentiment" has nothing to do with emotion, but is rather an embodiment of reason. Surprisingly, Johnson says nothing of the difference between his understanding of "sentiment" and Warton's—despite the importance of the term to the *Essay*'s argument. Warton's rejection of the aesthetics of Pope's poetry should have aroused a spirited rebuttal from the temperamentally skeptical Johnson, yet he offers nothing on this point apart from the following brief and rather nerveless statement:

> The revival of learning, mentioned in this poem, affords an opportunity of mentioning the chief periods of literary history, of which this writer reckons

five, that of *Alexander*, of *Ptolemy Philadelphus*, of *Augustus*, of *Leo* the tenth, of queen *Anne*. These observations are concluded with a remark which deserves great attention: "In no polished nation, after criticism has been studied, and the rules of writing established, has any very extraordinary book ever appeared."[59]

Another instance of Johnson's critical timidity can be found toward the end of the review:

> These are the pieces examined in this volume; whether the remaining part of the work will be one volume or more, perhaps the writer himself cannot yet inform us. This piece is however a complete work, so far as it goes, and the writer is of the opinion, that he has dispatched the chief part of his task; for he ventures to remark, that the reputation of Pope, as a poet, among posterity, will be principally founded on his *Windsor-Forest*, *Rape of the Lock*, and *Eloisa to Abelard*, while the facts and characters alluded to in his late writings will be forgotten and unknown, and their poignancy and propriety little relished; for wit and satire are transitory and perishable, but nature and passion are eternal.[60]

Johnson does indeed touch upon Warton's controversial outlook on Pope and Augustan poetics here, but his commentary represents Warton's central thesis as nothing more than an incidental observation.

Even in the concluding paragraph of the review, where a mild Parthian shot at Warton's central thesis would have done little harm, Johnson persists in his obliging treatment. "In this extract it was thought convenient to dwell chiefly upon such observations as relate immediately to Pope, without deviating with the author into incidental inquiries," Johnson declares, "We intend to kindle, not to extinguish curiosity, by the slight sketch of a work abounding with curious quotations and pleasing disquisitions."[61] Clearly Johnson means to encourage a sympathetic reception for Warton's *Essay*. No reader would be put off by Johnson's courteous and carefully hedged-about criticisms, and the overall tone of the review is favorable. But equally clear is that Johnson cannot bring himself to offer convincing praise of a work that conflicts so sharply with his own views of Pope's poetics. The best that Johnson can do for Warton is to applaud the worthiness of the subject matter, make vaguely approving remarks about the thoroughness of Warton's scholarship, praise a specific observation here and there, and encourage readers to investigate the work themselves.

Johnson's obliging treatment of Warton is set in relief by competing reviews published in the two leading review journals. Warton's *Essay* was reviewed in the *Critical* by Tobias Smollett. Johnson and Smollett reviewed many of the same books during 1756, so it is worth pausing here to compare their manner of proceeding, because the *Literary Magazine* and *Critical* reviews of Warton's *Essay* exemplify nicely the differences that separate Johnson's reviewing technique from Smollett's.[62] To begin with, both Johnson and Smollett shared a belief in the high social and moral purposes of authorship; both were disappointed in the state of reviewing when they began work as editors of review journals (we recall Johnson's remark in his diary about the "infelicity" of contemporary review journals). Much like Johnson, Smollett chose the material he extracted from the works under review with some care, as James Basker has shown. A third similarity is that both authors wrote a far greater number of favorable reviews than they did negative ones. Of Johnson's forty reviews in the *Literary Magazine,* not one is entirely dismissive, and only two—the Blackwell and Jenyns pieces—contain more critical than appreciative commentary. Smollett wrote thirty-six full-length (eight- to twelve-page) reviews in 1756: eighteen are distinctly favorable, nine reviews contain mixed commentary, and the remaining nine—one-quarter—are distinctly negative.[63]

Significant differences, however, separate Johnson's reviewing technique from Smollett's. Johnson, for instance, crafts his reviews so that ordinary readers can derive pleasure and profit from them whether they are familiar with the subject area of the book under review or not. By contrast, Smollett's reviews often demand a greater fund of knowledge than the book under review itself seems to call for. Indeed, some of the reviews in the forthcoming edition of Smollett's works contain more than one hundred annotations.[64] The Warton review is a good example of Smollett's pedantry, with its references to medicine, classical literature, the plays of Shakespeare, poetical works from the previous decade, and the like. A second difference is the temperament of each reviewer. With few exceptions, Johnson's voice as a reviewer is rather muted, as he leaves the final decision regarding a work's merit to the public. Smollett's reviews are often self-referential and domineering—the Warton piece is a good example, as we shall see—the purpose of which, evidently, is to emphasize the primacy of the *Critical Review* as an arbiter of taste and literary reputation. Finally, Smollett's reviews reflect a consistent and near-obsessive concern with linguistic and grammatical purity, a feature on display in the Warton review. Indeed, some of Smollett's reviews may strike us as the work of a copy editor rather than that of a literary critic. Scotticisms in particular agitate Smollett—perhaps because he does not want his journal, which employed two other Scottish reviewers besides himself, to be seen as going easy on fellow Scots. Johnson is remarkably tolerant of what he considers to be sensible use of jargon; indeed, Johnson often defends the prerogative of authors to write for their prospective readerships, even if doing so requires authors to depart from received English.[65]

As the previous commentary suggests, Smollett's review of Warton's *Essay* in the *Critical* (April 1756) could scarcely differ more from Johnson's. Indeed, Smollett's reviewing technique is neatly encapsulated in the Warton review, so it is worth analyzing in some detail. The review opens in the following way:

> The man of taste must expend his labours in reforming the judgment and enlightening the understanding of these pretenders [incompetent modern critics], and other novices of sensibility, before they are qualified to maintain the character they assume. This charitable task of improvement, the learned, who enjoy their ease, ought to undertake for the benefit of mankind. This is the professed aim of us, who publish our monthly lucubrations in the *Critical Review*; and we cannot help looking upon the author of the Essay now before us, as one of our coadjutors in the laudable scheme we have projected.[66]

Rather than engage the reader's interest and get the critical commentary underway as Johnson does, Smollett here insists on pausing to herald the *Critical*'s immense cultural significance: professional letters would plunge further into chaos were it not for the intellectual philanthropy of the *Critical;* readers who happen to disagree with the *Critical* essentially give proof of their ignorance, and so forth. Mention is made here of Warton's volume, but even these brief and rather vague remarks are swathed in praise for the *Critical*.

Obtrusive self-promotion of this kind would be forgivable if it were followed by a discerning and well-ordered assessment of Warton's achievement. But almost immediately after congratulating the *Critical* for its insightfulness, Smollett sets off in dogged pursuit of what at times prove to be rather trivial or obscure occasions to contest Warton. Take for instance the review's initial critical assertion, which does justice neither to Smollett nor to Warton:

> We shall first mention a few inaccuracies in the language by which we should judge the author to be a North-briton; for, he uses the word *adduce*, a verb peculiar to the *Scotch* dialect, and several uncouth phrases, which do not seem to be of *English* growth; such as *attention irresistibly awoke,— developement, untuneableness, musicalness, seeming originality.* . . .[67]

The anonymous author of the *Essay*, of course, was not Scottish. Born in Surrey, Warton was educated at Oxford and, after accepting holy orders, served the Anglican Church for many years as a curate in the greater London area. Warton was employed as an usher at his alma mater, Winchester College, when the *Essay* appeared.[68] Smollett's opening commentary thus tells us more about his zeal for rooting out Scotticisms—real or imagined—than it does about Warton's *Essay*.

The remainder of the review is largely taken up by digressive and pettifogging observations, as Smollett seems to have hastily assembled a clutch of notes in order to meet the publishing deadline. Unrelated criticisms are abruptly joined together with dashes, and as Smollett's opening remarks would suggest, there appears to be little rhyme or reason behind the critical weight given to this aspect of the *Essay* or that. At one point in the review, for instance, Smollett begins a paragraph with this observation. "In pag. 122. we are told that *Hogarth*'s picture of *Richard* the third, *impresses* terror and amazement. Surely the critic meant to say, it *denotes* terror and amazement."[69] No further context is given here, nor are readers told why this particular point merits attention.

Elsewhere, the better half of a page is given over to a ham-fisted analysis of what amounts to an extremely minor aside. In briefly disputing the status awarded to Petronius in Pope's *Essay on Criticism*—"Fancy and Art in gay *Petronius* please," Pope writes, "The *Scholar's Learning*, with the *Courtier's Ease*"—Warton points out that the Roman poet wrote little criticism, and in any case Petronius's style, particularly his use of metaphor, scarcely warrants high praise. To illustrate his observation, Warton gives an example of a Petronian metaphor, in which "animal conception and delivery, are confounded with vegetable production." Not only does Smollett fail to provide the necessary context for Warton's remark—that the reference to Petronius appears in the *Essay on Criticism*—but he spends a great deal of space, first, quibbling about whether or not the biological metaphor quoted was as poor as Warton claimed, and, second, quoting from and remarking on fellow *Critical Review* writer John Armstrong's poem the *Art of Preserving Health* (1744), which, as Smollett reminds readers, thoughtfully explores "the idea of the earth as the general parent" of all living things.[70] Thus what we see on display here are Smollett's knowledge of medicine, his familiarity with classical literature, and his respect for the talents of a colleague rather than an intelligent interest in Warton's critical views.

Easily the most important illustration of the review's eccentric priorities is that Smollett says little in the way of substance regarding Warton's advocacy of a post-Augustan poetics—"In his dedication to Dr. *Young*, he seems to undervalue the merit of versification, which we apprehend, has not yet been considered in a proper point of view" is the extent of Smollett's commentary on the matter—and no mention is made whatsoever about Warton's controversial ranking of Pope and other English poets.[71] What is more, at the end of a review largely given over to disjointed and at times niggling criticisms, readers are again tantalized by indefinite praise for Warton's volume:

> On the whole, we pronounce the *Essay on the Writings and Genius of* Pope,
> a work of taste and learning, animated with many strokes of manly criti-
> cism, replete with knowledge, and diversified with a number of amusing
> incidents and observations.[72]

To be sure, there is no shortage of material in Smollett's review that, taken
by itself, is of critical interest. Smollett's brief analysis of the "impropri-
eties" of some of Shakespeare's characters is a case in point, as is Warton's
observation on the stultifying effects of formal criticism, which Smollett
quotes in full. As James Basker has demonstrated, moreover, the review
offers revelatory insights into Smollett's underlying critical thought.[73] Nevertheless, the spasmodic quality of Smollett's commentary may very well
have alienated contemporary readers; it is hard to believe that Warton himself was much pleased with the piece, even though there is no reason to
suspect that Smollett's intention here is to discourage sales of the *Essay*.

Writing in the June 1756 issue of the *Monthly Review*, James Grainger
offers a coherent, rigorous, and balanced assessment of Warton's *Essay*.
Much to his credit—Johnson and Smollett failed to do as much—Grainger
opens his review by evaluating both Warton's advocacy of a post-Augustan
poetics and his revisionist outlook on Pope:

> Of all eminent men, none have been so much the butt of censure, and the
> subject of praise, as the poets; and among these none, perhaps, ever suf-
> fered more from either, than POPE; with this felicity, however, that if he has
> had a Zoilus in Gildon, he has had an Aristarchus in Spense, and in the
> Author of the present Essay. But though we think very highly of the critical
> and literary abilities of our unknown Essayist, and have perused his work
> with no less profit than pleasure, yet can we not implicitly subscribe to all
> his decisions, and illustrations. As he has ventured, in some things, to dif-
> fer from the received opinion, so shall we be the less scrupulous in dissent-
> ing from him.[74]

True to his word, Grainger goes on to scrutinize Warton's ranking of English poets, his reproach of Warton for placing Dryden beneath Otway and
Lee being an especially noteworthy point of criticism.[75] In fact, it is possible that by focusing on material that goes largely ignored in the *Critical*,
Grainger strives to make his review superior to Smollett's piece, which had
appeared three months earlier. Grainger and Smollett would become enemies later in the decade, but the two Scots may have already seen themselves as rivals by mid-1756. "I never heard of any personal Cause of dislike between him and Smollett," writes Thomas Percy (1729–1811), a friend
of Grainger's, in a letter to the physician Robert Anderson (1750–1830),
biographer of Smollett and Johnson, "and therefore suppose with you their

hostility proceeded from their being inlisted under the Banners of 2 Reviews that were in a State of declared Warfare."[76]

Equally significant is that Grainger's commentary frequently bears more than a coincidental resemblance to Johnson's observations in the *Literary Magazine* review of six weeks earlier.[77] It turns out that Grainger filched what have since become known as Johnson's most effective criticisms of the *Essay*, which prompts speculation on whether Johnson approved—or even knew—of Grainger's piracy. *Rambler* 143 speaks of plagiarism as a crime: writers are "convicted" of stealing from other authors; plagiarism "stigmatizes" its perpetrators, and so on. The *Dictionary* is equally unambiguous: "Plagiarism" is defined as "Theft; literary adoption of the thoughts or works of others." Certainly Soame Jenyns's plagiarism of Pope's *Essay on Man* further encouraged Johnson in his scathing criticism of *A Free Inquiry into the Nature and Origin of Evil* (discussed later in the chapter).[78] It is thus possible that Johnson resented Grainger's plagiarism, just as he would any other species of scholarly dishonesty. On the other hand, Grainger might have sought permission to borrow from Johnson's review of Warton and Johnson might have obliged, perhaps happy to see the *Essay* given the unvarnished analysis it deserved.[79]

The first instance of Grainger's plagiarism centers on the imagery of the bee versus the bird in Warton's analysis of Pope's pastorals. Here is Johnson:

> The critic prefers the image of *Theocritus* [who uses a bee] as more wild, more delicate, and more uncommon. It is natural for a lover to wish that he might be any thing that could come near to his lady. But we more naturally desire to be that which she fondles and caresses, than that which she would avoid, at least would neglect. . . . Which of the two images was less common in the time of the poet who used it, for on that consideration the merit of novelty depends, I think it is now out of any critic's power to decide.

And Grainger, writing one month after Johnson:

> The Critic prefers the image of Theocritus as more pastorally wild, more delicate, and more uncommon. It is natural for a lover to wish to be metamorphosed into any thing that may approach his mistress. . . . But as a lover would rather wish to be changed into what his fair one caresses, than into that which she shuns, we cannot help thinking, that the Bird is more pastoral and delicate than the Bee. Which of the two images was least common in the days of Theocritus, (for upon that the merit of novelty alone depends), no Critic can now determine.[80]

Here is Johnson on Warton's analysis of *Windsor Forest:* "On *Windsor-Forest*, he declares, I think without proof, that descriptive poetry was by no means the excellence of *Pope*. . . . He must inquire whether *Windsor-Forest* has in reality any thing peculiar." Grainger quotes directly Warton's remarks about *Windsor Forest*—Johnson epitomizes—and adds the following comment: "But it ought first to be enquired, whether Windsor-Forest has in reality any peculiar beauties, and whether Pope has omitted these."[81]

Here is Johnson on Warton's analysis of Pope's odes: "He mentions, with great regard, Pope's ode on *solitude*, written when he was but twelve years old, but omits to mention the poem on *Silence*, composed, I think, as early, with much greater elegance of diction, music of numbers, extent of observation, and force of thought." Grainger's treatment of the subject essentially mirrors Johnson's:

> The ode on Solitude, written by Pope at twelve years of age, recalls our critic from his literary ramble. This little piece he considers as a strong instance of the contemplative and moral turn, which he calls the distinguishing characteristic of Pope's mind. His poem on Silence, composed two years after, would have afforded the critic a better proof, as it certainly surpasses the other in elegance of language, harmony of numbers, and power of thought.[82]

Grainger also parrots Johnson's criticism of Warton's credulity regarding the *Essay on Criticism*'s provenance:

> [A]fter having detailed the felicities of condition, to which he imagines Pope to have owed his wonderful prematurity of mind, he tells us that he is well informed, this essay was first written in prose: There is nothing improbable in the report, nothing indeed but what is more likely than the contrary; yet I cannot forbear to hint to this writer and all others the danger and weakness of trusting too readily to information.

Here is Grainger's treatment of the same anecdote:

> Then detailing the other felicities of condition *(c)*, to which, he imagines, Pope owed his astonishing prematurity of mind, he tells us, he is well informed, this essay was first written in prose. Tradition seldom lies so much, as when she talks of men of genius; and daily experience must teach every one how much we ought to be upon our guard against her informations. . . . It is, however, not improbable, that the plan of the essay on criticism was sketched out in prose; but that the whole was first composed in that dress, is not so probable.[83]

In yet another instance, Grainger mimics Johnson's treatment of Warton on the *Essay on Criticism:* Warton "proceeds on examining passage after passage of this essay," Johnson argues, "but we must pass over all these criticisms to which we have not something to add or object, or where this author does not differ from the general voice of mankind." Grainger makes the same point in his discussion of Warton's commentary on Pope's *Essay on Criticism*, though he alters the context a bit:

> In the prosecution of this article, we shall not undertake to analyse the whole of our Author's observations. Where he has advanced any thing new, that we shall select; where any thing may with propriety be added, that we shall endeavour to supply: and where we conceive our Critic to be in an error, that we shall, with due deference, attempt to correct.[84]

Johnson's disagreement with Warton's criticism of the Alps simile also finds its way into Grainger's review: "We cannot agree with him in his censure of the comparison of a student advancing in science with a traveller passing the *Alps*, which is, perhaps, the best simile in our language," Johnson argues, "that in which the most exact resemblance is traced between things in appearance utterly unrelated to each other."[85] Johnson adds that "*the last line conveys* no new IDEA is not true, it makes particular what was before general." Grainger says this about Warton's characterization of the Alps simile as unoriginal:

> Here we beg leave to dissent from him; for as the poet has traced the most exact resemblance between things which, in appearance, are utterly unrelated to each other, so also does he, in the last line, really *add a new idea*, by making that particular, which before was general. In fine, we shall not easily be prevailed on, not to look upon this as one of the best similes in our language.[86]

What this instance of plagiarism shares with Grainger's other borrowings from Johnson's review is its piercing illumination of the flaws in Warton's reasoning. The not infrequent failures of Warton's critical intelligence, readers are thus led to believe, raise serious questions about the *Essay*'s attitude to Pope's achievement and Augustan poetics in general.

The fifty-two-page review closes as it began, as Grainger strives to reconcile his disapproval of the *Essay*'s thesis with his respect for Warton's scholarly talents: "Upon the whole, altho' we judge that this Essay is partly calculated to sink Mr. Pope's reputation to a lower degree in the poetical scale than he has hitherto been stationed at, yet do we hope, that the ingenious Author will continue his Observations." Grainger adds that a "Gentleman of so fine a taste, and master of so much learning, cannot fail of throwing out many beautiful and interesting particulars."[87] What to make of these three reviews? On balance, the Grainger piece is perhaps the most accomplished, though this is due in no small measure to its Johnsonian elements. But Johnson's review is no trifling achievement either, given the competing demands placed on it by Johnson's firmly held critical opinions and his personal regard for Warton. As an exercise in concision, moreover, the Warton review remains one of Johnson's finest, exhibiting Johnson's talent at composing lucid, cogent abstracts of difficult, dense material.

James Hampton (1721–78), *The General History of Polybius, in Five Books, Translated from the Greek*. Reviewed by Johnson, 15 May 1756; reviewed by John Berkenhout in the *Monthly*, April 1756; reviewed by Thomas Francklin in the *Critical*, May 1756. An ordained cleric by profession, James Hampton enjoyed a measure of celebrity among his contemporaries not for any ecclesiastical achievement but on account of his English-language version of Polybius's *History*, which went through at least seven editions between 1756 and 1823. Indeed, it was Hampton's success as a translator of Polybius that prompted Lord Chancellor Robert Henley (1708–72) to arrange for Hampton to be presented with the wealthy rectorate of Monkton-Moor, Yorkshire, in 1762.[88]

In the essentials—the absence of dogmatic pronouncements; a heavy reliance on extracted material; a keen awareness of the circumstances surrounding the composition of the work, in this case the particular challenges of translation—Johnson's commentary on Hampton's *Polybius* very much typifies his manner of proceeding as a reviewer in the *Literary Magazine*. Even so, most readers would probably agree that on the whole the Hampton piece stands out as one of Johnson's most appreciative reviews. Almost all of Johnson's criticism appears in the review's first six sentences, quoted here:

> This appears to be one of the books which will long do honour to the present age. It has been by some remarker observed, that no man ever grew immortal by a translation; and undoubtedly translations into the prose of a living language must be laid aside whenever the language changes, because the matter being always to be found in the original, contributes nothing to the preservation of the form superinduced by the translator. But such versions may last long, tho' they can scarcely last always; and there is reason to believe that this will grow in reputation while the *English* tongue continues in its present state. The great difficulty of a translator is to preserve the native form of his language, and the unconstrained manner of an original writer. This Mr. *Hampton* seems to have attained in a degree of which there are few examples. His book has the dignity of antiquity, and the easy flow of a modern composition.[89]

While there is no question that Johnson thinks highly of Hampton's work and that he is reasonably sure most readers will too, it is worth noting that his commentary here is tentative and carefully hedged about: "there is reason to believe" that the translation will endure; Hampton's work "appears to be" and "seems" worthy of public approval. Johnson's reticence does not reflect a critical sloppiness or an underlying ambiguity toward Hampton's translation. Rather, what we see at work here are Johnson's well-known views on the primacy of popular judgment and the inevitably provisional nature of criticism directed at living writers. As a reviewer Johnson is duty-bound to direct attention to meritorious authors, but his proposition that Hampton's volume may become a landmark in English translation of ancient texts can only be realized by posterity.

Also of importance here is the cogent expression of Johnson's views on translation. Writing three years later in *Idler* 69, Johnson may have had Hampton's *Polybius* in mind when he argued the following point. "There is undoubtedly a mean to be observed" between loose paraphrase and word-for-word exactness when translating ancient texts; "he therefore will deserve the highest praise who can give a representation at once faithful and pleasing, who can convey the same thoughts with the same graces, and who when he translates changes nothing but the language." Twenty years later, Johnson would elaborate on the argument advanced here and in the Hampton review in the "Life of Denham." Sir John Denham "appears to have been one of the first that understood the necessity of emancipating translation from the drudgery of counting lines and interpreting single words. How much this servile practice obscured the clearest and deformed the most beautiful parts of the ancient authors may be discovered by a perusal of our earlier versions, some of them the works of men well qualified, not only by critical knowledge, but by poetical genius, who yet by a mistaken ambition of exactness degraded at once their originals and themselves."[90] As mentioned earlier, Johnson's reviews are important because they exemplify his broad outlook on the exalted social and moral purposes of authorship and the worthy but subordinate role of the literary critic. Equally true is that many of Johnson's reviews convey critical opinions, such as his views on translation, that are elaborated on in Johnson's better-known works such as the *Rambler* and the *Lives of the Poets.*

Scarcely less interesting in the *Polybius* review is Johnson's toleration of Hampton's failure to include historical and technical footnotes:

It were, perhaps, to be desired that he had illustrated with notes an author which must have many difficulties to an *English* reader, and particularly that he had explained the ancient art of war: But these omissions may be easily supplied by an inferior hand from the antiquaries and commentators. To note omissions where there is so much performed, would be invidious, and to commend is unnecessary where the excellence of the

work may be more easily and effectually shown by exhibiting a specimen.[91]

Johnson's willingness to excuse Hampton's scholarly negligence and his
insistence that readers look up unfamiliar terms for themselves should come
as a surprise to students of Johnson's literary criticism. Indeed, Johnson's
refusal to rebuke Hampton on this point stands at odds with the principles
he had set forth in the *Proposals for Printing the Dramatick Works of William Shakespeare*, which appeared a few weeks before the *Polybius* review. "The business of him that republishes an ancient book, is, to correct
what is corrupt, and to explain what is obscure," Johnson states in the *Proposals*. Two months after the *Polybius* review appeared, Johnson would
again remark on the importance of explanatory notes in his self-review of
the second edition of Browne's *Christian Morals*. "Many allusions, which
to common readers must appear obscure, are explained in short notes,"
Johnson observes. [92] Johnson's characterization of his annotations as mere
"short notes" very much underplays the erudition they display, as O M
Brack has demonstrated. Johnson would apply a similar degree of scholarly thoroughness in the annotations he provided for Roger Ascham's *English
Works* (1761).[93] Why, then, does Johnson applaud Hampton's translation,
citing in particular its mass appeal, when crucial terms and concepts are
inscrutable to the very readers that the work is intended to reach? Hampton's
prefatory essay may help explain Johnson's indulgent commentary.

   The major part of Hampton's preface is devoted to a survey of Polybius's
achievement as an historian, but in the final two pages readers are offered
an explanation for the missing annotation.

> [W]hen I first engaged in this work many years ago, my intention was, to
> have joined with the translation such observations and remarks, as might
> have served not only to explain the difficulties, but to illustrate also and
> enforce the strong sense and wise selections, that are spread through all the
> following History: to have cleared the obscurity, which arises sometimes
> from remote allusions, or an imperfect detail of facts: to have opened those
> peculiarities of customs and manners, which, whenever they occur, raise
> doubt and hesitation in the unlearned reader: to have pointed out the uses,
> or defects, of various institutions, in religion, laws, and government: and
> above all the rest, to have traced, step by step, the advancement of Roman
> greatness. . . .[94]

Hampton thus intended to include the necessary annotation, but "various
accidents," readers are told, kept him from assembling the necessary material. "I have now neither leisure, nor inclination, to complete" the edition
as it was originally conceived, Hampton admits.

Yet as I had gone through the most difficult and irksome, as well as the most useful part likewise of the whole performance, I was not willing intirely to suppress it. For I flatter myself, that the publick will owe me some acknowledgement, if this Translation should prove the means of spreading into many hands a treasure of inestimable value, which the roughness and inelegance, and numerous difficulties that occur, both in the language, and construction, and sense of the Original, have hitherto confined to a few.[95]

The importance of proper annotation is thus duly acknowledged in Hampton's prefatory note, but so too is the inevitable frailty of human nature, which left Hampton to choose between abandoning the project completely and publishing an imperfect but meritorious edition of Polybius. Johnson's many commentaries on the hazards of authorship tell us that he read Hampton's frank self-assessment with great sympathy. A central theme of Johnson's *Rambler* essay serial is that our capacity to imagine ambitious achievements is often much greater than our power to realize them, and as *Rambler*s 2, 16, and 21 make clear, authors are especially prone to overestimating their abilities. Hardly less relevant here is that Johnson himself had faced similar difficulties a few years earlier with the *Dictionary*—"when it shall be found that much is omitted," Johnson declares in the preface, "let it not be forgotten that much likewise has been performed"—so it scarcely taxes credulity to argue that Johnson's obliging commentary at some level reflects his own recent experiences with preparing an ambitious scholarly work for the marketplace.[96] Far better that Hampton's worthy volume should reach the bookstalls, Johnson appears to have thought, than for the work to have been abandoned for want of material that readers might easily supply on their own.

One other point is worth making about Johnson's review. Johnson suggests that he chose the 1,755-word extract from Hampton's volume more or less randomly—the "passage" is not distinguished by "any peculiar excellence," Johnson declares. Nevertheless, the quoted material echoes familiar Johnsonian opinions in ways that give the review something of an eccentric character. In particular, elements of the extract conform nicely to Johnson's well-known loathing of Roman empire-building, his contemptuous attitude toward the French, and his advocacy of the didactic value of literature, particularly biography. To begin with, Polybius's history sought to explain how Rome came to dominate the Mediterranean basin. "For what man is there, so sordid and insensible," Polybius asserts, "that he would not wish to be informed, in what manner, and through what kind of government, almost the whole habitable world, in less than the course of fifty-three years, was reduced beneath the Roman yoke?"[97] Yet the six pages of material that Johnson extracts from Hampton's 559-page volume center on the humiliating defeat inflicted on the Romans by Hannibal at Lake Trasimene during the Second Punic War, a selection that may reflect Johnson's belief in the fundamental injustice of Rome's conquests.[98] The avaricious Romans, in other words, had it coming to them as far as Johnson was concerned. At one point in the passage Polybius quotes Hannibal proclaiming to Roman allies taken prisoner that his campaign against Rome was designed "to restore to all the inhabitants of *Italy* their ancient freedom; and to assist likewise each particular state to recover again those towns and territories of which the *Romans* had deprived them." The emphasis in the passage on Roman tyranny complements nicely Johnson's review of Thomas Blackwell's *Memoirs of the Court of Augustus*, which had appeared in the very same issue. "I know not why any one but a schoolboy in his declamation should whine over the commonwealth of *Rome*," Johnson argues in his searing criticism of Blackwell, "which grew great only by the misery of the rest of mankind. The Romans, like others," Johnson adds, "as soon as they grew rich grew corrupt, and, in their corruption, sold the lives and freedoms of themselves, and of one another."[99]

The passage Johnson extracts in the Hampton review also carries scornful descriptions of Hannibal's Gallic allies, who, we are given to understand, were renowned for their "fickleness," dishonesty, "effeminacy," and cowardice—a viewpoint that brings to mind Johnson's chauvinism regarding the French as expressed in *Boswell's Life* and elsewhere. The latter half of the passage dwells on the timeless lessons to be drawn from Hannibal's generalship, and here Polybius's commentary reads like a *Rambler* essay tailor-made for military officers. "For all men, even of moderate discernment, must acknowledge, that nothing is more useful or of greater importance in the conduct of a general," Hampton's translation reads, "than to examine with the nicest care into the character and natural disposition of the opposite commander."[100]

Hampton's translation was reviewed in the *Monthly* by former Prussian army officer John Berkenhout, so it is not much of a surprise to find Polybius given center stage while his modern English interpreter goes largely ignored. Almost all of Berkenhout's review is given over to summary and extract strung together with interpositions that refer to Polybius without even so much as the slightest of references to Hampton. Here is a good example of Berkenhout's manner of proceeding:

> In the second chapter of this book, our Historian, after having given us a geographical description of that part of Italy which was inhabited by the Gauls, proceeds in his concise, but accurate, narrative of all the wars between that people and the Romans; by which, however, the former were, at last, entirely subdued. He [Polybius] concludes his recital with the following sensible and instructive reflections.[101]

Clearly, Berkenhout's interest in the scholarly and aesthetic demands of translating ancient Greek into modern English can scarcely be described as exacting, and what little scrutiny there is of Hampton is not merely narrow-minded but emphatically eccentric.

Five pages into the review, for instance, we find Berkenhout reproaching Hampton for criticizing an earlier French translation by the military author Jean Charles Folard (1669–1752), which in Hampton's opinion was so sloppily done that even military scholars and enthusiasts might find parts of it unintelligible. In commenting on this point Berkenhout avers that descriptive analysis of ancient warfare necessarily depends on a specialized idiom, and that Folard succeeded admirably in making Polybius not only readable but also highly relevant to the modern-day soldier:

> [I]f Mr. Hampton had read M. Folard's Commentary with attention, he would have found that his notes frequently tend to illustrate and remove the difficulties of the original; that his system is founded on that of the antients; that his design was, by comparing the modern art of war with that of the Greeks and Romans, to convince us of our own weakness, and their superiority; and, by adapting their principles to our own times and weapons, to form a compleat system of military art.[102]

Hampton actually sought to make Polybius's *History* accessible to the lay English reader, so Berkenhout here fails completely in his attempt to rebut Hampton's prefatory criticism of Folard's translation. Of greater significance is that Hampton's offhanded criticism of his French predecessor, which is carried in a footnote, inspired Berkenhout to draft his fifty-three page review in the form of an apologia for Folard rather than as a review of Hampton's work as a translator.[103] "We shall also, as we go along, endeavour to give our readers some idea of M. Folard's commentary," Berkenhout declares,

> by selecting from it such parts as may tend to illustrate our transcripts from Mr. Hampton's book. This part of our labour cannot, we hope, but be acceptable to those who are unacquainted with the French language, or who may not chuse to purchase seven expensive quartos, the subject of which is chiefly military; yet, probably we have not a single reader who will not be glad to have some notion of a work which may be found in every library on the continent: and this the rather because we never expect to see a translation of Folard into English, as there are scarce military readers enough in this nation to purchase an impression of any thing beyond the A B C of a soldier.[104]

As the review unfolds we find that Hampton is forced to compete—at times unsuccessfully—with Folard for Berkenhout's attentions. Almost every page of Berkenhout's review carries at least a brief reference to Folard, and it is not at all unusual on any given page to find that extracts from Folard's translation eclipse the material taken from Hampton's text. Such is Berkenhout's concern for the reputation of Folard's edition that at the close of the first installment of the review Berkenhout thought it necessary to implore readers "to look upon these, and our subsequent, Notes to this Article, as a mere skeleton of Mr. Folard's Commentary."[105] The heavy reliance on Folard is enough to give Berkenhout's review a firmly idiosyncratic character, but equally significant is that Berkenhout takes no notice whatsoever of Hampton's failure to include explanatory notes—an unintended yet telling reflection of the extent to which the *Monthly* notice is shaped by Berkenhout's personal biases rather than by a desire to offer readers a discerning survey of the work actually under review.

In his closing remarks Berkenhout does manage to squeeze in a word or two about the version of Polybius he professes to review, claiming that the excellence of Hampton's rendition is amply demonstrated by the extracts and so requires no elaboration.

> As some of our Readers may possibly think, that we ought not to take our leave of this work, without mentioning a word or two, concerning the merit of Mr. Hampton's performance, we may here observe, that this has been rendered unnecessary, by the various specimens given; and which the learned peruser may, for his own satisfaction, compare with the original: whilst Readers less qualified, or less curious, will, perhaps, deem it sufficient, if we assure them, without enumerating particulars, that we look upon Mr. Hampton's Polybius as one of the best translations that has appeared in the English language.[106]

It would be much easier to take Berkenhout at his word here—rather than to suspect him of concealing his dereliction on this point behind a veil of perfunctory praise—were it not for his previous dismissal of the two earlier English translations:

> The first of these we have not seen; but Mr. Dryden, in his character of Polybius, and his writings, tells us, "that the Greek historian in his English dress appeared under such a cloud of errors, that his native beauty was not only hidden, but his sense perverted in many places." The second was done by Sir Henry Shears, who, in his preface he confesses, that to have done Polybius exact justice, he ought to have studied him longer.[107]

Given the *Monthly*'s opinion of itself as a preceptor of literary taste, one might have expected Berkenhout at some point in his lengthy review to instruct readers on precisely why Hampton's translation improves upon its predecessors. Prospective book buyers who endured Berkenhout's lengthy commentary in the hopes of learning something about the worthiness of Hampton's edition of Polybius would justifiably have felt let down when they reached the conclusion.

Writing for the *Critical*, Thomas Francklin offers an account of *Polybius* that is satisfactory without being in any way exceptional.[108] Readers are given a substantive and appreciative introduction to Hampton's volume—thanks in large measure to the nearly ten pages worth of direct quotation, including a judiciously chosen extract from Hampton's preface—but there is an overall frothy quality to Francklin's commentary that falls short of a compelling endorsement. Interestingly, Francklin's critical interjections that introduce and follow the extracted material perhaps bear an unseemly resemblance to the commentary in Johnson's review, which had appeared two weeks earlier.[109] Regius Professor of Greek at Cambridge since 1750, Francklin was as qualified as anyone else to evaluate Hampton's volume. What might have happened is that Francklin, an admirer of Johnson's and possibly an acquaintance of his at the time he wrote the review as well, found himself in agreement with the earlier *Literary Magazine* piece and, pressed for time perhaps, decided to build his own review around what he assumed was Johnson's trustworthy assessment.[110]

Francklin's review opens, as does Johnson's, with a spirited but nonspecific approval of Hampton's work—"we take this opportunity of congratulating the literary world on so valuable an acquisition" (cf. Johnson: Hampton's *Polybius* "appears to be one of the books which will long do honour to the present age"). Next in the way of criticism comes a brief remark on Hampton's inadequate annotation, expressed in a manner that can be read as a slapdash paraphrase of Johnson's commentary. Explanatory notes "would certainly have rendered the work more perfect, and been of great service to the unlearned reader," Francklin observes. "But since Mr. *Hampton* is otherwise engaged, we must content ourselves with the translation only" (cf. Johnson: "It were, perhaps, to be desired that he had illustrated with notes an author which must have many difficulties to an *English* reader. . . . But these omissions may be easily supplied by an inferior hand from the antiquaries and commentators"). The similarities here between Johnson's handling of the missing notation and that of his *Critical Review* counterpart are not nearly so significant as the one point of difference: reasonably well educated readers—or at least those who thought of themselves as other than "unlearned"—who bought Hampton's *Polybius* on the advice of the *Critical* and were later surprised by the extent to which their comprehension of the work hinged on perusing military dictionaries might very well have felt misled. Six pages of extract follow.[111]

The final two paragraphs of Francklin's review praise Hampton in terms that recall the *Literary Magazine* piece—Hampton "has preserved an elegance in his copy, without sacrificing his fidelity to the original" (cf. Johnson: Hampton's "book has the dignity of antiquity, and the easy flow of a modern composition")—and, interestingly, offer what seems to be an allusive attack on Berkenhout's earlier review. "As we apprehend, that to enter into a minute detail of the subject or merit of the *original,* would be foreign to the design of our *Review,*" the writer for the *Critical* declares, "we have presented our readers with this short specimen of the *translation;* which, we imagine, is the only thing that can properly come under our inspection."[112]

All things considered, the *Literary Magazine* offers the most effective of the three reviews of Hampton's *Polybius*. If you are not terribly bothered by looking up military terms for yourself, Johnson advises prospective book buyers, then Hampton's *Polybius* will almost certainly prove to be worth anyone's money. By contrast, readers of the *Critical* are encouraged to bring expectations to Hampton's translation ("so valuable an acquisition" to the literate world) that it cannot possibly live up to—unless, of course, a discerning word is said about the extra work entailed by the missing annotation. Francklin's sloppiness on this point is particularly crucial, given that Hampton's translation was directed at the very kind of reader—the nonspecialist—for whom the explanatory notes would have been a necessity. As for the *Monthly,* those who consulted Berkenhout's review may be forgiven if they could not recall Hampton's name, even if they were moved to a keener appreciation of Polybius and his modern French translator.

Thomas Blackwell (1701–57), *Memoirs of the Court of Augustus*. Reviewed by Johnson, May 1756; reviewed by William Rose in the *Monthly,* March 1756; reviewed in the *Critical* by John Armstrong, January/February 1756. The first volume of the *Memoirs of the Court of Augustus* appeared in 1753, the handiwork of Thomas Blackwell, a widely respected classicist. The second volume, which Johnson reviewed, appeared in 1756; the third volume was published posthumously in 1763.[113] Scholars generally agree that Johnson's review of the second volume of Blackwell's *Memoirs* exemplifies his conservative political instincts and his irascible impatience with authors who attempt to sentimentalize the past, points neatly summarized by John A. Vance in his essay on Johnson's attitude toward historiography:[114]

> The [Blackwell] review is most valuable not just because it demonstrates the power of Johnson's censure and arguments, but rather because it shows Johnson the skeptical historical thinker, debunking with considerable vigor romanticized impressions of the past, warning his readers to avoid facile

comparisons of Rome and modern Britain, and rebuking a historian who lowered the esteem of historical writing with an awkward, inflated, and at times incomprehensible style.[115]

Interestingly enough, Vance is the only critic who takes notice of the final paragraph of the Blackwell review, where Johnson's disposition changes suddenly from contemptuousness to appreciation. "But having thus freely mentioned our author's faults, it remains that we acknowledge his merit, and confess that this book is the work of a man of letters, that it is full of events displayed with accuracy and related with vivacity," Johnson observes. And "though it is sufficiently defective to crush the vanity of its author, it is sufficiently entertaining to invite readers."[116]

What might account for Johnson's abrupt change in attitude? "One may be tempted to argue that Johnson did not write the concluding paragraph or that he was encouraged by others or by a slightly guilty conscience to say something kind about the well-respected scholar," Vance speculates. "In any event, Johnson could be assured that these kinder words did little to soften the powerful blows delivered in the review."[117] Vance's surmises are plausible but ultimately unsatisfying. In the first place, it is hard to imagine the review editor who would insist on "'the choice of my subject'," to recall Johnson's conversation with Dr. Adams when he was pondering a review journal of his own, blithely accepting alterations to what would turn out to be one of his most forceful reviews.[118] It is conceivable, certainly, that in the final sentence Johnson sought to temper slightly the searing reproaches that dominate the critical portion of the review. But why are these mollifying remarks not blended into the argument itself, as is the case for the Hanway and Jenyns reviews, rather than inserted at the end, where they are plainly ineffective, as Vance admits? As I hope to show, Johnson's magnanimity in the final sentence is in no way inconsistent with the rest of the review if we read the entire piece as at the core an exemplum of the dangers of authorial vanity.

To begin with, what Johnson does in the final sentence of the review is shift the emphasis away from Blackwell's self-delusion in order to squeeze in a due word of praise for the work itself. It must be said, after all, that Johnson finds nothing historically inaccurate in the *Memoirs* ("It is not our design to criticise the facts of this history"). Nor can Blackwell be accused of charlatanism ("If this author's skill in ancient literature were less generally acknowledged") or of choosing an irredeemably vapid subject.[119] From what the final paragraph suggests, Johnson looks upon the *Memoirs* as an undistinguished but inoffensive history—flawed in ways that should puncture Blackwell's inflated sense of achievement but, on balance, not unworthy of readers. What irritates Johnson is Blackwell's irresponsible and superficial political views, in particular his "furious and unnecessary zeal for liberty"—that is, his endorsement of radical political innovation and his approval of factional overzealousness—an outlook that in Johnson's view can be used to justify tyranny and social disorder. "By reference to Johnson's well-reasoned opinions on liberty and subordination, we may infer the cause of his impatience with the story of the Roman downfall," writes E. A. Bloom. "The necessity of change in the public welfare he never denied, but change brought about through violence and rebellion he abhorred."[120] Indeed, Johnson's reference in the Blackwell review to "liberty" clearly anticipates his later commentary on the subject, particularly in the *Lives of the Poets*. "He certainly retained an unnecessary and outrageous zeal for what he called and thought liberty—a zeal which sometimes disguises from the world, and not rarely from the mind which it possesses, an envious desire of plundering wealth or degrading greatness," Johnson declares in the "Life of Akenside," "and of which the immediate tendency is innovation and anarchy, an impetuous eagerness to subvert and confound, with very little care what shall be established."[121]

Also provoking Johnson's wrath are Blackwell's witless and annoying obtrusions, particularly his dishonest portrayal of the *Memoirs* as a pioneering achievement, even though the work largely amounts to a rehash of familiar material. Johnson's treatment of Blackwell is perhaps clarified by way of a contrasting example. Jonas Hanway's *A Journal of Eight Days' Journey* (discussed at length later) is plainly an unsatisfactory piece of scholarship in Johnson's view. One might even argue from Johnson's commentary that the *Journal* has less going for it than does Blackwell's *Memoirs*. Yet Hanway is treated charitably because his is a delusion for good. Hanway's pomposity blinds him to the inadequacies of what are essentially benevolent designs. By contrast, Blackwell squanders a chance to offer a fresh and stimulating retelling of an overfamiliar but important topic, choosing instead to place worthy historical material in the service of vanity and what Johnson sees as foolish and potentially dangerous political attitudes. Writing on the subject of authorial vanity in the *Idler* 70 three years after the Blackwell reviewed appeared, Johnson sets forth in general terms his contempt for the habits of mind that he had earlier claimed were embodied in Blackwell's *Memoirs*. "If an author be supposed to involve his thoughts in voluntary obscurity, and to obstruct, by unnecessary difficulties, a mind eager in the pursuit of truth," Johnson declares, "if he writes not to make others learned, but to boast the learning which he possesses himself, and wishes to be admired rather than understood, he counteracts the first end of writing, and justly suffers the utmost severity of censure, or the most afflictive severity of neglect."[122] It seems possible that Johnson here is alluding to Blackwell and his own sternly worded review. Whatever Johnson had in mind when he wrote *Idler* 70, it is clear that he held no sympathy whatsoever for self-aggrandizing writers who were demonstrably indifferent to what he saw as the exalted calling of authorship.

In March 1756 both the *Critical* and the *Monthly* published rather mixed reviews of the *Memoirs of the Court of Augustus*, each journal concluding that Blackwell's conspicuous pedantry blights an otherwise engrossing and well-researched subject. "It ought never to appear, that the chief purpose of an author is to shew his erudition," writes John Armstrong in his review for the *Critical:*

> but a too constant attention to this object has, in some measure, hurt even the plan of this performance; for we find the course of the narration sometimes interrupted by philological and critical observations, which however curious, ingenious, or amusing, happen to be so foreign to the historical events, that they would make rather a whimsical appearance, even in the shape of notes.[123]

Armstrong offers no further analysis of Blackwell's scholarship but the rest of the review is noteworthy for its detailed criticisms of Blackwell's usage, such an emphasis here and elsewhere in the review journals being a reflection of the broader debates surrounding the English language in Johnson's day.[124] Also in play here, certainly, is the intense concern with linguistic correctness that characterized the *Critical Review* under the editorship of Tobias Smollett.[125]

Writing for the *Monthly*, William Rose also berates Blackwell for his abrasive lack of modesty:

> [H]e starts so frequently from his subject, and runs into digressions, often curious, indeed, but introduced, principally, as would appear, to display his reading. He keeps himself, indeed, almost constantly in view, and stares the reader full in the face; but notwithstanding this fondness of shewing himself, his figure is far from being graceful, or his dress elegant: there is a pompous solemnity that strikes us, but the true dignity of a historian is wanting.[126]

It is important to note that these criticisms, which appear in the review's final paragraph, follow Rose's earlier endorsement of Blackwell's vindication of Brutus for murdering Caesar. Blackwell "observes very justly," Rose states,

> that a public tye surpersedes all private obligation; that the rescuing the laws and liberties of a noble nation, from the yoke of a tyrant, is the most glorious of all human actions; and that the obligation which every free citizen lies under, to contribute to it to the utmost of his power, cannot be cancelled by the tyrant's being his friend, relation, or benefactor.[127]

The impression Rose leaves us with, ultimately, is that the *Memoirs* provides an accurate, stirring, and highly relevant account of Augustan Rome, though readers are warned that Blackwell's incautious self-promotion occasionally grates.

It is certainly possible that the *Monthly*'s endorsement of Blackwell's political outlook inspired Johnson to review the *Memoirs* in the manner that he did; perhaps the *Critical*'s rather toothless evaluation played a part as well. What we can be reasonably certain of is that Johnson looked upon Blackwell's *Memoirs* as an apt occasion to deal concretely with authorial self-deception and its consequences, a timeless issue, to be sure, but one that Johnson believed had become particularly troublesome in recent years if his scathing attacks on deluded authors in "Reflections on the Present State of Literature" (*Universal Visiter,* April 1756) and *Adventurer* 115 (December 1753) are any indication.[128] Of special interest to Johnson is Blackwell's boastful preface—

> BETWEEN the end of Julius Caesar's MEMOIRS, or rather of Hirtius' Supplement, and the beginning of Tacitus's Annals, there is a GAP in the most interesting part of the Roman History. . . . It was no part of the original Plan of these MEMOIRS to supply this Deficiency, and retrieve the grand Period of the Roman Story: but being once engaged in the Series of Affairs, and having forged a Link or two of the Chain; the consequence and curiosity of the Materials, and their strict connection with the Subject, insensibly drew in the Author to fill up the Chasm. WHEN this was done, it became a Point of choice, either to sacrifice this historical Period, or to add a Volume to the Work beyond the first Design; and both the nature of the Transactions, and the Characters of the Actors (being such as hardly any other Age has produced), seemed to bespeak the Subscriber's Candor, and promise Forgiveness to the Writer, if he undesignedly doubled his own Labour.[129]

—which works nicely as kindling for the opening paragraphs of the *Literary Magazine* review.

> The first effect which this book has upon the reader is that of disgusting him with the author's vanity. He endeavours to persuade the world, that here are some new treasures of literature spread before his eyes; that something is discovered, which to this happy day had been concealed in darkness; that by his diligence time has been robbed of some valuable monument, which he was on the point of devouring; and that names and facts doomed to oblivion are now restored to fame. How must the unlearned reader be surprised, when he shall be told that Mr. Blackwell has neither digged in the ruins of any demolished city; nor found out the way to the library of *Fez*; nor had a single book in his hands, that has not been in the possession of every man that was inclined to read it, for years and ages;

and that his book relates to a people who above all others have furnished employment to the studious, and amusements to the idle, who have scarcely left behind them a coin or a stone, which has not been examined and explained a thousand times, and whose dress, and food, and houshold stuff it has been the pride of learning to understand.[130]

Clearly, Johnson means to rebuke Blackwell for his hubris rather than to offer readers a rigorous survey of the *Memoirs*. To grasp fully the extraordinary severity of Johnson's criticisms here one must be familiar with his four dozen or so other reviews. As mentioned in chapter 1, Johnson's relation to the authors under review is best understood as that of defense attorney and client: often Johnson will make a case for the worthiness of the book at hand but leave matters in the hands of the reading public. Johnson often dwells upon a favorable feature of a given work that otherwise might go unnoticed or misunderstood, or he will point out extenuating circumstances when discussing an author's shortcomings. Whatever the specifics, as a rule Johnson pleads a case for the authors he has chosen to review and then turns the matter over to the jury—readers, that is—for the final decision. In this review, however, we find Johnson playing the role of judge, jury, and jailer in an attempt to punish Blackwell for demeaning the profession of letters with his bombast.

Rarely does Johnson refrain from calling attention to instances in which Blackwell's erudition is betrayed by his vanity. In the commentary quoted below, for example, we find Johnson making a careful distinction between Blackwell's pomposity and the essential worthiness of his subject matter:

> I do not mean to declare that this volume has nothing new, or that the labours of those who have gone before our author, have made his performance an useless addition to the burden of literature. . . . But after all, to inherit is not to acquire; to decorate is not to make, and the man who had nothing to do but to read the ancient authors, who mention the *Roman* affairs, and reduce them to common places, ought not to boast himself as a great benefactor to the studious world.[131]

The thematic material here is developed further in the second installment of the review, which appeared four months after the first. One issue that looms large for Johnson in the latter portion of the review is the extent to which Blackwell's language is debauched by his self-delusion. Blackwell's "great delight is to show his universal acquaintance with terms of art, with words that every other polite writer has avoided or despised"; "In his choice of phrases he frequently uses words with great solemnity, which every other mouth and pen has appropriated to jocularity and levity"; "His epithets are of the gaudy or hyperbolical kind." In his preface to the *Dictionary* Johnson points out that words merely convey—they do not determine, nor can they be used to refashion—the nature of things ("Language is only the instrument of science [knowledge], and words are but the signs of ideas"). Blackwell's inflated phraseology exemplifies this very point—in reverse. What Blackwell is up to with his choice of words, Johnson would have us believe, is nothing more than scholarly alchemy. The unseemly terminology, the bathetic phrases, the "gaudy" epithets: all of this amounts to an attempt to transform a series of shopworn observations into bold revelations about Roman history.[132]

The climax of the review arrives when Johnson evaluates Blackwell's discussion of the politics of pre-Augustan Rome. Blackwell's "furious and unnecessary zeal for liberty," Johnson declares, is just one of many "affectations." Reasonable people may differ over political philosophy, Johnson admits, but Blackwell's apologia for Caesar's assassins is superficial and sentimental to the point of self-parody: "[W]ho can bear the hardy champion, who ventures nothing?," Johnson asks, who "in full security undertakes the defence of the assassination of Caesar, and declares his resolution *to speak plain*"?[133] Elsewhere in the review Johnson makes the same point with even greater intensity.

> Dr. *Blackwell*, however, seems to have heated his imagination so as to be much affected with every event, and to believe that he can affect others. Enthusiasm is indeed sufficiently contagigious [*sic*], but I never found any of his readers much enamoured of the *glorious Pompey*, the *patriot approv'd*, or much incensed against the *lawless Caesar*, whom this author probably stabs every day and night in his sleeping or waking dreams. . . . It is not easy to forbear laughter at a man so bold in fighting shadows, so busy in a dispute two thousand years past, and so zealous for the honour of a people who while they were poor robbed mankind, and as soon as they became rich robbed one another. Of these robberies our author seems to have no very quick sense, except when they are committed by *Caesar*'s party, for every act is sanctified by the name of patriot.[134]

Of particular interest here is Johnson's ironical use of "patriot." Johnson's *Dictionary* (1755) offers a terse but firmly appreciative definition of the term: "One whose ruling passion is the love of his country." Little more than a year after the Blackwell review appeared, Johnson would pause briefly in his scathing attack on *A Free Inquiry into the Nature and Origins of Evil* to laud Jenyns for asserting that "No immoral man then can possibly be a true patriot."[135] What Johnson is doing here with "patriot" is underscoring the moral and scholarly irresponsibility that finds expression in Blackwell's careless use of language. On the whole, the severity of Johnson's commentary can be said to spring from his anger with Blackwell for portraying himself as courageous when he is merely deluded, for expressing intense passion for "a dispute two thousand years past," and for trying to pass off a collection of essentially commonplace observations as groundbreaking research. Like many of Johnson's other reviews, the Blackwell piece embodies Johnson's understanding of authorship as an essentially beneficent profession. The Blackwell review can also be read as a complement to Johnson's many moral essays—*Rambler* 16 and *Idler* 55 come to mind—on the danger of authorial self-delusion.

Sir Isaac Newton (1642–1727), *Four Letters From Sir Isaac Newton to Doctor Bentley, Containing Some Arguments in Proof of a Deity.* Reviewed by Johnson, 15 June 1756; reviewed by William Rose in the *Monthly,* June 1756; not reviewed in the *Critical,* though the work is given notice in the "List of Pamphlets" section, May 1756. The letters contained in the volume that Johnson reviewed in 1756 were written over an eleven-week period between mid-December 1692 and late February 1693 and number among the most important of Newton's letters that appeared in print before Cambridge University Press published the entire collection over three decades, beginning in the 1950s.[136] Queries from Dr. Richard Bentley (1662–1742), who later became famous for unmasking the spuriousness of the *Epistles of Phalaris*, provided the specific occasions for the four letters. In 1691 Bentley was awarded the Boyle lectureship, an endowed annual series of eight sermons, given in one of London's churches, that were expected to defend religion against infidelity. The sermons were delivered in the spring of 1692, but before their publication Bentley wrote to Newton with the intent of making sure that he had accurately represented Newton's ideas in his Boyle lectures. Newton's four responses remain of interest because they embody the connection Newton perceived between natural laws and God's providential scheme, in particular Newton's belief that gravity was "best accounted for by a direct action of the divine power, rather than by some mechanism created once for all at the beginning of the world."[137]

The *Four Letters* was published by two of the sponsors of Johnson's *Dictionary:* Robert and James Dodsley. Like many of the other titles produced by booksellers who also happened to publish works by Johnson, the *Four Letters* cannot be said to receive special treatment in the *Literary Magazine.* To begin with, Johnson's review appeared nearly five weeks after the publication of the thirty-five-page pamphlet and about two weeks after the *Critical*'s notice appeared, so it seems unlikely that the Dodsley brothers gave Johnson any sort of advance word regarding the *Four Letters.* Johnson's own commentary suggests that he decided to review the book based on its captivating subject matter and the renown of its author.

Perhaps the publication announcement of the book in the 12 May 1756 number of the *Public Advertiser* caught Johnson's attention; he also might have taken note of the appearance of Newton's *Four Letters* as he glanced at the May issue of the *Critical*.[138]

Though one of Johnson's shortest reviews—commentary and extract together total some thirteen hundred words, about the size of a typical *Rambler* essay—the Newton piece exemplifies well Johnson's habit of fashioning his book reviews into independent essays that are easily understood by the common reader even though the volume under review is directed at the specialist or the scholar. Johnson begins by calling attention to the crucial absence of Bentley's letters and by warning readers of the chasm that may separate the expectations raised by the name on the title page and the scholarly value of the letters themselves.

> It will certainly be required, that notice should be taken of a book, however small, written on such a subject, by such an author. Yet I know not whether these letters will be very satisfactory; for they are answers to inquiries not published: and therefore, though they contain many positions of great importance, are, in some parts, imperfect and obscure, by their reference to Dr. *Bentley*'s letters. Sir *Isaac* declares, that what he has done is due to nothing but industry and patient thought, and indeed long consideration is so necessary in such abstruse inquiries, that it is always dangerous to publish the productions of great men, which are not known to have been designed for the press, and of which it is uncertain, whether much patience and thought have been bestowed upon them. The principal question of these letters gives occasion to observe how even the mind of *Newton* gains ground gradually upon darkness.[139]

Perhaps the point of the final sentence is easy to miss in light of the carefully hedged commentary that precedes it, but what Johnson does here is to draw out a moral lesson from material that, by his own reckoning, is "imperfect," "obscure," and not necessarily a reliable reflection of Newton's intellectual powers, given that the letters were not written for publication.

The remaining portion of Johnson's review comprises extract and summary from six of the pamphlet's thirty-five pages of text. Of interest is Johnson's deft arrangement and epitome of Newton's arguments. What Johnson does is to turn Newton's correspondence with Bentley into a quasi-*Rambler* essay in which Newton, much the way "Mr. Rambler" handles moral issues, begins by taking a fresh look at a commonly held attitude—in this case a belief in a divinely created universe—then explores fully competing positions, and concludes with a stronger, more intelligent grasp of the original commonplace.[140]

Johnson reprints the key passage of the first letter, in which Newton acknowledges the plausibility of a materialistic explanation of the origins of the sun and the planets. Newton's doubts of such a view are recorded, but so too is his rather lukewarm endorsement of the creationist viewpoint. In the first letter Newton ultimately finds himself "'forced to ascribe'" the creation of our solar system "'to the counsel and contrivance of a voluntary agent.'" Johnson then offers a recapitulation of Newton's reasoning—leaving out the reluctant edge of Newton's religious account of the nature of the universe. Johnson moves on to quote from Newton's second letter, which considers the materialist understanding of the laws of gravity, though again Newton acknowledges the possibility of a providential design. Following this passage Johnson editorializes, rebuking Newton for awarding what Johnson sees as an unwarranted plausibility to a materialist account of the origins of the universe: "[I]n my opinion, this puzzling question about matter is only, how *that could be that never could have been,* or what a man thinks on when he thinks on nothing. Turn matter on all sides," Johnson goes on to say, "make it eternal, or of late production, finite or infinite, there can be no regular system produced but by a voluntary and meaning agent. This the great Newton always asserted, and this he asserts in his third letter." Johnson then quotes from the third letter, in which Newton unhesitatingly argues that the laws of gravity reflect a providential plan.

> [T]he hypothesis of matter's being at first evenly spread through the heavens, is, in my opinion, inconsistent with the hypothesis of innate gravity, without a supernatural power to reconcile them, and therefore it infers a Diety. For if there be innate gravity it is impossible now for the matter of the earth, and all the planets and stars, to fly up from them, and become evenly spread throughout all the heavens, without a supernatural power; and certainly that which can never be hereafter without a supernatural power, could never be heretofore without the same power.[141]

Had Johnson sought succinctly and accurately to represent Newton's position in the *Four Letters,* he need only have quoted this passage, in which Newton endorses firmly a position he characterizes merely as plausible in earlier letters. The circumstances of the *Four Letters,* after all, boil down to this: Bentley asks whether the universe could have come into existence without divine intervention; Newton's response, in a word, is "No." Clearly, Johnson infuses Newton's letters with a measure of drama that they do not necessarily possess in order to make a case for a religion-centered explanation for the origins of the universe.

Read in their entirety, the letters can be said to function as tutorials, with Newton guiding the inquisitive Bentley through a complicated reasoning process. Newton's skepticism, in other words, is more apparent than real; it is largely a position he stakes out as a means of helping Bentley move from ignorance to understanding. Yet Johnson would have us believe that the letters record a religious conversion of sorts, with Newton's faith gaining strength in direct proportion to improvements he makes in his grasp of physics. Significantly, Johnson does not quote from the fourth letter. The letter essentially reiterates technical arguments made in previous pieces, so Johnson may have felt that quoting from the piece was unnecessary. Even so, at one point the skepticism of the first two letters creeps into the fourth, thus invalidating Johnson's claim that the correspondences show Newton's mind gaining gradually upon darkness. "That gravity should be innate inherent & essential to matter so that one body may act upon another at a distance through a vacuum without the mediation of anything else by and through which their action or force may be conveyed from one to another," Newton states, "is to me so great an absurdity that I believe no man who has in philosophical matters any competent faculty of thinking can ever fall into it." In the next sentence, however, Newton refuses firmly to associate the laws of gravity with divine agency. "Gravity must be caused by an agent acting constantly according to certain laws, *but whether this agent be material or immaterial is a question I have left to the consideration of my readers* [emphasis added]."[142] The *Four Letters* thus reflects Newton's belief that the action of a divine power best explains the origins of the universe, but to argue that the letters reveal a significant shift in Newton's outlook on physico-theology is to ignore the context in which they were written. What the *Literary Magazine* review of the *Four Letters* illustrates is Johnson's willingness to employ the book review not merely as a survey of a recently published title but also as a moral essay that stands apart from the book under review.

E. A. Bloom offers a competing outlook on Johnson's decision to review the *Four Letters*. Johnson "probably felt impelled by journalistic competition to undertake a consideration of the *Four Letters*," Bloom argues. Otherwise, Johnson would not have bothered to review the work because of its controversial subject matter. This reading seems implausible for several reasons.[143] To begin with, Johnson's contributions to the *Literary Magazine* often reflect indifference—or at times active hostility—to the prevailing tastes of the marketplace. Johnson reviews no novels in spite of the public's robust appetite for the genre, it is worth recalling, and many of his political essays embrace belligerently unpopular positions. Equally relevant here is that, contrary to Bloom's claim, the *Critical* all but ignored the *Four Letters,* while the *Monthly* offered readers what can only be described as mere pettifogging criticisms of the work. In his review for the *Monthly*, William Rose takes note of the absence of an introduction/preface before moving on to complain about the exorbitant cost of the slim volume: "[T]ho' they [Newton's letters] are swelled out very artfully," Rose declares, "it is with difficulty that they are stretched to the size of a six-penny pamphlet.— O the Pick-pocketry of Booksellers!" Rose concludes his review with an extremely brief extract from the *Four Letters*.[144]

Johnson may have felt ill at ease with what he may have interpreted as Newton's lukewarm embrace of physico-theology, but Johnson respected Newton's standing as a scholar. If "Newton had flourished in ancient Greece," Johnson is alleged to have said, "he would have been worshipped as a Divinity." [145] And given Johnson's pledge in the *Literary Magazine*'s prefatory essay to review only those works that have met basic scholarly or aesthetic standards, it is hardly surprising that Johnson felt duty-bound to alert the public to an intellectually significant volume irrespective of the editorial decisions made by the leading review journals. To ignore the *Four Letters* because he personally recoiled from Newton's accommodation of the materialist viewpoint, moreover, would have been to indulge the very sort of critical arrogance that Johnson professes to despise in *Ramblers* 3 and 93, "Reflections on the Present State of Literature," and elsewhere. Johnson instead stakes out a middle ground, offering readers a competent introduction to an important work while retailing the least appealing aspects of the *Four Letters* in a manner that serves what Johnson sees as a morally improving end.

Sir Thomas Browne (1605–82), *Christian Morals: The Second Edition, with a Life of the Author, by Samuel Johnson, and Explanatory Notes*. Reviewed by Sir Tanfield Leman in the *Monthly,* May 1756; reviewed by Johnson, 15 July 1756; not reviewed in the *Critical*. Educated at Winchester and Pembroke College, Oxford—the same college Johnson attended in 1728–29—Sir Thomas Browne enjoyed a reputation in his lifetime as a successful physician, antiquarian, and moral philosopher. The first edition of Browne's *Christian Morals* appeared in 1716, thirty-four years after Browne's death; the second edition followed four decades later. The publication of the second edition was underwritten by the bookseller John Payne, a friend of Johnson's and the publisher of the *Rambler*, the *Adventurer*, and the *Universal Chronicle*, which carried Johnson's *Idler* papers. Johnson provided the annotation for the text of the *Christian Morals;* he also wrote the biography of Browne that prefaces the second edition.[146]

Writing in the *Monthly*, Sir Tanfield Leman offers a rousing if rather vaguely worded endorsement not only of the second edition of the *Christian Morals* but also of Johnson's biography—though for some reason Leman declines to include any sort of extract from the work itself that might validate his lofty praise. Browne's character is "so generally known, that to enlarge upon it would be needless and impertinent, especially with regard to the learned," Leman declares. And the "compiler of Sir Thomas's life, has animated his narration with many spirited and judicious remarks: as might, indeed, be naturally expected from the known abilities of Mr. Johnson."[147] The *Literary Magazine* review of Browne's *Christian Morals* is by comparison much more substantive, thanks largely to the 2,000-word extract that reproduces the last ten pages of Johnson's sixty-one-page prefatory biography. Johnson's review opens with tersely neutral critical commentary:

> This little volume consists of short essays written with great vigour of sentiments, variety of learning and vehemence of style. Many allusions, which to common readers must appear obscure, are explained in short notes. The narration prefixed contains rather observations on the author's character, than incidents of his life, which, like that of other learned men, appears to have passed without any extraordinary adventures or revolutions of fortune: It is closed with the following remarks on his writings and opinions.

Noteworthy about this passage is Johnson's principled restraint. What we see here, in other words, is Johnson refusal to go beyond what he sees as the acceptable bounds of reviewing, even when his own literary reputation might have benefited had he done so. Johnson may have refrained from making an impassioned case for his own work, but from the literary historian's viewpoint the Browne piece nevertheless must rank as one of Johnson's most accomplished reviews. A plausible criticism of Johnson's reviews is that they are intellectually uneven, as commentary from the "Great Cham" of letters is diluted or overshadowed by extracts from what are at best indifferent works by minor or forgotten authors. What sets the Browne piece apart is that we are offered a review of Johnson by Johnson, which means that the piece takes on a stylistic and critical unity not found in any other of his reviews.

Of particular interest is Johnson's choice of extract, which exemplifies his habit of employing the book review as a scholarly essay in its own right. Johnson's modest introductory commentary may suggest otherwise, but the extract from Johnson's biography actually touches upon several intellectually weighty subjects. Readers of Johnson's review, for instance, are treated to a rigorously impartial survey of Browne's achievements— "there is no science, in which he does not discover some skill; and scarce any kind of knowledge, profane or sacred, abstruse or elegant, which he does not appear to have cultivated with success"—and Browne's imperfections. In evaluating Browne's style here, Johnson employs a phrase that anticipates his criticism of the metaphysical poets in the "Life of Cowley." Browne's "style is, indeed, a tissue of many languages; a mixture of heterogeneous words brought together from distant regions, with terms originally appropriated to one art, and drawn by violence into the service of another."[148] The extract also includes Johnson's eloquent defense of Browne from charges of impiety and, what is more, contains a passage on the psychology of atheism that can be said to match the eloquence found in the *Rambler* series. As is the case with so many of Johnson's reviews, the Browne piece is much more intellectually substantive than a quick glance would lead us to believe. Brief though it is, the Browne piece reflects Johnson's views on the proper role of the scholarly editor ("Many allusions, which to common readers must appear obscure, are explained in short notes"), Christian orthodoxy ("Men may differ from each other in many religious opinions, and yet may retain the essentials of *christianity*"), literary aesthetics (Browne's "heterogeneous" terms), and the biographer's duty to weigh different kinds of evidence ("The opinions of every man must be learned from himself: concerning his practice, it is safest to trust the evidence of others").[149]

Robert Keith (1681–1757), *A Large New Catalogue of the Bishops of the Several Sees within the Kingdom of Scotland, Down to the Year 1688*. Reviewed by Johnson, 16 August 1756; not reviewed in the *Monthly* or the *Critical*. Robert Keith, bishop of Fife, made a name for himself in the world of professional letters in 1734 with the publication of *The History of the Affairs of the Church and State of Scotland from the Beginning of the Reformation to the Retreat of Queen Mary*. His second major work, *The Catalogue of Scottish Bishops*, appeared some twenty years later and is generally regarded as inferior in scholarly rigor to its predecessor.[150]

Johnson's 3,500-word review of the *Catalogue* is almost entirely composed of direct quotation preceded by the following introductory commentary: "This book, though perhaps not likely to find many readers, will give great pleasure to those who are studious of the *Scotish* ecclesiastical antiquities, which the author, an antient bishop of the church of *Scotland*, appears to have studied with great diligence." Johnson's brevity here is less remarkable than the fact that he bothered to review the 234-page quarto volume at all. As Johnson himself remarks, Keith's *Catalogue* is directed at an extremely narrow readership—chiefly antiquarians, ecclesiastical scholars, and historians of Scotland. Indeed, the *Catalogue* is unlike almost any of the other books Johnson reviews in the *Literary Magazine*, insofar as the others can be said more or less to address a general readership: works of practical science, journalistic compilations, political tracts, translations and adaptations of well known works, and the like. It is also worth noting that the *Catalogue* was not reviewed in the two leading review journals, perhaps because of its provincial subject matter.[151]

E. A. Bloom speculates that Johnson decided to review Keith's work because "the Scottish bishops were loyal to the Stuarts [which] may well have disposed Johnson in favor of the *Catalogue*." This is a plausible interpretation of Johnson's review. As J. C. D. Clark has pointed out, Johnson's writings and conversation show a distinct sympathy for the Stuart cause.[152] Also lending credence to Bloom's reading is the implicitly depreciative viewpoint that the second extract in particular takes of King William III, whom Johnson plainly despised. King William "was arbitrary, insolent, gloomy, rapacious, and brutal," Johnson declares in his review of the duchess of Marlborough's *Memoirs* (1742).[153] Even so, we must keep in mind that Johnson's commentary is devoid of any of the overt political point making one finds in, for instance, the Blackwell, Byng, Cleeve, Evans, Hanway, or Lucas reviews. A more attractive reading is that Johnson, perhaps made aware of the work by the advertisement in the *London Evening-Post* (17 June 1756), admired Keith's scholarly effort and wanted to give his *History* favorable publicity.[154] Johnson made his living largely as a journalist, but we should not forget that he began his career as an aspiring historian and antiquarian. Thus, Johnson may have looked upon Keith as a man very much after his own heart, committed to ordering and preserving material of historical worth even though his effort would likely go largely unnoticed by the contemporary literary marketplace.

Further evidence for this reading can be found in Johnson's choice of extracts. The first of two is a brief but historically significant biographical account of Robert Leighton (1611–84), a Presbyterian minister and author of devotional works whose place in history rests on his acceptance of two Anglican bishoprics during the reign of Charles II in an attempt to bring the two faiths together. The following passage, which discusses Leighton's success at uniting the two faiths, may tell us why Johnson appreciated Keith's contribution to history. "Mr. Leighton did behave himself with so much piety, and a due inspection into the state of his diocese of *Dunblane* first, and next of *Glasgow*, that many of the Non-conformists in these dioceses have acknowledged, that in him all the good qualities of a primitive bishop seemed to be revived."[155] In Johnson's view, evidently, Keith's volume presents readers with a biographical sketch of an exemplary Christian minister: a cleric not only conscientious in discharging his pastoral responsibilities[156] but, of equal importance, committed to emphasizing the central tenets of faith that unite all Christians while at the same time underplaying the issues that might aggravate underlying suspicions or other strains of ill will. As Maurice Quinlan has pointed out, Johnson scorned the cultivation of animosity between Protestant and Catholic, Dissenter and Anglican, even though Johnson understood and very much respected the doctrinal issues that separated the various branches of Christianity. We need only turn to

Johnson's preface to his translation/adaptation of Jeremy Lobo's *Voyage to Abyssinia* (1735), in which Johnson decries the unprincipled proselytizing of the Jesuits, or consult Johnson's "Sermon 11," which argues for sympathy and compassion among all Christians, to find evidence of this point.[157] Johnson's choice of extract, then, can be read as an exemplum that might benefit the bishop and the lay person alike.[158]

The second extract, which takes up most of the review, reproduces a 2,600-word letter from Alexander Ross (1647–1720), "the last Bishop of *Edinburgh*," King William having abolished the Scottish episcopacy in 1689 and reestablished presbyterianism one year later. By way of an introduction to the passage, Johnson acknowledges that Keith's research is destined to reach far fewer readers than it perhaps should—which provides the *Literary Magazine* with all the more reason generously and judiciously to quote from the *Catalogue*. Ross's letter "contains many curious particularities relating to the revolution," Johnson declares, "which, as this book is not likely to fall into many hands, we may have copied as useful to the knowledge of that great event." Ross's letter was written in 1713 and addressed, as Keith points out at the end of the letter, to the "Honorable *Archibald Campbell*, bishop" (1668–1744), a nonjuror whom Johnson is reported to have spoken highly of when he traveled to Scotland in 1773.[159] Ross's letter provides a captivating firsthand account of the political turmoil that confronted the Scottish bishops—who wished to remain loyal to King James II—from October 1688, on the eve of the landing of William of Orange, to the new king's arrival in London in December 1688.

By his own reckoning, Johnson extracted from Keith's otherwise abstruse history two passages that had the best chance of appealing to the public at large. Certainly, the extract on Bishop Leighton reflects the moral and civic importance Johnson attached to biography. The Ross extract can be said to embody Johnson's views on biography as well, but the piece also illustrates Johnson's adversarial temperament and his sympathy for underdogs—the consequences of the Glorious Revolution on the Scottish Church not having been much told—more than it does his alleged Jacobite leanings.

Johnson's review of Keith's *Catalogue*, then, can be said to accomplish two objectives. First, book buyers are given an evenhanded survey of an essentially meritorious, if rather specialized, volume. Second, Johnson departs from conventional expectations of the book review when he de-emphasizes the commercial viability of the work and instead takes Keith's most valuable contributions to history and reprints the material in the general-interest *Literary Magazine*. Johnson's commentary on the *Catalogue* works well enough as a review, certainly. Equally important is that, like

Johnson's other reviews, the *Catalogue* piece also functions as an expository essay—or rather, as a pair of essays—on what Johnson clearly viewed as an important, if little-studied, historical subject.

Charles Parkin (1689–1765), *An Impartial Account of the Invasion under William Duke of Normandy.* Reviewed by William Rose in the *Monthly,* June 1756; reviewed by Johnson, 16 August 1756; not reviewed in the *Critical.* Cambridge educated and an antiquarian by avocation, Charles Parkin served as rector of Oxburgh, Norfolk, from 1717 until his death. Parkin's thirty-six-page *Impartial Account* basically offers readers a tendentious, rehashed survey of the massive administrative, social, and political upheavals—in particular, the displacement of the English aristocracy— that followed in the wake of the Norman Conquest. Evidently, Parkin's nationalistic history was occasioned by the growing hostility between Britain and France, which was formalized with a declaration of war three days after Parkin's pamphlet was published on 12 May 1756. Parkin may also have been moved to write the *Impartial Account* by his continuation of the work of the antiquarian Francis Blomefield (1705–52), whose five-volume *Topographical Account of the County of Norfolk* (published posthumously, 1775) records some of the changes in land ownership brought about the Norman Conquest.[160]

Writing in the *Monthly,* William Rose offers readers an extremely brief and mildly patronizing review of Parkin's *Impartial Account.* "The reverend Author has given himself the trouble of this recital, to put us on our guard against the perfidious and enterprizing French, by a detail of the fatal consequences this nation once experienced from a successful invasion."[161] Johnson's review, which appeared some six weeks later, begins by echoing its predecessor in the *Monthly.* "This pamphlet is published to prove what nobody will deny, that we shall be less happy if we were conquered by the *French.* The intention of the author is undoubtedly good," Johnson declares, "but his labour is superfluous at a time when all ranks of people are unanimously zealous and active against our enemies; and when indeed there is no great danger of invasions while we have the sea covered with our ships, and maintain fifty thousand men in arms on our coasts." In the next sentence, Johnson introduces what is, as Donald Eddy points out, Parkin's only meritorious observation: that an assumption by the antiquary and historian Sir Henry Spelman (misspelled by Johnson and Parkin as "Spilman") regarding the transfer and return of lands in Norfolk following the Norman Conquest is false.[162] The 1,200-word extract is taken from pages 30 to 34 of Parkin's pamphlet, a passage meant to refute the view implicit in Spelman's narrative that the Norman conquerors were capable of generosity and leniency. According to Spelman, a large tract of land awarded to

"'Edwin, a Dane,'" by King Canute the Great (d. 1035), was taken over by William de Albini, William the Conqueror's butler, and William Earl Warren at the time of the Conquest. A portion of the land was returned following Edwin's pledge to William the Conqueror that he never acted against him. Parkin goes on to point out that Spelman bases his argument on an unreliable sixteenth-century manuscript. Parkin, whose own case rests on material from the *Domesday Book*, asserts that the land in question was never in the possession of Edwin, William de Albini, or William Earl Warren. Thus, William the Conqueror's magnanimous gesture of returning a tract of land to its rightful English owner in fact never took place.[163]

Following the extract, Johnson concludes by questioning the significance of Parkin's attempt to rebut Spelman. "To this we shall only add, that the story, whatever be decided concerning it, proves very little, since it is plain, that the restoration, if any such there was, could be only considered as an act of favour, and a grant from the Conquerer." The coherence and thoroughness of the material taken from Parkin's volume might easily captivate the historian, the antiquarian, or the indiscriminately curious general reader. Yet Johnson's introductory and concluding commentary, which would have us believe that the pamphlet overall is of negligible scholarly worth, raises questions about Johnson's decision to review the *Impartial Account* in the first place. Given the demands of superintending a monthly general-interest magazine, Johnson must have known that the quality of the books available for review each month would be uneven, so he had to assign considerable critical weight to an author's potentially admirable intentions if he wanted to avoid the censoriousness that in his view had done so much to undermine the worthy activity of reviewing. Authors such as Parkin who demonstrate what Johnson interprets as a desire to spread worthwhile knowledge are entitled to be treated sympathetically even if their actual achievement lacks merit. Surely Parkin's painfully obvious thesis irritated, or carried the potential to irritate, Johnson's scholarly sensibilities. Even so, Parkin's patriotism, anti-Gallic sentiments, and sedulousness as an antiquarian command a measure of respect from Johnson—who, as the Blackwell review (and, as we shall see, the Jenyns review) bears out, did not shrink from bludgeoning authors whose literary dullness was aggravated by their vainglory or self-centeredness.

Johann Georg Keyssler (1693–1743), *Travels through Germany, Bohemia, Hungary, Switzerland, Italy, and Lorrain,* **vol. 1.** Reviewed by Gregory Sharpe in the *Monthly,* May 1756; reviewed in the *Critical* (reviewer unknown), July 1756; reviewed by Johnson, September 1756. Keyssler's massive, encyclopedic *Travels through Germany*—four quarto volumes, nearly two thousand pages—was one of the most popular examples of the genre produced during the eighteenth century. Essentially, Keyssler's *Travels* emphasizes observation at the expense of reflection, much as its title page would suggest ("Giving a True and Just Description of the Present State of those Countries . . ."), so it is scarcely surprising that tourists in particular—the most famous being Edward Gibbon—used it as guidebook of sorts during Johnson's day, much the way modern visitors to Europe rely on the *Thomas Cooke Travellers*.[164]

The English translation of Johann Keyssler's *Travels through Germany*, published by Andrew Millar, Robert Dodsley, and W. Shropshire in late 1755, was warmly welcomed in the two leading review journals. Writing in the *Monthly*, Gregory Sharpe asserts that the *Travels through Germany* exemplifies the best sort of travel narrative, insofar as it offers accurate observations on the history, politics, and geography of several continental nations. Sharpe's counterpart in the *Critical* is similarly appreciative. Keyssler's volume "abounds" with "many useful and entertaining remarks," the reviewer argues. As a means of validating their lavish praise, both reviewers allocate the bulk of their lengthy reviews to direct quotation from the 520-page first volume of Keyssler's *Travels*.[165] In short, the *Monthly* and the *Critical* offer readers wholly serviceable accounts of Keyssler's narrative. Both reviewers reprint a mass of material from the work so that readers can make up their own minds—though in their roles as arbiters of literary merit they do not shy from attempting to condition the reaction of readers to the extracted material.

Johnson's review of Keyssler's *Travels* is of interest, to begin with, because we can read it as an attempt to deflate what Johnson may have interpreted as unreasonably lofty praise of the work published previously in the two leading review journals. Much like his counterparts in the *Monthly* and the *Critical*, Johnson relies heavily on extracted material in his review of the Keyssler volume. What makes Johnson's review stand out from its competitors, however, is that Johnson stops well short of lauding the *Travels* in the *Literary Magazine* and instead merely acknowledges that Keyssler's is an "agreeable narrative." More significantly, Johnson goes on to advise prospective book buyers that "in the opinion of most readers the only objection to his [Keyssler's] performance is, that he has visited only those countries which every man visits, and therefore has only seen what every man sees." Fully to understand Johnson's criticism here requires that we recall his discussion of travel narratives in *Idler* 97, published a few years afterward. "Every writer of travels should consider, that, like all other authors, he undertakes either to instruct or please, or to mingle pleasure with instruction," Johnson argues. "He that instructs must offer to the mind something to be imitated or something to be avoided; he that pleases must offer new images to his reader, and enable him to form a tacit comparison of his own state with others."[166] For Johnson to claim that the "only objection" to Keyssler's volume is that it offers readers nothing really new is on the order of saying that the only fault consumers will find with a given manufacturer's raincoat is that it occasionally lets in water—though wearing the coat will give certain proof of its owner's fashion sense. Johnson clearly believed that Keyssler's travel narrative was basically worthy of the public's attention—in fact, some twenty years later Johnson would speak well of Keyssler's observations in private conversation—but as a reviewer he could not bring himself to praise unhesitatingly a rather bulky travel book that failed to present a fresh perspective.[167]

Johnson may not have thought all that highly of Keyssler's skill at crafting an account of his journey across continental Europe, but he does discern a latent worthiness in some of Keyssler's incidental observations as well as in the biography that accompanies the English translation. The importance Johnson attaches to biography, for instance, finds expression in his first extract, which is taken not from the translation of Keyssler's *Travels* but from the anonymous translator's prefatory biography. The biographical extract totals some thirteen hundred words—about the size of a *Rambler* essay—and emphasizes Keyssler's early education and its relation to his resolute moral sense. The first paragraph of the extracted material must have been especially pleasing to Johnson, who valued biography particularly for its inspirational value. Indeed, the first extract exemplifies the prescriptions for biography set forth in *Rambler* 60 by paying scant attention to Johann Keyssler's public affairs and focusing on his private moral life instead.

> [Keyssler's father] took an extraordinary care of his education; and the sincere piety which he imbibed in his childhood from his mother, strongly influenced him during his whole life. His early years were not squandered away in the dissipations of youth, but seriously consecrated to the great author of being. He was so well fixed in his religious principles, that he never was carried away by the torrent of libertinism, or tainted by the prevalence of custom and fashion in a degenerate age.[168]

Elsewhere in the extract, we learn that Keyssler spent the last years of his life not in "a culpable inactivity" or in "a lazy indolent repose" but adding to his library and building up his collection of "natural curiosities." We are also told of the equanimity with which he greeted death. "The serenity of his mind in that awful crisis, shewed that his hopes were full of immortality, and the whole tenor of his life demonstrated, that these hopes were well grounded."[169] Johnson's lead extract thus encourages us to admire Keyssler for his moral and intellectual excellence while the humdrum aspects of his travel narrative go largely ignored.

The next block of extracted material is chosen with equal care, as Johnson passes over the first third of Keyssler's volume and reprints a pair of moral exempla from page 153 of the *Travels*. The first paragraph of the extract surveys a "remarkable hermitage" endowed with "a chapel, oratory, steeple, hall, refectory, kitchen, rooms, stairs, cellar, well and other conveniences, all hewn out of a rock." The life and death of its pious occupant are also discussed. The second paragraph describes the similarly sophisticated mountain hideaway of a criminal. "One cannot but reflect on the different motives of these two solitaries," Johnson declares, as he draws out a general moral point that Keyssler largely overlooks. "To retire from the world to the service of God was rational in a man who thought innocence best secured, and God best served by retirement. But what can be thought of him who lived in a cavern to rob, and robbed to live in a cavern. Surely in every sense all wickedness is folly."[170]

Johnson's review closes with an additional pair of extracts, the first describing the court of Charles of Sweden, which Johnson believes will "interest many of our readers," and the second surveying the "laws and practices" of the University of Tübingen, which Johnson believes may "promote the interest of learning." Thus, at first glance Johnson's review of Keyssler's *Travels* may strike readers as a rather halfhearted response to what is at best a mildly interesting volume. But when we take into account the critical decisions Johnson makes as he selects and arranges the extracted material, the review takes on a much greater stature, functioning as a series of moral, historical, and cultural essays.

Charlotte Lennox (1720–1804), trans., *Memoirs of Maximilian De Bethune, Duke of Sully, Prime Minister to Henry the Great*. Reviewed in the *Monthly,* June, July, and August 1756 (reviewer unknown); reviewed by Johnson, 15 October 1756; not reviewed in *Critical*. In regard to format, the *Monthly*'s review of Charlotte Lennox's translation of the *Memoirs of the Duke of Sully* is very much typical of what one finds in review journals of the period, as it comprises a brief critical comment followed by lengthy extracts from the work under consideration. Lennox's translation "is judiciously executed," the reviewer declares, and "the language is easy, and proper for the subject, and such as may well become the fair hand to which the public is obliged for the *Female Quixote*, and *Shakespear Illustrated*." The reviewer goes on to tell readers that, given the popularity of the *Memoirs*—the book appeared more than six months before the publication of the *Monthly*'s review—there is little left for him to do apart from reprinting portions of the work, which may help readers unfamiliar with the work to understand the public's great fondness for Lennox's 1,500-page, three-volume translation.[171]

The first thing that one notices about Johnson's review of his friend Charlotte Lennox's book is its tardiness, for which there seems to be no ready explanation. Johnson's review appeared nearly one year after the publication of the *Memoirs* and some eleven weeks after its counterpart appeared in the *Monthly Review*. [172] True, Johnson's *Literary Magazine* review does contain a measure of timeliness, insofar as it announces the imminent publication of a "cheaper edition" of the *Memoirs*—a five-volume octavo version was published in late 1756—but when we recall that Johnson reviewed Lennox's *The Female Quixote* within a month of its publication, the lateness of his review of *Sully's Memoirs* seems all the more difficult to understand, particularly if we accept J. L. Clifford's surmise that Johnson helped Lennox with the translation. [173] What also surprises is the relative brevity of Johnson's review. In the October 1756 number of the *Literary Magazine* the thousand-word *Memoirs* review precedes Johnson's review of Elizabeth Harrison's *Moral Miscellanies*, which is more than five times as long. Other reviews by Johnson in the October number are of about the same size as the Harrison piece, if not longer, thus underscoring further the relative shortness of the *Memoirs* review. Nevertheless, Johnson's commentary is decidedly favorable if not particularly original, as it mirrors its predecessor in the *Monthly* by acknowledging both the popularity of the *Memoirs* and Lennox's skill at translation. "This translation has been already so well received by the public that we can add little to its reputation by the addition of our suffrage in its favour," Johnson observes in his opening sentence, adding a bit later that Lennox's translation combines "the variety of romance with the truth of history." Lennox's style, Johnson goes on to say, "is easy, spritely, and elegant, equally remote from the turgid and the mean." Johnson fleshes out his review with a block of text from pages 266–68 of the first volume of the *Memoirs*, which he selects "because it can be understood alone, and requires little room, not because it is otherwise preferable to other passages." [174]

What might account for Johnson's conservatively appreciative survey of Lennox's *Memoirs*? As Johnson's reviews of Birch's *History of the Royal Society*, Warton's *Essay on the Writings and Genius of Pope*, and his own edition of Browne's *Christian Morals* demonstrate, Johnson seems to have been particularly concerned about the temptation to peddle fulsomeness when reviewing in the *Literary Magazine* works written by friends. In the review of *Sully's Memoirs*, Johnson evidently refused to let his fondness for Charlotte Lennox transcend what he understood to be the critical limits of reviewing. In his capacity as a reviewer, in other words, Johnson could not possibly justify doing more for Lennox than recording popular approval of her translation and calling attention to the soon-to-be-published octavo edition.

Apart from taking note of Lennox's praiseworthy work as a translator, Johnson's review also offers readers brief but perceptive observations on the enduring relevance of history and autobiography. *Sully's Memoirs* "contain[s] an account of that time in which France first began to assume here superiority in Europe," Johnson declares. Thus the work is of special interest because it "exhibit[s] a nation torn with factions, and plundered by tax-gatherers, rescued by a great king and an honest minister. There can be no age or people to which such a history may not be useful and pleasing," Johnson goes on to argue, "but it must more particularly invite the attention of those who like us are now labouring with the same distresses, and whose duty it is to endeavour at the same relief."[175] Maximilien de Béthune, duke of Sully (1559–1641), enacted a series of bold reforms during his tenure as King Henry IV's chief finance minister, including the abolition of many useless government offices and the institution of an efficient and basically estimable tax collection system. In his capacity as advisor to the king, moreover, Sully encouraged civic, economic, and military projects that contributed significantly to France's status as a world power. Sully resigned his public office in 1611, following the assassination of King Henry. Sully's *Memoirs* appeared in 1638, three years before his death and more than a quarter of a century after his withdrawal from public life.[176] Clearly, Johnson's review was designed to encourage the reading public, who were witnessing the birth of England as a supreme world power, to draw all the right lessons from Sully's conduct during a period in French history that compared favorably to contemporary English circumstances.

The *Literary Magazine* review of the *Memoirs* thus tells us that Johnson trusted completely Sully's account; he admired in particular Sully's honesty, intelligent civic-mindedness, and courage—a significant point given the robust skepticism that Johnson brought to the reading of such works.[177] Indeed, the *Sully* review can be said to exemplify Johnson's broader outlook on the value of autobiography, properly written. "The high and the low, as they have the same faculties and the same senses, have no less similitude in their pains and pleasures," Johnson observes in *Idler* 84. "Men thus equal in themselves will appear equal in honest and impartial [auto]biography; and those whom fortune or nature place[s] at the greatest distance may afford instruction to each other."[178] *Sully's Memoirs* is the best sort of autobiography, Johnson would have us believe, as it illuminates the inner life of a major historical figure in ways that yield valuable moral lessons that apply equally to the aspiring head of state and the common reader.

Elizabeth Harrison (fl. 1724–56), *Miscellanies on Moral and Religious Subjects*: Reviewed by Johnson, 15 October 1756; reviewed by John

Berkenhout in the *Monthly,* November 1756; not reviewed in the *Critical.* The privately printed *Moral Miscellanies*—a 384-page (octavo) collection of inspirational poems and short fictional pieces—was created to raise money to support the compiler's aging and ill father. The volume holds some interest for scholars today not only because Johnson chose to review the work but also because both he and John Hawkesworth subscribed to the volume.[179]

Given Johnson's connections with the *Moral Miscellanies*, it is not much of a surprise to find him writing favorably of the work in the *Literary Magazine,* even though his praise is characteristically provisional. It is noted, for instance, that the contributing authors "*attempt* to employ the ornaments of romance in the decoration of religion [emphasis added]," and that they "have laboured" to infuse their narratives with "brightness of imagery" and "purity of sentiment." Also remarkable here is Johnson's observation that the *Miscellanies* "will not be generally read," because it is "published only for the subscribers," a circumstance that may have prompted readers to wonder why Johnson devotes considerable space—at twelve columns, the Harrison review is one of Johnson's longest—to a work not widely available. It is impossible to do more than make an educated guess, given the available evidence, but a likely explanation is that Johnson admired the moral sense of the contributing authors and sought to award them their due mead of favorable publicity. The inclusion of extensive extracts, moreover, may have been a deliberate attempt to highlight what Johnson saw as the proper ends of fiction at a historical moment when scandalous "secret histories," bawdy poems, and similar sorts of lowbrow material were regularly given notice in the *Monthly* and the *Critical* (though such reviews were almost invariably condemnatory). Equally likely is that Johnson hoped either to generate marketplace demand for a second edition, or to ensure the sale of any unsold copies from the first printing.[180]

Johnson's review opens with an ambitious comparison of Harrison's contributors to Isaac Watts (1674–1748) and Elizabeth Rowe (1674–1737), two Dissenters whose writings enjoyed great popularity during the first half of the century.[181] "The authors of the essays in prose seem generally to have imitated or tried to imitate the copiousness and luxuriance of Mrs. *Rowe*," Johnson states. The contributing poets, meanwhile, "have had Dr. *Watts* before their eyes, a writer who, if he stood not in the first class of genius, compensated that defect by a ready application of his powers to the promotion of piety."[182] Johnson then proceeds to survey the history of religion-centered fiction.

> The attempt to employ the ornaments of romance in the decoration of religion was, I think, first made by Mr. *Boyle's Martyrdom of Theodora*, but

Boyle's philosophical studies did not allow him time for the cultivation of stile, and the completion of the great design was reserved for Mrs. *Rowe*. Dr. *Watts* was one of the first who taught the dissenters to write and speak like other men, by shewing them that elegance might consist with piety. They would have both done honour to a better society, for they had that charity which might well make their failings forgotten, and with which the whole christian world might wish for communion.[183]

Johnson goes on to assert that the enduring fame of Watts and Rowe is the legitimate expectation of all "writers who please and do not corrupt, who instruct and do not weary."[184] To lend weight to his point that Harrison's contributors exemplify the noblest traditions of fiction, Johnson devotes a great deal of space—eleven columns altogether, or roughly twice the size of the review of Blackwell's *Memoirs of the Court of Augustus*—to extracts. The first piece is a letter from a man who writes to a woman from beyond the grave, telling her to "turn your thoughts from this lifeless clay, and that dark and silent grave wherein it is interred, to these blissful realms, at which my more noble part is safely arrived." The second piece quoted is an exemplum on the duty of charity and its ennobling qualities. Two poems included in the extract are entitled, respectively, "Truth's Answer to a Man's Enquiry" and "Virtue and Vice."[185] Clearly the Harrison review reflects Johnson's intense religious feeling, but it also encapsulates Johnson's general outlook on the high moral seriousness of even the lower forms of fiction. The worthiness of the material quoted in Johnson's review is meant to stand in direct contrast to the silly, licentious, and often badly written familiar histories, petty verse, and so forth, regularly given notice in the "Monthly Catalogue" sections of the two leading review journals.

One interesting aspect of the review is Johnson's conspicuous silence with regard to the occasion for the work. Why Johnson eschewed comment on this matter is open to conjecture, but he may have surmised that appeals to leniency or pity would overshadow the considerable merit of the *Miscellanies;* perhaps he suspected that such remarks would evoke public cynicism rather than goodwill. The *Monthly*'s review of the *Miscellanies* suggests that Johnson acted wisely by keeping the review on a strictly literary level. The reviewer for the *Monthly*—possibly John Berkenhout—takes into account Harrison's difficulties but does so in a particularly ham-handed fashion:

As the publication is the work of benevolence, and a sacrifice, not to vanity, but to PIOUS OLD AGE, and INDUSTRIOUS POVERTY; it has a natural claim upon us, to an entire exemption from any criticism that might tend, in the least, to obstruct the progress of so worthy an intention.[186]

The *Monthly*'s self-congratulation here is obvious enough, but what about the worthiness of the *Miscellanies* itself? Are we to read the comments here as a bit of paralipsis? Lucky for Harrison, in other words, that her circumstances evoke compassion. Or is the reviewer merely a clumsy rhetorician who really does mean to encourage a sympathetic reading of the work? Either way, it is difficult to imagine that this review pleased Harrison, her contributors, or her subscribers.

Soame Jenyns (1704–87), *A Free Inquiry into the Nature and Origin of Evil*. Reviewed by Johnson, 17 May–17 July 1757; reviewed by William Rose in the *Monthly,* April 1757; reviewed in the *Critical,* May 1757 (reviewer unknown). Soame Jenyns was a prominent figure in the social and political establishment of his day, serving in Parliament for some forty years and, beginning in 1755, acting as one of the commissioners of the board of trade and plantations. Jenyns also authored numerous poems and works of prose.[187] The most famous of his writings—thanks in no small portion to Johnson's review—is the *Free Inquiry*, a clumsily argued exposition of the optimistic philosophy widely associated with Alexander Pope's *Essay on Man* (1733-34) and later fiercely attacked by Voltaire's *Candide* (1759). Essentially, the *Free Inquiry* attempts to prove that evil occupies a legitimate place in the moral order and that all misery ultimately serves a humanitarian end.[188] Johnson's rather vitriolic response to the work has been frequently commented upon. Donald Eddy, for instance, correctly points out that Jenyns is ridiculed with such intensity because Johnson was "morally offended" by the irresponsible ideas advanced in *A Free Inquiry*. R. B. Schwartz avers that Johnson was chiefly irritated by Jenyns's incompetent scholarship. One reason "behind the vehemence of Johnson's attack," Schwartz argues, "is the disparity between the enormity of the subject and the shallowness of Jenyns' treatment of it." Johnson was moved to review the *Free Inquiry* in the first place, Schwartz adds, because he wanted to keep its arguments from encouraging complacency about the plight of the poor, the ad hominem rebukes being the most effective means of delegitimating Jenyns's ideas.[189] These assessments are certainly accurate, but an additional word needs to be said about the ways in which the Jenyns piece embodies Johnson's general views on authorial self-deception. True enough, Johnson plainly despises shallow optimism as portrayed by Jenyns. But it is important for us to recognize that the critical emphasis in the *Literary Magazine* review falls as much on Jenyns's hubris as it does on the philosophical issues in themselves.

In the lead paragraph of the review, for instance, we find Johnson chastising Jenyns not for his advocacy of optimism per se but for assuming that the immensely complex issues addressed in the *Free Inquiry* can be disposed of with ease:

> This is a treatise consisting of six letters upon a very difficult and important question, which I am afraid this author's endeavours will not free from the perplexity, which has entangled the speculatists of all ages, and which must always continue while *we see* but *in part*. He calls it a *Free* enquiry, and indeed his *freedom* is, I think[,] greater than his modesty. Though he is far from the contemptible arrogance, or the impious licentiousness[,] of *Bolingbroke*, yet he decides too easily upon questions out of the reach of human determination, with too little consideration of mortal weakness, and with too much vivacity for the necessary caution.[190]

Certainly the nature of evil is a worthy subject to pursue, Johnson acknowledges here, and Jenyns at some level probably means well. What is so vexing for Johnson is the aura of self-satisfaction surrounding the work. Jenyns is convinced that the *Free Inquiry* resolves philosophical conundrums that have stymied the greatest thinkers from antiquity onward, even though his arguments amount to nothing more than an apologia for self-centeredness that many readers will find compelling precisely because of its simplemindedness.

As the review unfolds, we find that Johnson rarely strays from rebuking Jenyns for his irresponsible authorship. To be sure, Johnson does provide readers with a rigorous and largely evenhanded survey of the major issues touched upon in the *Free Inquiry*. Indeed, so thorough is Johnson that, as Donald Eddy points out, the review contains quotations from 51 of the treatise's 181 pages of text.[191] But it is the fiery personal reproaches of Jenyns's hubris and self-delusion that define the review. "I am told, that this pamphlet is not the effort of hunger," Johnson observes as he berates Jenyns for manufacturing the second of the *Free Inquiry*'s six letters almost entirely out of material extracted from Pope's *Essay on Man:*

> What can it be then but the product of vanity? and yet how can vanity be gratified by plagiarism, or transcription? When this speculatist finds himself prompted to another performance, let him consider whether he is about to disburthen his mind or employ his fingers; and if I might venture to offer him a subject, I should wish that he would solve this question, Why he that has nothing to write, should desire to be a writer.[192]

In another instance Johnson asserts straightforwardly that the polemical failures of the *Free Inquiry* are less of an irritation than is Jenyns's conviction that his muddled or superficial observations are clearheaded and profound.

I do not mean to reproach this author for not knowing what is equally hidden from learning and from ignorance. The shame is to impose words for ideas upon ourselves or others. To imagine that we are going forward when we are only turning around. To think that there is any difference between him that gives no reason, and him that gives a reason, which by his own confession cannot be conceived.[193]

In what is perhaps Johnson's most memorable attack, Jenyns is "hoist by his own petard." At one point Jenyns attempts to explain away human suffering by claiming that it brings pleasure to higher life forms. These same "beings," Johnson says in response,

> now and then catch a mortal, proud of his parts, and flattered either by the submission of those who court his kindness, or the notice of those who suffer him to court theirs. A head thus prepared for the reception of false opinions, and the projection of vain designs, they easily fill with idle notions. . . . Then begins the poor animal to entangle himself in sophisms, and flounder in absurdity, to talk confidently of the scale of being, and to give solutions which himself confesses impossible to be understood.[194]

The remarks here could easily serve as the cornerstone for one of Johnson's *Rambler* or *Adventurer* essays on the evils of self-deception. Indeed, the Jenyns piece is important to our understanding of Johnson's outlook on not only authorial self-delusion but the beneficent purposes of all literary activity as well. Jenyns arouses Johnson's anger chiefly because he abuses the authorial role of social and moral luminary. As R. B. Schwartz and others have shown, Johnson fully realized that the concepts advanced in *A Free Inquiry* might easily undermine beneficent activity on both public and private levels: if human misery serves a greater moral good, why tamper with the grand schemes of the Deity? Though Johnson generally does live by his own numerous warnings against domineering or excessively harsh criticism, the potentially inhumane consequences of the ideas advocated in the *Free Inquiry* cried out for a commensurably strong response. In fact, we can read the Jenyns review as an endorsement of the brief but significant exemption to critical reticence allowed for in *Rambler* 93. "There is indeed some tenderness due to living writers," Johnson argues, except "when they attack . . . those truths which are of importance to the happiness of mankind."[195] As far as Johnson is concerned, Jenyns fits squarely into this category. The *Free Inquiry* effectively attempts to legitimate the meanest of human impulses, and so its author richly deserves to be thrashed in full view of the public.

Do reviews in the two leading journals tell us anything about Johnson's treatment of Jenyns? William Rose's fifteen-page review for the *Monthly* is largely taken up by extract and summary, though Rose does remark on the *Free Inquiry*'s intellectual flimsiness in the beginning of his review (Jenyns's ideas, he says, bear a "strong resemblance to those Nostrum-Advertisements we so frequently meet with in our News-papers") and in his closing remarks ("our Author reduces Omnipotence to numerous difficulties, and endeavours to extricate it by very bungling expedients"). Rose ultimately rejects the *Free Inquiry*, as does Johnson, but missing is the passionate indignation found in the *Literary Magazine* piece. Rose's essay has a rather routine, workaday quality to it: his brief criticisms largely refer to the forensic qualities of the treatise. The appreciative review of Jenyns in the *Critical*, meanwhile, essentially validates Johnson's assumptions about the attractiveness of Jenyns's facile optimism. In spite of its minor flaws the *Free Inquiry* can be summarized as "a performance of distinguished merit, and apparently the work of an able and judicious writer," the reviewer declares. Whether Johnson managed to read this review before writing his own is impossible to say—the second and third segments of Johnson's review appeared in June and July, after the publication of the *Critical Review* piece in May—but such ill-considered praise must have made Johnson's biting remarks seem all the more necessary.[196]

It is also worth noting that the thirty-page preface to the fourth edition of the *Free Inquiry* (1761) offers a rebuttal to Johnson and other critics of earlier editions. In a manner reminiscent of *Rambler* 16's "Misellus" and *Idler* 55's "correspondent," Jenyns attributes the worst motives to his critics—"senseless misapprehensions, and malicious misconstructions"—while resolutely defending what he believes are the compelling merits of his work. There is "nothing in the sentiments which ought to be retracted," Jenyns asserts, though it is true that stylistic blunders occasionally blight an otherwise meticulously argued thesis.[197] Clearly, the publication of an unfavorable review aroused in Jenyns, who was widely known for his geniality and wit, a surprising and wholly irrational acrimony. In his frequent discussions of authorship in the *Rambler* and elsewhere, Johnson persistently characterizes writing for the marketplace as an emotionally hazardous venture, a gamble of sorts between fame on the one hand and disgrace or oblivion on the other, with aspiring authors being well advised to assume that the odds are against them. Jenyns reaction to Johnson's review in the *Literary Magazine*—the stubborn refusal to confront even obvious weaknesses; the combative disposition toward legitimate criticisms; the impulse to justify one's imagined achievement despite overwhelming evidence to the contrary—dramatizes this very point, thus highlighting further Johnson's keen understanding of the modern authorial sensibility as expressed in his journalistic writings.

The third installment of the Jenyns review (15 July 1757) proved to be

Johnson's final contribution to the *Literary Magazine*. Why Johnson left the magazine is not known, nor can it be determined whether he resigned or was fired. Jonas Hanway's accusation in the spring of 1757 that Johnson's review of Hanway's *A Journal of Eight Days' Journey* defamed him and sullied the reputation of the Foundling Hospital—an incident discussed at length in the next chapter—almost certainly hastened Johnson's departure, as did Johnson's antigovernment essays, which probably cost the magazine readers. It is hard to believe that Johnson was hoping for a long-term arrangement with the *Literary Magazine* in any case. "The circulation of the magazine was discouragingly small," Donald Eddy observes, "and it must have hurt his professional pride to be furnishing well-written material to a periodical which few people ever saw." Nothing was keeping Johnson at the *Literary Magazine*, in other words, but there were plenty of good reasons for him to quit.[198]

The sour note that concludes Johnson's tenure at the *Literary Magazine* should not eclipse his generally solid performance as a reviewer of literary, philosophical, and historical titles—nor, for that matter, of journalistic and scientific works, as subsequent chapters shall demonstrate. The Blackwell, Hampton, Jenyns, and Warton reviews are justly famous, because they convey Johnson's specific views on historiography, translation, moral philosophy, and poetry. The Blackwell and Jenyns reviews, moreover, can be said to reflect Johnson's core belief in the lofty moral and social purposes of authorship and, correspondingly, the duty of the critic to rebuke writers who plainly betray those aims. But the other reviews discussed in this chapter are worthy of study—the Sully, Browne, and Keyssler pieces, for instance—because they too embody aspects of Johnson's broader critical and moral outlook.

In several of his *Rambler* papers, Johnson warns of the inherent fallibility of the critical intelligence, particularly when it is directed at the work of the critic's contemporaries. By the same token, other *Rambler* essays, as well as Johnson's introductory essays to the *Literary Magazine* and the *London Chronicle*, tell us that Johnson also believed that the literary world would benefit from a temperate strain of criticism. As far as Johnson was concerned, effective book reviews introduce readers to apparently worthy works even as they stop short of offering heavy-handed or dogmatic judgments that would almost certainly prove to be inaccurate and would needlessly skewer public perceptions of a given work. As a reviewer of literary, philosophical, and historical titles in the *Literary Magazine*, Johnson manages to offer the reading public discerning surveys of evidently meritorious new titles even as he refrains from assigning to himself the authority of passing final judgment on such works, a privilege that in Johnson's view should remain in the hands of the reading public. Johnson's critical restraint, of course, does not mean that his reviews lack spirit or intellectual rigor. Quite the contrary: often his selection of extracts in itself is interesting—the Birch, Hampton, and Harrison reviews come immediately to mind—as readers are given what in fact amount to collaborative essays, written by Johnson and the author under review, that make broad ethical or historical points that transcend what one expects to find in book reviews of the period.

3

Johnson as a Reviewer of Journalistic Publications, Fugitive Pieces, and Books on Public Affairs in the *Literary Magazine*

As mentioned in chapter 1, Johnson's pioneering contribution to the theory and practice of journalism, which was emerging as an independent profession just as Johnson's literary career was getting underway, has been discussed at length by Donald Greene, E. A. Bloom, and others.[1] Johnson's exalted view of journalism helps us to understand the high priority—roughly 25 percent of both the titles reviewed (ten) and pages allocated (fifty-one)—that Johnson assigned to news writing, a practice that contemporaries thought of as among the meaner sorts of literary activity. Johnson thought equally well of pamphlet writing, or "fugitive pieces," as his "Introduction to the *Harleian Miscellany*" (1744) bears out.[2] Pamphlets and other sorts of occasional essays bearing on contemporaneous controversies illustrate "the progress of every debate; the various states to which the questions have been changed; the artifices and fallacies which have been used, and the subterfuges by which reason has been eluded," Johnson observes. "In such writings may be seen how the mind has been opened by degrees, how one truth led to another, how error has been disentangled, and hints improved to demonstration."[3] Pamphlets and occasional essays are indispensable vessels of information in a society made up of self-governing citizens, Johnson would have us believe, even as they prove to be important, if at times unjustly ignored, historical artifacts.

Generally speaking, the reviews Johnson writes of journalistic and fugitive publications contain little in the way of ambitious literary criticism. Johnson instead fills his reviews with large portions of extracted material, quoting from or paraphrasing, for instance, 142 of the 287 pages of text that the five Byng pamphlets collectively comprise. Johnson does indeed take firm stands on some of the issues raised in the pamphlets he reviews—he vigorously opposed the court-martial of Admiral Byng, just as he did Great Britain's expansionist designs on North America—but he also allows those holding competing views the necessary space fully to express their positions. Johnson's reviews of David Mallet's defense of the Newcastle ministry's prosecution of Admiral Byng and Lewis Evans's attempt to justify Great Britain's colonization of the Ohio valley, for instance, can be profitably studied as exchanges of editorial essays between Johnson and the authors under review. Johnson's ultimate intention, clearly, is to make sure that readers of the *Literary Magazine*—even if they choose not to purchase the items reviewed—acquire a sound understanding of the various controversies of the day so that they can reach intelligent decisions about matters on their own. Under Johnson's direction the *Literary Magazine*'s reviewing section functions as something of a digest of leading opinion on some of the major issues confronting the English at mid-century. Put another way, Johnson's practices as a reviewer of journalistic and fugitive publications exemplify the general positions he stakes out in *Rambler* 145, the "Introduction to the *Harleian Miscellany*," and elsewhere, namely, that journalistic writings and fugitive pieces provide not only contemporaries but historians with various perspectives on how this or that major issue took shape and came to be resolved. Indeed, Johnson's attitude to journalism both as a writer of and as reviewer of such pieces embodies his basic political belief in "the importance of a public well informed on political matters."[4]

What of Johnson's commentary on books related to public affairs and current events? Johnson's review of Jonas Hanway's 723-page, two-volume *Eight Days' Journey* contains discerning criticisms that reflect, as we shall see in due course, Johnson's intelligent understanding of England's contemporary social ills. By contrast, the reviews of the four works related to the John Douglas/Archibald Bower controversy are critically slight pieces. Nevertheless, Johnson's generous extracts leave readers with plenty of material to evaluate the worth of these volumes and to ponder the broader issues that prompted their publication.

On the whole, Johnson's reviews of the Hanway and Douglas/Bower titles, as well as his reviews of journalistic and fugitive pieces, deserve a greater measure of scholarly regard than they have received thus far. Not only do these reviews offer us a glimpse of the major issues that confronted the English during the mid-eighteenth century, but these pieces also demonstrate that Johnson's reviewing of humbler sorts of literary activity can be read as extensions of his generalized commentary on what he saw as the socially and morally uplifting purposes of authorship.

JOURNALISTIC PUBLICATIONS

Arthur Murphy (1727–1805), *The Gray's-Inn Journal, in 2 vols.*
Reviewed by Johnson, 15 May 1756; not reviewed in the *Critical* or the
Monthly. Arthur Murphy enjoyed a modestly successful career as an actor,
playwright, and journalist, but he is perhaps best known nowadays for his
biographical account of Johnson, which from 1792 until well into the nineteenth century prefaced numerous editions of Johnson's works. Johnson
and Murphy had been friends for two years or so when this review appeared. In fact, it was the plagiarism of a *Rambler* essay in the *Gray's-Inn
Journal* that brought Johnson and Murphy together.[5] In considering possible topics for the 15 June 1754 number of his weekly essay serial, Murphy
decided to follow a friend's suggestion by translating an oriental tale recently published in a French periodical. Readers immediately brought it to
Murphy's attention that the piece was in fact *Rambler* 190 (11 January
1752). Murphy apologized for the incident in the next issue of the *Journal*
and shortly thereafter approached Johnson to explain the matter in fuller
detail. From the moment they met, the two men, as J. L. Clifford puts the
matter, "got along famously." Indeed, Murphy would eventually work for
Johnson as a reviewer in the *Literary Magazine*.[6]

The *Gray's-Inn Journal* began life on 21 October 1752 as a column in
the biweekly *Craftsman* and was issued separately from 29 September 1753
until 21 September 1754. The *Gray's-Inn* essay serial follows conventions
established by the *Spectator* and the *Tatler*. Murphy adopts the amiable
persona of "Charles Ranger," and writes, generally with discernment, on
various contemporary social and literary issues.[7] Johnson reviewed the two-
volume collected edition of the *Journal*, which contained the entire run of
its 104 numbers. On the whole, Murphy's work is given a hospitable wel-
come in the *Literary Magazine:*

> THOSE who remember the entertainment which these essays gave them in
> the weekly publication, will be well pleased that they are collected into
> volumes, with the author's corrections. Those who have not read the single
> papers will probably be awakened to inquiry after them by the following
> specimen [number 93, an oriental fable that deals with the "vanity of hu-
> man wishes" theme, is given in full].[8]

Murphy's decision to include the "True Intelligence" section of every number, however, is greeted with less warmth:

> At the end of every essay are some ludicrous articles under the title of TRUE
> INTELLIGENCE, which are drawn up with sprightliness and humour; but as

they often relate to some topic of the day already forgotten, many of them might have been omitted without loss in a book designed to last longer than such slight incidents are kept in remembrance. Some of them, however, touch upon facts that will be retained in history, and some upon subjects of general and perpetual concern. Part of them therefore can never be unseasonable, and part may shew at distant times what was the voice of the people concerning particular events, when they were yet recent, or particular questions while they were yet in agitation.[9]

The "True Intelligence" section was almost certainly designed to bolster sales of individual issues of the *Journal* as they came out and, doubtless, Johnson speaks for many prospective book buyers here when he remarks on the evident pointlessness of including at least some of this material in the collected edition of the *Gray's-Inn* essays. What makes Johnson's commentary significant is his acknowledgment of the potential historical value of what most people—including, perhaps, even Murphy himself—probably looked upon as mere ephemera. What we see in operation here, in other words, is Johnson's attitude to journalism as expressed in the introduction to the *Harleian Miscellany* (1744), *Rambler* 145 (1751), the introductory essays to the *Universal Chronicle* (1758), and elsewhere. Journalists are de facto historians, Johnson argues in these pieces, and their writings may provide future generations with an indispensable record of the day-to-day circumstances that, though in themselves of little importance, collectively shape in some measure the direction of consequential events. Johnson invites readers to think of the *Gray's-Inn* "True Intelligence" section in just this light, though we are also warned that some of this material will inevitably prove to be as useless to posterity as it is to those reading it a few months after its initial publication.

Arthur Murphy, Henry Fox, et al. *The Test: A New Political Paper*. Owen Ruffhead, Philip Francis, et al., *The Con-Test*. Both periodicals are reviewed by Johnson, 15 January 1757; neither compilation is reviewed in the *Monthly* or the *Critical*. The *Test* and the *Con-Test* were composed of, respectively, thirty-five and thirty-eight issues, each six pages in length. The earliest number of *The Test* carries a date of 6 November 1756; the last a date of 9 July 1757. The thirty-eight issues of *The Con-Test* are dated from 23 November to 6 August 1757. Essentially, these papers served as opposing forces in a public relations war between Henry Fox and William Pitt, who replaced Fox as secretary of state for the Southern Department in late 1756. Donald Eddy believes that Johnson reviewed the two periodicals to help Robert Dodsley, a longtime friend of Johnson's and one of the sponsors of Johnson's *Dictionary*, who was involved in a dispute with

Charles Spens, editor of the *London Chronicle*. Dodsley was for a brief time one of the copublishers of the *London Chronicle*. According to Eddy, Dodsley withdrew his support of the newspaper chiefly because Spens routinely published invective and satire—including samples of the *Test* and *Con-Test*—a practice that offended Dodsley. Eddy asserts that Johnson's review, which comprises an extract followed by the passage quoted below, is designed to validate Dodsley's criticism of Spens's editorial decisions.[10]

> Of these papers of the *Test* and *Con-test* we have given a very copious specimen, and hope that we shall give no more. The debate seems merely personal, no one topic of general import having been yet attempted. Of the motives of the author of the *Test*, whoever he be, I believe, every man who speaks honestly, speaks with contempt. Of the *Con-Test*, which being defensive, is less blameable, I have yet heard no great commendation. The language is that of a man struggling after elegance and catching finery in its stead: the author of the *Con-test* is more knowing; of wit neither can boast, in the *Test* it is frequently attempted, but always by mean and despicable imitations, without the least glimmer of intrinsic light, without a single effort of original thought.[11]

Eddy's reading of the review, and of this passage in particular, is certainly plausible but another possible interpretation of Johnson's commentary is simply that *The Test/Con-Test* review can be said to reprise the theme of Johnson's much earlier "Letter to Mr. Urban" in the *Gentleman's Magazine* and, in effect, foreshadows his criticism in his *Universal Chronicle* essay, "Of the Duty of a Journalist," of journalists who subordinate truth to political expediency. Indeed, it is worth pausing here to consider the standards Johnson set for himself as a contributor to the *Universal Chronicle* (1758–60), which not only carried Johnson's *Idler* papers but also several editorials by Johnson that strenuously objected to England's conduct of the war with France. "If the writer of this journal shall be able to execute his own plan," Johnson declares in "Of the Duty of a Journalist," "if he shall carefully enquire after truth, and diligently impart it; if he shall resolutely refuse to admit into his paper whatever is injurious to private reputation; if he shall relate transactions with greater clearness than others, . . . he hopes that his labours will not be overlooked."[12] In his double review of *The Test* and *The Con-Test*, then, Johnson basically asserts—just as he does in the earlier and later pieces on journalism—that the best news writers and political polemicists always measure their work by strict standards of accuracy and eloquence. In other words, Johnson insists that the news writer and the political pundit strive to match the moral essayist in regard to wit, intelligence, and commitment to purveying truth.

PAMPHLETS AND OCCASIONAL ESSAYS

Bourchier Cleeve (1715–60), *A Scheme for Preventing a Further Increase of the National Debt, and for Reducing the Same.* Reviewed in the *Monthly* (reviewer unknown), May 1756; reviewed by Johnson, 15 August 1756; not reviewed in the *Critical*, though the work is noted in the "List of Pamphlets" for April 1756. Bourchier Cleeve made his living in London as a pewter merchant; his sixteen-page quarto pamphlet on national finance is one of two titles that Cleeve is known to have published, the other being a similarly brief treatise on the staffing His Majesty's Navy.[13] Cleeve's concern with retiring, or at least reducing, the national debt was very much a timely one. In 1739 the national debt stood at forty-six million pounds sterling; chiefly on account of the War of the Austrian Succession, the debt had climbed to seventy-six million pounds sterling by 1749. Reductions in the armed forces and the restructuring of the debt by Henry Pelham (1695–1754; first lord of the treasury, 1746–54) over the next several years brought down the cost of funding the debt, but with the opening of formal hostilities with France in May 1756, the problem of borrowing large sums to finance Britain's war effort resurfaced.[14] Basically, Cleeve's "scheme" for attacking the national debt called for the imposition of a considerable tax on property and—not surprisingly, given Cleeve's connections to the merchant class—the repeal of an equivalent amount on commodities and duties.

The extremely brief notice of Cleeve's *Scheme* in the *Monthly Review*'s "Catalogue of Books" section does little more than assert the implausibility of Cleeve's proposal.[15] By contrast, Johnson's review is not only considerably more substantial than its predecessor in the *Monthly* but also distinctly appreciative, though Johnson criticizes Cleeve's style and the banality of some of his assertions.

The core of Johnson's commentary appears in the opening two sentences. "This pamphlet seems to be written with a very honest intention by a man better acquainted with arithmetic than with style," Johnson declares. "He begins with asserting what no man doubts, and no honest man pretends to doubt, that the *French* have gained upon our commerce, and that the national debt has swelled so high that it can be no longer safely enlarged." Johnson thus begins with an unflattering assessment of Cleeve's talents as a writer and an observer of the contemporary political and economic scene, but he quickly moves on in effect to endorse Cleeve's point of view by offering readers a generous selection from the *Scheme*. In fact, Johnson ends up reprinting roughly half of Cleeve's pamphlet—including Cleeve's graphs and forecasts. Cleeve may not be the most eloquent critic of British trade and monetary policy, Johnson would have us believe, but his basic outlook on these matters deserves serious consideration. What we thus see in the Cleeve piece is Johnson's remarkable ability to encourage a sympathetic reception of a work even as he refrains from making anything that resembles dogmatic pronouncements on its literary merits.

The Cleeve review also offers us a glimpse of Johnson's broader political views. Indeed, the basic ideas contained in the extracts Johnson selects echo the political arguments Johnson makes elsewhere in the *Literary Magazine*. Take for instance the following example, in which Cleeve calls attention to what he sees as the recent alarming expansion of French international trade.

> Should it be said, that trade in general is increased in *Europe*, I wish I could say our trade and navigation are increased in the same degree as the *French* trade is; but this no one can presume to say. As reflections on this topic seem to me to have been quite neglected, the consequence thereof (if not timely taken into consideration) will be, that the *French* in a few years commerce will leave us little enough to look after.[16]

Cleeve's observations here basically conform to the thesis of Johnson's essay, "An Introduction to the Political State of Great Britain," which was the lead article of the *Literary Magazine*'s inaugural issue. In this essay, Johnson portrayed the relationship between England and France as fundamentally based on economic rivalry rather than, say, on cultural or religious differences.[17]

Johnson's anti-Newcastle ministry views, and his general suspicion of concentrated political power, also find expression in the review.[18] There is, for instance, Johnson's commentary on Cleeve's aim of reducing the debt specifically to forty million pounds sterling. "Why should it not be reduced to twenty,—why not to nothing?" Johnson wonders. "[W]hy should not all these wretches that live on the public misery, commissioners of excise, and officers without number, be at once, if it be possible, discarded, and sent to gain a living by honest industry, or to beg it of those whom they are now insulting?" Johnson's *Dictionary* definition of "Excise" is worth considering here: "A hateful tax levied upon commodities, and adjudged not by the common judges of property, but wretches hired by them to whom excise is paid." Cleeve's pamphlet may not be a particularly illuminating or well considered economic tract, but clearly Johnson sympathized with Cleeve's basic position that taxes on commodities are too great, and that the money is being used for selfish rather than civic ends.

We see additional evidence of this in Johnson's commentary on Cleeve's attempt to defuse possible objections to his idea. Here is Cleeve on the potential criticisms of his tax plan:

That the ministry will lose their power; second, That the ministry, and those in great places, will not then have so many ways of serving their friends; and the third, That such a scheme will hurt those who now enjoy places, salaries or have reversionary grants under the government, as most places will then be rendered useless.[19]

Cleeve's answer to these potential charges is as follows: first, the government, freed from obligations of raising great sums of money, can then devote all energies to foreign policy, which is in the true national interest. To the second objection, Cleeve states that the civic and economic health of the nation is all that need be considered. The third objection, Cleeve says, can be met by essentially enforcing a sunset clause; that is, the treasury would continue to pay those currently occupying sinecures, receiving pensions, and the like, but no more of such offices would be awarded. Johnson's response is succinct and expressive of the populist streak in his broader political outlook: "It had been surely better to say, that those objections are the reasons for which every wise and honest man desires the immediate execution of the scheme." Johnson is receptive to Cleeve's idea not because the numbers work out perfectly, a point plausibly disputed by the *Monthly* in its review. Rather, Johnson is attracted to the political effects of a tax on property and the corresponding abolition of duty and commodity taxes. Thus, the Cleeve review complements nicely Johnson's better-known political writings in the *Literary Magazine* and elsewhere. The Cleeve piece also exemplifies Johnson's resourcefulness as a book reviewer, as Johnson skillfully abridges Cleeve's pamphlet, retailing the worthy core of his scheme to readers of the *Literary Magazine*—who thus are given the chance to weigh Cleeve's ideas whether they buy the *Scheme* or not. In other words, Johnson's review functions as a de facto essay on contemporary economic policy.

Lewis Evans (1700–1756), *Geographical, Historical, Political, Philosophical, and Mechanical Essays, the First Containing an Analysis of a General Map of the Middle British Colonies in America,* **second edition.** First edition printed in Philadelphia and sold in England by Dodsley & Co.[20] Reviewed by John Berkenhout in the *Monthly,* January 1756; second edition reviewed by Johnson, 15 October 1756; not reviewed in the *Critical.*[21] Lewis Evans was born in Wales but spent the last twenty years of his life in North America, where he made his living as a cartographer, surveyor, and occasional lecturer on scientific topics. Evans's *Map* was designed to facilitate the English settlement of—and the expulsion of the French from—what we today know of today as a large section of the upper Midwest, that is, Ohio, Indiana, southern Michigan, and the western portions of New York and Pennsylvania.

In his introductory commentary in the Yale Edition of Johnson's political writings, Donald Greene points out that Johnson's review of Evans's
Map exemplifies his broader political outlook in regard to British colonial
expansion and, of equal importance, notes that, though Johnson does indeed attack the presumption that the conventional "system of national ag-
grandizement by European powers was productive of universal happiness,"
the *Literary Magazine* review "is not, on the whole, a hostile one." Johnson
points out, for instance, that Evans's map of the Ohio Valley "is engraved
with sufficient beauty, and the treatise is written with such elegance as the
subject admits."[22] What Greene's introduction fails to consider is the apparent relationship between Johnson's review of Evans's thirty-two-page
pamphlet and its predecessor in the *Monthly*.

John Berkenhout opens his review in the *Monthly* by emphasizing the
commercial importance of geographical knowledge and the meritorious-
ness of Evans's cartography.[23] After providing a generous extract from
Evans's pamphlet, Berkenhout goes on to applaud Evans's argument that a
strong English military presence is needed in North America: "We may
now conclude with remarking, that we want a military Force in America, if
this, by any Method, could be established, and the Men kept, even in Time
of Peace, in Action and Discipline, our Colonies would, of themselves, be
an Over-match for the French." Berkenhout, who served previously in the
Prussian army, declares:

> Our Plantations were always of great Consequence, but they are now of
> the utmost Consequence to the Nation; for at least one Half of our Com-
> merce depends upon them, as the Whole of our Strength and Happiness
> depends upon our Commerce. Our Wealth produces Liberty, and our Wealth
> was produced by Trade; whatever affects the latter will lessen the former:
> And whenever we lose our Trade, we must certainly feel the Effects of
> Poverty and arbitrary Power.[24]

Berkenhout thus endorses Evans's call for military and political efforts to
restrict French control of strategically valuable waterways in North America.

Johnson reviews a later edition of Evans's *Map*, but he chooses to quote
one of the key passages in Berkenhout's review[25] and, not surprisingly given
his harsh criticisms of colonial expansionism earlier in the Evans review
and elsewhere in his writings, argues against the position that Evans advocates and Berkenhout seconds. "This great country for which we are so
warmly incited to contend, will not be honestly our own though we keep it
from the French," Johnson argues in his review.

> It will indeed, he [Evans] says, be deserted by its inhabitants, and we shall
> then have an addition of land greater than a fourth part of Europe. This is a

magnificent prospect, but will lose much of its beauty on a nearer view. An increase of lands without increase of people gives no increase of power or of wealth, but lies open to assaults without defenders, and may disgrace those who lose it without inriching those that shall gain it.[26]

There is no way to prove that Johnson here means allusively to rebut Berkenhout's review, but such a reading stands as an attractive possibility. What might have happened is that Johnson, having decided to examine Evans's *Map* after reading the *Monthly* piece, specifically crafted his review as an alternative to Berkenhout's sanguine interpretation of Evans's political commentary. Once again, we see Johnson employing the book review as an independent essay. Rather than write an editorial opposing colonial expansion in North America, Johnson here reviews a popular book on the subject, and in doing so incorporates a rebuttal to the conventional outlook on Britain's North American policy.

Paul Whitehead (1710–74), *A Letter to a Member of Parliament in the Country, from His Friend in London, Relative to the Case of Admiral Byng;* **John Shebbeare,** *An Appeal to the People: Containing, The Genuine and Entire Letter of Admiral Byng to the Secr. of the Admiralty.* Reviewed by Johnson, 15 October 1756; reviewed by James Ralph in the *Monthly,* October 1756; reviewed in the *Critical* (reviewer unknown), October 1756.[27] The *Letter to a Member of Parliament* and the *Appeal to the People* both oppose the Newcastle ministry's decision to court-martial Admiral John Byng, who was charged with cowardice and negligence following the loss of Minorca to French forces during the opening weeks of the Seven Years' War. The pamphlets were published in early October 1756, five months after the series of engagements that led to the preferment of charges against Byng and about twelve weeks before his trial got underway. Essentially, the duke of Newcastle, Thomas Pelham Holles, and the first lord of the admiralty, George Anson, held Byng accountable for what was in fact their imprudent deployment of naval forces in the weeks before the start of the war with France. Byng, commanding an inadequately sized and poorly supplied squadron, basically found himself in an impossible situation when in May 1756 he was expected to defend the British garrisons at Minorca and Gibraltar against superior French forces, even as the necessary reinforcements sat idle in British ports—thanks to the ministry's wrongheaded conviction that a French invasion was imminent. Byng's squadron failed to keep Minorca from falling into French hands, and in a later engagement Byng decided to withdraw from a confrontation with a much larger French force, as he knew that a defeat would have further endangered the English garrison at Gibraltar.

The court-martial of Admiral Byng began in December 1756. A guilty verdict was returned on 27 January 1757, and Byng was executed by firing squad about seven weeks later, on 14 March. "The trial and execution of Admiral the Hon. John Byng was one of the most cold-blooded and cynical acts of judicial murder in all British history," claims Dudley Pope in his study of the case. "Although many of the people perhaps realised that the Ministers were at least partly to blame, they knew these men—the Duke of Newcastle, Hardwicke, Fox, and Anson particularly—were all well beyond their reach; but Byng, the proffered victim, was not," Pope goes on to argue. "In their anger the mob wanted a sacrifice; in their anger, as is the way with all mobs, they were not particularly concerned whether they had the right victim or not. It was important, and quite sufficient, to have a victim."[28] Given Johnson's own highly refined sense of humanity and his legendary capacity to sympathize with underdogs, not to mention his willingness publicly to decry the knavery and tomfoolery of government officials, it is not at all surprising to find him coming down firmly on the side of Admiral Byng in his *Literary Magazine* reviews of these pamphlets.

Like most of his other reviews, Johnson's double notice of the *Letter to a Member of Parliament* and the *Appeal to the People* is largely taken up by extract and summary. Nevertheless, Johnson's deeply held belief that Byng was being used as a scapegoat for the defeat of the British fleet at the battle of Minorca finds expression in the review's introductory paragraph.

> To hear both parties, and to condemn no man without a trial are the unalterable laws of justice. The man who lately commanded the *English* fleet in the *Mediterranean;* after having had his effigies burnt in a hundred places, and his name disgraced by innumerable lampoons after having suffered all that malice of wit or folly could inflict on his reputation, now stands forth, and demands an audience from those who have almost universally condemned him, but condemned him in his own opinion without justice, and certainly without any calm or candid examination.[29]

Johnson's concluding declarations are equally pointed.

> It appears to us that *Byng* has suffered without sufficient cause. That he was sent to the relief of *Minorca*, when relief was known to be no longer possible. That he was sent without land forces, the only forces that could raise the siege. That his fleet was inferior, and long before the battle was known at home to be inferior to that of the *French*. That he fought them, and retreated only when he could fight no longer. That a second engagement would only have increased the loss suffered in the first. That a victory at sea would not have saved *Minorca*. That there was no provision for the chances of a battle. That the nation has been industriously deceived by false and treacherous representations.[30]

From a political perspective, Johnson's review could not differ more from competing pieces published in the *Monthly* and the *Critical*.

Shebbeare's pamphlet, writes James Ralph in the *Monthly*, levels "many strange" and "unwarrantable" charges against the Newcastle administration. The *Critical Review* offered similarly harsh condemnations of the attempt to exonerate Byng. *An Appeal to the People* amounts to nothing more than "the work of an hireling pen, fruitful, not in argument but invective, old, inanimated, and poisonous," argues the reviewer. Shebbeare's "justification of the adm——l is a tedious, diffuse, and perplexing declamation."[31] Johnson's review appeared a couple of weeks before the *Monthly* and *Critical* reviews, but he must have had some sense of where the weight of popular opinion lay regarding Byng's innocence. What we find here and in the other pieces related to the Byng affair is Johnson using the book review as a means of intervening in a major contemporary controversy, even though his own opinions, though conveyed with intensity, are relatively brief and are kept subordinate to those of the central antagonists. We have no doubt as to where Johnson stands on the matter, but he is careful to leave the final decision in the hands of the public. Indeed, in this review and in the others on the subject, we find Johnson hewing closely to his belief in the essay "Observations on the Present State of Affairs" that "every Englishman expects to be informed of national affairs," and thus "has a right to have that expectation gratified."[32]

Paul Whitehead, *Some Further Particulars in Relation to the Case of Admiral Byng, by a Gentleman of Oxford*. Reviewed by Johnson, 15 November; reviewed by James Ralph in the *Monthly,* November 1756; not reviewed in the *Critical*.[33] Johnson's review of Paul Whitehead's seventy-page pamphlet offers little in the way of straightforward literary criticism. Even so, Johnson's lengthy extract reflects his own belief in Byng's innocence and can read as an apologia for Byng in its own right. Johnson begins his review with remarks that at first glance seem to be at odds both with Johnson's own position and with the extracted material that follows.

> Why a gentleman of Oxford should be supposed particularly qualified to examine and defend the conduct of Mr. *Byng*, or how his defence is much recommended by such a title, whether truly or not bestowed upon his advocate, we are not able to discover. But as we are willing to hear every pleader in this important cause, we shall make a faithful extract from this pamphlet, and oppose to it what the friends of the ministry have offered, however denominated, or where educated.[34]

Johnson's remarks here convey a surprising degree of skepticism toward Whitehead's pamphlet and, implicitly, toward the charges leveled at Byng as well. Interestingly enough, the extracted material that follows amounts to a coherent 3,600-word account of the great difficulties Byng faced in staffing his ships properly and in marshaling his plainly inadequate forces to meet the French aggressors. Reading the narrative—which comes across as a dispassionate, evenhanded survey of the pertinent facts surrounding the case—we are left with the impression that Byng was assigned a pair of incompatible objectives: defend Minorca *and* engage a superior fleet at sea. Of particular significance is the following extract from Whitehead's pamphlet. The extract conforms perfectly to Johnson's own views on the Byng affair, though one would not have thought so given Johnson's opening remarks. Indeed, the passage below can be said to echo points that Johnson himself argues at the conclusion of his review of Shebbeare's *An Appeal to the People*. Difficult as his tactical situation was at the time of the Minorca battle, Whitehead declares, Byng "has now more dangerous enemies to combat with":

> When the proper time comes, every man that is open to conviction, will be convinced, that he [Byng] acted in all respects suitably to the great trust repos'd in him; that without impairing the honour, he never once lost sight of the real interest of his country;——that in every order he gave, he made the best use that he could possibly make of his understanding;——that even what seems to be so inexplicable, with regard to his ordering the *Deptford* out of the line, will receive the most satisfactory explanation;——that the odious imputations thrown on his personal behaviour, are as groundless as wicked;——that he had indeed the pleasure to see the enemy give way to the impressions made upon them;——and that nothing could equal his mortification in not being in a condition to follow them.[35]

The spirited advocacy in this passage can be reconciled with the chilly critical commentary that opens the *Further Particulars* review in this way. Johnson may have felt that the most effective means of endorsing Whitehead's position was, first, to accommodate the viewpoint of skeptical or disinterested readers. After all, the rhetorical question embedded in Johnson's comment—why *should* readers accept the authority of "A Gentleman from Oxford" on this matter?—is sensible enough. Johnson probably hoped that readers who read the extract would be persuaded by the facts of the case and, rather than nursing doubts about the qualifications of the pamphlet's author, would accept Johnson's implication in the opening paragraph that the compiler of the details is far less important than the details themselves.

Johnson's deft handling of Whitehead's artless yet earnest defense of Byng—a good thing badly done, as Johnson might have described Whitehead's efforts in conversation—is highlighted further by the competing review that appeared in the *Monthly* a couple of weeks later. James

Ralph begins by attacking the abilities of the pamphlet's author. "By the number of mistakes, and absurdities, which have escaped the press, in this performance, one would think the author of it had never communicated his thoughts to the Public before," Ralph declares. Ralph goes on to argue, essentially, that the pamphlet's author is a committed if rather inept antiministry partisan in the Byng affair. A four-page extract from White-head's pamphlet follows, but clearly Ralph has worked to condition our reading of this material. We are led to expect little in the way of disinter-ested or even competently expressed argumentation. Ralph's closes by de-ferring to the public—"With what regard to truth and justice all this is said, it is fit every Reader should judge for himself"—but these remarks amount to a mere gesture toward impartiality given the harshly dismissive com-mentary that opens the review.[36] On the whole, the *Monthly* and the *Liter-ary Magazine* both offer basically satisfactory accounts of Whitehead's pamphlet. Ralph does indeed take a firm stand in his review, but the *Monthly*'s generously sized extract allows Whitehead a chance to make his own case. What makes Johnson's review distinctive is his clever rhetorical strategy, whereby Johnson maintains an aura of impartiality even as he en-courages readers to accept the arguments advanced in Whitehead's pamphlet, which, as far as Johnson is concerned, are on behalf of a man condemned to death in order to save the reputations of inept and devious politicians.

David Mallet (1705–65), ***The Conduct of the Ministry Impartially Examined***. Reviewed by Johnson, 15 November 1756; reviewed by Tobias Smollett in the *Critical,* November 1756; reviewed by James Ralph in the *Monthly,* November 1756.[37] David Mallet's pamphlet *The Conduct of the Ministry Impartially Examined* was commissioned by the Newcastle min-istry to rebut opposition to the imminent court-martial of Admiral Byng. In keeping with his conviction that Byng was a victim of governmental mal-feasance, Johnson pulls no punches in his review of the pamphlet and opens with a direct assault on Mallet's integrity. "When a man appeals to himself for what only himself can know, he may be very confident of a favourable sentence. This author may perhaps think as he writes, for there are men who think as they are bidden."[38] *The Conduct of the Ministry* review ends in a manner similar to Johnson's earlier reviews of Shebbeare's *Appeal to the People* and *A Letter to a Member of Parliament in the Country*, with Johnson offering readers a series of strongly worded resolutions that sup-port Byng's innocence. "To what has been said already on the case of Mr. *Byng*, I shall add," Johnson declares,

> That *Byng* has been treated since his return with indignities and severities, neither decent nor needful. That papers have been industriously given away to inflame the populace against him. That since the prosecution of *Laud*,

no such zeal for vindictive justice has been ever shewn. That from such diligence of persecution there is reason to believe some latent enemies interested in the accusation, who defame him that he may be less invidiously destroyed. That whatever be the fate of *Byng*, the justice of the nation ought to hunt out the men who lost *Minorca*.[39]

Johnson's impassioned apologia for Byng commands our attention but equally significant here is that Johnson's arguments have been validated by history. As Dudley Pope has demonstrated, Byng was indeed systematically maligned in an attempt to cover up the ineptitude of the king's ministers.[40]

In sharp contrast to Johnson's review of *The Conduct of the Ministry Impartially Examined*, the *Monthly* and the *Critical* both praise Mallet as an example of rhetorical and polemical excellence. "Of all the pamphlets that have appeared since the return of admiral Byng, this is the most sensible and spirited," declares Tobias Smollett in the *Critical*. "The style is elegant and manly, the arguments are well conceived and artfully arranged, and an air of moderation and candour is diffused through the whole performance. In a word, the author has exposed the weak side of those writers who have entered the lists against the ministry, and said every thing that imagination, ruled by good sense, could say in behalf of an administration, which, we are afraid, is not to be entirely justified from the imputation of misconduct." James Ralph offers readers a similarly appreciative review. "Of all the pamphlets which either the passions or interests of men have lately given rise to," Ralph states, "this is, on many accounts, most worthy of serious consideration." Perhaps the most interesting part of the review is Ralph's uncritical acceptance of Mallet's professions of disinterestedness, which contrast sharply with Johnson's attack on Mallet's claims to impartiality. Mallet is to be admired, Ralph states, for declaring that "he intends neither panegyric nor abuse; that he has no cause to serve, but that of Truth and his Country; that if he any where imposes on his readers, he has first been imposed upon himself; that he has, however, left nothing undone to avoid such a misfortune, but on the contrary, has exerted his best endeavours to procure every light, every information, which a private man could, by the most deliberate research, arrive at knowledge of."[41] Thus, a comparative analysis of Johnson's review with competing notices published in the leading review journals highlights Johnson's courage and independence of mind, in particular his willingness to use the book review as a forum for protesting political wrongdoing.

Anonymous. A Letter to a Gentleman in the Country, from His Friend in London, Giving an Authentick and Circumstantial Account of the Confinement, Behaviour, and Death of Admiral Byng, as Attested by the Gentlemen who were present. Reviewed by Johnson, 16 April 1757; reviewed in the *Monthly* (reviewer unknown), April 1757; not reviewed in the *Critical*. For readers of Johnson's earlier reviews of pamphlets related to the Byng case there is nothing new here apart from the elegiac tone, Byng having been executed by firing squad on 14 March 1757, a month or so before Johnson's review appeared.[42] The *Letter* "relates a number of curious anecdotes of this unhappy gentleman, who has at length paid the forfeit of his life, and fallen a sacrifice to the justice of his country," Johnson states in the review's opening paragraph. What follows is a generous extract: Johnson quotes from forty of the pamphlet's forty-eight pages. By contrast, the *Monthly* reviewer approaches the pamphlet with the sort of skepticism one finds in Johnson's review of Mallet's *The Conduct of the Ministry Impartially Examined*. The pamphlet offers readers a well-written and "pathetic account" of Byng's tribulations, the reviewer observes. Nevertheless, the *Letter* "has much the air of a studied endeavour to set off his [Byng's] memory to the best advantage, and, at the same Time, to convey a vengeful stroke at the Admiral's enemies."[43] What the reviewer says here, in effect, is that the pamphlet lacks a market: readers sympathetic to Byng will learn nothing from it, while apologists for the Newcastle ministry and their followers, having won the day with the conviction and execution of Byng, can safely ignore the *Letter*.

As mentioned earlier, Johnson's reviews of pamphlets related to the Byng trial offer very little in the way of literary analysis that transcends the circumstances of Byng's court-martial. As examples of his reviewing technique, moreover, Johnson's reviews of the Byng pamphlets are conventional insofar as they are made up largely of extract and summary strung together with terse critical observations. Nevertheless, these pieces are of interest to students of Johnson's thought, because they dramatize his willingness to take unpopular stands on public affairs, especially when he thought justice was being sacrificed to political expediency. This group of reviews also can be said to reflect Johnson's broader outlook on journalism. Johnson believed strongly in Byng's innocence, but he also was careful as a reviewer to make sure that contemporary readers—and posterity— was aware of both sides of the debate.

Books on Public Affairs

John Douglas (1721–1807), *Six Letters From Archibald Bower to Father Sheldon; Provincial of the Jesuits in England; Illustrated with Several Remarkable Facts, Tending to Ascertain the Authenticity of the Said Letters, and the True Character of the Writer*. Archibald Bower (1686–1766), *Mr. Archibald Bower's Affidavit, in Answer to the False*

Accusation Brought against Him by the Papists. Both titles reviewed by Johnson, 15 July 1756. The *Six Letters* was reviewed by William Rose in the *Monthly,* July 1756; reviewed in the *Critical* (reviewer unknown), July 1756. Bower's *Affidavit* was reviewed in the *Critical* (reviewer unknown), July 1756; reviewed by William Rose in the *Monthly,* August 1756.

John Douglas, *Bower and Tillemont Compared: Protestant History of the Popes*. Archibald Bower, *Mr. Bower's Answer to a Scurrilous Pamphlet*. Both titles reviewed by Johnson 15 January 1757; reviewed by William Rose in the *Monthly,* January 1757; and reviewed in the *Critical* (reviewer unknown), January 1757. Archibald Bower was a controversial figure in the world of eighteenth-century English letters, as the titles of the four works discussed here would suggest. Scottish-born and educated by the Jesuits in Rome, Bower left Italy for England in 1726 and immediately repudiated the Roman Catholic faith, allegedly because of what he came to believe was the underlying fraudulence of church doctrine and the pointless cruelty of the Inquisition. The first volume of Bower's most important achievement, *History of the Popes*, appeared in 1748; the second and third volumes followed, respectively, in 1751 and 1753. What occasioned the publication of John Douglas's 102-page *Six Letters* was a series of epistles that revealed Bower's continued private embrace of Roman Catholicism even as he profited from his reputation as a courageous, principled apostate and loyal Anglican. John Douglas, who at the time enjoyed a measure of fame for debunking William Lauder's claim that Milton plagiarized contemporaneous Latin poets (1750), assembled the letters and added commentary that shed light on Bower's duplicity.[44] Bower responded almost immediately, publishing his 49-page riposte on 1 July 1756, three days after Douglas's exposé appeared. Douglas's subsequent attempt to unmask Bower's fraudulent character, the 106-page *Bower and Tillemont Compared*, appeared on 6 January 1757 and, apart from commenting further on Bower's rancid character, asserted that volume 1 of Bower's *History of the Popes* was essentially a translation of earlier scholarship by Sébastien Le Nain de Tillemont (1637–98), a French priest and ecclesiastical historian. Bower published on the same day, 6 January 1757, a 127-page apologia, *Mr. Bower's Answer to a Scurrilous Pamphlet*, which sought to rebut further Douglas's *Six Letters*.

Johnson's double review of Douglas's *Six Letters* and Bower's *Affidavit* appeared a couple of weeks before competing notices in the *Monthly* and the *Critical* and roughly two weeks or so after the two works were published. Noteworthy about Johnson's review is its dispassionate temperament, even though the Bower/Douglas controversy plainly aroused intense feelings among Johnson's contemporaries. "Thus we have laid before the public a summary of the charge against Mr. Bower, with the evidence on which it is founded, which those who shall consult the masterly pamphlet from which this extract was made, will find that we had no desire to aggravate," Johnson states following several columns of extracted material from both titles. "[W]e hope Mr. *Bower* has some answer to make more cogent than his own testimony, but would remind him that silence is better, at least more modest than a weak plea."[45] Clearly, Johnson accepted Douglas's argument, but we should also note that Johnson is careful to allow Bower his say on the matter: fourteen of the *Affidavit's* thirty-seven pages of text are quoted from in the *Literary Magazine* review. Scarcely less important is that Johnson's brief editorializing comes at the very end of the review. What Johnson does here is to set before the public both sides of a controversial issue. Johnson does offer his own opinion on the matter, but the brevity and placement of Johnson's views make the point clearly enough that Johnson wants the public to reach its own conclusion as to Bower's alleged self-aggrandizing deviousness.

By contrast, William Rose in the *Monthly* takes up Douglas's cause with great gusto. Douglas's *Six Letters* "contains such instances of Bower's zeal for Popery, and his connexions with Jesuits, long after his coming into England, as seem to carry but too much conviction along with them; and he who has laid these facts before the public, whoever he is, [the volume did not carry Douglas's name on the title page] appears to us to have acted, in this respect, the part of a good citizen, of a friend to truth, and of a sincere Protestant." The *Critical* offers a similarly appreciative review of Douglas's volume. Douglas is "entitled to the thanks and approbation of the public," his work embodying "that honest zeal and warmth, which it becomes every honest man to exert in the detection of falshood, and a laudable search after truth."[46] Not surprisingly, the *Critical* raises questions about the credibility of Bower's *Affidavit*. "This is no defence at all," the reviewer declares. Though "we are very loth to believe any man guilty of wilful and deliberate perjury, yet we are far from imagining Mr. *B——r*'s affidavit is an indisputable proof of his innocence, because the man who is capable of committing one bad action, is often drove into others, and perhaps worse, to shelter himself from punishment." William Rose essentially agrees in his review for the *Monthly*, claiming in his brief survey of the work that Bower's demonstrable public shiftiness undermines completely any claims he might make to be taken at his word.[47]

Somewhat surprisingly, the reviews of Douglas's *Bower and Tillemont Compared* and Bower's *Answer to a Scurrilous Pamphlet* are bland in comparison to the pieces published six months or so earlier—at least as far as straightforward critical commentary is concerned. The *Monthly* and the *Critical* were almost certainly expected to review the two works, given the notoriety of the Douglas/Bower feud, but it seems that the two reviewers concluded that, on the whole, everything that needed to be said on the matter had been said in earlier reviews of related material.[48] Douglas, then, ultimately comes across in the *Monthly* and the *Critical* as a talented and dauntless academic muckraker, while Bower's flamboyant dishonesty is more or less taken for granted. Johnson's review is almost entirely given over to extract and summary, as are competing notices in the *Monthly* and the *Critical*. What makes Johnson's review stand out is the evident moderation of the mildly dismissive attitude of Bower's case expressed in Johnson's earlier double review of Douglas's *Six Letters* and Bower's *Affidavit*. In his review of *Bower and Tillemont Compared*, Johnson ignores Douglas's analysis of Bower's alleged plagiarism of Tillemont and instead essentially reprints the final eighteen pages of Douglas's volume, which contains Douglas's account of Bower's recollection of the Inquisition as practiced in Macerata, Italy—"taken," Douglas's title page tells us, "from his own Mouth." Juxtaposed to this passage is Bower's own account of the very same episode as published in the *Answer to a Scurrilous Pamphlet*, which Johnson introduces in a manner that undermines Douglas's attempt to portray Bower as nothing more than a self-promoting peddler of studied deception. "Mr. *Bower* has at last published an account of his escape [from Macerata to England, which gave him the opportunity to apostatize], in an *Answer to A Scurrilous Pamphlet, & c*. The narrative which he has printed is conformable enough," Johnson states, "to that which he is said to have given in conversation, the slight disagreements between them being, as Mr. Bower himself allows, only failures of memory, and geographical mistakes."[49] Johnson here essentially sticks up for Bower, at least insofar as he suggests that Douglas's case might be at least slightly overblown. What we see at work here, first, is Johnson's reflexive suspicion of monolithic political and intellectual opinion on current topics. Having been vilified in the reviewing press as well as in Douglas's publications, Bower was evidently a sympathetic—if not an admirable—figure in Johnson's eyes. To be sure, Johnson does not take up Bower's case in the manner that he did Admiral Byng's. Nevertheless, his reviews function as a necessary counterweight to the prevailing attitudes to Bower's truthfulness. On a broader level, the series of reviews on the Bower/Douglas controversy illustrate Johnson's use of the book review as a means of airing competing views on a subject of wide public interest.

Jonas Hanway (1712–86), *A Journal of Eight Days' Journey, to which is added an Essay on Tea*. Reviewed by Johnson, 17 May 1757; Johnson's response to Hanway's 26 May riposte in the *Daily Gazetteer* published 17 June 1756; reviewed in the *Critical,* July 1757 (reviewer unknown); reviewed by Oliver Goldsmith in the *Monthly,* July 1757.[50] A merchant known for his philanthropy and his prolific writings on subjects ranging from British trade with Arab nations to pressing domestic social concerns, Jonas Hanway also achieved a measure of fame in his day for bringing into fashion the use of the umbrella.[51] Hanway's 723-page *Journal* is best understood as an epistolary travel narrative interspersed with reflections of differing lengths on various subjects. The first of its two volumes amounts to a rather humdrum miscellany of historical, philosophical, and religious essays on topics ranging from "buildings and nunneries" to "reflections on the vanity of life." The second volume is given over to a consideration of the tea trade, and what commands attention here is the breathtaking hubris of Hanway's proposals. The "Essay on Tea" is meant to provide a justification for a massive shift not only in public policy—especially in regard to tax, trade, and monetary laws—but also in social norms as well: witness Hanway's bizarre declaration in "letter twenty-one" that if matters were left to him he "would abolish the custom of *sipping*" and allow "no liquids used hotter than they could be drank, in small quantities, without the least pain; and they should always be *drank*, except when they were eaten as soop mixed with *bread*, or other consistency."[52]

The *Literary Magazine* piece is best remembered nowadays for Johnson's mirthful observations on tea drinking—Hanway is to expect "little justice from the author of this extract, a hardened and shameless tea-drinker." But it is also important to recall that the controversies ignited by the review contributed in some way to Johnson's departure from the *Literary Magazine*. At one point in the review Johnson criticized what he understood to be the inadequate religious instruction at the Foundling Hospital, which Hanway generously supported:

> I know not upon what observation Mr. *Hanway* founds his confidence in the governors of the *Foundling Hospital*, men of whom I have not any knowledge, but whom I intreat to consider a little the minds as well as bodies of the children. I am inclined to believe irreligion equally pernicious with gin and tea, and therefore think it not unseasonable to mention, that when a few months ago I wandered through the hospital, I found not a child that seemed to have heard of his creed or the commandments. To breed up children in this manner, is to rescue them from an early grave, that they may find employment for the gibbet; from dying in innocence, that they may perish by their crimes.[53]

The *London Chronicle* reprinted Johnson's observations here, and threats of libel soon followed. Johnson's reply in the *Literary Magazine* to Hanway's published response to the review rebuts charges of dishonesty and malice. Even so, the owners of the *Literary Magazine* apparently concluded that, having had enough already of Johnson's incendiary anti-war essays, the time had finally come for him to hand in his resignation.[54] Eye-catching circumstances that they are, the aside on tea drinking and the Foundling Hospital controversy have encouraged Johnson scholars to dwell on either the humorous or the censorious aspects of the review. Bloom, Boswell, and Eddy, for instance, interpret the tea-drinking commentary as a witty interlude between Johnson's otherwise unrelentingly sharp criticisms of Hanway's book. Robert DeMaria, meanwhile, finds a streak of testiness in the remark about tea. "Jonas Hanway arouses Johnson's anger," DeMaria observes, "partly by giving useless, unfounded advice on the imaginary economic and physical evils of tea-drinking" and also because Hanway advocates what Johnson sees as a needlessly "prudish reduction in the small stock of innocent human enjoyment." These readings are tenable, but they seem to disregard Johnson's basically appreciative intentions. What the Hanway review amounts to, in fact, is a sympathetic treatment of an author whose altruistic objectives are thwarted by an overly sanguine understanding of his competence as a social critic.[55]

True, Johnson does criticize Hanway's unpolished prose and his at times facile analysis. But equally true is that Johnson gives Hanway ample credit for attempting to grapple with England's troubled civic culture. If Hanway's "character may be estimated by his book," Johnson declares in the first paragraph, "he is a man whose failings may well be pardoned for his virtues." As if to make certain that readers admire Hanway personally even though his treatise may disappoint, in the second paragraph Johnson is careful to soften criticisms of Hanway's style with praise for his benevolence. "We wish indeed, that among other corrections he had submitted his pages to the inspections of a grammarian," Johnson states, "but with us to mean well is a degree of merit which over-balances much greater errors than impurity of stile."[56] Elsewhere in the review Johnson acknowledges the underlying legitimacy of Hanway's outlook on England's contemporary social ailments, though Hanway's attempt to blame tea drinking for various disorders is rejected out of hand:

> Of these dreadful effects, some are perhaps imaginary, and some have another cause. . . . That the diseases commonly called nervous, tremours, fits, habitual depression, and all the maladies which proceed from laxity and debility, are more frequent than in any former time, is, I believe, true, however deplorable. But this new race of evils, will not be expelled by the prohibition of tea. This general languor is the effect of general luxury, of general idleness. If it be most to be found among tea drinkers, the reason is that tea is one of the stated amusements of the idle and the luxurious.[57]

Hanway is right to ponder the social and medical ramifications of a mass craving for luxury, Johnson suggests here, but the solutions to these problems are far more complicated or elusive than Hanway is perhaps capable of comprehending.[58] Significantly, Johnson might easily have resorted to sarcasm or searing censure in discussing Hanway's simpleminded analysis— much as he does in the Blackwell and Jenyns pieces—but he chooses instead to treat Hanway with remarkable charity.

Nevertheless, Johnson goes beyond mere politeness on the few occasions when he portrays Hanway as a much better writer and thinker than the *Journal* on the whole would have us believe. Johnson offers a judiciously abridged version of the third "letter" of the *Journal*'s second volume, for instance, which is described as a "truly curious" survey of the "rise and progress of tea-drinking."[59] Hanway's denunciation of gin drinking, meanwhile, receives a rousing endorsement, and it is worth noting that on the one issue where the *Journal* is compellingly persuasive, Johnson quotes Hanway's argument in its entirety:

> From tea the writer digresses to spirituous liquors, about which he will have no controversy with the *Literary Magazine*, we shall therefore insert almost his whole letter, and add to it one testimony, that the mischiefs arising on every side from this compendious mode of drunkenness, are enormous and insupportable; equally to be found among the great and the mean; filling palaces with disquiet and distraction, harder to be born[e], as it cannot be mentioned; and overwhelming multitudes with incurable diseases and unpitied poverty.[60]

Here, we find Johnson reprising an argument first put forth some thirteen years earlier in his "Parliamentary Debates," published in the *Gentleman's Magazine*.[61]

Interestingly, the closing paragraphs of the review betray an ambivalence in Johnson toward the position he stakes out earlier. We are left with the impression that Johnson—in spite of his assumptions about the harmlessness of tea and the prevailing dim-wittedness of Hanway's analysis— finds common ground with Hanway when it comes to the economics of the tea trade. Hanway rightly points out that tea drinking has left England with an unfavorable balance of trade with China, Johnson avers, though Hanway is not quite consistent when he refuses to lay some of the blame for the ills of tea drinking with the East India Company. If "Mr. *Hanway*'s computation" of the trade with China "be just," Johnson declares, then the "importation" of tea—and not merely "the use of it"—"ought at once to be stopped by a penal law."[62]

On a related point, Johnson asserts that Hanway concedes more than he should to the opposition when he admits that tax revenues from the tea industry are a boon to the nation's treasury. "The author allows one slight argument in favour of tea, which, in my opinion, might be with far greater justice urged, both against that, and many other parts of our naval trade." To begin with, the money raised by a levy on tea cannot be said to deter luxury—itself a dubious employment of tax law, Johnson suggests—because the poor love tea no less than do the rich. And in any case imposing a tax on a universally popular commodity encourages black-marketeering. But of much greater significance is the loss of life attendant on the tea trade. Of the roughly six hundred sailors employed in the China tea trade, Johnson observes,

> I am told, that sometimes half, commonly a third part perish in the voyage; so that instead of setting this navigation against the inconveniences already alleged, we may add to them, the yearly loss of two hundred men in the prime of life, and reckon, that the trade to *China* has destroyed ten thousand men since the beginning of this century. If tea be thus pernicious, if it impoverishes our country, if it raises temptation, and gives opportunity to illicit commerce, which I have always looked upon as one of the strongest evidences of the inefficacy of our law, the weakness of our government, and the corruption of our people, let us at once resolve to prohibit it for ever.[63]

What follows is a list of the many philanthropic projects that Hanway claims might easily be financed by the money currently spent on the tea industry: "public gardens"; "paving and widening of streets"; "rendering *rivers* navigable"; building "neat and convenient *houses*, where are now only *huts*"; "*draining* lands." A deeply compassionate man, Johnson could not help but assent to Hanway's impassioned if somewhat implausible argument. "Our riches would be much better employed to these purposes," Johnson declares in his closing sentence, "but if this project does not please, let us first resolve to save our money, and we shall afterwards very easily find ways to spend it."[64] Perhaps reluctantly, Johnson is led to conclude that Hanway may be right in arguing that England's robust appetite for tea comes with a measure of social and economic hazard, though it is also suggested here that tea-drinkers themselves—and not government ministers, whose calculations will prove to be self-interested rather than philanthropic—must decide whether to abstain or not. Clearly, Johnson discerned an essential worthiness in Hanway's *Journal*. Many of Hanway's specific claims are risible in themselves—tea's effect on the genetic fitness of the English people, for instance—but one or two of his observations are insightful, and the *Journal* on the whole deserves recognition, if only for the praiseworthy moral sensibility it displays.

Somewhat surprisingly, Hanway responded to Johnson's kindhearted review with an imperious, menacing, and rather foolish riposte in the *Daily Gazetteer*. No copy of the 26 May issue of the *Gazetteer* is known to have survived, but Johnson's reply in the June number of the *Literary Magazine* tells us a great deal about the contents of Hanway's letter. Hanway evidently censured Johnson for his general insolence—"see the fate of ignorant temerity! I now find, but find too late, that . . . I have irritated an important member of an important corporation; a man who, as he tells us in his letters, puts horses to his chariot"—before specifying the grounds on which charges of libel could be brought: "I am asked, whether I meant to *satirize* the man or *criticise* the writer"; "I am yet charged more heavily for having said, that *he has no intention to find any thing right at home*"; the observations on the Foundling Hospital were made "with folly and malice." It also seems that Hanway concluded with a vague but strongly worded threat: Hanway "advises me to consult my safety when I talk of corporations."[65] Taken together, Hanway's letter and Johnson's rebuttal are significant on two counts. The episode not only sheds light on Johnson's talents as a reviewer—doubtless Hanway's resentment was inspired at some level by the intelligence of Johnson's commentary—but it also validates Johnson's general observations on the hazard of authorial self-delusion as expressed in *Rambler* 16, *Idler* 55, and elsewhere. By everyone's reckoning, Hanway was a decent, affable man who justly acquired no small measure of public esteem on account of his philanthropic activity. Yet such was Hanway's sense of vulnerability to an unfavorable book review, and to such an extent was his self-regard exaggerated by the marketplace's capacity to confer celebrity, that Johnson's commentary—hardly adulatory but unquestionably fair-minded—elicited from Hanway an uncharacteristic malevolence. It is possible that Hanway came to recognize Johnson's evenhandedness, if his conspicuous silence in the weeks following far less charitable notices of his work in the two leading review journals is any indication.

Johnson's remarkably sympathetic review is indeed set in relief by the reception of the *Journal* in the *Critical*. Quite unlike Johnson, for instance, the reviewer for the *Critical* dwells on the vapid aspects of the *Journal,* while Hanway's benevolent intentions go largely ignored. Hanway "should have consider'd, that there are some truths which every mortal is as well acquainted with as himself, and which it is therefore quite unnecessary to obtrude upon the public," the reviewer declares.

> [S]uch are the trite and vulgar topics of morality, which, however just, are yet extremely insipid, when they come recommended by no elegance of style, enforc'd by no strength of argument, and embellished by no graces of the imagination. If this be the case, we apprehend that little entertainment or instruction can be gathered from that extravagant profusion of reflections, with which Mr. H———'s work abounds, and which are in truth

as hackney'd and as beaten as the road from Portsmouth to Kingston-upon-Thames.[66]

Brief mention is made of Hanway's philanthropic intentions, but this mite of kindliness is swept away by the final verdict. Hanway's "humanity and worth," the reviewer declares, are "discredited" by a "total want of that distinguishing taste which might enable him to become acquainted with the nature of his own talents, and to select such materials as might be proper for the inspection of the public."[67] It is important to note that Johnson and the reviewer for the *Critical* agree on the essentials: the *Journal* fails to live up to its commendable objectives, thanks to Hanway's maladroit analysis and crude style. What each reviewer chooses to emphasize, however, speaks volumes about his attitudes toward authors and the role of reviewing. Hanway's altruism entitles him to a sympathetic review from Johnson in spite of the *Journal*'s intellectual flimsiness. By contrast, the *Critical* sees little reason to do more than sneer at Hanway's bungling commentary.

The *Journal of Eight Days' Journey* was reviewed in the *Monthly* by the then twenty-nine-year-old Oliver Goldsmith, who in joining Ralph Griffiths's staff a few months earlier had inaugurated his career as a professional author.[68] In terms of critical efficiency and impartiality, Goldsmith's is as good a review as one is likely to find in the major journals of the period. Equally significant is that Goldsmith and Johnson are in basic agreement in their survey of the strengths and imperfections of Hanway's work. Like Johnson, for instance, Goldsmith refrains from harping on the *Journal*'s prevailing fatuity and instead emphasizes the considerable gap between the nobility of Hanway's objectives and the vacuousness of his commentary. Hanway "takes every opportunity (and sometimes forces one) to indulge his propensity to moralizing," Goldsmith observes, and in "this capacity, indeed, he shews great goodness of heart, and an earnest concern for the welfare of his country." Unfortunately, Hanway is manifestly incapable of transfiguring his worthy intentions into an engrossing narrative. "Novelty of thought, and elegance of expression," Goldsmith declares, "cannot be reckoned among the excellencies of this Gentleman; who generally enforces his opinions by arguments rather obvious than new, and that convey more conviction than pleasure to the Reader."[69]

Another similarity between the *Monthly* piece and its predecessor in the *Literary Magazine* is that Goldsmith pays relatively little attention to the *Journal*'s first volume and devotes the majority part of the review instead to a discussion of the controversial second volume. Predictably, Hanway's willingness to ascribe almost every major physical malady to excessive tea-drinking is politely yet unequivocally dismissed, and here it is worth noting that Goldsmith the practicing physician (bachelor of medicine,

Trinity College, 1756) steps forward to present an interesting contrast to Johnson, whose personal fondness for tea drinking brought forth a humorous rather than a grave response. When Hanway "treats of Tea in his assumed medical capacity," says Goldsmith,

> he speaks by no means like an adept in physic: indeed it is not to be expected, that every Gentleman can be acquainted with a science that requires so much time and industry in the acquisition, and therefore we may forgive his errors without pointing them out: but if to be unacquainted with the medical art, indicates no want of general knowledge, yet, perhaps, it argues some want of prudence, to speak of subjects to which our acquirements are not adequate.[70]

Goldsmith is to be commended here not only for his critical discernment but also for the refinement of his scholarly manners, as he manages to unmask the intellectual emptiness of Hanway's thesis without resorting to the heavy-handed ridicule found in the *Critical* notice. Nevertheless, when compared with Johnson's, Goldsmith's review comes across as rather pallid, if only because Johnson's notice can stand alone as a moral essay. Even readers who are indifferent to, or who despise, Hanway's *Journal* can derive much pleasure and profit from Johnson's review, with its wryly humorous aside on tea drinking, its historical and economic survey of the tea trade, and its timeless observations on what were, strictly speaking, contemporary issues.

The Hanway review stands out as one of Johnson's more famous pieces of criticism directed at the work of living writers, but we should also remember that most of Johnson's other reviews of titles related to current events can be said to embody the attributes that make the Hanway review interesting. Like the Hanway review, for instance, many of Johnson's reviews offer readers generous extracts that allow the public to make an informed choice of whether the work under review is worth buying and, of equal significance, keep readers abreast of what evidently meritorious authors were saying about major topics of the day such as the trial of Admiral Byng and the alleged deviousness of Archibald Bower. Scarcely less important is that most of Johnson's other reviews of works dealing with current events, no less than the Hanway piece, exemplify Johnson's understanding of the relationship between the literary marketplace and public affairs. Johnson's reviewing of titles related to current events demonstrates that, as far as he was concerned, the humbler sorts of literary activity in particular—journalism, pamphleteering, and books on transparently ephemeral subjects—were pivotal components in a society made up of free and responsible citizens and so should be characterized by clarity, honesty, and thoroughness.

4

Johnson as Reviewer of Works in the Physical, Practical, and Natural Sciences in the *Literary Magazine*

Roughly one-quarter of the titles Johnson reviews in the *Literary Magazine* can be categorized as works in the physical, practical, and natural sciences, about the same number of reviews that Johnson devotes to publications bearing on current events. Johnson's reviews of such works, moreover, at first glance are wholly conventional, comprising largely extract and summary interspersed with brief connective remarks and introduced, and perhaps concluded, by a sentence or two—a paragraph at the most—of critical commentary. Nevertheless, readers who study Johnson's reviews of what we might term technical books inevitably will be struck by the breadth and depth of Johnson's interest in all sorts of scientific subjects. After all, in the *Literary Magazine* we find Johnson evaluating, or at the very least abridging with a no small measure of discernment, works that deal with bleaching, military science, water distillation, anthropology, balneology, botany, climatology, geography, pathology, zoology, apiculture, electricity, and so on. Johnson enjoys a reputation nowadays chiefly as a moralist and literary historian—we like to refer to him as "Dictionary Johnson," "Mr. Rambler," the editor of Shakespeare, author of the *Lives of the Poets* and *Rasselas*—but the reviews discussed in this chapter tell us that Johnson possessed a remarkably full understanding of scientific inquiry.[1] In fact, Johnson's reviews of scientific books total somewhere in the range of forty-five thousand words, which means that they would fill a small volume all by themselves.

The second thing one notices about these reviews is their persistently appreciative character. Unlike the other categories of literature reviewed by Johnson in the *Literary Magazine*, Johnson really has nothing seriously negative to say about a single one of the scientific works he gives notice to.

Two or three of the eleven reviews of scientific works offer readers mixed commentary—Johnson reproves Samuel Bever for relying on parochial military terms, just as he regrets the agnosticism that finds its way into some of the material contained in the *Philosophical Transactions*—but Johnson clearly respects what these authors have achieved, and he wants to ensure that their works are given a fair chance at success in the literary marketplace. Indeed, Johnson's commentary on scientific titles stands out in particular because roughly one-third of his reviews—Browne's *Natural History of Jamaica,* Russell's *Natural History of Aleppo,* Home's *Experiments on Bleaching,* Lucas's *Essay on Waters*—appear to be written as rebuttals to competing notices published earlier in either the *Monthly* or the *Critical,* while another, the review of Lovett's *Subtil Medium Prov'd,* evidently attempts to forestall the sorts of captiousness that greeted Browne, Russell, Home, and Lucas in the two leading review journals. Generally speaking, as a reviewer in the *Literary Magazine* Johnson casts himself as an apologist for projectors, calling attention to their innovations while at the same time mitigating their failures and neutralizing their detractors.

As is the case for Johnson's reviewing of literary titles and works related to current events, we must turn to Johnson's major essay serials to understand his manner of proceeding as a reviewer of scientific titles. A handful of Johnson's 335 periodical essays help us fully to appreciate Johnson's sympathetic treatment in the *Literary Magazine* of the publications of scientists and innovative artisans. "A projector generally unites those qualities which have the fairest claim to veneration, extent of knowledge and greatness of design," Johnson declares in *Adventurer* 99 (1753). "That the attempts of such men will often miscarry, we may reasonably expect," Johnson goes on to say, "yet from such men, and such men only, are we to hope for the cultivation of those parts of nature which lie yet waste, and the invention of those arts which are yet wanting to the felicity of life."[2] In this passage and throughout *Adventurer* 99, Johnson offers a general apologia for scientific pioneers that would later find specific expression in his reviews of works by Stephen Hales, Richard Lovett, Charles Lucas, and others.

Rambler 9 (1750) similarly encourages readers to value the contributions of scientists; what makes this essay significant is that Johnson is careful to illuminate fully the complementary relationship between the scientific theorist and the pioneer of the lower arts. "Who, when he saw the first sand or ashes, by a casual intenseness of heat melted into a metalline form, rugged with excrescences, and clouded with impurities, would have imagined, that in this shapeless lump lay concealed so many conveniencies of life, as would in time constitute a great part of the happiness of the world?"

Johnson declares as he surveys the far-reaching benefits that the humble art of glass blowing has yielded and continues to yield.

> Yet by some such fortuitous liquefaction was mankind taught to procure a body at once in a high degree solid and transparent, which might admit the light of the sun, and exclude the violence of the wind; which might extend the sight of the philosopher to new ranges of existence, and charm him at one time with the unbounded extent of the material creation, and at another with the endless subordination of animal life; and, what is yet of more importance, might supply the decays of nature, and succour old age with subsidiary sight. Thus was the first artificer in glass employed, though without his own knowledge or expectation. He was facilitating and prolonging the enjoyment of light, enlarging the avenues of science, and conferring the highest and most lasting pleasures; he was enabling the student to contemplate nature, and the beauty to behold herself.[3]

The outlook expressed here explains Johnson's willingness as a reviewer to rebut what he believed were unfair attacks on scientists in the leading review journals and Johnson's aggressive emphasis in his reviews on the humanitarianism of projectors of all sorts. As Richard Schwartz has pointed out, projectors were routinely ridiculed in Johnson's day, a circumstance that Johnson acknowledges and spiritedly objects to in *Rambler* 9, *Adventurer* 99, and elsewhere.[4] We need only recall, for instance, Jonathan Swift's parody of projectors in part 3 of *Gulliver's Travels* (1726) to understand why Johnson saw fit to use the lofty genre of the moral essay to exalt both scientific theorists and pioneers in the practical arts, whose courage and civic-mindedness were unjustly despised as far as Johnson was concerned.

A word needs to be said here about Johnson's outlook on natural history in particular. Johnson reviews three works in this field—one written by a medical doctor (Patrick Browne), the other two by Fellows of the Royal Society (Alexander Russell, also an M.D., and William Borlase)—though we might easily include the *Philosophical Transactions* (the plague in Constantinople) and the *History of the Royal Society* (a survey of the climate and wildlife of Greenland) in this category because of the topicality of the extracted material Johnson includes in his reviews. Natural historians are not mentioned specifically in *Adventurer* 99 or in *Rambler*s 9, 83, or 137, but certainly Johnson's broader commentary on scientific innovators is meant to include those who help us better to understand the natural world. Johnson's reviewing of natural histories leads us to believe that the natural scientist—no less than the pioneer in electrical experimentation or the balneologist—is rightly thought of as a humanitarian. Thanks to the natural historian, Johnson's reviews would have us believe, the English

reading public are allowed to compare their own provincial experiences—
the difficulties presented by climate and geography, their manner of con-
ducting business and social affairs, how they cope with disease, and so
on—with those of foreign lands. *Idler* 97 focuses on travel narratives, but
Johnson's observations here apply just as easily to the natural historian if
we take his reviews of Patrick Browne, William Borlase, and Alexander
Russell as a guide. "The adventurer upon unknown coasts, and the de-
scriber of different regions, is always welcomed as a man who is able to
enlarge our knowledge and rectify our opinions," Johnson asserts. "Every
nation has something peculiar in its manufacturers, its works of genius, its
medicines, its agriculture, its customs, and its policy," he goes on to argue.
"He only is a useful traveller who brings home something by which his
country may be benefited; who procures some supply of want or some
mitigation of evil, which may enable his readers to compare their condition
with that of others, to improve it whenever it is worse, and whenever it is
better to enjoy it."[5] The principle stated here, as we shall see in due course,
can be said to govern Johnson's choice of titles and manner of proceeding
as a reviewer of natural histories in the *Literary Magazine*.

Works in the Physical and Practical Sciences

Stephen White (1696?–?), *Collateral Bee-Boxes; or a New, Easy,
and Advantageous Method of Managing Bees*: Reviewed by Johnson, 15
May 1756; reviewed by Sir Tanfield Leman in the *Monthly*, May 1756. The
Bee-Boxes is given notice without comment in the *Critical's* "List of Pamphlets" section for April 1756. In 1714 Stephen White was admitted to St.
John's College, Cambridge, as a sizar (a commoner of limited means). White
earned his B.A. in 1718 and was awarded the M.A. in 1721, one year after
taking holy orders. White served as rector of Holton in Suffolk from 1733
until, presumably, his death. In 1734 White was appointed as chaplain to
Lucius Charles, seventh viscount of Falkland (d. 1785). White managed to
publish one of his sermons, *A Dissuasive from Stealing: A Sermon Preached
at Holton, in Suffolk*. The sermon evidently enjoyed a measure of popularity: thirteen editions of the twenty-four-page (duodecimo) work appeared
between 1745 and 1821.

The son of a carpenter, White grew up surrounded by the English countryside—he was born in the village of Wing, Rutland (about fifteen miles
west of Peterborough)—so it is not much of a surprise to find White publishing a work on agriculture that relies heavily the sort of skills he likely
would have learned from his father. By White's own reckoning, the *Collateral Bee-Boxes* amounts to his life's work. As White tells us in his prefa-

tory note, the sixty-three-page volume was forty years in the making, which means that he began working on the project while an undergraduate at Cambridge.[6]

White's relative obscurity today—most Johnson scholars, when they mention the White review at all, treat it as a reflection of Johnson's capacity for eccentricity or as a reflection of his indiscriminate curiosity—perhaps tells us something about why Johnson's reviews have gone largely neglected thus far. Here we have Johnson expending attention on what surely is insignificant material, written by an author justly invisible to literary history. Yet, as we shall see, White is the very sort of contemporary author who earned Johnson's respect, or at least his sympathy. By studying Johnson's reviews of the *Collateral Bee-Boxes* and other minor works written by long-forgotten authors, we gain a finer appreciation of Johnson's understanding of the contemporary literary world, in particular the value Johnson as a reviewer attached to the civic-mindedness of authors working in fields of knowledge that, however insignificant they might appear to us nowadays, were of some importance in the mid-eighteenth century.

Exemplifying the traditional outlook on Johnson's least-known reviews, Donald Greene would have us believe that the White review amounts to nothing more than a petty curiosity; he observes in his brief attribution statement that the piece is noteworthy strictly for its illustration of "Johnsonian humor at its driest." Greene does not elaborate, but he seems to assume that only good-natured irony can account for Johnson's spirited approval of such trifling material (*Collateral Bee-Boxes* is "delightfully-entitled" in Greene's view).[7] More importantly, Greene's commentary fails to consider fully the context of Johnson's review. It is worth noting, for instance, that the White review is not relegated to the magazine's "Books and Pamphlets Published" section, which would have spared Johnson the bother of extraction and commentary, but is situated as the lead review in the magazine's premier issue. And when we recall Johnson's keen interest in manufacturing and agricultural economics—see, for instance, his commentary on the wool trade—we can scarcely regard Johnson's decision to review the *Collateral Bee-Boxes* in the first place as an exercise in condescension or whimsy. Indeed, we should not forget that Johnson himself spent his youth in the country. Lichfield sits in the middle of what is even today an agricultural area, and the countryside is no more than a quarter of an hour's walk from the Johnson Birthplace Museum. Doubtless Johnson was drawn to review White's volume based on his considerable experience with rural life. What is more, apiculture—the study of bee culture and the production of honey—was by no means viewed by Johnson's contemporaries as a frivolous or shallow occupation, as Greene evidently assumes, but was in fact a rigorously studied field of knowledge, as the publication of numerous books on the subject during the period bears out. Sixty-six separate works related to beekeeping appeared during Johnson's lifetime, and most of these titles were published in multiple editions. White's *Collateral Bee-Boxes* appeared in four editions between 1756 and 1766.[8] Thus, it seems likely that Johnson looked upon the *Collateral Bee-Boxes* not as a handbook for the avocational gardener, as is suggested by Greene. Rather, Johnson almost certainly gave notice to the work because he understood it to be a worthy example of the widespread contemporary interest in agricultural production and beekeeping in particular, an outlook that has been validated by history.[9]

Greene's reading of the White piece seems off-target for other reasons as well. Comprising as it does two and a half columns—the same amount of text as is given over to Johnson's appreciative review of Charlotte Lennox's three-volume, 1,500-page translation of the duke of Sully's *Memoirs*—the White review represents a generous allocation of space for a mere sixty-three-page volume. More significantly, Johnson's selection of extracts demonstrates that he evaluated *Collateral Bee-Boxes* with some care. In the review's first paragraph Johnson quotes directly from White's introduction; the seven paragraphs that follow deftly summarize chapters 1 through 6, while the ninth paragraph epitomizes the remaining six pages of the book.[10] Equally important is that the White review deftly conveys Johnson's general outlook on the beneficent purposes of even the humbler sorts of literary activity.

Take for instance the opening paragraph of the *Literary Magazine* review, where we find Johnson directing attention to White's authorial virtues—his benevolence, modesty, and resourcefulness—while assigning relatively less weight to the technical substance of the *Bee-Boxes*. "The reverend author of this little treatise appears to be a man of ingenuity, candor, and, what is far more valuable, of piety," Johnson declares, "willing to communicate his knowledge for the advantage of others, and careful to learn before he presumes to teach, having, as he declares, tried every method before he found the right, and *been almost forty years in making a bee-box*." Summary and extract take up the next few paragraphs, but even in the connective commentary Johnson manages to squeeze in an additional reference to White's altruism and industriousness ("The ingenious author having given these plain and benevolent directions").[11]

Indeed, it is worth pausing to consider here the extent to which Johnson amplifies what are in fact occasional and rather offhanded revelations of authorial character in White's volume. In the preface to *Collateral Bee-Boxes* White surveys the history of beekeeping science, only mentioning at the conclusion of the preface his own forty-year effort to build a more efficient bee box. Yet Johnson gives White's tenacity some prominence, paraphrasing White's remarks in the review's first sentence and placing them in italics. The volume itself deals mostly with the nuts-and-bolts aspects of bee-box construction and beekeeping. In the closing pages White mentions that his modest innovation will not eliminate hunger, nor can he promise that his theories will improve honey production in every region of England. Nevertheless, White is convinced that in some small way his new bee box can be used to alleviate human misery. Johnson includes these observations in the review, eschewing summary for the more emphatic direct quotation. Though White "'cannot promise great things,'" he does "'hope that by my method the poor will be benefited, though not inriched.'"[12] By its own definition, White's book is nothing more than a self-help manual for beekeepers whose product is consumed chiefly by their rural neighbors, yet Johnson builds the critical core of his appreciative review around what are in fact incidental disclosures of authorial personality.

Johnson closes his review by recommending White's book to those readers who happened to hold an interest in subjects of this sort, and it is worth noting that here—as is the case for the review overall—Johnson manages to leave a highly favorable impression of White's volume without resorting to dogmatic pronouncement. "No one, who intends the pleasure or profit of a bee-garden, should be contented with this abstract," Johnson states, but should "consult the original treatise."[13] White's authorial attributes entitle him to serious consideration, Johnson thus argues, but it is the marketplace—and not the *Literary Magazine*—that shall determine the true value of the *Collateral Bee-Boxes*.

That the White review embodies Johnson's general outlook on the beneficent purposes of authorship, and in particular his views on the subordinate standing of the critic and the primacy of the author/reader relationship, is given greater clarity by the *Monthly*'s rather condescending treatment of the *Collateral Bee-Boxes*. Here is the entire critical commentary, written by Sir Tanfield Leman:

> Tho' we do not pretend to be adepts in the constitution of this female monarchy, yet we imagine the method recommended by Mr. White will answer every thing he says of it himself, in the title. The construction of his bee boxes are plain and easy to any one that can drive a sufficient number of nails, to hold four square pieces of wood together,—In his conclusion he takes notice of an error frequently fallen into by *bee fanciers*, which is, that they are fond of enlarging their stock, without considering how they are to be provided for.[14]

Leman glanced at White's diagrams and read the title and conclusion, but he appears to have missed completely the underlying humanitarian objective of White's project. More significantly—and doubtless worrisome for

an author whose prospects hinged on the pronouncements of reviewers—
Leman seems disdainful of White. The patronizing edge to the lead sentence of Leman's review, the haphazard selection of details, the characterization of beekeepers as *"bee fanciers"* (with its implication of eccentricity and dabbling) all suggest that Leman dismissed White's book as unde-
serving of serious attention. By contrast, Johnson's commentary is informative and appreciative, yet free of even the slightest hint of exaggeration.
The *Literary Magazine* review manages to convey White's earnestness and
his mechanical ingeniousness, in other words, without overselling his contributions to modern husbandry.

Francis Home (1719–1813), *Experiments on Bleaching.* Reviewed
by Johnson, 15 July 1756; reviewed by Tobias Smollett in the *Critical,*
March 1756; reviewed by Sir Tanfield Leman in the *Monthly,* May 1756.
Francis Home made his living as a physician and as a professor of medicine at the University of Edinburgh. Home also managed to publish eight
books on topics ranging from the one under consideration here to virology
and surgical procedure. Before discussing the reception of *Experiments on
Bleaching,* Home's second book, it is worth pausing to consider Home's
prefatory "Advertisement," which illuminates key circumstances behind
the publication of his 330-page volume. Of particular interest here is that
the *Experiments* is sponsored by a provincial trade organization and is directed specifically at fellow artisans, so prospective book buyers would
naturally expect to find the work peppered with specialized terms and re-
gional expressions.

> At the desire of the Honourable Board of Trustees for the improvement of
> fisheries and manufactures in North Britain, the following treatise was com-
> posed, read in different lectures, and the experiments, so far as it was pos-
> sible, were performed before the bleachers of this country. It is now pub-
> lished in consequence of a petition presented by the bleachers to the
> Honourable Board of Trustees.[15]

A glance at the table of contents underscores the volume's highly specialized subject matter. Part 1 discusses the relation between chemistry and the
practical arts and surveys the *"Different practical methods of bleaching."*
Part 2 evaluates the *"application of lyes"* and *"acids,"* and also explains
the means of *"Hand-rubbing with soap and water"* and also touches upon
"rubbing-boards." Part 3 examines the various sorts of *"ashes"* and concludes with a discussion of the *"Methods of manufacturing these ashes at
home."* Part 4 analyzes *"the cause and effects of hard water, and the methods of softening it,"* the *"effects of steel and coal waters on cloth, and the*

cure," and finishes with *"Some considerations with regard to the further improvement of the linen manufacture."*

Though the "Advertisement" and table of contents are as clear as one may reasonably expect in spelling out the occasion for the work and its objectives, Tobias Smollett chose to downplay in particular Home's prefatory declarations, even though he neatly paraphrases the remarks in the opening paragraph of his review for the *Critical*. To be sure, Smollett acknowledges Home's good intentions (he deserves credit "for having dedicated his time and talents to the improvement of the linen manufacture which is the staple commodity of his country") and Smollett does offer a kindly word for discrete observations found in the work (Home's "remarks upon the inconveniences that attend the common methods of bleaching, are extremely judicious").[16] But it is significant that Smollett ultimately censures the very features of Home's work that its prospective readers would have found congenial, if not indispensable. Home's "experiments"—the heart of his treatise, after all—"are painfully described," Smollett asserts in the review's concluding paragraph:

> Surely there is a less unpalatable way of communicating natural knowledge. Any reader will peruse with pleasure the chymical works of *Boerhaave, Stahl,* and *Homberg*; but we believe no person, but a mere whitster, or a writer in either REVIEW, will ever drudge through Dr. Home's treatise on bleaching; which nevertheless, we pronounce a valuable performance, though like the green linen he describes, *steeped and rinsed clean of all flummery and dressing.*[17]

It would be tempting to attribute Smollett's imperiousness here to a commendable if rather heavy-footed attempt to enforce standards in scholarly discourse, but there seems to be more at work here than well-intentioned fastidiousness in matters of diction.

It is worth noting, for instance, that Smollett ignores the stipulations of Home's prefatory remarks when he insists on making what can only be described as unreasonable comparisons of the *Experiments* to the works of Wilhelm Homberg (1652–1715), Georg Ernst Stahl (1660–1734), and Herman Boerhaave (1668–1738).[18] True, like Home these men were trained in medicine and at various points published scholarly works on chemistry. But in *Experiments on Bleaching* Home clearly addresses an unscholarly class of reader—and in the service of a commercial end rather than an academic one. To write at the level of a Homberg or a Stahl would be self-defeating on the order of, say, hoping to meet the demands of today's do-it-yourself automobile repair market by substituting a Purdue University Ph.D. dissertation on mechanical engineering for one of the popular self-help manuals. As a novelist, playwright, poet, and journalist, Smollett must have been keenly sensitive to authorial efforts to calibrate one's material to a specific class of reader. Why, then, does Smollett insist on evaluating Home's treatise against a standard it was not designed to meet? It is a matter that cannot be proved conclusively, but one credible explanation is that Smollett seeks to validate what he sees as the adjudicatory function of reviewing. Literary works have no artistic merit outside of what the *Critical Review* assigns to them, so authors hoping for a favorable review are well advised to take into account the literary tastes of the *Critical Review*. Home's book meets the expectations of its intended readership well enough, Smollett admits, but we are also given to understand that Home's vulgar tonalities offend the refined scholarly sensibilities of the *Critical Review*, a fact that determines the character of the review at least as much as its suitability for those interested in advanced techniques in bleaching. Indeed, we can read Smollett's review of Home as exemplifying his near-obsessive loathing of Scotticisms.[19]

Sir Tanfield Leman's review in the *Monthly* is noticeably more sympathetic than its *Critical Review* predecessor: "genius or science" cannot be "more advantageously employed," Leman declares, "than when they are directed to disquisitions that immediately tend to facilitate or improve such particular branches of trade or commerce, as serve to find continual business for numbers, and consequently bring a considerable increase to the national wealth." *Experiments on Bleaching* "promises greatly to answer so commendable a design; at the same time that it also evinces, how far commerce may be benefitted by the aid of philosophy." Given Johnson's own views on the symbiotic relation between practical arts and "philosophy," it is at least possible that Leman's appreciative review encouraged Johnson to consult Home's treatise.[20]

Johnson's review of Home appeared in July, two months after Leman's. *Experiments on Bleaching* "is one of the few books which philosophy has condescended to give mankind for the improvement of the lower arts," Johnson declares in the lead sentence, perhaps consciously seconding Leman's earlier judgment. Most of Johnson's review is given over to extract and summary, though the occasional interjections reminding readers of the usefulness of Home's treatise (it "may justly excite curiosity"; his commentary on hard water "is of great importance"; one section contains "very curious experiments") manage to sustain the distinctly favorable tone of the opening sentences.[21] At one point Johnson allows Home to speak for himself on the beneficial potential of his innovative water filtration system, a secondary discovery in relation to the stated objectives of *Experiments*, certainly, but one that promises a usefulness far beyond the bleaching trade:

This method which we have discovered of softening hard waters, is easy, expeditious, and cheap; qualities absolutely necessary to render it useful to the public. It is easy, as the most ignorant can do it; expeditious, as it becomes fit for all family uses immediately, and for drinking in half an hour; and cheap, as the material costs but a mere trifle; nay, may be prepared by any person.[22]

Home's research on bleaching thus led to the discovery of a simple yet effective water-processing technique that offers poor and lower-middle-class readers a means to remove a nagging inconvenience from their lives. While it is true that Smollett makes mention of Home's section on hard water, and Leman devotes two pages to a summary of this portion of Home's book, only Johnson gives emphasis to the philanthropic potential of Home's innovation in water processing. In the *Literary Magazine* Home is ultimately portrayed as a humanitarian rather than a mere mechanic or artisan. By contrast, the two major review journals cast Home either as a resourceful but obscure technician whose work bears no meaningful relation to the lives of most people (Smollett: "no person, but a mere whitster, or a writer in either REVIEW, will ever drudge through Dr. Home's treatise"), or whose achievement is noteworthy chiefly for its shimmering, remote symbolic value (Leman: "how far commerce may be benefitted by the aid of philosophy").

Of additional significance is that Johnson's apologetic treatment of Home's provincial expressions can be read as a counterpoint to Smollett's earlier criticisms. There is no conclusive evidence that Johnson writes with the *Critical* in mind here, though in the following quotation Johnson walks a fine line between acknowledging Home's diction for what it plainly is— an impediment to sales in the relatively lucrative English market—and defending Home's prerogative to write in an idiom commensurate with his subject matter and his intended readership. Indeed, Johnson apparently believes that the *Experiments* can reach a readership far greater than its author realizes, provided of course that the English public are prepared in advance to tolerate Home's reliance on obscure terms and expressions:

[Home's] performance is indeed rather useful than pleasing, sometimes obscured by the use of terms, which none but bleachers understand, and sometimes made unpleasing to an *English* ear, by words and phrases never uttered on this side of the *Tweed*. But the author wrote for his countrymen [Scots], and his business was rather to instruct than to delight. It had yet been proper to have told the meaning of words peculiar to the trade on which he treats, but we seldom suspect others of ignorance in things which daily use has made familiar to ourselves.[23]

Experiments occasionally makes difficult reading for the nonspecialist and the non-Scot, and Home probably should have added at least a few explanatory notes, given the broader significance of some of his observations. But such minor imperfections should not be held against the author, Johnson argues, nor should the overall worthiness of Home's work be doubted.

It is worth noting that on the whole Johnson and Smollett agree on basic critical matters: the roughness of Home's language, the virtuousness of his intentions, the soundness of his scientific method. What separates the two reviews is the attitude each takes towards its subject matter. To one degree or another Smollett strives to exalt the *Critical* at the expense of Home. By contrast, Johnson acts as a broker of sorts, introducing the general public to a work that carries a much broader appeal than is suggested by its title. Significantly, Johnson's observations on this point turned out to be right on the mark: *Experiments* was soon translated into French and German, earning along the way a "gold medal" from the Edinburgh Society for the Improvement of Arts and Sciences.

Stephen Hales (1677–1761), *An Account of a Useful Discovery to Distill Double the usual Quantity of Sea-Water*. Reviewed by Johnson, 15 July 1756; reviewed by Sir Tanfield Leman in the *Monthly,* May 1756. The *Critical* gives notice to the *Discovery*, without commentary, in its "List of Pamphlets" section for April 1756. Parish priest, physiologist, inventor, and Fellow of the Royal Society, Stephen Hales devoted much of his life to philanthropic causes.[24] Essentially, the fifty-eight octavo pages of Hales's *Useful Discovery* argue that distilling fresh water from seawater is more efficient than carrying onboard ship sufficient quantities of fresh water. Hales not only describes in detail the method and mechanics of the scheme, but he also includes time-employed/fuel-burned studies to prove that distilling fresh water from seawater using his coal-fired process saves weight and space, and also delivers water that is more hygienic than that stored in barrels on the date that a ship sails.[25] "Of all Hales's technological work, the highest value, retrospectively, is assigned to his technique to improve the efficiency of distillation," argue D. G. C. Allen and R. E. Schofield in their biography of Hales. Hales's "distillation process works, today as it did in Hales day," Allen and Schofield also point out.[26]

The *Useful Discovery* was among the last and, clearly, the most successful of a procession of works by Hales that addressed humanitarian concerns, so it is hardly surprising to find Sir Tanfield Leman paying homage to Hales's altruism ("This worthy and assiduous philosopher, whose labours have been long devoted to serve the real interests of mankind") in his brief but appreciative review in the *Monthly*. Equally unremarkable, given the significance of the material, is that Leman promptly moves on to make undoubtedly pertinent but rather arcane observations on water distillation: "[F]rom our Author's experiments it appears, that chalk in the proportion of half an ounce to a gallon of water, answers all the intention of Mr. Appleby's *lapis infernalis*, and calcined bones; and Dr. Butler's capital soap-lees," and so on.[27]

The *Literary Magazine* also published an appreciative review of the *Useful Discovery*. But quite unlike his *Monthly Review* counterpart, Johnson insists on making Hales's humanitarianism and highly refined scholarly manners the centerpiece of his review, while the scientific aspects of the *Useful Discovery* are very much underplayed. In the following passage, for instance, we find Johnson striving to bring out the inspirational value of Hales's researches, and the "useful discovery" itself is characterized as of secondary importance: "There was still wanting some method of quickning distillation, and this Dr. *Hales* has at length discovered, and imparted with candour more to be admired than even his sagacity; for he has ingenuously traced it from the first hint, that he may receive no more than his due share of honour."[28]

The suggestion here is that the potential economic and political impact of Hales's discovery was such that he may have been tempted to grab much more of the credit than he really deserved. England, after all, was growing increasingly reliant on its navy and the transoceanic trade, and the projector who managed to improve dramatically the efficiency of these operations would quite justifiably earn the gratitude of the nation. Yet Hales avoids using his discovery as an occasion for self-aggrandizement. Indeed, he seems to have gone to great lengths to portray his own contributions as nothing more than the pinnacle of a grand edifice. Brief though it is, the passage quoted above illustrates the extent to which Johnson's book reviewing embodies his general views on the socially uplifting ends of professional letters. Johnson understood well the inherent instability of scientific inquiry, today's discoveries in his view being subject to reversal, extension, qualification, or irrelevancy by future investigations.[29] So rather than offer what might turn out to be unwarranted praise for the "useful discovery," Johnson instead places the emphasis on Hales's exemplary conduct as an author.

That Johnson intends to celebrate Hales more for his general authorial qualities than for his expertise in hydrology also finds expression in the extracts chosen for the review. Take the lead quotation, for instance, where Hales's unpretentiousness and his eagerness to credit predecessors are on display: "Mr. *William Baily* of *Salisbury-Court*, the author of many ingenious contrivances, shewed me, in a small model of a tin vessel, a method by which he has happily increased the force of the engine to raise water by fire." Observing this experiment led Hales "'to think that a greater quantity of liquor might also by this means be distilled.'"[30] Even Hales's scientific manner of proceeding is mined for its underlying humanistic lessons. "We shall exhibit the process of his discovery," Johnson says in his introduction to the extract portion of the review, "for the art of improving hints, and tracing one consequence from another, is of more importance than the distillation of ten waters." The commentary that accompanies the technical quotations is far less appreciative, and in a few instances we find Johnson expressing doubts about Hales's accuracy and comprehensiveness. The technique recommended for removing salt "appears to be a great improvement; yet I am not certain whether it can be turned to much advantage," Johnson declares, because "Speculation is fallacious," and "experiments in small quantities deceive." Elsewhere in the review Johnson questions some of Hales's mathematical calculations, though he admits that in doing so he addresses "what the Doctor understands better than I."[31] Johnson is predictably reluctant here and throughout the review to characterize Hales's scientific conclusions as flawless or definitive. What is not open to question, however, are Hales's altruism, academic scrupulousness, and his commendably earnest pursuit of the truth.

Charles Lucas (1713–71), *Essay on Waters*. Reviewed by Johnson, 15 August 1756; reviewed by Tobias Smollett in the *Critical,* May 1756; reviewed in the *Monthly,* August 1756 (reviewer unknown). Charles Lucas made a name for himself initially as a political reformer. In 1748 Lucas campaigned in his native Dublin for a seat in the House of Commons, publishing as part of his candidacy several pamphlets decrying parliamentary corruption. Arrested at one point for his allegedly treasonous writings, Lucas managed to escape an almost certain prison sentence by fleeing to London in late 1749. Lucas eventually managed to transcend his status as a fugitive from justice. In 1752 he completed his training in medicine at the University of Leyden, setting up a practice in London shortly afterward. His career as an author of medical works, however, was not without controversy.

Lucas's three volume *Essay* professes to examine the chemical properties of water and to consider fully its far-reaching medical and economic applications. A collateral aim of the *Essay* is to reform English spelling— though Lucas's "system" of orthography is not merely unpersuasive, but eccentric to the point of self-parody.[32] It is important to note here that Lucas's work is heavily polemical—particularly the third volume—being as it is one salvo in a much broader contemporary controversy surrounding the exact nature of the mineral spas at Bath and Bristol.[33] Also very much in the foreground are Lucas's political struggles of the 1740s. In his dedication to the Prince of Wales, Lucas declares unwavering loyalty to King George II, whose government a few years earlier had bent all the rules in an attempt to silence his dissent:

> Yet, pardon mine ambition, to let YOUR ROYAL HIGHNESS see my sentiments of loyalty and gratitude upon this occasion; though I am, I hope, the Onely [*sic*] living subject, that can of a truth complain of having been denied the potection [*sic*], that even criminals enjoy from our laws; having notoriously suffered the Oppressor's Wrongs, the Laws Delay, and the Insolence of Office, to say no more; and that, without any taste or prospect of redress; Notwithstanding, I can call upon my bitterest enemies to attest, that it has not been in the power of persecution and adversity to pervert my senses, so far as to make me impute the unauthorised outrages of Substitutes to the PRINCIPAL, or make me one moment disregard or forget the DELIVERERS of my country, the RESTORERS and PRESERVERS of our most valuable, our POLITICAL HEALTH.[34]

These remarks give us some idea of the great obstacles facing Lucas. Despite the passage of the better part of a decade, Lucas still sees a necessity in refuting lingering accusations of treachery, and even this rather straightforward task appears to be fraught with much hazard if the remarks here are any indication.[35] In reminding the public of his steadfast adherence to noble political principles in the face of flagrant government oppression, Lucas assumed, probably correctly, that the slightest suggestion of disloyalty to the house of Hanover would jeopardize whatever chance he still might have of putting to rest his lingering reputation as a political agitator. Lucas's sense of estrangement becomes even more discernible in the preface, where he rebukes critics in the scientific community for dredging up long-dormant legal problems in an effort to undermine the credibility of his research. "Of all the various ill-natured means of detraction, that have yet been devised" by those who disagree with the balneological theories advanced in the *Essay*, Lucas declares,

> the most remarkable, are the calling my moral and political character, and even mine understanding, in question, and attempting to cast reflections from my late profession.—"Who is this," says one, "that is come to decry our waters?"—"A fellow," answers another, "that was forced to fly his own country, and will never be quiet, till he is forced to fly this. . . ." "Ay," says a third, "I have heard of him; no body will mind him; a mere mad man!"[36]

With all of these circumstances pressing on him, Lucas undoubtedly nursed keen hopes that the *Essay*'s fate in the marketplace would not only vindicate his controversial balneological theories but also set him free, finally, from the vestigial popular view of him as a rabble-rouser.

How did Lucas and his *Essay* fare in the press? Writing for the *Critical*, Tobias Smollett offers readers a thoroughgoing and basically well conceived critique of Lucas's researches—hardly a surprise, given Smollett's formal medical training and his intelligent avocational interest in the physical sciences.[37] What makes the *Critical* review interesting is not this technical remark or that, however, but Smollett's intense dislike for Lucas, which surfaces repeatedly in his choice and treatment of material and leads Smollett, ultimately, to dismiss Lucas's *Essay*.

It is important to point out here that Smollett himself had written a treatise on balneology some four years earlier. Smollett's *Essay on the External Use of Water* amply demonstrates that he and Lucas were essentially in agreement on the contemporary controversies surrounding balneology, particularly with regard to what Lucas sees as the maladroit administration of the spas at Bath. Yet we find Smollett reproving Lucas in the *Critical* for assertions that he himself had advanced in his own *Essay on the External Use of Water*.[38] Take for instance Smollett's commentary on Lucas's general outlook on the hygienic conditions at Bath. "After having read this learned treatise of Dr. *Lucas*, we cannot help wondering how the hot-springs of *Bath*, acquired their reputation," Smollett observes rather sneeringly, "considering how injudiciously they have been administered—Is it possible that any person could ever return alive from the use of the waters at *Bath*"?[39] Smollett's earlier treatise sought to call attention to "the necessity of reforming" the Bath spas and to root out the numerous "evils and defects" inherent in the administration of these enterprises, so it is something of a surprise to find him criticizing Lucas for embracing the same cause.[40] Indeed, Smollett's volume is hardly destitute of the very kind of hyperbole that makes Lucas's *Essay* such an enticing subject for ridicule. Witness the following dire prophecy that precedes Smollett's eleven proposals to reform the Bath spas:

> [W]e have reason to believe, that some attention will be paid to those fountains flowing with health, which, at a very moderate expence, might be so improved as to become the greatest boast, ornament, and blessing of these kingdoms. —But, if our expectations from the legislature should be disappointed, and the Corporation of *Bath* still turn a deaf ear to the proposals which have been made; the proprietors of other Baths, either in this, or in any other country, will probably take the hints which they have rejected, and then they may chance to see their Springs deserted, and their town utterly impoverished and ruined.[41]

When set side by side, the works of Lucas and Smollett would lead us to believe that the two are soul mates, not only in regard to their positions on balneological controversies but also in their mutual preference for alarmist idiom.

Why Smollett takes stands in the *Critical* that directly contradict the views expressed in his own treatise on balneology is never stated forthrightly, but there is plenty of evidence to suggest that Smollett is irritated not by the propositions contained in the *Essay* itself—which, as his own writings tell us, Smollett largely agrees with—but by Lucas's overweening vanity and his scholarly dishonesty, not to mention what Smollett sees as Lucas's irresponsible political activities during the 1740s. Smollett evidently looks upon Lucas as a raffish pretender, an unscrupulous, irascible crank who is completely out of place in the exalted environs of professional letters. Smollett's review thus means to cement this very image of Lucas in the public mind. Smollett dare not endorse what are in some instances Lucas's sensible ideas on balneology, for fear of engendering an unwarranted respect for the man himself.

That Smollett aims to blacken Lucas's character—or, more accurately, to unmask what Smollett sees as his unjustified claims to respectability—manifests itself in the emphasis placed on Lucas's troubled past and his eccentric, abrasive personality. Take for instance Smollett's lead sentences, which are heavily freighted with malevolent irony:

> NATURE still continues to produce great and stupendous geniuses, howsoever they may be over-looked or opposed by the ignorance or envy of mankind. Two such have lately appeared like comets in our hemisphere; in the contemplation of whose labours, we know not whether most to admire, the acuteness of penetration, the extent of learning, the strength and solidity of argument, the candour, modesty, patriotism, or singularity in station, study and circumstance, that denote them so consummate and congenial. Both are apothecaries, chemists, physicians and politicians. Both have shone like *Phosphorus* amidst the mists of ignorance and prejudice: both have corroded like the *lapsis infernalis*, an imposthumated administration big with foulness and corruption; and both have been over-whelmed and well nigh dissolved in the discharge that ensued. Many moons have not revolved since one of these illustrious adepts obliged the world with a performance, in which he plainly demonstrated the absurdity of the practice adopted by all his contemporaries, and blew up their whole medical system by means of a mine kindled with electrical fire. . . . That judicious reformer's worthy compere is the learned author of the treatise which now falls under our examination.[42]

By the time this review was published in May 1756 Smollett had already written a scathing, personally abusive review of Lucas's political apologia, *An Appeal to the Commons . . . by the last Free Citizen of Dublin* (March

1756), and an equally searing ad hominem review of a political pamphlet by the other author alluded to here, John Shebbeare (January/February 1756).[43] The review of the *Appeal to the Commons* suggests that Smollett looked upon Lucas not as a legitimate participant in contemporary political controversies but as a deluded, noisy pest whose flamboyant lawlessness and inane yet provocative writings made him into something of a celebrity. "Some people unacquainted with the real character of" Lucas, Smollett says in his review of the *Appeal to the Commons*, "might be apt, from the circumstances of his expulsion and the nature of this appeal, to look upon him as a turbulent partisan, who wanted to fish in troubled waters; who having miscarried in his own country, endeavours to foment factions and disturbance in the city of *London:* to us, however, he appears in the light of a weak, enthusiastic democratic; who, had he lived in the reign of *Charles* I, would, with *Leighton, Pryn,* and *Lilburn,* have received more flagrant marks of the ministry's regard."[44] Far from being a dispassionate, impartial consideration of a new work, then, Smollett's review of the *Essay on Waters* means to take up where his earlier review of Lucas's *Appeal* had left off.

That Smollett intends to defame Lucas also finds expression in the ridicule directed at the *Essay*'s rather fulsome dedicatory addresses to the Prince of Wales and Lord Chesterfield. "Such is his patriotic zeal," Smollett observes, "that even in this performance, his political principles seem to glow warmer than the waters of *Aken*," adding that "it is not impossible that the doctor studied medicine, on purpose to unite in his own person, the body-healer and the physician of the state."[45] Essentially an accurate observation, to be sure, but rather mean-spirited as well when we bear in mind that bombast of this sort was a matter of convention when it came to dedicatory essays. Smollett's assertions here might easily be used to characterize Johnson's numerous dedications to members of the peerage and the royal family. Indeed, Lucas's fustian language in the dedicatory addresses might very well be the most prominently orthodox aspect of the entire *Essay*.

Curiously, Lucas's bizarre attempt to employ the *Essay* as a vehicle to overhaul accepted orthographical practices elicits relatively tepid criticism from Smollett. Lucas "offers his reasons in the preface for differing from all other authors, which indeed may be cohobated or concentrated into this one maxim," Smollett observes with more than a hint of parody, "namely, he holds himself wiser than all the rest of the world."[46] A few examples are given to illustrate Lucas's irrational spelling innovations, but on a point that might easily have unleashed a torrent of abuse, Smollett conducts himself with surprising restraint.

Certainly the most significant aspect of Smollett's review are the charges of incompetence and deceitfulness leveled at Lucas, exemplified in the following passage:

> [N]otwithstanding all he has copied from *Hippocrates, Aristotle, Dioscorides, Celsus, Galen, Aretaeus, Vitruvius, Plinius, Cardanus, Trallianus, Platerus, Prosper Alpinus, Caelius Aurelianus, Avicenna, Paracelsus Bombast, Van Helmont, Boerhaave, Hoffman, Stahl, Homberg, Muschenbreck, Becher, Lister, Wallerius, Guidot, Floyer, Rowzee, Linden, Shaw*, and some more modern tracts which he has not thought proper to name, we will venture to pronounce him a true original.[47]

The basic point here is obvious enough: so heavily does Lucas borrow from existing works—and not all of this material is properly credited—that there is good reason to doubt whether there are any original observations in the *Essay* worth remarking on. What is not nearly so obvious is that Smollett means to accuse Lucas of filching from his (Smollett's) own *Essay on the External Use of Water*, a point suggested by the allusion to "some more modern tracts which he has not thought proper to name."

The insinuation that Lucas plagiarized Smollett's earlier treatise is repeated elsewhere in the review. "We do not find any thing new in his account of the medicinal properties of simple water (page 166.)," Smollett observes in commenting on the first volume, "but we apprehend he has made free with *Boerhaave, Hoffman*, and some other authors of smaller account, to whom he has forgot to make proper acknowledgments." Perhaps the most revelatory instance of Smollett's accusations can be found in the discussion of the third volume of Lucas's *Essay:*

> The improvement of the baths which he so strenuously recommends, has been inculcated by repeated plans and proposals presented to the corporation of *Bath;* particularly by the late Mr. *Wood*, the architect, and Dr. *Cleland*, whose proposals have been constantly opposed by the faculty, and rejected by the corporation at *Bath*, with a species of rancour which Dr. *Lucas* would have construed into persecution. The candour of this curious chymist, would have therefore appeared more conspicuous, had he taken some notice of those gentlemen and others from whom he seems to have almost literally borrowed many of his most valuable hints of reformation. . . .[48]

It is important to note here that the proposals of Cleland and Wood are discussed at length in Smollett's earlier survey of the problems with the Bath spas. As far as Smollett is concerned, then, Lucas quite deliberately sought to pass off the work of others as his own—including most especially material presented in Smollett's own *Essay on Waters.*

Clearly it is Smollett's contempt for Lucas personally and professionally—

and not any particular scientific fault with the *Essay* itself, or an ulterior desire to elevate the status of reviewing—that is behind the censorious disposition of the *Critical* notice. The earlier notice of the *Appeals to the Commons* shows that Smollett despised Lucas the politician. Lucas's plagiarism of Smollett's earlier work in writing up the *Essay on Waters* adds a personal dimension to matters, intensifying further Smollett's existing opinion of Lucas as an unprincipled and clownish firebrand, eager to attract publicity at whatever cost. It is thus not surprising to find Lucas portrayed in the *Critical* not as a competent though unexceptional researcher, but as a buffoon: besotted with himself, prone to embrace patently foolish ideas, and a brazen pilferer of intellectual property who is richly deserving of the severest public rebukes.

Did Johnson consult Smollett's notice before writing his own review of Lucas's *Essay*? Almost certainly. Appearing with the Lucas piece in the May 1756 issue of the *Critical* is the review of Russell's *Natural History*, aspects of which, as we shall see, Johnson attempts to refute in the June 1756 number of the *Literary Magazine*. The May number of the *Critical* also carries a review of Charlotte Lennox's *Memoirs of the Countess of Berci*, which Johnson claims to have read in a letter to Lennox dated 30 July, two weeks before the appearance of his review of Lucas's *Essay*.[49] That Johnson reviews the *Essay* with Lucas's controversial reputation foremost in his mind becomes clear in his opening sentences, where a discussion of the work itself is put on hold while Lucas's public-spiritedness and moral courage are extolled. Johnson's assertiveness on this point is almost certainly calibrated to neutralize correspondingly strong prejudices against Lucas, which had recently found expression in Smollett's reviews of the *Appeal to the Commons* and the *Essay on Waters:*

> The author of this book is a man well known to the world for his daring defiance of power when he thought it exerted on the side of wrong, the popularity which he obtained, and the violence to which the *Irish* ministers had recourse, that they might set themselves free from an opponent so restless by his principles, so powerful by his conduct, and so specious by his cause; they drove him from his native country by proclamation, in which they charged him with crimes of which they never intended to be called to the proof, and oppressed him by methods equally irresistible by guilt and innocence. Let the man thus driven into exile for having been the friend of his country be received in every other place as a confessor of liberty, and let the tools of power be taught in time that they may rob but cannot impoverish.[50]

Lucas acted in the best interests of his fellow citizens, the government's case was willfully dishonest, and we should all celebrate the author of the

Essay on Waters as an exemplar of the highest civic ideals. Johnson's own willingness to speak out against the wrongdoing of politicians is evident enough here. But what invests these remarks with even greater significance is that Johnson offers a spirited endorsement of the self-image Lucas himself sought to project in both the *Essay* and the earlier *Appeal*, neither of which made much headway in the public mind if the reviews of these works in the *Monthly* and *Critical* are any indication.[51] In the next few sentences Johnson turns his attention to the *Essay* itself:

> In the book which we are now to examine is treated one of the most important and general of all physical subjects, the nature and properties of a body justly numbered among the elements, without which neither animal nor vegetable life can subsist. This subject our author has examined with great diligence, not only by consulting writers, but by numerous and careful experiments, which he has tried upon more mineral springs, than perhaps any single man had ever examined.[52]

Perhaps in response to Lucas's fears of being widely thought of as a scientific quack, Johnson is careful to emphasize the erudition on display in the *Essay*. It is also possible that Johnson here means to rebut the charges of scholarly incompetence leveled at Lucas in the *Critical*. Having said so much in Lucas's favor, however, Johnson is by no means reluctant to point out that the bizarre spelling innovations in the *Essay* undermine what are in fact Lucas's basically legitimate claims to scholarly respectability.

Lucas's zeal for orthographical reform should have been inhibited by Johnson's *Dictionary*, which had authoritatively addressed irregularities in English spelling when it appeared in April 1755. Yet Lucas presses ahead with his poorly conceived program anyway, anchoring his case in the presumption that the act of publishing one's writings in itself makes one a de facto orthographer: "Let then every writer propose his corrections and amendments of our stile and diction, to the public," Lucas declares, "without that religious, or rather blind, attachement to the authority of predecessors, with which some sensible men seem pinioned."[53] We can easily read Lucas's remarks here as a thinly veiled attack on Johnson's cautious, precedent-based approach to orthography in the *Dictionary*—"I have endeavoured to proceed with a scholar's reverence for antiquity," Johnson states in the preface—so it is hardly surprising to find Johnson bluntly censuring Lucas on this point, even though the review ultimately strives to help Lucas gain respectability in the public eye and to encourage a sympathetic reading of the *Essay*.

> This author has been induced by an affected fondness for analogy and derivation, to disfigure his pages with new modes of spelling, which indeed

gives his book a forbidding aspect, and may dispose many to conclude too hastily, that he has very little skill in questions of importance, who has so much leisure to lavish upon trifles. Every book, I suppose, is written to be read: the orthographical innovator very little consults his own interest, for I know few faults so likely to drive off the reader as perpetual and glaring affectation. He that studies singularity, should at least compensate that disgust which his disapprobation of custom naturally produces in all who follow it, by taking a better way than that which he leaves; he that despises the countenance of example should supply its place by the power of truth. But Dr. *Lucas*'s changes are sometimes wrong upon his own principles. . . .[54]

Particularly in the third paragraph of the review, Johnson addresses readers not as a reviewer primarily but as an experienced orthographer reproving an incompetent amateur. A glance through the *Essay* reveals that Johnson's admonitions are very much in order. But it is also worth noting that Johnson's criticisms—pointed though they are—are blended into the review in a manner that minimizes their impact. Had Johnson not established beforehand the prevailing worthiness of Lucas's effort and thus set his spelling oddities in a proper perspective, readers might understandably—but in Johnson's view "too hastily"—conclude that such problems betray a general incompetence. Indeed, in an effort to encourage readers to think of the spelling problems as trivial, Johnson makes a point of asserting at the close of the review's critical portion—eighteen columns of extract follow, stretched over two issues—that Lucas's orthographical blunders "do not lessen the usefulness of his book, though they may diminish the pleasure of perusing it."[55] Though let down by needless tampering with accepted spelling practices, Johnson argues here and in the review as a whole, the *Essay on Waters* will reward readers with its insightful observations on balneology.

A word must be said about the eighteen columns of extract that conclude Johnson's review of the *Essay on Waters*. E. A. Bloom finds this portion of the review, as well as everything else Johnson says apart from his political and orthographical commentary, to be of negligible interest ("anticlimatic" is how Bloom puts the matter).[56] Such a reading makes a certain amount of sense. Samuel Johnson's linguistic and political observations understandably interest modern scholars, while none but the most specialized scientific historian or antiquarian would read the review to learn more about Lucas's contribution to balneology. Plausible though it is, Bloom's position takes insufficient notice of the contemporary circumstances that give Johnson's review its force and coherence. After all, Johnson's chief aim is to win for a deserving but much maligned author a critical mass of readers, and all four parts of the review make interrelated and indispensable contributions to that end. The spirited defense of Lucas's political activities that begin the review are meant to redress his besmirched reputation. Having conditioned readers to read with an open mind if not sympathetically, Johnson then praises Lucas's scholarly thoroughness in the hopes of creating interest in the *Essay*. Indeed, Johnson's commentary on this point would make suitable material for today's dust jackets. The discussion of Lucas's orthography that follows contributes an aura of impartiality and scholarly rigor while defining the spelling problems as a subordinate issue. The extensive extracts come last and are intended to whet further the curiosity created by the preceding material, though here as elsewhere in Johnson's reviews—the Hales and Warton pieces come to mind— Johnson occasionally endorses, qualifies, or questions Lucas's method.

For example, Johnson notes that "every part" of Lucas's rather exotic definition of water—which Lucas treats not "'as a mere element,'" but as it "'occurs to our senses'"—is validated "by experiments."[57] Elsewhere, Johnson takes issue with Lucas's claim that a lifelong habit of bathing in cold water is conducive to robust health, but he does so in a manner that takes for granted the legitimacy of Lucas's standing as a physician and as a scientist.

> It is incident to physicians, I am afraid, beyond all other men, to mistake subsequence for consequence, to use the fallacious inference *post hoc*, ergo *propter hoc*. "The old gentleman," says Dr. *Lucas*, that uses the cold bath, "enjoys in return an uninterrupted state of health." This instance does not prove that the cold bath produces health, but only, that it will not always destroy it. He is well with the bath, he would have been well without it. I have known, every man has known, old men scrupulously careful to avoid cold, who enjoyed in return an uninterrupted state of health.
>
> The caution not to bathe with a full stomach is just, though it is violated every summer day without hurt.
>
> The rules about the posture to be used in the bath, and the directions to forbear to speak during the action of the water, are refinements too minute to deserve attention, he is past much hope from baths to whom speech or silence can make any difference.[58]

Here and for the review as a whole, Johnson proceeds on the assumption that Lucas deserves to be taken seriously, even though some of his prescriptions are, on mature consideration, ill-conceived or overwrought. We are left with the impression, in other words, that *An Essay on Waters* makes stimulating reading even when one finds it necessary to disagree with this or that specific observation.

The *Monthly*'s assessment of the *Essay on Waters* appeared in August 1756, and like Johnson's, which was published two weeks earlier, it acknowledges Lucas's diligence ("If industry may be admitted any part of a writer's merit" Lucas is entitled to "the favour of the public") and firmly but not uncharitably criticizes his orthographical excesses ("though they render him less agreeable, they do not make him less instructive"). But unlike Johnson, the reviewer for the *Monthly* demonstrates little sympathy for Lucas's embittered but largely justifiable defiance of critics and his nagging sense of social isolation. The "candid reader will be more offended at the asperity with which he treats those from whom he dissents," the reviewer declares.[59] Something of a benighted remark, perhaps, but certainly a tenable observation. Indeed, it would be proper to say that the *Monthly* offers a basically serviceable account of Lucas's *Essay*, as does the *Critical*. But the *Literary Magazine* review remains distinctive, because Johnson manages to address the interests of both the author and the reading public without straying beyond what he sees as the proper bounds of contemporaneous criticism. Readers are given a well-informed and thorough introduction to a stimulating and at times politically and pedagogically controversial work. Lucas is treated with every bit of the respect his scientific attainments entitle him to, though Johnson refuses to tread lightly when it comes to the spelling affectations that blight an otherwise worthy treatise.

Philosophical Transactions, Giving Some Account of the Present Undertakings, Studies, and Labours, of the Ingenious, in Many Considerable Parts of the World. Vol. XLIX. Part I. For the Year 1755. Reviewed by Tobias Smollett in the *Critical*, July–September 1756; reviewed by Johnson, 16 Aug 1756; reviewed in the *Monthly* by various writers, September–October 1756. The *Philosophical Transactions*, "the oldest scientific journal in the English-speaking world," began publication in 1665. The annual volumes of the *Philosophical Transactions* comprise abstracts of pioneering experiments in the physical, natural, and practical sciences, summaries of recently published scientific books, papers read at meetings of the Royal Society, correspondence of leading scientific scholars of the day, and the like.[60] Johnson's review of the first part of the forty-ninth volume of the *Philosophical Transactions* offers a rather mixed appraisal of the 444-page work. The appreciative commentary in the first couple of sentences is qualified in the latter half of the paragraph, where Johnson rebukes the compilers for their indifference to religion and the standards of received English. "THIS volume contains many entertaining and many useful narratives and observations," Johnson declares in the opening sentence of his review.

> Many more of equal value might be taken, but we desire to promote, not to hinder the sale of these valuable collections, which have done so much honour to the English nation. We wish, however, that the editors of these

papers would have some regard to the purity of our language, which is too frequently vitiated by their correspondents and translators, and yet more to the sacrosanctity of religion, which seems to be treated with too little reverence when it is represented as hypothetical and controvertible, that all mankind proceed from one original.[61]

Several of Johnson's better-known critical positions surface in this passage. The attack on inept translation, for instance, brings to mind a similar declaration in the preface to the *Dictionary*. "The great pest of speech is frequency of translation," Johnson argues in the preface. The "idleness and ignorance" of careless translators, "if it be suffered to proceed, will reduce us to babble a dialect of *France*." The nationalism embedded in Johnson's praise for English scholars in the *Philosophical Transactions* review not only echoes Johnson's assertion in the preface to the *Dictionary* that the "chief glory of every people arises from its authours," but also anticipates similar commentary published a couple of years later in the *Idler* series. "He that is delighted with experiments, and wishes to know the nature of bodies from certain and visible effects," Johnson states in *Idler* 91 (1760), "is happily placed where the mechanical philosophy was first established by a publick institution [the Royal Society], and from which it was spread to all other countries." The charge of impiety leveled at the compilers of the *Transactions* exemplifies Johnson's embrace of a physico-theological viewpoint—that is, scientific inquiry, properly understood, reveals a providential scheme. Here, Johnson almost certainly means to attack Article V, "A Supplement to the Account of a Distempered Skin," by Henry Baker.[62]

Baker's article is a sequel to a report published nearly a quarter of a century earlier in the *Transactions*, which centered on the extraordinary skin disease afflicting fourteen-year-old "Edward Lambert." Baker examines Lambert in 1755 and discovers that his ailment—"an innumerable company of warts, of a dark-brown colour, and a cylindric figure, rising to a like height, and growing as close as possible to one another; but so stiff and elastic, that, when the hand is drawn over them, they make a rusting noise"—has been passed on to his six children. Here is Baker's conclusion:

> It appears therefore past all doubt, that a race of people may be propagated by this man, having such rugged coats or coverings as himself: and, if this should ever happen, and the accidental original be forgotten, 'tis not improbable they might be deemed a different species of mankind: a consideration, which, would almost lead one to imagine, that if mankind were all produced from one and the same stock, the black skins of negroes, and many other differences of the like kind, might possibly have been originally owing to some such accidental cause.[63]

What irritates Johnson is that Baker—by his own reckoning—awards an unjustified plausibility to the idea that the human species might have evolved and might continue to do so, or that we might in some way be susceptible to mutation, a point of view that clearly stands at odds with Johnson's orthodox Christianity. Brief though it is, the critical portion of the *Literary Magazine* review neatly embodies Johnson's broader critical outlook.

What makes Johnson's review of further interest is the 2,500-word extract, which reproduces Article XXI, pages 96–107, of the *Philosophical Transactions*. Here, the review takes on something of an eccentric air, as Johnson offers readers not a block of text from a treatise on the physical sciences, but an anthropological survey of the inhabitants of Constantinople. The extract reprints a letter from Sir James Porter (1710–86), British ambassador to Constantinople from 1746 to 1762.[64] Porter's letter is addressed to Dr. Mathew Maty (1718–76), whose captious review of Johnson's *Dictionary* prompted the following response from Johnson in the Spring of 1755, when Dr. Adams mentioned his name as a possible assistant editor of Johnson's proposed scholarly journal: "the little black dog! I'd throw him into the Thames."[65] Porter's letter to Maty answers in some detail the following seven questions:

> 1. Whether we may know with any certainty, how many people are generally carried off by the plague at *Constantinople?*
> 2. Whether the number of inhabitants in that capital may be ascertained?
> 3. Whether what has been advanced by some travellers, and from them assumed by writers on politics, be true, that there are more women than men born in the east?
> 4. Whether plurality of wives is in fact, as it was confidently affirmed to be, in the order of nature, favourable to the increase of mankind?
> 5. What is the actual state of inoculation in the east?
> 6. What is become of the printing-house at *Constantinople?* And are there any original maps of the *Turkish* dominions, drawn from actual surveys?
> 7. What sort of learning is cultivated among the *Greeks*, and among the *Turks?*[66]

Johnson's choice of extract can be said to reflect his sympathetic curiosity in non-Western cultures. It is worth recalling that Constantinople provides the setting for Johnson's tragedy, *Irene* (1749). *Rasselas* (1759), "The Vision of Theodore, the Hermit of Teneriffe" (1748), and Johnson's translation/adaptation of Jeremy Lobo's *Voyage to Abyssinia* (1735) are also set outside of Western Europe. The choice of extract can also be read as an expression of Johnson's wide-ranging interests, particularly in medicine and the history of publishing.[67] Interestingly enough, Porter's answer to the query about the Turkish book trade expresses views that very much accord with Johnson's. Indeed, Porter's sentiments parallel Johnson's own commentary on the mid-eighteenth-century London book trade, which is discussed in chapter 1. "The sole drift and end of their [the Turks] study is gain," Porter observes, and "there does not seem the least emulation towards true knowledge: so that the state of letters may be said to remain deplorable, without the least glimmering, or remote prospect of recovery."[68] It is thus possible that the inclusion of Porter's commentary was meant as an oblique criticism of what Johnson viewed as destructive trends in the contemporary British publishing industry.

Equally significant is that Johnson's choice of extract exemplifies his habit of fashioning his book reviews into de facto independent essays that carry a much broader appeal than do the works themselves. As Johnson suggests in the opening paragraph of his review, the various contributions to the *Transactions* are of uneven quality and are plainly intended for a highly specific readership in any case, but the discussion of Constantinople in "Article XXI" makes for captivating copy for the specialist and ordinary reader alike. As we see in many of the reviews Johnson writes of abstruse, or at least bulky, scholarly works—the Birch, Keith, Keyssler, and Lovett volumes come to mind—the extracted material transmits worthwhile knowledge to readers of the *Literary Magazine* whether they are in the market for scholarly works or are content to read popular contemporary magazines strictly for amusement or diversion.

Tobias Smollett's review of the *Philosophical Transactions* in the *Critical* begins by criticizing the indifferent editing practices of the compilers. "We could have wished that this performance had been better weeded before it was presented to the public," Smollett observes. "At present it looks like a collection of rude drawings in a school of young painters, among which we, now and then, meet with the sketches of a master." Extensive extracts of various scientific experiments follow over the next two numbers of the *Critical*. The *Monthly* review of the *Transactions* is very similar to its counterpart in the *Critical*, insofar as it attempts to give readers a solid idea of the *Philosophical Transactions* by quoting generously from the work. On the whole, the two leading review journals offer readers substantive introductions to the work. Book buyers who purchased the *Philosophical Transactions* based on reviews in the *Monthly* or the *Critical*, in other words, would have had no grounds to complain that they were given inadequate or misleading information.[69] Johnson's review stands apart from competing pieces published in the two leading review journals because it reflects both his robust intellect and his desire to fashion his review into a cogent, informative essay regardless of whether readers are moved to purchase the *Philosophical Transactions* or not.

Richard Lovett (1692–1780), *The Subtil Medium Proved.* Reviewed by Johnson, 15 September 1756; reviewed by John Berkenhout in the *Monthly,* December 1756; not reviewed in the *Critical.* A lay cleric at Worcester Cathedral from 1722 until his death, Richard Lovett also authored a handful of treatises on electricity, thus exemplifying the burgeoning interest in scientific experimentation during the eighteenth century among both occasional projectors and serious scholars alike.[70] How Lovett's *Subtil Medium* came to Johnson's attention is not known. The volume was not reviewed previously in the two leading review journals, nor does it appear that Johnson knew Lovett or his copublishers, John Hinton and William Sandby. Johnson's public and private writings reveal a keen and intelligent interest in groundbreaking developments in the physical sciences—particularly electricity, as Richard Schwartz and William K. Wimsatt have shown—so it is not hard to imagine him being moved to consult the *Subtil Medium* after reading an advertisement for the work, or after hearing of it through casual conversation.[71]

Johnson's review comprises a half-dozen sentences of critical commentary, which are quoted here, followed by five columns of extract.

> ELECTRICITY is the great discovery of the present age, and the great object of philosophical curiosity. It is perhaps designed by providence for the excitement of human industry, that the qualities of bodies should be discovered gradually from time to time. How many wonders may yet lie hid in every particle of matter no man can determine. The power of Electricity is sufficient to shew us that nature is far from being exhausted, and that we have yet much to do before we shall be fully acquainted with the properties of these things which are always in our hands and before our eyes.
>
> The writer of this pamphlet pretends not to learning, but he seems at least to be diligent in his enquiries, and faithful in his relations. The main works we shall perhaps not examine, but we exhibit here his introduction which contains a history of Electricity that may give some entertainment to those who are not yet much versed in philosophical studies.[72]

Perhaps it would be correct for us to conclude that Johnson is much more interested in electricity as a concept than he is in the specifics of Lovett's book. Even so, we should not forget that it is Lovett's investigations that spark the eloquent observations on scientific inquiry here—Johnson's review of Hoadly and Wilson's *Electrical Experiments* is uninspired by comparison— and that on the whole Lovett would have had little reason to bemoan his reception in the *Literary Magazine.* Indeed, a survey of Lovett's preface demonstrates that Johnson's commentary very much conforms to the *Literary Magazine*'s prefatory pledge to advance the interests of worthy authors and to alert book buyers to the recent availability of meritorious titles.

Lovett's preface is conventional in essential matters of form: the occasion for the work is discussed, readers are introduced to the topics addressed in the volume, issues of scholarly methodology are considered, and so forth. Relevant here is the discussion of Lovett's overarching aim, which is to inspire a wider interest in the practical aspects of electrical experimentation, the traditional view of electricity as "of so abstruse a Nature, as to be scarce explicable on any rational Principles whatsoever" being no longer valid if the experiments set forth in the *Subtil Medium* are any indication. Also of note in the preface is Lovett's frank self-assessment. Readers are asked to forgive the author's sporadic grammatical mistakes and his paltry knowledge of Greek and Latin. Elsewhere in the preface Lovett admits that the *Subtil Medium* contains "some Things which may appear a little heterodox, and something different from certain Philosophical Points, which, for a considerable Time past, have been settled, as undeniable, by the greatest Philosophers." But such should not put off readers, Lovett adds, if only because the scholarly rigor on display here and the potential significance of the subject matter entitle the *Subtil Medium* to a "fair" and "candid" "Hearing" in the marketplace.[73]

In what manner does the *Subtil Medium*'s prefatory essay bear on the *Literary Magazine* piece? We can read the first four sentences of Johnson's review as a solid endorsement of Lovett's call for further attempts to determine the properties of electricity. Lovett is on the mark, Johnson suggests here, when he argues that the boundaries of electrical experimentation—especially its practical applications—have yet to be reached. Johnson's remark about Lovett's scholarly trustworthiness ("he seems at least to be diligent in his enquiries, and faithful in his relations"), meanwhile, addresses Lovett's worry that the absence of learned terminology might foster unwarranted doubts about his competence as a projector—hardly a minor point when we recall that being a projector in the eighteenth century did not presumptively command the esteem of contemporaries, as Johnson's *Adventurer* 99 (1753) points out.[74] Also worth noting are the five columns of extract, which are drawn from Lovett's prefatory account of the history of electrical experimentation rather than from the main body of the work because, as Johnson says, it is hoped that the review will arouse interest in the *Subtil Medium* among "those who are not yet much versed in philosophical studies."[75] Lovett's prefatory history is successful enough in conveying the drama of what was in 1756 an emerging field of scientific inquiry (e.g., "This sudden and wonderful discovery," Lovett writes as he describes an experiment performed in 1746, "amazed the whole European world for some time"), but what gives the extract a much greater impact is its relation to Johnson's eloquent commentary on physico-theology that precedes it.[76] What the review ultimately amounts to, in other words, is a deftly executed philosophical essay on electricity, coauthored by Johnson and Lovett. Johnson interprets the humanistic and theological significance behind the recent headline-grabbing experiments in electricity, while Lovett provides the necessary historical context.[77]

The *Monthly*'s three-page notice of Lovett's treatise hardly qualifies as impartial or even as particularly discerning criticism. As Lovett himself would put the matter two years later in his rebuttal to critics, the *Subtil Medium* was quite unfairly "knock'd o'the Head by the *Monthly Review*."[78] The reviewer—perhaps John Berkenhout—begins by calling attention to the *Subtil Medium*'s needlessly prolix subtitle (157 words) and Lovett's unscholarly idiom. "Mr. Lovett has saved us the trouble of telling the Reader what he may expect to meet with in this pamphlet, the above title being a compendious Epitome of the whole performance. It will also be sufficient to apprise" readers, the reviewer continues, "that whatever discoveries may be contained in it, they are not delivered in a very elegant style." These are essentially legitimate observations, of course, but rather superficial, and in the case of Lovett's style unwarranted as well, given Lovett's own remarks on the matter in the prefatory note (which the reviewer quotes). Berkenhout does make mention of Lovett's "candour and sincerity," and a word of praise, however grudging, is said on behalf of Lovett's illuminating discussion of the medical applications of electricity. But ultimately Lovett is portrayed as a well-meaning but eccentric dabbler who, almost in spite of himself, has managed to make a useful observation or two on electricity and medicine. The *Subtil Medium* "may, at least, be of as much advantage to Society as many others that are written in a more scientifical, and more elegant manner," Berkenhout declares. Even so, Lovett is plainly ignorant "of the common principles of the Newtonian Philosophy; and, consequently, but indifferently qualified to account for the many surprising Phaenomena of Electricity."[79]

Reviewing Lovett's work amounts to a minor affair for both the *Literary Magazine* and the *Monthly,* but the differences between the two commentaries are instructive nevertheless. Johnson would never dwell on shortcomings admitted to in the preface, as his counterpart does here. Nor would Johnson bother to criticize a detailed and accurate, though perhaps overly long, title page, a feature that many prospective book buyers may have viewed as advantageous in any case. More significantly, Johnson's review can stand alone as an intellectually weighty yet widely accessible essay on an emerging field of knowledge.

Benjamin Hoadly (1706–57), F.R.S., and Benjamin Wilson (1721–88), F.R.S., *Observations of a Series of Electrical Experiments*. Reviewed by Johnson, September 1756; reviewed in the *Monthly,* November 1756 (reviewer unknown); not reviewed in the *Critical*. Unlike the amateur Richard Lovett, Messrs. Hoadly and Wilson were established scholars who were well regarded for their pioneering work in the physical sciences when the *Observations* appeared in 1756. It is also worth noting that, quite apart from their reputations as projectors, both Hoadly and Wilson enjoyed success in fields far removed from the laboratory. Hoadly, who was elected Fellow of the Royal Society in 1728, gained a measure of literary fame from the production of his comedy, *The Suspicious Husband* (1747), which featured David Garrick in the lead role. Wilson's work as a painter rivaled that of his achievements as a projector. A friend of Hogarth's, Wilson was commissioned to paint portraits of Thomas Gray, Lord Lyttleton, and other prominent contemporaries. The *Observations* was Wilson's third publication; his first appeared in 1746, his second in 1750, one year before he was elected Fellow of the Royal Society. Seven other works related to electricity followed over the next three decades and complemented the fifteen papers Wilson published as part of the *Philosophical Transactions* series.[80]

In fact, versions of the experiments contained in the *Observations* first appeared in the forty-eighth volume of the *Philosophical Transactions*, published in 1754. A second edition of the *Observations*—eighty-six quarto pages in length, ten pages longer than the first edition—appeared in 1759. Both editions were published by Thomas Payne (1719–99), brother of William Payne (d. 1779?), who authored in *An Introduction to the Game of Draughts* in 1756. Johnson wrote the preface and dedicatory address of William Payne's *Game of Draughts*. Given his interest in electricity, perhaps Johnson became interested in the *Observations* through his connections with William Payne, the publisher Thomas Payne's brother. It is also possible that Johnson may have come across a copy of the *Observations* in Thomas Payne's bookshop, where "the chief book-lovers of the day used to assemble."[81]

As is the case with his review of Richard Lovett's the *Subtil Medium Prov'd*, Johnson's commentary on Hoadly and Wilson's volume reflects his interest in cutting-edge experiments in electricity. Curiously, Johnson eschews substantive evaluation of the experiments themselves and the broader significance of electrical experimentation, in direct contrast to his review of Lovett's *Subtil Medium*, and instead focuses his critical commentary on the celebrity of the two authors:

> This series of observations and experiments will undoubtedly be received with uncommon regard by the inquisitive and speculative, being the product of two men, of whom one is eminent for mathematical learning, and the other for experimental curiosity, and both at once the favourites of those who cultivate the abstruser and politer arts. One has already published the *Lectures on Respiration*, and the other *Electrical Experiments*.[82]

Johnson plainly thinks highly of Hoadly and Wilson, but he introduces material taken from their work by warning readers of its limited appeal. What is going on here? It seems that in the Hoadly and Wilson piece, if not in most of his other reviews, Johnson gestures toward the sort of reviewing he had in mind when he considered founding a learned review journal in 1755. It is worth noting, for instance, that the extract basically recapitulates recent breakthroughs in electrical experimentation made by Benjamin Franklin in the late 1740s, specifically the concept of polarity and the concept that there existed only one kind of electricity rather than two.[83] Johnson's extract reprints the first seven pages of the volume, in which the authors introduce their subject and place their work in a historical context, and pages 68 through 74, which is the point at which Hoadly and Wilson summarize the results of their investigations.[84] Johnson's 3,300-word extract begins by making a case for the fluidlike nature of electricity, its ubiquity, and, most important, its unity. "[E]very body we have it in our power to make any experiment upon," Hoadly and Wilson write, "has naturally within it (before it is disturbed by our experiment) one certain quantity of this fluid, in such a state of rarity or density, as is most agreeable to the nature of each particular body." Readers of the *Literary Magazine* review next are introduced to the concept of polarity, that is, the rubbing together of two items leaves one with an excess charge, the other with a deficiency. When "we say a body is electrified . . . either the body has by the force of the experiment made in order to electrify it, been forced to part with a share of this electrical fluid, that naturally belonged to it during the experiment, and to remain without it some time after the experiment is over: or to admit more than it naturally had within it, during the experiment, and to remain so overloaded, some time after the experiment is over."[85] As these passages demonstrate, the extracted material can be characterized as technical, perhaps dauntingly so, to those unfamiliar or uninterested in electrical experimentation. Nevertheless, the extract amounts to a coherent introductory essay on the nature of electricity. In the Hoadly and Wilson review, then, Johnson essentially moves toward bridging the gap between reviewing for a popular readership and publishing abstracts of works meant for a narrow, learned readership—much as he does in his reviews of Keith's *Catalogue of Scottish Bishops* and the *Philosophical Transactions*.

One other point is worth making about the extract. In one of his connective remarks Johnson straddles the line between firmly endorsing the work and leaving matters completely up to prospective purchasers of the volume. "Many experiments are mentioned, which seem to have been made with great exactness, and have been considered with uncommon subtilty of reasoning," Johnson declares, "but as the experiments are connected with each other, and the theory arising from them cannot be well understood without them, this treatise does not well admit of an abstract." As is typical of his manner of proceeding when evaluating the work of contemporaries, Johnson here introduces readers to what *seems* to him to be a meritorious work, but it is the reading public—and not Johnson in his capacity as a reviewer—who will determine the value of Hoadly and Wilson's volume.

Though much shorter than Johnson's, the review of the *Observations* in the *Monthly* bears a striking and perhaps an unseemly resemblance to the *Literary Magazine* piece that preceded it by two and a half months. The *Monthly* review begins with a general and rather humdrum statement about the rigors of modern scientific method, whereby no principle or hypothesis is allowed credit unless it is validated by experimentation. The block of extract that follows, however, basically amounts to an abridgment of Johnson's review. The *Monthly* reprints about two-thirds of material that also happens to appear in the *Literary Magazine* piece and contains nothing not found in Johnson's review. What is more, the *Monthly* reviewer's rationale for not reproducing complete experiments conforms at least vaguely to Johnson's remarks on the same point and also parrots Johnson's observation in the beginning of his review that Hoadly and Wilson's book will appeal only to "the inquisitive and the speculative." Here is what the *Monthly* reviewer says on the matter: "As it is impossible to give the substance of their experiments, without transcribing too much from their pamphlet, we must refer our Philosophical Readers to the whole."[86] Here is Johnson on the same point: because "the experiments are connected with each other, and the theory arising from them cannot be well understood without them," Johnson declares, "this treatise does not well admit of an abstract."[87] It is at least possible, then, that the *Monthly* reviewer abridged Johnson's earlier piece without ever having laid eyes on Hoadly and Wilson's *Observations*. Indeed, it strains credulity for us to believe that the *Monthly* reviewer, confronted with the seventy-six page *Observations*, chose to approach the volume in exactly the same manner as Johnson did and, in so doing, extracted the very same material.

Samuel Bever (fl. 1756), ***The Cadet: A Military Treatise, by an Officer****.* Reviewed by James Grainger in the *Monthly,* October 1756; reviewed by Tobias Smollett in the *Critical,* October 1756; reviewed by Johnson, 15 November 1756. The anonymous *Cadet*—the title page merely tells us that its author is "an Officer"—was actually written by Samuel Bever. At the time of the publication of *The Cadet* in early October 1756, Bever held the rank of captain. He was promoted to the rank of major shortly afterward, perhaps on account of what certainly has proved to be his substantive contribution to British military science. The volume's popularity finds expression in the appearance of at least three later editions between 1756 and

1762. [88] Bever's 244-page volume (octavo) is part military commonplace book and part tactics and training manual. Its purpose is to make available to the British army's junior officers the best that has been thought and said—chiefly by continental soldiers—on military theory and practice. "In the Course of reading from which the following Attempt is drawn, I have endeavoured to collect every Thing applicable to, or corresponding with, our Service," Bever writes in his dedicatory address to the duke of Cumberland, "and what perhaps may be of Use to some of your Officers who don't understand the Originals, or who have too much Employment or too little Curiosity to peruse those Treatises throughout."[89] The book comprises twenty-four chapters: the first seven concern military administration and discipline; chapters 8 through 19 examine the various branches and ranks of the army; the final five chapters discuss military ethics and honor. Bever's volume thus can be said roughly to correspond to the early and midcareer officer education programs run by the U.S. armed services, in which enrollees are taught the history and traditions of their profession and branch of service as well as the latest developments in strategy and tactics.

The appearance of the first edition of *The Cadet* can be said to reflect, at least in a minor way, both the growing concern in Britain with the staffing and performance of its army and the marketplace demand for reading material of every sort.[90] With Britain engaged since May 1756 in what was in effect a global war with France, the means of raising and training land forces was a prominent political issue when *The Cadet* appeared, as Johnson's own editorials in the *Literary Magazine* bear out.[91] From the perspective of the military historian, *The Cadet* is a good example of the many drill books that sought to help the British army reform itself following the lackluster performances during the War of the Austrian Succession.[92] Bever's volume should also interest students of the eighteenth-century book trade, as *The Cadet* obviously was expected to make a profit for its publisher, William Johnston, who evidently assumed that the subject matter would appeal to a critical mass of England's increasingly diversified reading public.[93] Indeed, the subject matter of *The Cadet*, as well as the timing of its publication, vaguely anticipates the sorts of popular books on warfare—in particular those written by military members that dwell on the minutiae of technology and tactics—that cluttered the bookshelves of *Barnes and Noble*, *Waldenbooks*, and the other major chain stores during and immediately after the Persian Gulf War in 1991.

The Cadet received a warm reception in the two leading review journals. The *Monthly* and the *Critical* each provide a neat and remarkably comprehensive survey of *The Cadet*, and while this or that particular point is criticized, both journals wholeheartedly endorse Bever's effort. "Upon the whole, it appears to us, that tho' this gentleman is a modest, he is not the less an intelligent, writer," observes James Grainger in the concluding paragraph of his review in the *Monthly*. "[T]here is no doubt but his work will be found useful to every rank of military men." Writing in the *Critical*, Tobias Smollett has equally good things to say about Bever's volume, which in his view is "the effect of judgment, reflection, study and experience." Smollett concludes by recommending Bever's volume "to the attention of all the youths that embrace a military life; in full confidence that they will find it replete with useful maxims, the result of judgment, candour and experience."[94] *The Cadet*, then, was praised in strong terms by the two leading review journals of the day—a not inconsiderable achievement for the only publication of a soldier by trade.

In contrast to what one finds in the reviews published a couple of weeks earlier in the *Monthly* and the *Critical*, the *Literary Magazine* offers readers a mixed account of *The Cadet*. The first half of Johnson's review is temperamentally rather peevish, perhaps foreshadowing *Idlers* 5 and 8 (1758), which mock British infantrymen. It is also possible that Johnson's dismissive tone in the opening of the review is meant to offset what Johnson must have construed as excessively appreciative reviews published two weeks earlier in the *Monthly* and the *Critical*. "This book consists of quotations chiefly from French authors not ill connected, with some remarks by the compiler. The book is of no great use but to military men," Johnson adds, and so not surprisingly it is "written in a dialect which none but they can understand." An extract on field maneuvers, approximately four hundred words in length, follows. Johnson's opening critical observation certainly should strike us as grossly out of character. Indeed, the dismissive commentary here is unique in Johnson's reviewing canon, because we are encouraged to despise not the book itself, but the field of knowledge it surveys. Johnson might easily have said similar things about White, Home, Hales, Hoadly and Wilson, and Russell, yet these authors are treated charitably, if not always deferentially, in regard to the assumptions they make about their prospective readerships and, in particular, their reliance on professional jargon. All the more surprising is that, unlike the Hampton, Lovett, and Russell reviews in particular, Johnson ignores Bever's self-deprecatory remarks in his prefatory address to his intended readers, fellow military officers. "I wish I could have added a few *English* Names to the following List of Authors," Bever declares in his prefatory "To the Officers of the Army," "but I am sorry to say, that a disappointed Search for Books of this Kind in our Language, exonerates me from the Guilt of Plagiarism from my Countrymen." Bever goes on to apologize for the roughness of his translations and invites readers to offer more polished alternatives, which we are told "shall be received with Gratitude."[95] Johnson's mildly unfavorable review at some level reflects, perhaps, his sympathy for the Stuart cause. The volume, after all, is dedicated to the duke of Cumberland, who won fame for crushing the Jacobite forces at the battle of Culloden in 1746. It is also possible that Bever's indifferent abilities as a translator annoyed Johnson, who was himself an accomplished translator of a book written in French, *The Voyage to Abyssinia* (1735). But Bever admits to his inadequacies as a translator up front and emphatically reminds readers that his chief purpose is to transmit important military maxims. Declarations of this sort normally earn authors a charitable review from Johnson, especially if their books are otherwise meritorious, as Bever's in fact is.

Indeed, history does not appear to have validated Johnson's depreciative assessment of the volume. *The Cadet* "displayed a selection of material the choice of which was both judicious and economic," observes J. A. Houlding in his scholarly study of British army training during the eighteenth century. "Though hardly deep," Bever's volume "was a useful introduction of the service to young officers and might also have stimulated them to further reading."[96] Given the standards by which Johnson judges every other work he reviews, *The Cadet* should have received spirited praise. After all, by everyone else's reckoning Bever meets the objectives he sets for himself, that is, to provide the British military with sound, historically grounded advice on how to improve operations. The subject of *The Cadet* is a timely one, moreover, and Bever's dedication to William Augustus, duke of Cumberland, and his prefatory address to fellow military officers provide notification enough to prospective book buyers of Bever's intended readership and the nature of his commentary. What we see in the first half of the *Literary Magazine* piece, evidently, is Johnson's loathing of a professional military, an attitude that surfaces prominently in several of his political writings of the 1750s, most notably the *Idler*s mentioned previously and his "Speech on the Rochefort Expedition" (1757).[97]

The second half of Johnson's review is, by comparison, more appreciative. "One of the most remarkable and entertaining passages" in Bever's volume "is an account of a military academy," Johnson observes, perhaps revealing his own interest in the details of military training.[98] An extract that discusses the German military academy at Neustadt is followed by Johnson's grudging affirmation of the importance of a professional military. "If an army is necessary, it is fit that the duties of an army should be known, and this book may be fitly recommended conducive to that knowledge."[99] Johnson's acknowledgment here of the potential worthiness of Bever's volume may simply be an accommodation to the press of contemporary circumstance. Britain needed a well-trained land army if it hoped to secure its North American possessions (a policy that Johnson opposed) and, perhaps more important to readers of the *Literary Magazine*, if Britain hoped to thwart any invasion that France might undertake. All things considered, the Bever review is one of Johnson's least successful, as not one of his other reviews can be said to offer book buyers what is in truth a cramped understanding of its subject.

WORKS IN THE NATURAL SCIENCES

Alexander Russell (1715–68), *Natural History of Aleppo.* Reviewed by Johnson, 15 June 1756; reviewed by John Armstrong in the *Critical,* May 1756; reviewed by Gregory Sharpe in the *Monthly,* August 1756. Scottish born and educated, Alexander Russell worked in Aleppo from 1740 until 1753 as the resident physician for an English industrial project. Russell eventually managed to make a name for himself with his medical and biological researches: in May 1756—the month when the *Natural History* was published—he was elected Fellow of the Royal Society.[100] Russell's *Natural History* can be said to exemplify the interests of the age. Travel narratives of all kinds, including natural histories of foreign locations, were amongst the most popular forms of literature produced during the eighteenth century. It is thus no surprise to find Johnson's *Literary Magazine* and the two major review journals allocating space to Russell's essentially meritorious but at times ineptly conveyed commentary on the climate, population, and natural features of an Arabic city and its environs. The *Monthly* review of Russell's *Natural History,* the last of the three, offers mostly bland summary and extract, the few appreciative remarks that come at the end perhaps telling us more about contemporary England's indiscriminate curiosity about distant parts of the world than about the *Natural History* itself: "We should own our obligations to such writers as the Author of the Natural History of Aleppo," asserts Gregory Sharpe, "who, with great fidelity, and sufficient abilities, adds to our store of knowledge, both in natural and political history."[101] Generous remarks as far as they go, certainly, but Sharpe's review otherwise offers no analysis that might validate his lofty generalizations.

John Armstrong also writes approvingly of Russell's *Natural History* in his review for the *Critical,* but the commendation that concludes his piece—Russell's account is "distinct, concise," and his scholarly method "rational, judicious, and simple"—bears no substantive relation to the analysis that precedes it, apart from contradicting the brief and rather controversial reproaches of Russell for his overreliance on "*Greek* and *Latin* names" (the traditional lingua francas of science and medicine) and his inclusion of extensive meteorological tables (too much detail is probably better than too little in ambitious studies of the impact of climate on human health).

Perhaps not surprisingly, given the intense contemporary debates surrounding English usage and the *Critical*'s view of itself as an arbiter of literary standards, the bulk of Armstrong's review is given over to a detailed survey of Russell's various stylistic blunders. What does come as a surprise, however, is that Armstrong—who was trained as a physician—neglects to say anything of substance regarding Russell's observations on the plague and other local diseases, which take up the major part of the *Natural History*.[102]

In his prefatory "Advertisement" Russell asks readers to make allowances for his graceless style, the inevitable by-product, he says, of many years lived where English is not spoken. "When it is considered that the Author resided many years abroad, and conversed daily in other languages more than in his own, which he had but little leisure to cultivate, the defects in his stile, it is hoped, will be forgiven."[103] Armstrong briefly acknowledges this point but goes on to make Russell's solecisms the centerpiece of his review anyway. Such an emphasis makes sense in light of the intense contemporary interest in matters of usage, certainly, but one is left to wonder why more is not said in regard to the general character of the *Natural History*.[104] The need to convince the public of its usefulness and literary discernment in this instance, it seems, impels the *Critical* to embrace an antagonistic relation with Russell even though common sense would counsel otherwise. Indeed, readers interested in accounts of remote locations—and they must have been legion, given the great contemporary popularity of travel works—who looked to the *Critical* for insight on Russell's volume almost certainly would have been disappointed with Armstrong's review.

Johnson's review is remarkable chiefly for its relation to the *Critical* piece. In the absence of conclusive evidence one cannot be sure, of course, but it appears that Johnson either decided to peruse Russell's work after reading the notice in the *Critical* or, having already selected the *Natural History* for review when the *Critical* piece appeared, chose to craft his review in the form of a rebuttal. Though by no means a prodigious achievement, Johnson evidently concluded, Russell's *Natural History* exhibits an essential worthiness and was thus entitled to an evenhanded and illuminating review.

Johnson makes no dogmatic pronouncements in the *Literary Magazine* review, but he does offer prospective book buyers a sympathetic survey of Russell's volume. The lead sentence of Johnson's review, for instance, deftly condenses Russell's aims as stated in the *Natural History*'s prefatory "Advertisement." Russell initially set out to catalog the diseases of Aleppo and its environs, Johnson states, but he was "insensibly led to enlarge his plan, into an account of the natural productions of the place and the customs of the inhabitants." In the next two sentences the review more obviously takes on the character of a rebuttal. Russell "makes no magnificent professions, and has performed as much as he promised," Johnson declares in what can be read as a response to *Critical*'s emphasis on the *Natural History*'s various inadequacies. "His accounts have all the appearance of truth, and his stile, though it has been censured, is not more vitious than that of many writers, who have had better opportunities of cultivating our language."[105] Russell is a trustworthy if not a particularly eloquent natural historian, in other words, and while his volume cannot be ranked with the greatest of its kind, it is worth recalling that his objectives were rather modest to start with. Interestingly enough, Johnson here pauses to vindicate Russell from the criticisms directed at his style by the *Critical*. This is a distinctive trait of Johnson's reviewing: we often find him attempting at some level to negate what we might term exploitative censures found in the *Monthly* or the *Critical*, that is, attacks centering on imperfections admitted to in the prefatory material of the work under review. In this case Johnson believed, first, that Russell's stylistic problems were not quite the nuisance suggested by the *Critical* and, second, that Russell's admission of such problems in the prefatory material—far from warranting censure— reflects an admirable forthrightness.

More significantly, in the twelve columns of extract that flesh out the Russell review Johnson avoids quoting from the weakest sections of the *Natural History*, though these areas are noted: "there is nothing very observable" in Russell's descriptions of diseases; Russell's meteorological tables are similarly unremarkable. Instead, Johnson emphasizes the more attractive aspects of Russell's work. Nearly five columns are devoted to an abridgment of Russell's descriptive analysis of the plague, observations that, Johnson claims, "deserve particular regard." Readers are also introduced to Russell's survey of Aleppo's exotic wildlife ("the *sheep* with the *great tail*"; "*Hyenas* . . . of which our author had the opportunity of examining one that was killed"; "*serpents* extremely venomous") and the day-to-day lives of Aleppo's inhabitants ("their beds which consist only of a matrass and a coverlet, are made in summer on the top of the house"; "When they are at home they amuse themselves with chess"). It is worth noting here that Johnson relies not on direct quotation in relating details of this kind but on skillful summary. Indeed, Johnson's narration creates the impression that Russell is a much better stylist than he actually is.[106] All things considered, the Russell review very much lives up to the pledges Johnson makes in the *Literary Magazine*'s prefatory note: an attempt is made to defend a worthy author from unreasonable criticisms, while readers are given an appreciative introduction to a flawed work, certainly, but one hardly devoid of meritorious observations, as the generous amount of extracted material demonstrates. Readers nowadays may be inclined to dismiss this review as a trifling bit of commentary—a view not without justification, given the paucity of forthright, trenchant criticism. But if we try to put ourselves in the position of a contemporary reader with an interest in natural history who also happened to read Armstrong's earlier piece, Johnson's review takes on much greater critical force. This is particularly true with regard to the discerning selection of quotation and the intelligent abridgments, which may have been just enough to convince even skeptical book buyers that Russell's volume was worth consulting.

William Borlase (1695–1772), *Observations on the Ancient and Present State of the Islands of Scilly*. Reviewed by Johnson, 15 June 1756; reviewed by Tobias Smollett in the *Critical,* January/February 1756; reviewed by Sir Tanfield Leman in the *Monthly,* May 1756. William Borlase's literary career, much like that of Johnson's friend Thomas Birch, provides an example of the enduring importance of traditional forms of patronage to aspiring authors in mid-eighteenth-century England.[107] After taking his B.A. and M.A. from Oxford University, Borlase was ordained an Anglican priest and given a living near Penzance in Cornwall. Borlase soon acquired a reputation as a conscientious and diligent cleric, but it was the patronage of Charles Lyttleton (1714–68), bishop of Carlyle, that led to his election as a Fellow of the Royal Society in 1750.[108] The relationship between traditional patronage and mid-eighteenth-century literary careers finds expression in the opening sentences of the *Observations*, which is framed as a letter from Borlase to Lyttleton:

> If I fall short of any one of my obligations to you, don't let it be imputed to my negligence, but to the number of those obligations, and the difficulty of leveling accounts where there is so much due: among the rest, since you are not contented with the short sketch I have already given you of the SCILLY ISLANDS, I acknowledge my promise to give you a particular account of my little voyages to them, and instead of apologizing for not doing it sooner, I proceed to acquit myself of that engagement as well as I can.[109]

We are given to understand that Lyttleton provided Borlase with moral and, perhaps, with material support as well. Readers are led to believe here that Lyttleton functioned as an academic supervisor of sorts, encouraging Borlase to expand on the worthy but inadequate commentary on the Scilly Islands that Borlase had published two years earlier in the *Philosophical Transactions*.[110]

Borlase's 140-page anthropological, historical, and topographical account of the Scilly Islands received a rather tepid reception in the two leading review journals. Both the *Monthly* and the *Critical* applaud Borlase for calling attention to the contemporary strategic significance of the islands—which he does briefly, between pages 129 and 132—but neither journal seems much impressed by Borlase's contribution to natural history. Tobias Smollett points out in the closing sentence of his review that Borlase's volume makes "some just observations on the importance of these islands to the *British* nation, and offers some judicious hints for rendering them still more important and defensible."[111] Nevertheless, Smollett opens his review by characterizing the *Observations* as a dull, tumid work. Borlase's "subject is so rocky and barren, that it cannot produce much entertainment or instruction," Smollett declares.

> The inhabitants boast neither antiquity, history, nor tradition.—Except the coarse, uncultivated soil and naked rocks, all that presents itself to the eye amount[s] to no more than a few rude stones, supposed to be the remains of temples consecrated to the worship of the Druids, a very few burrows of the pagan burying places, karns, or heaps of stones, the ruins of an abbey, the fragments of an old fortification, wretched farm-houses, one or two miserable villages, and a curious light-house.

Smollett adds that Borlase has made the *Observations* bulkier than its subject warrants by describing the flora, fauna, and landscape in very great detail, and by adding "a very dry historical or rather chronological account of charters, and some conjectures."[112] Discriminating book buyers, Smollett would thus have us believe, will find that they get little value for their money should they choose to purchase Borlase's volume.

Sir Tanfield Leman basically agrees with Smollett, asserting in his review for the *Monthly* that Borlase "does not greatly excel" as a naturalist. Even so, Borlase "has judiciously and clearly pointed out the importance of these islands to Great Britain; the prejudice that accrue[s] from their falling into an enemy's hands; what is wanting for their protection and encouragement."[113] Clearly, a potential invasion from France was much on the minds of the two reviewers as they evaluated Borlase's work, the Seven Years' War having begun a couple of weeks after Leman's review appeared at the end of May 1756. Certainly, war must have appeared imminent when Smollett wrote his review eleven weeks or so before the formal declaration of hostilities between England and France on 18 May 1756.

The reviews in the *Monthly* and the *Critical* must have come as a great disappointment to Borlase, if only because the one aspect of the *Observations* given favorable attention was incidental to the aims of the work. In fact, it seems at least possible that Borlase added the passages on the military significance of the islands strictly as a means of improving the volume's prospects in the marketplace. Borlase's article on the Scilly Islands in the *Philosophical Transactions* (volume 48, part 1), which served as a precursor to the *Observations*, and the substance of the *Observations* itself tell us that Borlase's true interests are scholarly rather than political.

The *Literary Magazine* review of the *Observations* differs significantly from its two predecessors and must have pleased Borlase on account of its evenhandedness and thoroughness. It seems that Johnson's review is meant to rebut Smollett's piece in the *Critical*, which had appeared two and a half months earlier. To begin with, Johnson says nothing about the strategic importance of the Scilly Islands—though the final paragraph of the review contains Borlase's claim that the islands "are of great importance to the trade of *England* both in peace and war"—and instead offers brief but spirited praise of Borlase's achievement as a natural historian. "This is one of the most pleasing and elegant pieces of local enquiry that our country has produced," Johnson declares, allusively rejecting Smollett's suggestion that the work is dull-witted and swollen beyond reason. A 5,000-word block of extract follows. What is noteworthy here is that Johnson either quotes from or paraphrases fifty of the volume's 140 pages of text, thus offering readers a judiciously assembled introduction to Borlase's volume.[114] Johnson's extract, moreover, can be interpreted as a series of responses to Smollett's discrete criticisms in the *Critical*. For example, Johnson reprints Borlase's ethnographical and economic history of the Scilly Islanders, which we can read as a rebuttal to Smollett's claim that the inhabitants "boast neither antiquity, history, nor tradition." What is more, Johnson introduces Borlase's survey of the ancient economy of Scilly in terms that can be read as a rejoinder to Smollett's specific claim that Borlase's "conjectures" are "dry" and essentially useless. "Mr. *Borlase* makes a curious enquiry after the ancient *British*," Johnson states, "who traded with the *Phoenician* and *Roman* merchants, and delivers his conjecture in these words."[115] The concluding portion of the extract that discusses the history of the Scilly Islanders warrants particular attention, because it exemplifies Johnson's characterization of the narrative as "curious"[116] and, correspondingly, specifically refutes Smollett's assertion that the inhabitants possess no heritage worthy of scholarly attention:

> I [Borlase] conclude therefore, that these islands have undergone some great catastrophe, and besides the apparent diminution of their islets by sea and tempest, must have suffered greatly by a subsidence of the land (the common consequence of earthquakes) attended by a sudden inundation in those parts where the abovementioned ruins, fences, mines, and other things of which we have no vestiges now remaining, formerly stood. This inundation probably destroy'd many of the ancient inhabitants, and so terrified those who survived, and had wherewithal to support themselves elsewhere, that they forsook these islands, by which mean the people who were the *Aborigines*, and corresponded so long with the *Phoenicians*, *Greeks*, and

Romans were reduc'd to the last gasp. The few poor remains of the desolation might soon lose sight of their ancient prosperity and eminence, by their necessary attention to food and rayment; no easy acquisitions, when their low-lands, ports and towns were overwhelmed by the sea.[117]

Contrary to what Smollett contends in the *Critical*, Borlase's narrative as retailed by Johnson contains no shortage of engaging material. Essentially, we are given to understand here that the tiny Scilly Islands, an isolated and sparsely populated part of the British nation, was once the center of a bustling civilization that suddenly and violently came to an end.

Also included in Johnson's review is Borlase's lengthy and arresting description of the *"Giants-Castle,"* a promontory near the water's edge once used by pirates as a hiding place. Borlase's descriptions of Druid ceremonial and burial grounds and the remains of the abbey on the island of St. Nicholas are inserted as well, thus implicitly rebutting Smollett's dismissive remarks on these topics and allowing prospective book buyers a means of making up their own minds about the merits of Borlase's narrative.[118] On the whole, Johnson's review amounts to a deftly constructed survey of the major topics discussed in Borlase's *Observations*. When we compare the *Literary Magazine* commentary with that of the *Critical*, Johnson's review appears as a restrained, artfully executed response to Smollett's depreciatory assessment of the *Observations*. Almost every specific objection raised by Smollett is answered either in Johnson's introductory remarks or in his choice of extract. What Johnson does in the Borlase review, then, is to protect, or patronize, a meritorious author who is the victim of a rather obtuse and captious review. Johnson manages to do this without stooping to the sort of bickering and sniping by and between reviewers that, as Johnson makes clear in his preface to the *London Chronicle* and elsewhere, had done so much to deface the contemporary literary landscape.

Johnson almost certainly chose his extracts with Smollett's review in mind, but we should also note that the extracted material embodies Johnson's broader outlook on natural history and travel narratives, which as it applies to the Borlase volume allows readers to compare their state with that of their fellow citizens who live in a remote part of the kingdom.[119] Johnson complements the historical account of the Scilly Island economy, for instance, by reprinting what can arguably be called a romantic description of contemporary Scilly Islanders. The "present islanders are handsome, and civil, and speak good *English*," Borlase declares. "The men are active and hardy, much busied in fishing and fowling, and therefore ready and nimble both on land and water." The inhabitants, "if sober, live long, and there are few distempers among them. Perhaps, if carefully observed, among any single thousand, the diseases would not be many." The Scilly Islanders are abstemious, hard-working, and productive, and as a result enjoy lengthy and satisfying lives—a manner of living, perhaps, that is meant by Johnson to be a rebuke to the contemporary obsession among the English with luxury and consumerism.[120] In fact, the excerpt on the Scilly Islanders' physical robustness makes an apt companion to Johnson's observation in the Hanway review, published some eleven months later, that many diseases peculiar to modern England—"tremours, fits, habitual depression, and all the maladies which proceed from laxity and debility"—can be traced to the age's pursuit of high living.[121]

Also of note is the extract on the inadequacies of the civil and ecclesiastical government of the archipelago. Essentially, Borlase decries the absence of any significant administrative mechanism to enforce social order. As "far as I could learn," Borlase states, the Scilly Islanders:

> want authority, want rules and precedents, want power to compel the payment of small debts, want penalties and punishments for the stubborn and wicked, a bridewell for the idle, and a regular, strict administration of justice and law for all. So that the people are left too much to their own will, (happy effects of liberty without law!) and as the islands have but the shadow of government, the good feel not the benefit of it because 'tis but a shadow, nor the wicked the weight of it for the same reason.[122]

The observations here certainly echo Johnson's own views on subordination as expressed in his conversation, in "Sermon 24," and elsewhere.[123]

Quite apart from rebutting Smollett's depreciatory criticism, then, Johnson's review works as an intelligently assembled digest of the *Observations on the Ancient and Present State of the Islands of Scilly*, with summaries connecting what Johnson plainly believed to be the most captivating passages from Borlase's volume. The review of Borlase, in other words, functions as a discrete essay on a subject that promises to appeal to the general public. Like almost every other of Johnson's reviews, the Borlase piece embodies Johnson's view that the journalist and the critic should contribute to culture. Johnson gives prospective book buyers enough material here to evaluate the *Observations*, certainly, but he also makes available to the general public worthy information on a little-studied aspect of English geography, history, and ethnography.

Patrick Browne (1720–90), *Natural History of Jamaica.* Reviewed by Johnson, 16 August 1756; reviewed by Tobias Smollett in the *Critical,* June 1756; reviewed by Sir Tanfield Leman in the *Monthly,* July and October 1756. Born in Ireland and educated at the University of Leyden, where he obtained the degree of M.D. in 1743, Patrick Browne practiced medicine for two years in London before removing to Jamaica, where he spent ten years studying the island's natural features. What immediately impresses about Browne's *Natural History* are the references in the title page and prefatory essay to a nonexistent section on Jamaica's climatology and diseases. Browne does in fact own up to the error, but for some reason his explanation is placed at the end of the work, on page 490, rather than on an errata slip or in a prominent place near the beginning where it belonged. "I would willingly have added the Three Dissertations I proposed to publish with this work," Browne declares,

> but as it has already swelled to the limits I designed, and the season is too far advanced to finish the whole this year, I determined to publish the Civil and Natural History alone; leaving those, with another on Worm-fevers, &c. which will make a small volume in 8*vo*, to be printed the ensuing season.[124]

Writing for the *Critical Review*, Tobias Smollett is careful to make mention of the *Natural History*'s never-completed segment—

> [T]he third part which we should expect to be the most useful of the whole, is no where to be found, but in this paragraph [the preface] and the title page, where it makes a considerable figure, and no doubt helped the doctor to the greater part of his subscribers. . . .[125]

—though not of Browne's apology. Indeed, if the remainder of the review is any indication, the missing section raised doubts in Smollett's mind about Browne's basic competence as a scholar. A few sentences later, for example, we find Smollett reproaching Browne for his very slight misdating of Columbus's initial sighting of North America (he is off by one day) and for mistakenly claiming that the island that first came into Columbus's view was Hispaniola rather than St. Salvador. Elsewhere in the review Smollett accuses Browne of duplicating the researches of Sir Hans Sloane, whose natural history of Jamaica and other Caribbean islands had appeared a generation or so earlier.[126] To be sure, Browne's insightfulness as a botanist and the quality of his accompanying illustrations are recognized in the closing paragraph, but at the end of the day Smollett cannot bring himself to endorse the *Natural History:*

> On the whole, we can say in favour of this performance . . . that the plants are neatly engraved; and that the author may claim some merit among botanic writers: but, we cannot recommend it, as a compleat natural history; because we apprehend it deficient in the fossile productions of the island; contains no account of the trade-winds, the rainy season, the earthquakes, exhalations, or diseases of the climate; nor is it provided with a thermometrical table of the weather.[127]

Sir Tanfield Leman reached much the same conclusion in his review for the *Monthly*, though unlike Smollett Leman did manage to stumble across Browne's note on the missing chapter. In the second segment of his review (published eleven or so weeks after Johnson's) Leman acknowledges Browne's apology but levels charges of dishonesty nevertheless: "[I]s this keeping his word with his subscribers? nay, is not every one who buys this book, upon the credit of its title-page, deceived in his purchase?" Leman declares. "In short, what would have been highly culpable in a jobbing bookseller, is more inexcusable in a scholar, and a gentleman."[128] Readers interested in subjects of this kind who happened to consult both leading review journals likely would have come away with a very low opinion of Browne's volume.

Published in mid-August 1756, Johnson's review of Browne appears to have been designed chiefly to answer Smollett's criticisms of two months earlier. Take the lead sentences, for instance, where Johnson points out that Browne's work is remarkably free from the kinds of scholarly sloppiness that disfigure, when they do not invalidate, most other natural histories:

> NATURAL HISTORY was in former times so filled with fabulous narratives, that there is scarcely any part of knowledge in which less help has descended to us from our ancestors; and the desire of relating something wonderful has at all times prevailed so much on physiologists, that they have with too much readiness adopted the tales of the vulgar, and, with too much credulity admitted the testimonies of such as observe grossly or relate inaccurately. From this fault Dr. *Browne* seems to be more free than most other writers, and therefore they who look rather for amusement than truth may perhaps find themselves disappointed.[129]

One wonders if it is possible to write a more resourceful vindication of Browne from charges of dullness and fraudulence. Given the temptations to exaggerate one's findings—the impossibility of refutation; the universal appeal of fantastical observations—Browne deserves praise for sticking to the truth even though he almost certainly knows that many readers, accustomed as they are to finding "amusement [rather] than truth" in natural histories, may reject his work because it departs sharply from the disreputable practices of most other authors who write in this genre.

Johnson develops this point in the next sentence when he calls attention to the eyewitness authenticity of Browne's account. Of particular interest are Johnson's comments on Hans Sloane, which seem to answer Smollett's claim that Browne pointlessly duplicates the work of his renowned predecessor. "How much he has added to the history of Sir *Hans Sloane* we are not able to tell, having not compared them," Johnson declares, "but [we] have reason to believe that he has generally trusted his own eyes, and then, though he should have discovered no new animals or vegetables, his book is still useful, as the accounts of two observers necessarily illustrate one another." Browne's *Natural History* does indeed fill a legitimate scholarly niche, Johnson thus argues.[130]

As the critical portion of the review draws to a close, Johnson persists in offering appreciative interpretations of what are described in the *Critical* as instances of Browne's incompetence. Browne's failure to limit his discussion to novel aspects of Jamaican life, for example, is portrayed by Johnson as a net benefit to readers: "we are very far from intending to insinuate" that Browne "has added nothing" to our knowledge of Jamaica, Johnson asserts. True enough, Browne's natural history often reflects what is best described as an "unnecessary diligence. He has described many products of *Jamaica* which are equally to be found in other parts, perhaps in every part of the known world." But overzealousness of this kind ultimately amounts to a venial rather than a grave failing, Johnson adds, because "every man is fond of the country that he inhabits, and is willing to multiply its products, and celebrate its fertility." Even in the choice of extracts that conclude the review we find Johnson working to counterbalance the dismissive commentary published in the *Critical*.

Unlike Smollett, who quotes from the least attractive portions of Browne's work, Johnson chooses the more interesting passages from the *Natural History*. In "the account of any country, those things should be selected, that are peculiar to it, that are distinguished by some permanent and natural difference from the same species in other places," Johnson says by way of introduction to the nineteen columns of extract that conclude the review. "Upon these principles we have extracted the following particulars without intending to prefer them to many others, for which we have no room." Readers of the extracts Johnson chooses would learn something about the following subjects: the "'manufacture of rum'" and the sugar cane plant on which the industry depends; worm grass, which "'takes its present denomination from its peculiar efficacy in destroying worms; which . . . it does in so extraordinary a manner, that no other simple can be of equal efficacy in any other disease as this is in those that proceed from these insects, especially when attended with a fever or convulsions'"; the cotton shrub, which is exported to "'*Manchester*, where . . . there are no less than 120,000 people, constantly employed in the different branches of the manufacture of this single staple'"; the firefly: "'A person may, with great ease, read the smallest print by the light of one of these insects, if held between the fingers and moved gradually along the lines, with luminous spots immediately over the letters.'" Other creatures discussed in the extract include the yellow snake, the galley wasp, and the large gray house spider. The *Natural History* contains plenty of meritorious observations, readers of Johnson's review are thus encouraged to believe, though Browne occasionally offers more information than most readers might want.[131]

It is worth speculating as to why Johnson avoids discussing Browne's missing section. The representative nature of Johnson's citations—as well as his habit of scrutinizing prefaces—suggest that he knew of both the nonexistent section and Browne's apology for it.[132] Solid evidence is lacking, but one likely possibility is that Johnson accepted Browne's apology on account of his forthright—though clumsily placed—acknowledgment of the error and, more importantly, because the omissions were in some measure beyond Browne's control, the weather and marketplace considerations being the chief factors in this case rather than incompetence or sloth. Johnson may also have believed that Browne had already received more than his share of abuse at the hands of the *Critical*.

In many ways, the Browne piece neatly embodies Johnson's manner of proceeding as a reviewer of various sorts of scientific books. In the first place, the Browne review is not merely appreciative but apologetic, thus exemplifying both Johnson's respect for ambitious scientific inquiry and his awareness of the popular willingness to think disparagingly of projectors. Of equal importance is that we find Johnson in the Browne review, as in his reviewing for other scientific works, emphasizing the humanitarianism of the author. Browne is a reliable purveyor of truth, Johnson would have us believe, in sharp contrast to what the *Monthly* and the *Critical* assert, and his highly detailed survey of Jamaica allows English readers to compare their provincial circumstances with life in the Caribbean.

5

Johnson as an Occasional Reviewer
in the *Gentleman's Magazine*
and the *Critical Review*

In MARCH 1742 THE *GENTLEMAN'S MAGAZINE* PUBLISHED SAMUEL JOHNSON'S FIRST book review, or what was in fact a proto book review; Johnson's final contribution to the practice appeared nearly twenty-three years later in the *Critical Review*. In between, Johnson published two additional reviews in the *Gentleman's Magazine* and three others in the *Critical Review*. Johnson's work as an occasional reviewer in these two publications, scattered as it is over more than two decades, at first glance does not lend itself to the sort of systematic analysis that applies to the *Literary Magazine*, the editorship of which Johnson held between May 1756 and July 1757. Nevertheless, we can make a couple of useful generalizations about Johnson's practices as an occasional reviewer.

To begin with, six of Johnson's seven occasional reviews—the Lennox piece, which is largely composed of an extract taken from an earlier review by Henry Fielding, may be the exception—deserve to be considered as among his most thorough and provocative. Indeed, the trenchant commentary one finds in the Churchill and Tytler reviews is, or should be, familiar to every serious student of Johnson's critical outlook, and the four reviews Johnson contributed to the *Critical* contain a surprising measure of assertive criticism, especially when we bear in mind Johnson's temperamental reluctance to make dogmatic pronouncements on the works of contemporaries. Six of the seven works reviewed by Johnson—the Churchill volume is the exception—were written by friends or acquaintances, so we can say that Johnson's boldness is in some degree a manifestation of his legendary camaraderie. Also worth noting is that three of the seven reviews—the Tytler, Graham, and Grainger pieces—are apparently crafted as rebuttals to criticisms published earlier in competing review journals, which necessarily gives them a more pointed critical edge. It is almost certainly true, more-over, that the critical forwardness of Johnson's occasional reviews reflects the influence on Johnson of the evolution in book reviewing, which from the late-1750s onward—when Johnson's most assertive reviews appeared—increasingly moved away from being essentially abstracts introduced and interspersed with brief commentary and came to take on the character of the modern book review, today's reviews centering largely on the opinion of the critic and offering much less in the way of direct quotation.

The second generalization worth making is that every one of Johnson's occasional reviews is either of imaginative or historical literature. Clearly, Johnson's decision to review such titles in the *Gentleman's* and the *Critical* cannot be said to reflect anything like a grand design, but the handful of occasional pieces do help to balance Johnson's work in the *Literary Magazine*, where two-thirds of Johnson's reviews are of scientific works or titles that bear in some way on current events or public affairs.

In terms of sheer volume, Johnson's work as an occasional reviewer amounts to an extremely minor portion of his vast output as a literary critic. Nevertheless, these few pieces carry some of Johnson's most probing observations on historiography and, perhaps, on drama and poetry as well; they also reflect Johnson's understanding of the contemporary literary scene, particularly in regard to the difficulties aspiring authors face as they strive to gain a measure of literary reputation and to the demonstrably important role book reviewing plays in determining a given title's fate in the literary marketplace.

THE *GENTLEMAN'S MAGAZINE*

Samuel Johnson may have authored as many as four-dozen book notices and reviews in the *Gentleman's Magazine* between 1750 and 1769, or so attribution arguments advanced by Donald Greene, Arthur Sherbo, and others would have us believe. These attribution arguments are based almost entirely on internal evidence and in many cases amount to nothing more than brief surmises that Johnson *might* have authored this piece or that. A given sentence sounds like a passage from Johnson's known works, we are told; Johnson may have been acquainted with the author whose book is reviewed, or Johnson is known to have indulged an interest in the subject treated by a given title, and so on.[1]

John L. Abbott argues much more persuasively that nearly all of the *Gentleman's Magazine* notices attributed to Johnson are almost certainly the work of John Hawkesworth. In his 1982 biography of Hawkesworth,

Abbott sets forth three factors that in his view presumptively tilt the scales away from Johnson's authorship of the contested pieces: Hawkesworth held the literary editorship of the *Gentleman's Magazine* from the late 1740s until the early 1770s, thus leaving him in a much better position to have written the notices attributed to Johnson, who left the *Gentleman's* in 1746 to begin work on the *Dictionary;* the reviews published in the *Gentleman's* between 1747 and 1773 are "marked by an unmistakable unity of approach and language," thus suggesting that they are "the work of a single man"; and Hawkesworth was highly adept at imitating Johnson's prose style, which necessarily undermines the attribution of reviews to Johnson based strictly or largely on such evidence.[2]

To Abbott's arguments one must add the following considerations. True enough, Johnson contributed a clutch of pieces to the *Gentleman's Magazine* after he left in 1747 to work full-time on his *Dictionary*. The editorial piece "'O.N.' on the Fireworks" (1749) and the review of Charlotte Lennox's *Female Quixote* (1752) come to mind, as do Johnson's prefaces to the 1753 and 1754 annual volumes of the *Gentleman's Magazine*, not to mention his brief but affecting life of Edward Cave (1754) and his exposé, "An Account of the Detection of the Imposture in Cock-Lane" (1762). Nevertheless, we must ask ourselves this: with the *Dictionary* (completed in mid-1754), the *Rambler* (1750–52), and the *Adventurer* (1753–54) making persistent demands on his time during the period when he is alleged to have written almost all of reviews attributed to him, why would Johnson put himself to the trouble of reading, or at least scanning, a number of books merely for the purpose of writing a sentence or two of commentary on each one? Why would Johnson bother with such petty literary activity when he clearly had better things to do with his time? By contrast, Hawkesworth's duties as editor would have required him to perform duties of this kind.

We should also take into account the opinion of the eminent Johnson scholar James L. Clifford. In his 1979 biographical study of Johnson's middle years, *Dictionary Johnson*, Clifford makes the following observation:

During 1749 and 1750 Johnson's connections with the *Gentleman's Magazine*, which had been his chief means of support in the early 1740s, were, at best, tenuous. Although he kept in close touch with what was going on through Hawkesworth and other friends, it is unlikely that he did much regular writing for Cave. It must be admitted that Donald Greene and other modern scholars have made persuasive attempts to identify Johnson's hand in some dramatic criticism, as well as in other reviews. But Hawkesworth had learned to imitate Johnson's style so perfectly that it is risky to use stylistic evidence, or internal details of any sort, as conclusive proof of authorship.[3]

We can allow for the possibility, then, that Johnson *might* have written at least some of the many notices attributed to him in the *Gentleman's Magazine,* even as we weigh the considerable evidence that tells us that he likely had nothing to do with these pieces. Complicating matters further is that most of the questionable notices are brief and rather tepid, so attribution arguments that lack conclusive external evidence, as Clifford points out, will inevitably appear undernourished. As matters stand now, however, Johnson is known to have written reviews of three works—Sarah Churchill's *Account of the Conduct of the Dowager Duchess of Marlborough,* Charlotte Lennox's *The Female Quixote,* and William Tytler's *Enquiry into the Evidence Produced against Mary Queen of Scots*—in the *Gentleman's Magazine.*[4]

Published on 2 March 1742, *An Account of the Conduct of the Dowager Duchess of Marlborough* attempts to justify Sarah Churchill's controversial actions during her service as a member of Queen Anne's inner circle.[5] Not surprisingly, Churchill's firsthand observations of life at court immediately commanded wide public interest. In keeping with the *Gentleman's* emphasis on contemporary issues, Cave asked Johnson, or allowed Johnson, to write a commentary on the memoir for the March 1742 issue.[6] Johnson's analysis begins with a general discussion of historiography, with particular attention given to the proper treatment of primary sources. Autobiographical accounts such as Churchill's are important, Johnson argues, because "those who write in their own Defence, discover often more Impartiality, and less Contempt of Evidence, than the Advocates which Faction or Interest have raised in their Favour." But scholars always must keep in mind that "the Parent of all Memoirs, is the Ambition of being distinguished from the Herd of Mankind, and the Fear of either Infamy or Oblivion." The desire to determine one's standing in history, "cannot but have some Degree of Influence, and which may at least affect the Writers Choice of Facts, though they may not prevail upon him to advance known Falshoods." Hence the historian must be guided by two apparently contradictory but in fact closely related habits of mind: skepticism and a desire to get at the truth. Distrust "is a necessary Qualification of a Student in History," Johnson observes. It "quickens his Discernment of different Degrees of Probability, animates his Search after Evidence, and perhaps heightens his Pleasure at the Discovery of Truth; for Truth," Johnson adds, "though not always obvious, is generally discoverable." Johnson lauds the *Account* for its revelations of the private and public lives of Churchill's contemporaries, though it cannot be recommended as a forthright exposé of "the Character which it is principally intended to preserve or to retrieve." The remainder of the piece comprises evenhanded and rather unvarnished commentary on Churchill's depiction of King William, Charles II, and Queen Anne.[7]

Clearly, the Marlborough "review" is important for its revelation of Johnson's attitude toward historical method, contemporary politics, and autobiography.[8] But the piece is by its own definition not a review but an "essay" that takes the form of a letter to the *Gentleman's Magazine:*

> SIR,
> THE Account of the Conduct of the Duchess of Marlborough, having been so eagerly received, and so attentively considered, as to become even at this Time of Business, Contests, Wars, and Revolutions, the most popular Topic of Conversation, you may be perhaps willing to admit into your Collection this short Essay upon it, which does not appear written with an Intention to please or offend any Party.[9]

Clearly, Johnson here means to examine the significance of Sarah Churchill's well-known and much-commented-upon critique of court life rather than to announce the publication of the work itself. That the "essay" contains no publishing or bibliographic data—a common feature of eighteenth-century book reviews—further suggests that the essay should not be categorized as a book review per se, at least not in the same sense as Johnson's *Literary Magazine* pieces. In fact, the Marlborough "Essay" has far more in common with those *Rambler* essays that obliquely remark on recent, consequential titles—numbers 4, 139, and 154 come to mind, as do *Adventurer* 85 and *Idler* 65—than it does with the four-dozen or so book reviews known to have been written by Johnson, which strive to direct public attention to unknown but meritorious books.[10] As a general interest periodical the *Gentleman's Magazine* had no compelling reason to review regularly new books—Why devote great amounts of space to material of an as yet unknown value?—and in any case there really was no precedent in 1742 for the kind of reviewing initiated by the *Monthly Review* seven years later. Even so, the rigorous nature of the *Memoirs* essay is relevant here, because it exemplifies Johnson's belief in the essential legitimacy of criticism directed at recently published titles, particularly criticism in the form of what would eventually become the modern book review.

Ten years would pass before Johnson would again publish a substantive commentary on a new work. Johnson and Charlotte Lennox (1720–1804) had known each other for at least two years when Johnson's notice of *The Female Quixote* appeared in the March 1752 issue of the *Gentleman's Magazine.* Apart from writing a favorable review of the work—the only time he bothered to review a novel—Johnson is also known to have contributed the dedication to the *Female Quixote.* Johnson also awarded Lennox a rare distinction by quoting from *The Female Quixote* eleven times in his *Dictionary* (1755).[11] Equally significant is that the *Female Quixote* piece is the earliest example of Johnson's use of the book review as a means of helping a meritorious but relatively unknown author triumph over the indifference of contemporary readers and the hostility of critics.[12] The entire critical portion of the review, which follows a two-sentence plot summary, is quoted here:

> The solemn manner in which she [Lennox] treats the most common and trivial occurrences, the romantic expectations she forms, and the absurdities which she commits herself, and produces in others, afford a most entertaining series of circumstances and events. Mr. Fielding, however emulous of Cervantes, and jealous of a rival, acknowledges in his paper of the 24th [of March], that in many instances this copy excels the original; and though he has no connection with the author, he concludes his encomium on the work, by earnestly recommending it as a most extraordinary, and most excellent, performance. "It is, (says he) indeed, a work of true humour, and cannot fail of giving a rational, as well as very pleasing amusement, to a sensible reader, who will at once be instructed and highly diverted."[13]

The assertive praise here is not all that surprising if we bear in mind Johnson's personal fondness for Charlotte Lennox and his keen understanding of the scarcity of literary fame, as expressed in numerous *Rambler* essays.[14] What does make this passage significant is Johnson's somewhat distorted representation of Henry Fielding's review of *The Female Quixote*, which had appeared a short time earlier in the *Covent-Garden Journal*.

In his review, Fielding strives to convey an aura of impartiality even though, as we shall see in moment, he too writes with the intention of stimulating brisk sales of the *Female Quixote*. As the title of the section of the *Covent-Garden Journal* that carries Fielding's remarks would suggest, "Proceedings at the Court of Censorial Enquiry, & c." mimics the structure of a courtroom hearing. Fielding identifies five ways in which Lennox's work surpasses its model, *Don Quixote*, four ways in which Cervantes's romance is the better of the two, and areas of comparison where the two works are on equal footing. Fielding's final "verdict" is reproduced accurately in the *Gentleman's Magazine* review, but clearly Johnson exaggerates matters at least slightly when he characterizes the rest of Fielding's piece as an "encomium." After all, Fielding does admit that the *Female Quixote* cannot compete with its legendary predecessor on the crucial points of originality (Cervantes is "intitled to the Honour of Invention, which can never be attributed to any Copy however excellent") and didactic significance (Cervantes "intended not only the Diversion, but the Instruction and Reformation of his Countrymen: With this Intention he levelled Ridicule at a vicious Folly, which . . . had almost converted a civilized People into a Nation of Cutthroats")—though these consequential differences are downplayed as much as possible in Fielding's *Covent-Garden* piece. We would expect Johnson to acknowledge such foundational distinctions himself—especially given his well-known views on these topics and his high opinion of *Don Quixote*—yet not a word is said about these issues in the *Gentleman's Magazine* review.[15]

Equally striking are Johnson's remarks about Fielding's disinterestedness ("though he has no connection with the author") and his assertion that Lennox's achievement is such that Fielding, who had every reason to fear that his own standing as England's premier novelist was at stake, was moved to applaud the work anyway ("Mr. Fielding, however emulous of Cervantes, and jealous of a rival"). This is a plainly false account of the circumstances surrounding Fielding's essay, as Johnson almost certainly knew when he wrote his review. As J. L. Clifford has pointed out, it was Johnson and, later, Johnson's friend Samuel Richardson who managed to persuade an evidently skeptical Andrew Millar to publish the *Female Quixote*. Millar, a friend of Fielding's and a shareholder in the *Covent-Garden Journal*, pressured Fielding, or asked him at least, to puff the *Female Quixote* in the *Covent-Garden Journal*—just as Fielding had done earlier for another of Millar's productions, the *History of the Portuguese*. Fielding's review appeared on Tuesday, 24 March 1752, two weeks or so before Johnson's and eleven days after the publication of the *Female Quixote*.[16] What follows is a bit of guesswork, but given the connection between Johnson and Millar (a financial sponsor of the *Dictionary*) and between Millar and Fielding—not to mention Johnson's legendary willingness to act on behalf of literary friends, most especially Charlotte Lennox—one wonders if Johnson encouraged Millar to seek an endorsement from Fielding. The actual details remain shrouded in mystery, but we can say that Fielding and Johnson make a point of hiding their advocatory aims behind a veneer of impartiality. Indeed, Johnson's review is a remarkably shrewd piece of work, given that he recasts—to the point of misrepresentation—the opinion of the most popular novelist of the day and transplants it from a fledgling twice-weekly to a well-respected journal with a nationwide circulation.[17]

Why Johnson chose to review *The Female Quixote* in the manner that he did is open to speculation. One credible explanation is that Johnson, aware of the overcrowding of the prose fiction market yet loath to make assertive pronouncements that might turn out to be reckless or foolish, saw the use of the Fielding excerpt as an acceptable compromise. Lennox's novel is given a crucial boost in publicity without Johnson himself having to say things he did not really believe, though his exclusion of details from Fielding's review that might discourage prospective buyers of the *Female Quixote* must have stretched to the limit Johnson's highly refined sense of scholarly manners.

The Female Quixote was reviewed in the April 1752 issue of the *Monthly Review*, four weeks or so after Johnson's review appeared. John Ward's twelve-page review is entirely given over to extract and summary, apart from an introductory remark establishing the *Monthly*'s neutrality. "Whether a plan, and character, of this kind, be agreeable to nature, or to the age and the country we live in," Ward declares after summarizing the basic plot of the novel, "our readers will determine for themselves."[18] Appended to Ward's review is an interesting bit of criticism written by Ralph Griffiths, the editor of the *Monthly:*

> N.B. We have been the more liberal of our extracts from this work, that our readers might be the better enabled to judge of the character given of it by the author of *The Covent Garden Journal*; who has not scrupled to prefer this performance, in many respects, to the inimitable *Don Quixote.*[19]

It seems that Griffiths here is suggesting that Fielding overestimated Lennox's achievement. The generous extracts published in the *Monthly*, we are given to understand, are meant to encourage readers to make up their own minds about the novel.

In October 1760 Johnson would publish the last of his reviews for the *Gentleman's Magazine*. Though Johnson does not go to quite the same lengths for William Tytler as he had for Charlotte Lennox eight years earlier, the review of *An Historical and Critical Enquiry into the Evidence Produced against Mary Queen of Scots* is remarkable nonetheless for the balance Johnson strikes between encouraging a sympathetic reading of the work and refraining from authoritative pronouncements.[20]

William Tytler's *Historical and Critical Enquiry* is entitled to a place in history distinct from its association with Samuel Johnson's *Gentleman's Magazine* review. Tytler's attempt to clear Mary's name from accusations of murder and adultery appeared in 1760, six years after an Edinburgh librarian, Walter Goodall, had argued in the *Examination of the Letters Said to Be Written by Mary, Queen of Scots*, that the letters between Mary and the earl of Bothwell, which supposedly proved that the two were involved in an adulterous relationship and had conspired to kill Mary's husband, Lord Darnley, were in fact forgeries. "To Goodall's mind," writes Jayne Elizabeth Lewis in her essay "Mary Stuart's 'Fatal Box': Sentimental History and the Revival of the Casket Letters Controversy," "local anachronisms, catachreses, inconsistencies with other documents and with Mary's own known literary style all proved the casket letters spurious."[21] Lewis observes that the controversy surrounding the "casket letters" (so called because, allegedly, the letters had been held in a silver casket before they were taken from Bothwell) had been a matter of enduring interest in the literary world, and in Johnson's day the issues surrounding the accusations against Mary proved to be heavily freighted with political and cultural significance. The casket letters "were not very subtly used to justify the Hanoverian succession," Lewis states. "In turn, to discredit the letters would be to sympathize with the Stuart cause."[22] Of equal significance is that the casket letters "became for Johnson's history-writing contemporaries at once an object of close scrutiny and a lively trope for the predicaments of modern British historiography, formal and informal alike":[23]

> Far more than her cousin Elizabeth, Mary exemplified the persisting problem that sixteenth-century matter posed for eighteenth-century method. Elizabeth may have masterminded many of the machinations that made sixteenth-century evidences so unreliable. But it was Mary, evidently knowable only through others' false but deeply felt constructions, who tried modern historiography to its limit. The intrinsic mystery of her personal "character" sorely tested the assumption that written characters were trustworthy transmitters of historical information.[24]

Lewis goes on to observe that "Ultimately, the casket letters controversy enlisted everyone from literary celebrities like Hume, Johnson, and Robertson to anonymous reviewers, mildly delusional antiquarians, and brilliant and meticulous French women writing in the twilight of the *ancien régime*."[25]

How Johnson came to write the review of William Tytler's book remains a mystery. His day-to-day involvement with the *Gentleman's Magazine* had ceased many years earlier, and his departure from the *Literary Magazine* in 1757 by all accounts marked the end of his brief career as a regular reviewer. Equally open to question is whether or not Johnson even knew Tytler (1711–92) personally at this time, though it is established that they met during Johnson's visit to the Hebrides in 1773. Thomas Tyers, one of Johnson's early biographers, suggests that Johnson wrote the review "at the instigation of an old acquaintance." E. A. Bloom makes a similar claim, asserting that the review was "probably a voluntary contribution motivated by personal conviction or prejudice," perhaps related in some way to Johnson's "Stuart sympathies." An arresting surmise, certainly, especially if we take into account Johnson's particularly strong admiration for Mary Queen of Scots: "[W]ho could let your Queen remain twenty years in captivity, and then be put to death, without even a pretence of justice, without your ever attempting to rescue her," Johnson remarked to Boswell at one point during the Hebrides tour, "and such a Queen too! as every man of any gallantry of spirit would have sacrificed his life for." Believing that Bloom overstates the Jacobite angle, John A. Vance argues that the Tytler piece chiefly intends "to make significant points about historical writing and evidence" and "to champion the spirit of independence that marks the best kind of historian."[26] Johnson's commentary speaks to all of these issues at some level, but we should not overlook the considerable extent to which the review is shaped by aspects of the contemporary literary marketplace. To begin with, the Tytler piece is first and foremost a book review that seeks to win a sympathetic reception for a presumptively unpopular work written by a meritorious but unknown author. Also influencing Johnson's analysis are the faintly condescending reviews published earlier in the *Monthly Review* (July 1760), the *Critical Review* (June 1760), and the *British Magazine* (June 1760).[27] As a means of helping Tytler triumph over these hazards, Johnson focuses on Tytler's benevolent intentions and scholarly fastidiousness, while at the same time avoiding the telltale dogmatic overreaching regularly found in the leading review journals, the final judgment of the work in Johnson's view being the proper responsibility of readers.

The review itself comprises about eight columns (four pages). Summaries, extracts, and connective remarks constitute all but the first few and final paragraphs of the review. Though proportionally meager, Johnson's critical commentary is carefully calibrated to soften conventional hostility to Tytler's historical revisionism. In the following passage, readers are called upon to admire Tytler's courageous attempt to correct firmly entrenched but deeply flawed popular opinions about Mary Queen of Scots:

> The writers of the present time . . . profess to serve no interest, and speak with loud contempt of sycophants and slaves. There is, however, a power from whose influence neither they nor their predecessors have ever been free. Those who have set greatness at defiance have yet been the slaves of fashion. When an opinion has once become popular, very few are willing to oppose it. Idleness is more willing to credit than enquire; cowardice is afraid of controversy, and vanity of answer; and he that writes merely for sale is tempted to court purchasers by flattering the prejudices of the publick. . . . Yet there remains still among us, not wholly extinguished, a zeal for truth, a desire of establishing right, in opposition to fashion.[28]

In his preface Tytler states that he intends chiefly "to convince any of the unprejudiced part of his readers" that history has unjustly branded Mary a murderer.[29] Given the popular state of mind regarding Mary and her descendants—"It has now been fashionable for near half a century to defame and vilify the house of *Stuart*"—Johnson knows that the disinterested readers whom Tytler hopes to reach will be extremely hard to come by. Hence the aim of the review is to encourage the public to approach Tytler's book with an open mind and, collaterally, to weaken the existing popular prejudices against Tytler's thesis that had recently found expression in the lead review journals. Indeed, it is possible that Johnson in the passage quoted above alludes to the reviews published previously in the *Monthly*, the *Critical*, and perhaps in the *British Magazine* as well—all three of which offer grudging approval of Tytler's historical method but ultimately reject his thesis.

Writing in the *Monthly* three months before the publication of Johnson's *Gentleman's Magazine* review, Owen Ruffhead insists that Tytler "has not been able to establish the innocence" of Mary, even though it now appears that the evidence against her is not as conclusive as once thought. Ruffhead cites the "indecency" of Mary's "hasty marriage with Bothwell, who was publicly accused of having murdered her husband" as reason enough to reject a complete rethinking of Mary's historical standing. The reviewer for the *Critical* reached basically the same conclusion in the preceding month, as he asserts that Tytler "has in general acquitted himself with great ability and address; he has invalidated the evidence against Mary" but her innocence has not been "fully established." We find a remarkably clear echo of the *Critical* commentary in the June issue of Smollett's *British Magazine*. The *British Magazine* and *Critical Review* notices appeared in the same month, thus raising the distinct possibility that Smollett authored both pieces.[30] Here is the *British Magazine* review in its entirety:

This champion, for the character of an injured and accomplished Lady, which for two centuries had been cruelly traduced, enters the lists with great intrepidity, against two of the most formidable antagonists whom the age could produce [Hume and Robertson]; and manages his weapons with such dexterity, that if he does not clearly demonstrate the innocence of Mary, he at least establishes very strong presumptions in her favour, which must warmly recommend her cause to the protection of the candid and humane.[31]

All three reviewers basically agree that Tytler's considerable talents are placed in the service of an essentially untenable cause. The reviewers are impressed with Tytler's scholarly thoroughness and impartiality, but they cannot bring themselves to endorse what they obviously take to be politically unacceptable conclusions. Even the *British Magazine* piece—easily the most appreciative of the three—carries a whiff of condescension insofar as the reviewer concludes that Mary's case will be heard sympathetically only by the most charitable and benevolent of readers. We are meant to feel sorry for Mary, certainly, but the *British Magazine* reviewer would also have us believe that Tytler is to be pitied as well, given the weight of scholarly and popular opinion against him—not to mention his apparent failure to "clearly demonstrate the innocence of Mary." The *British Magazine* review conveys a vague sympathy for its subject, in other words, even while it denies the essential validity of Tytler's argument. Johnson almost certainly speaks to this circumstance when he dwells upon Tytler's scholarly discernment and courageousness, such traits in his view being far more reliable indicators of truth than mere unexamined opinion and politically motivated prejudice. We are called to trust and admire Tytler, that is, and not to see him as an idealist whose observations are doomed to go unheeded.

Other aspects of the *Gentleman's Magazine* review suggest an attempt by Johnson to counter notices published in the *Monthly* and the *Critical*. Both journals make a point of rejecting the most ambitious of Tytler's arguments, which is that Mary's accusers, the earls of Murray and Morton, were chiefly responsible for the murder of her husband, Lord Darnley. Tytler "had done much better to have stopped at his vindication of Mary," writes Ruffhead; "after he had so ably invalidated the presumptive evidence against her, it was injudicious to build a charge against her accusers, on presumptions equally weak." The reviewer for the *Critical* also claims that Tytler has "brought strong presumptions against Murray and Morton, but he has not convicted them."[32] Johnson allusively disputes these arguments in the final paragraph of his *Gentleman's Magazine* piece when he declares that Tytler's *Enquiry* successfully shifts the burden of proof to those who would assert the innocence of Murray and Morton:

> The rest of this treatise is employed in an endeavour to prove that *Mary's* accusers were the murderers of *Darnley*; thro' this enquiry it is not necessary to follow him, only let it be observed, that, if these letters were forged by them, they may easily be thought capable of other crimes. That the letters were forged is now made so probable, that perhaps they will never more be cited as testimonies.[33]

Though nothing has been proved beyond a shadow of a doubt, Johnson admits here, the weight of the evidence clearly resides with Tytler's argument. In effect, what Johnson does here and throughout the review is to pit reason against prejudice. Tytler's work embodies the modern scholarly method, while the popular view of Mary as expressed in the review journals represents unexamined opinion and political prejudice.

That the *Gentleman's Magazine* review chiefly aims to clear away unreasonable hostility toward Tytler's thesis is evident enough, but what is Johnson's opinion of the work itself? In keeping with his normal reviewing practice, Johnson is reticent about endorsing Tytler's conclusions even though he amply praises Tytler's intellectual courage and scholarly thoroughness: Tytler "has attempted a vindication of *Mary*"; he has "undertaken to prove" that the incriminating letters are "spurious"; "That the letters were forged," Johnson says in the final sentence, "is now made so probable, that perhaps they will never more be cited as testimonies."[34] Johnson thus insists on honoring the line between persuasiveness and irrefutable fact. As something of a skeptic, Johnson realizes that additional evidence may surface to modify Tytler's conclusions. Even so, Johnson argues that Tytler's devotion to truth cannot be disputed. At once ambitious—especially in light of prevailing opinion and Tytler's lack of reputation—and yet typically restrained in its evaluative commentary, Johnson's review works to encourage a fair-minded reception for Tytler's *Historical and Critical Enquiry*.

To summarize matters: during the 1950s and 1960s Donald Greene, Gwyn Kolb, and Arthur Sherbo published articles asserting Johnson's authorship of some four-dozen book reviews that began appearing in the *Gentleman's Magazine* in early 1750. The section on Samuel Johnson in the 1971 edition of the *NCBEL*, compiled by David Fleeman, lists nearly all of these pieces as of questionable authenticity. We will probably never know for certain the full extent of Johnson's contributions to the *Gentleman's Magazine*, but scholarly opinion over the past twenty years has grown increasingly skeptical of the possibility that Johnson reviewed regularly in the *Gentleman's*. Significantly, Professor O M Brack's forthcoming three-volume edition of Johnson's shorter prose reprints only the reviews long accepted as Johnson's: the Churchill, Lennox, and Tytler commentaries. Brack's decision to reject the authenticity of the dozens of doubtful reviews seems all the more sensible when we recall the similarities between Johnson's writing style and that of John Hawkesworth, who took over the literary editorship of the *Gentleman's* following Johnson's departure in the late 1740s, and the fact that Johnson really had no good reason to contribute such material, given his other authorial responsibilities at the time. What can we say about the few titles that Johnson did review in the *Gentleman's*? As embodiments of Johnson's broad critical outlook, the Churchill, Lennox, and Tytler reviews are important not only for the critical opinions they convey but also because they illustrate Johnson's talent at reconciling his desire to help worthy authors triumph over the hazards of the contemporary book trade with his well-known reluctance to make dogmatic pronouncements on the works of living writers.

Samuel Johnson and the *Critical Review*

Why the fifty-something Samuel Johnson, who was busy at the time with his edition of Shakespeare's plays and had not written a review since July 1757, bothered to write a handful of reviews for the *Critical* beginning in late 1759 remains something of a mystery—though a plausible possibility is that Johnson wanted to promote works that represented a personal interest in some way, and he was impressed by both the *Critical's* popularity and its editorial policies.[35] The reviews of John Hawkesworth's

Oroonoko, James Grainger's *The Sugar-Cane*, and Oliver Goldsmith's *The Traveller* are of works written by friends (or, in the case of Grainger, an acquaintance), while the review of George Graham's *Telemachus* evidently sprang from Johnson's personal fondness for the dramatic poem.[36] Johnson and Tobias Smollett, the editor of the *Critical*, knew each other quite well by the late 1750s. A plausible scenario is that Johnson offered to review *Oroonoko* (December 1759) and *Telemachus* (April 1763) in the *Critical* and Smollett obliged, eager as he must have been to accept contributions from the man whom he had once described as the "great Cham of literature."[37] The editorship of the *Critical* following Smollett's departure in May 1763 was assumed by the journal's proprietor, Archibald Hamilton (1719–93), who often delegated the responsibility to William Guthrie (1708–70). Hamilton worked for some years as the manager of William Strahan's printing house before resigning in 1756, so he and Johnson probably became acquainted as Johnson's *Dictionary* was being prepared for publication. Guthrie was a colleague of Johnson's at the *Gentleman's Magazine* during the early 1740s. In fact, Johnson helped Guthrie compile the controversial parliamentary debates before taking on the entire project himself. It is thus not hard to believe that the reviews of *The Sugar-Cane* (October 1764) and the *Traveller* (December 1764) were published under circumstances similar to those surrounding the two earlier notices.[38]

Though scattered over five years and only four in number, Johnson's reviews in the *Critical* are important nevertheless, not only because they exemplify the skill and conscientiousness that Johnson routinely brought to reviewing but also because they reflect a fundamental change in Johnson's theoretical understanding of the practice. It is not at all unusual to find Johnson writing mildly appreciative reviews in the *Literary Magazine* and the *Gentleman's Magazine* on behalf of worthy authors struggling to find a readership in a fiercely competitive literary marketplace. In fact, nearly all of the forty-seven reviews that Johnson is known to have written are essentially favorable, if often rather tentative in their conclusions. But what does surprise about the four reviews that Johnson contributed to the *Critical* is their bold assertiveness, particularly the extravagant comparisons Johnson makes between the authors he reviews and legendary, or at least significant, literary figures. George Graham at one point is likened to William Shakespeare, while James Grainger and Oliver Goldsmith are favorably compared to, respectively, Virgil and Alexander Pope. Johnson also would have us believe that John Hawkesworth is much more talented than Thomas Southerne (1659-1746), the author whose tragedy Hawkesworth revises. When studied as a group, these four reviews tell us that by the end of the 1750s—about a decade after the publication of the *Monthly Review*'s inaugural issue—Johnson had convinced himself that the prospects of worthy but unknown authors pivoted on an ardent and perhaps even an exaggerated endorsement from the *Monthly Review* or the *Critical Review*. In other words, Johnson's four reviews in the *Critical* collectively amount to a rather pronounced rejection of, or at least a dramatic exception to, his previously enunciated critical position that dogmatic, authoritative pronouncements directed at the works of one's contemporaries inevitably prove to be unreliable.

John Hawkesworth, *Oroonoko.* Reviewed by Johnson in the *Critical,* December 1759; not reviewed in the *Monthly.*[39] John Hawkesworth's tragedy *Oroonoko* was an adaptation of an identically titled drama by Thomas Southerne, first performed in 1695. Southerne's play was itself an adaptation of Afra Behn's novel *Oroonoko: or, The History of the Royal Slave* (1688). The dramatic version of the narrative centers on Oroonoko, formerly an African prince but now forced to labor as a slave in an English colony in South America. Much to Oroonoko's surprise, his wife, Imoinda—whom Oroonoko had feared was dead, the result of his father's jealousy and treachery—turns up as a slave in the same colony. Outraged when he learns that the governor of the island has predatory designs on Imoinda, Oroonoko leads his fellow slaves in a revolt against the English colonists. Cornered by colonial forces and faced with certain defeat, Oroonoko helps his wife commit suicide, and then he kills the governor and himself.[40]

John Hawkesworth's version of *Oroonoko* had already earned the approval of the public by the time Johnson's review appeared in early January 1760. Hawkesworth's *Oroonoko* was first acted at the Drury Lane Theater on 1 December 1759, with David Garrick playing Oroonoko and Mrs. Cibber (1714–66) playing Imoinda. Seven more performances were given before the month was out—one by command of the Prince of Wales.[41] Why would Johnson bother to review a play that had already proved to be widely popular? That Johnson simply wanted to exalt a work he personally admired is a plausible explanation for the review, but a much more interesting possibility is that Johnson was writing on behalf of his friend John Hawkesworth, who at the time was planning to embark on a career as an author of original dramas. Hawkesworth and Johnson had been friends for nearly twenty years when the *Oroonoko* review appeared—they had worked closely together as editors of the *Gentleman's Magazine* during the 1740s, and together they founded the Ivy Lane Club, a social group that met regularly during the early 1750s—so it would not be at all unusual if Johnson reviewed *Oroonoko* strictly out of loyalty to a much-admired friend.[42]

The first of Hawkesworth's original dramas to reach the stage, *Edgar and Emmeline*, was not performed until 31 January 1761, thirteen months after Johnson reviewed *Oroonoko* in the *Critical*. But *Edgar* was completed, or nearing completion, by the early spring of 1759, as the following letter to Hawkesworth from David Garrick, whose Drury Lane Theater would stage the play, demonstrates: "[S]ome revolutions & unexpected Matters have arisen, which You shall know when I see You, that will absolutely hinder Us from performing the *Masque* [*Edgar and Emmeline*] next Year, if it was all ready & to our Wishes." Garrick's letter carries a date of 19 April 1759, thus establishing at least the possibility that at some point before the staging of *Oroonoko* in December 1759 Hawkesworth had mentioned to Johnson the imminent performance of *Edgar and Emmeline* and, though strictly a matter for conjecture, Johnson might even have offered critical advice on *Edgar*—and on *Oroonoko*, for that matter—just as he would do at some point in 1760 for an untitled, never-completed drama by Hawkesworth. Certainly Hawkesworth's grandiloquent praises of *Rasselas* in the April 1759 issue of the *Gentleman's Magazine*—Johnson's novel abounds "with the most elegant and striking pictures of life and nature, the most acute disquisitions, and the happiest illustration of the most important truths"—pleased Johnson and perhaps encouraged him to return the favor seven months later.[43]

That Hawkesworth stood to benefit from an appreciative review is suggested by the absence of any specific reference to him in the published version of the play, though the remarks, "Alterations in *Oroonoko* by Dr. Hawkesworth," appear in pre-performance advertisements.[44] The title page of *Oroonoko* announces Southerne's authorship without mentioning Hawkesworth, though an allusion to Hawkesworth's contributions ("with alterations") appears beneath Southerne's name, set in a smaller typeface and not italicized.[45] Neither the six-page prefatory essay nor the prologue mentions Hawkesworth by name. Not only does Johnson dwell on the fact that it was Hawkesworth's alterations that made the play performable in front of contemporary audiences, but readers are encouraged to believe that Hawkesworth, who at the time had no reputation at all as a dramatist, is a far more talented playwright than the widely respected Southerne. Interestingly enough, Johnson does not mention Hawkesworth by name in the *Critical* piece, probably because Johnson assumed that Hawkesworth's association with *Oroonoko* was already widely known. Even so, the various characterizations of Hawkesworth in the *Critical*—the "ingenious reviser" of the play; "the writer of the adventitious part"—are uniformly laudatory and are intended to remind readers that it was an adaptation of *Oroonoko*, and not the original, that pleased theatergoers.[46]

Johnson's intentions are made plain in the opening sentences of the review, where Hawkesworth's talents as a dramatist are highlighted against the inadequacies of Southerne's original work. "The original play, as it came out of the hands of Southern, is well known," Johnson declares, "and the public will only expect from us an account of its alterations. That it was necessary to alter it," Johnson adds, "cannot be denied: the tragic action was interrupted, not only by comic scenes, but by scenes of the lowest buffoonery, and the grossest indecency." What follows is Hawkesworth's twenty-two-line prologue, which emphasizes the necessity of reforming Southerne's essentially meritorious tragedy. Johnson then goes on to quote from Hawkesworth's prefatory essay, where his method of adaptation is set forth. A sequence of appreciative remarks on the material added by Hawkesworth comes next and, again, it is worth noting that the review focuses on the discernment of Southerne's modern-day editor rather than on the original work.[47] Hawkesworth "has very little indulged declamation, a mode of writing, to which modern tragedies owe much of their excellence, and much of their tediousness," Johnson observes. Hawkesworth has instead opted for short speeches, and he has "lengthened the action by a very rapid dialogue, animated with frequent changes of gesture, and expressions of emotion."[48] All of these ambitious changes, Johnson is careful to point out, have been carried out without compromising the play's dramatic unity. The "plan of the play proceeds with sufficient regularity, from the first act to the last," Johnson observes, "so well interwoven with the several insertions, that there is no loss of any thing omitted."[49]

Johnson concludes with a reprise of earlier praises. Significantly, Johnson here avers that revising Southerne's popular tragedy proved to be unworthy of Hawkesworth's great talents. The difficulties of adaptation—retaining unity of action and speech while purging undesirable elements; the necessity of restraining one's creative instincts even if superior to the original author's—are "obstructions, by which the strongest genius must be shackled and retarded, and the writer who can equal Southern under such difficulties, may be expected to excel greater authors, when he shall exert his natural powers without impediment, by adapting his own sentiments to his own plan."[50] Readers and theatergoers who enjoyed Hawkesworth's adaptation of Southerne's play, Johnson thus argues, should eagerly anticipate the day when the "ingenious revisor" of Southerne's *Oroonoko* offers the public an original composition.

While it is impossible to prove that Johnson wrote the *Oroonoko* review with the imminent production of *Edgar and Emmeline* specifically in mind, the evidence suggests strongly that he did so. For Johnson to employ the book review as a means of bolstering a friend's literary reputation, moreover, is not without precedent. Johnson's highly flattering review of Charlotte Lennox's *The Female Quixote* (1752) bears witness to this assertion and, to a lesser extent, so does the commentary on Joseph Warton's *An Essay on the Writings and Genius of Pope* (1756). But perhaps the most significant aspect of the *Oroonoko* review is that we find Johnson embracing a degree of critical assertiveness rarely seen in his earlier *Literary Magazine* reviews.

George Graham (1728?–67), *Telemachus, A Mask.* Reviewed by Johnson in the *Critical,* April 1763; reviewed by John Langhorne in the *Monthly,* February 1763. George Graham earned his living as a teacher and administrator at Eton College, where he was known amongst the students as "Gronkey Graham." Graham also entertained keen hopes of making a name for himself as a dramatist and a poet.[51] Graham's only published work, *Telemachus,* is actually an adaptation of *Télémaque* (1699), a didactic romance by François de Salignac de la Mothe Fénelon (1651–1715), which is based on the Odysseus legend. At first glance, Graham's choice of subject matter seems sensible. Quite apart from the fame associated with the character of Telemachus in Homer's *Odyssey,* Fénelon's narrative was itself widely popular during the eighteenth century. The "lofty sentiments and overt didacticism" of the *Télémaque* drew readers in great numbers, particularly in Great Britain. "Ministers, teachers, and parents often recommended the work to young people, and few must have escaped an encounter with a work so highly praised and so readily available in a large number of copies," observes Leslie A. Chilton in her introduction to a recent edition of Tobias Smollett's version of *Telemachus.*[52] The worthiness of its source material notwithstanding, Graham's version of *Telemachus* received a frigid reception in the *Monthly Review.* In his review, John Langhorne celebrates Graham's choice of genre but finds fault with the poem itself. "There is not in the province of Drama any species of composition so favourable to genius, and so capable of pure poetry, as the Mask," Langhorne declares in the opening sentence of his review. "Unrestrained by time or place, and inattentive to the rules of order and probability, the Poet is at full liberty to indulge all the powers of imagination, in description, passion, and machinery." Even so, readers aware of the full aesthetic possibilities of the mask are bound to be disappointed by *Telemachus.* Though Graham's "Muse is correct and decent," Langhorne states, his "images bear no marks of original genius; his moral sentiments are not uncommon, and his argumentative conversations are often flat, and always too long."[53] Graham's *Telemachus* amounts to a remarkably dull piece of poetry, Langhorne argues, all the more so given the possibilities of the genre it represents.

In direct contrast to the reception of *Telemachus* in the *Monthly,* Johnson found Graham's moralistic adaptation/translation of *Télémaque* to be very much in line with his own outlook on fiction. Indeed, Johnson so admired the Fénelon's narrative that years later he would persist in asking Boswell to send him a copy of a particularly fine edition of *Télémaque,* translated into English by Isaac Littlebury and Abel Boyer and published by the Foulis Press in 1755.[54] How Johnson came to review *Telemachus* in the first place is not quite clear. At some point—no date of any kind is available—Graham occupied a place in Johnson's constantly growing inventory of acquaintances, so it is not hard to imagine him seeking a favorable review from Johnson either personally or through their mutual friend, David Garrick.[55] What makes this an attractive possibility is that Johnson's review seems to concern itself chiefly with rebutting Langhorne's criticisms of two months earlier. Take for instance the opening remarks of Johnson's review, which answers Langhorne's claim that Graham relies too heavily on shopworn themes:

> The contention between pleasure and virtue, a struggle which will always be continued while the present system of nature shall subsist, has now furnished another author with the matter of a poem. We are far from any intention of charging him with the choice of a trite or exhausted subject, for the truth is, that there is no other to be chosen; for by this conflict of opposite principles, modified and determined by innumerable diversities of external circumstances, are produced all the varieties of human life; nor can history or poetry exhibit more than pleasure triumphing over virtue, and virtue subjugating pleasure.[56]

Graham is fully justified in choosing "not uncommon" moral sentiments, Johnson argues here, there being no others worthy of an author's attentions.

Certainly the most striking illustration of Johnson's attempt to answer the *Monthly*'s depreciative notice is the favorable comparison of Graham to Shakespeare. "Shakespear is admired for having brought upon the stage beings of a peculiar order, which exist only in his own imagination," Johnson observes. Graham "likewise has endeavoured to shew the effects of passion upon minds superior in powers to humanity, yet not exalted to impassive dignity." Not quite so striking but equally revelatory of Johnson's intentions is the commentary that follows an extract featuring an exchange between Calypso and Telemachus. "The poet has artfully made his hero use the very same argument afterwards in defence of pleasure," Johnson declares, "which he now offers for refusing it; so differently do we think of the same things in different states of mind." That Johnson wants his readers to think highly of Graham's narrative talents is obvious enough here, but these remarks can also be read as a rebuttal to Langhorne's claim that Graham's "argumentative conversations" lack spirit.[57]

The review concludes with vigorous praise: "[W]e recommend the fertility of imagination, the depth of sentiment, and the knowledge of passion, which are occasionally displayed," Johnson asserts, "to the observation of those readers who have skill to discern, and delicacy to taste them." Significantly, Johnson here answers Langhorne's most severe criticisms point for point: Graham's "images bear no marks of original genius; his moral sentiments are not uncommon, and his argumentative conversations are often flat, and always too long." As we often find in Johnson's book reviews, the *Telemachus* piece is designed to assist a worthy but fallible author—Johnson does admit that genius is only "occasionally displayed" in the poem—gain a foothold in the marketplace in the face of unjust criticisms published in one of the leading review journals.[58]

James Grainger (1721–66), *The Sugar-Cane*. Reviewed by Johnson in the *Critical,* October 1764; reviewed by John Langhorne in the *Monthly,* August 1764. A physician by profession, James Grainger also managed to carve a niche for himself in the world of belles lettres. Between 1756 and 1758 Grainger wrote some three-dozen notices for the highly influential *Monthly Review*, and his earlier "Ode to Solitude" was awarded a measure of status when it appeared in the fourth volume of Robert Dodsley's *Collection of Poems* (1755), which also included works by William Collins, Thomas Gray *(Elegy Wrote in a Country Churchyard),* Johnson *(Vanity of Human Wishes),* and Joseph Warton. In April 1759 Grainger traveled to the Caribbean as the attending physician of John Bourryau, an heir to extensive properties in the West Indies. Five years later Grainger published the *Sugar-Cane*, a poetical account of the region's sugar industry.[59]

Writing for the *Monthly*, John Langhorne offers readers a polite but firmly dismissive account of Grainger's poem. The provincial subject matter of the *Sugar-Cane* cannot possibly appeal to a "European" reader, Langhorne asserts, and the preponderance of "Terms of art" and the many references to "Indian names of trees, and herbs, and fruits" scarcely help matters.[60] Equally significant in Langhorne's view is Grainger's decision to model his style on that of Hesiod, even though a more ornate mode of expression patterned on Virgil's *Georgics* would have been more in keeping with contemporary tastes. "There could be no doubt that the learned and ingenious Author of the Sugar Cane," Langhorne argues,

> knew that he was writing to an age not less luxurious or refined, nor less impatient of whatever has merely the merit of serious utility than Rome itself, during the infancy of its imperial state.—He knew, surely, that the Ascrean simplicity was by no means characteristic of these days, and that to write more like Hesiod than like Virgil, would be to write in vain. Yet whether Dr. Grainger meant it as a compliment to the genius and disposition of his country, or whether something like ancient simplicity may not really exist in our Western Colonies, it is certain that he has made his Sugar Cane rather an useful than an entertaining poem.[61]

Langhorne does manage a word of praise for Grainger's scholarly notes, which are to be considered "both in their medical and botanical capacity, as a very valuable part of the work." And Grainger's reputation as a poet is duly acknowledged in the review's closing sentences. "The Reader had no need of these quotations to inform him of Dr. Grainger's poetical abilities," Langhorne states, but "we have quoted them for his [the reader's] entertainment, as well as to do the Author justice; and hope, that in neither of these respects we have laboured in vain."[62] Nevertheless, Langhorne ultimately leaves us with the impression that the *Sugar-Cane* will disappoint all but the least demanding of readers.

Not much is known about Johnson's relationship with James Grainger apart from the fact that Johnson admired Grainger's "Ode to Solitude"— he "often repeated the sublime introductory Stanza," recalls Thomas Percy in a letter to Robert Anderson—and that Johnson agreed to review Grainger's *Sugar-Cane* in the *Critical* in the fall of 1764. Grainger was rightly grateful to Johnson for doing so.[63] Though Johnson pauses to rebuke Grainger for his indifference to the slave trade, the *Sugar-Cane* review must stand as Johnson's most appreciative. Indeed, the extravagance of Johnson's praise is fully grasped only when we recall his blunt dismissal of the poem in private conversation. "What could he make of a sugar-cane?" Johnson told Boswell in 1777. "One might as well write 'The Parsely-bed, a Poem'; or 'The Cabbage-garden, a Poem.'" Also suggestive of Johnson's low opinion of the *Sugar-Cane*, perhaps, is the much blander and skimpier review that he and Thomas Percy wrote for the *London Chronicle* in July 1764.[64] E. A. Bloom claims that the later review, which appeared in the October 1764 issue of the *Critical*, was meant to address the *Sugar-Cane*'s stubbornly poor sales. This surmise is probably true, but we should not overlook the equally interesting possibility that Johnson wrote the *Critical* piece largely in response to John Langhorne's earlier review in the *Monthly*, which had appeared in August.[65]

Take for instance the lead sentences of Johnson's *Critical* piece, which evidently addresses Langhorne's claim that the *Sugar-Cane* fails to comply with contemporary tastes. Particularly noteworthy is Johnson's mimicry of Langhorne's reference to the "European" reader:

> There are some works in which the exertion of a poet's genius may be very great, and yet his success but moderate. To pursue the topic of the day, or to prop a declining party, are generally sure of immediate applause; but in proportion as such poets write to the present world, they must forego their claims to posterity. If we were to judge of the work before us from its reception among the public, or its aptitude to catch the attention of a common European reader, our criticism might only tend to encrease our ingenious author's displeasure.[66]

That the *Sugar-Cane* betrays an indifference to prevailing fashion, Johnson would have us believe, tells us little about the poem's worthiness and may even betoken a transcendent greatness.

Much of the rest of the review also develops around the criticisms published in the *Monthly*. The alleged dullness and obscurity of the *Sugar-Cane* is answered directly in what is for Johnson unusually lofty praise directed at a living writer. Of special interest is Johnson's comparison of Grainger to Garcilaso de la Vega and Luiz de Camoëns, two Renaissance poets renowned as much for their adventurous lives as for their literary achievements.[67]

> [T]he reader must not be deterred by the title-page, since the most languid will here find his passions excited, and the imagination indulged to the highest pitch of luxury. A new creation is offered, of which an European has scarce any conception; the hurricane, the burning winds, a ripe cane-piece on fire at midnight; an Indian prospect after a finished crop, and nature in all the extremes of tropic exuberance. It is, indeed, a little extraordinary how regions so poetically striking, and so well known to the merchant, have been so little visited by the muse: and that while the Spaniards boast their Garcillasso, and the Portuguese their Camoens, we have been destitute till now of an American poet, that could bear any degree of competition.[68]

The Sugar-Cane triumphantly unites the imagination with real-world experience, in other words. Ambitious and "languid" readers alike will take much delight in Grainger's insightful observations, conveyed as they are by a graceful poetic idiom. Far from being trifling and insipid, Johnson thus argues, Grainger's poem ultimately amounts to a substantial contribution to English letters.

Easily the most striking feature of Johnson's review are the many flattering comparisons of Grainger to Virgil. These comments are almost certainly meant to rebut Langhorne's claim that Grainger's style is somehow out of step with the contemporary appetite for Virgilian imitation. "The character of a good planter is beautifully described," Johnson observes at one point, "and will bring to the reader's memory Virgil's description of the pleasures of a husbandman."[69] Elsewhere, Johnson boldly argues that Grainger surpasses all other recent Virgilian imitators:

> It has been remarked of Virgil that he rises in every book: on the contrary Dyer, Philips, and some others, who have pursued his plan, grow languid as they proceed, as if fatigued with their career. Our poet happily improves in his progress; and as the *taedium* of reading increases, he makes the interest increase proportionably.[70]

Interestingly enough, Johnson ranks Grainger above John Dyer (1699–1758) and John Philips (1676–1709), authors whose poetry would eventually be included in the *Works of the English Poets*, an enterprise remembered nowadays chiefly for its association with Johnson's prefatory "Lives." Hardly less noteworthy here is Johnson's praise for the poem's capacity to delight readers from beginning to end, which can be read as a rejection of Langhorne's claim that the *Sugar-Cane* amounts to "rather an useful than an entertaining poem." Eye-catching though some of Johnson's specific observations may be, the review is significant not for any one critical principle conveyed here but for what it reveals about Johnson's understanding of the influence of book reviewing in the 1760s. Evidently, Johnson concluded that writing an appreciative review of the *Sugar-Cane* entailed the kind of fulsomeness he would have rejected out of hand ten years earlier.

Oliver Goldsmith, *The Traveller, or a Prospect of Society*. Reviewed by Johnson in the *Critical,* December 1764; reviewed in the *Monthly,* January 1765. By all accounts Johnson's friendship with Oliver Goldsmith began in 1759 and lasted until Goldsmith's death in 1774.[71] Though the two men did not always get along well—Goldsmith envied Johnson's fame; Johnson was occasionally irked by Goldsmith's clownish and pretentious disposition—their unwavering admiration of each other's literary abilities cannot be questioned.[72] It is worth recalling, for instance, that Goldsmith addressed the comedy *She Stoops to Conquer* to Johnson (1773). "It may do some honour to inform the public, that I have lived many years in intimacy with you," Goldsmith states in the dedication. "It may serve the interests of mankind also to inform them, that the greatest wit may be found in a character, without impairing the most unaffected piety." Johnson offered similarly high praise of Goldsmith in the "Life of Parnell" (1781). "The Life of Parnell is a task I should very willingly decline," Johnson states in the opening sentence, "since it has been lately written by Goldsmith, a man of such variety of powers and such felicity of performance that he always seemed to do best that which he was doing."[73] Hardly less significant is that Johnson helped Goldsmith at a crucial point in his career by contributing ten lines to the *Traveller*, the first of Goldsmith's works to carry his name on the title page. Johnson also arranged to review the *Traveller* in the *Critical Review*.[74]

Appearing within two weeks of the *Traveller*'s publication, Johnson's review features generous extracts strung together with occasionally flattering but hardly impassioned critical commentary, of which the following is a typical example.[75] "The author already appears, by his numbers, to be a versifier, and by his scenery, to be a poet," Johnson observes, "it therefore remains that his sentiments discover him to be a just estimator of comparative happiness." What makes this review memorable is its final sentence, in which Johnson rather abruptly compares the then largely unknown Gold-smith to Alexander Pope. "Such is this poem, on which we now congratu-late the public, as on a production to which, since the death of Pope, it will not be easy to find any thing equal." Johnson appears to be making two points here. The first and more obvious concerns the great merit of the *Traveller*, the handiwork of an up-and-coming poet. Less obvious but per-haps of greater significance is the possibility that Johnson here means to criticize the growing popularity of what we would think of today as roman-tic strains in poetry. The *Traveller* relies heavily on the very neoclassical devices—rhymed couplets, straightforward description rather than sugges-tion, and well-ordered progression from one idea to the next—that had been falling out of fashion at least since the late 1740s, a circumstance Johnson allusively bemoans when he characterizes the *Traveller* as the finest example of poetry since the death of the greatest of Augustan poets.[76]

Johnson's review of the *Traveller* amounts to a solid endorsement, yet in relation to the three earlier pieces in the *Critical* the Goldsmith review is remarkably subdued. There is no obvious explanation for Johnson's mod-eration. We know that *Critical* piece mirrored Johnson's private opinion of the *Traveller*, so we cannot assert that the comparatively restrained tone of the review indicates a reluctance in Johnson to make claims he really did not believe.[77] One plausible explanation for the relative blandness of the review is that it appeared ahead of competing notices published elsewhere, so there was no existing criticism for Johnson to refute.[78] Had the *Monthly* published a scathing rejection of the *Traveller* before Johnson got around to writing his review, it is at least possible that the *Critical* piece would have turned out much differently.

Johnson ceased writing reviews after the publication of the Goldsmith piece in 1764. His decision to do so comes as something of surprise, espe-cially when we recall the subsequent publication of works—many authored by close friends—that we can imagine him reviewing with some relish: Anna Williams's *Miscellanies in Prose and Verse* (1766), Goldsmith's *The Deserted Village* (1770), Adam Smith's *Wealth of Nations* (1776), John Howard's *State of the Prisons* (1777), Frances Burney's *Evelina* (1778), Thomas Davies's *Memoirs of the Life of David Garrick,* and George Crabbe's *The Village* (1783). That Johnson did not review *The Decline and Fall of the Roman Empire* (1776), written by fellow club member Edward Gibbon, or Gibbon's rebuttal to critics published in 1779, is particularly surprising given the controversy provoked by the disdainful treatment of Christianity in the *Decline*'s fifteenth and sixteenth chapters.[79] One might suppose that Gibbon's views were at least as worthy of Johnson's reproaches as was Soame Jenyns's shallow, breezy advocacy of optimistic philosophy or Thomas Blackwell's overly zealous republicanism.

One credible explanation for Johnson's refusal to write reviews after 1764 is that congenial platforms for reviewing no longer existed. Indeed, we can interpret the relative tepidity of the *Traveller* review as a sign that Johnson could no longer bring himself to write with the level of assertiveness that reviewing in the lead journals demanded from the mid-1750s onward.[80] Also possible is that Johnson, keenly aware of his vast and rather controversial reputation—"I believe there is hardly a day in which there is not something about me in the newspapers," he told Boswell in 1781—did not want his opinions to eclipse the work under review or to allow his reputation as the great Cham of literature to unduly influence popular judgment. Reviews were published anonymously during Johnson's lifetime, true. But as the reception of *Rasselas* (1759) had demonstrated, Johnson could not expect his identity to remain a secret for very long.[81]

Evidence of Johnson's views on the potential impact of his celebrity can be found in Thomas Tyers's brief biography, which appeared in the *Gentleman's Magazine* a few weeks after Johnson's death:

> He [Johnson] did not choose to have his sentiments generally known; for there was a great eagerness, especially in those who had not the pole-star of judgment to direct them, to be taught what to think or say on literary performances. "What does Johnson say of such a book?" was the question of every day. Besides, he did not want to increase the number of his enemies, which his decisions and criticisms had created him.[82]

Johnson's reluctance to make himself heard regarding the works of contemporaries from the mid-1760s onward was well justified, as H. L. McGuffie's bibliography of Johnson's reception in the contemporary press demonstrates. It is scarcely any wonder, then, that when Johnson set out to assist worthy authors during the last twenty years of his life, he did so discreetly by offering advice in private correspondence, for example, or by anonymously composing prefaces and dedications.[83]

What, then, is the final word on Johnson's achievement as a book reviewer? To begin with, Johnson cannot be said to rank among the most influential reviewers of his day—largely because he devoted an extremely small amount of his time to reviewing, most of his authorial career being taken up by heftier projects such as the *Dictionary*, the *Rambler*, the edition of Shakespeare's plays, and the *Lives of the Poets*. Nevertheless, Johnson's sporadic work as a reviewer yielded a surprisingly vast and on the whole intellectually rigorous volume of literary criticism. As mentioned earlier, the forty reviews Johnson wrote in the *Literary Magazine*, along with the seven he contributed to the *Gentleman's* and the *Critical*, total some 180,000 words. By comparison, Johnson's *Idler* and *Adventurer* essays together total some 130,000 words; his *Rambler* essays, some 260,000 words. True, the major part of Johnson's reviews comprise material taken from the works evaluated, but we should also bear in mind that Johnson's selection of extracts, and the understanding of the works embodied not only in Johnson's choice of extracts but in his critical commentary as well, reflects Johnson's highly refined critical intelligence to a much greater degree than most students of Johnson's thought have previously allowed for.

More specifically, we should value Johnson's reviews for three reasons. First, because collectively they exemplify Johnson's outlook on the morally and socially uplifting purposes of authorship as well as what Johnson understood as judiciousness and restraint in criticism directed at the work of living authors—an activity that, as Johnson makes clear in several *Rambler* essays, was particularly prone to extremes of praise and censure. Johnson's reviews are worth studying, moreover, because they show us Johnson contributing his share to the advancement of contemporary letters at a particularly turbulent moment in English literary history by reviewing only authors who plainly have something worthwhile to say, leaving the incorrigibly foolish and the dull to the obscurity they deserve. The frustrated or cynical book buyer, in other words, could rely on Johnson's reviews in the *Literary Magazine* for a survey of basically meritorious books—which is precisely what Johnson had in mind when he began his brief but prolific period of service as a reviewer in the *Literary Magazine*. The Jenyns and Blackwell pieces are famous exceptions to the overall appreciative tenor of Johnson's reviewing, but as the individual discussions of these reviews demonstrate, Johnson had compelling reasons for thrashing these authors in the manner that he did.

Finally, through his reviews Johnson reveals the vastness of his intellectual interests to an extent that is only surpassed by the *Dictionary* project. Indeed, Johnson's reviews illustrate further what Johnson's *Dictionary* proves well enough: that Johnson was one of the last great polymaths, a man equally comfortable discussing electrical engineering, national fiscal policy, English and Roman history, the editing of Shakespeare's plays, the prosody of *Paradise Lost*, balneology, and the climate, geography, and wildlife of Jamaica, Greenland, Syria, and the Scilly Islands. And because of Johnson's intelligent interest in such a wide variety of topics, his reviews often transcend the extract-married-to-brief-critical-comment that largely defined book reviewing at midcentury. Many of Johnson's reviews can be studied as moral, philosophical, political, literary, and scientific essays in their own right, as Johnson collaborates with the authors he reviews to produce perceptive and often provocative commentaries on an impressive array of subjects.

6

Book Reviewing in the Moral Essays: Johnson's Commentary on Recently Published Books in the *Rambler, Adventurer,* and *Idler*

We must read what the world reads at the moment.

—Johnson

[H]e that writes may be considered as a kind of general challenger, whom every one has a right to attack; since he quits the common rank of life, steps forward beyond the lists, and offers his merit to the publick judgment. To commence author is to claim praise, and no man can justly aspire to honour, but at the hazard of disgrace.

—Johnson

SAMUEL JOHNSON'S OUTPUT AS A LITERARY CRITIC INCLUDES A SIZABLE BUT LITTLE-studied body of published commentary directed at living writers, as the preceding chapters have demonstrated. Most of this criticism takes the form of the book review, of course; the remainder can be found in Johnson's essay serials, the *Rambler* (1750–52), the *Adventurer* (1753–54), and the *Idler* (1758–60). That a mere nine of Johnson's 335 essays—*Rambler*s 4, 77, 121, 139, and 154; *Adventurer*s 85, 92, and 137; and *Idler* 65—fall into this category is not at all surprising, given that Johnson in *Rambler*s 78, 106, 208, and elsewhere asserts that the moral essayist should avoid overtly topical subject matter. Nevertheless, the nine essays examined here are significant because they reflect Johnson's interest in the contemporary literary world, particularly his willingness to comment on, or to review, recently published titles.

Three of these essays are already known as commentaries on contemporaneously published works. Scholars generally agree that Johnson in *Rambler* 4 (March 1750) allusively criticizes Tobias Smollett's *Roderick*

Random (1748) and Henry Fielding's *Tom Jones* (1749).[1] The occasion for *Idler* 65 (14 July 1759), as Johnson himself points out, is the recent posthumous publication of the *Continuation of the History of the Grand Rebellion*, by Edward Hyde, earl of Clarendon (1609–74). Of special interest here is that Johnson's essay appeared within weeks of the work's publication and ahead of notices published in the *Monthly Review* and the *Critical Review*—both of which applauded the volume in terms similar to those of *Idler* 65.[2] The subject of the third essay, widely known as a criticism of a contemporary work, is less straightforward. James Woodruff makes a good—if not an airtight—case that the complaint about the recent profusion of Spenserian imitations in *Rambler* 121 refers to the *Four Seasons*, by Moses Mendez, and the *Progress of Envy*, by Robert Lloyd.[3] But a much more likely target of *Rambler* 121 is Gilbert West's *Education: A Poem in Two Cantos, Written in Imitation of the Style and Manner of Spenser's Faerie Queene.*

Number 121 appeared on 14 May 1751, a few weeks after the publication of *Education* on 28 March 1751—thus establishing the possibility that Johnson had read, or had at least known something about, West's poem before composing the *Rambler* essay.[4] Of greater significance is the similarity between Johnson's characterization of the leading practitioners of Spenserian imitations—*Rambler* 121 describes them as "men of learning and genius" who labor away on an unworthy poetical form—and what Johnson says about *Education* in the *Lives of the Poets*.[5] West's Spenserian imitations, Johnson writes in the "Life of West,"

> are very successfully performed, both with respect to the metre, the language, and the fiction; and being engaged at once by the excellence of the sentiments and the artifice of the copy the mind has two amusements together. But such compositions are not to be reckoned among the great achievements of intellect, because their effect is local and temporary; they appeal not to reason or passion, but to memory, and presuppose an accidental or artificial state of mind. An imitation of Spenser is nothing to a reader, however acute, by whom Spenser has never been perused.[6]

It is not hard to conclude that Johnson here simply reiterates critical opinions expressed in his journalistic writings many years earlier—just as he had done in his biographies of Milton, Pope, and Watts.[7]

While *Rambler* 4, *Rambler* 121, and *Idler* 65 are generally accepted as commentaries on recently published works, six other essays by Johnson can be tied to the contemporary literary world with reasonable certainty. As is the case for the previously discussed pieces, Johnson wraps his commentary in an aura of universality even as he leaves plenty of clues that would allow contemporary readers to draw connections between what "Mr.

Rambler" says and recently published titles. Johnson reconciles the conflict between the general language called for by the genre of the moral essay and the topicality that would attract ordinary readers, in other words, by emphasizing the timeless aspects of a given essay's contemporary source of inspiration.

The least obviously topical of the nine periodical essays in which Johnson criticizes contemporary works is *Rambler* 77, entitled "The Learned Seldom Despised but When They Deserve Contempt" by the editors the Yale Edition of the Works of Samuel Johnson. In many ways, number 77 typifies Johnson's manner of proceeding in the *Rambler*. Johnson begins by pondering a commonplace: the universal authorial habit of bemoaning the contemporary neglect of literary merit. "Among those, whose hopes of distinction or riches, arise from an opinion of their intellectual attainments, it has been, from age to age, an established custom to complain of the ingratitude of mankind to their instructors," Johnson observes, "and the discouragement which men of genius and study suffer from avarice and ignorance, from the prevalence of false taste, and the encroachment of barbarity." Johnson soon moves on to a discussion of "loose or profane" authors. Many writers "have dared to boast of neglected merit, and to challenge their age for cruelty and folly, of whom it cannot be alleged that they have endeavoured to increase the wisdom or virtue of their readers."[8] Johnson goes on to argue that the pains of hell are a condign punishment for writers who deliberately misuse their talents:

> Those, whom God has favoured with superior faculties, and made eminent for quickness of intuition, and accuracy of distinctions, will certainly be regarded as culpable in his eye, for defects and deviations which, in souls less enlightened, may be guiltless. But, surely, none can think without horror on that man's condition, who has been more wicked in proportion as he had more means of excelling in virtue, and used the light imparted from heaven only to embellish folly, and shed lustre upon crimes.[9]

Needless to say, *Rambler* 77 expresses Johnson's general outlook on the relation between literature and conventional morality. Even so, a comparison of the specifics of the essay and Johnson's "Life of Otway" (1779) suggests that at some level *Rambler* 77 means to address specifically the resurgent popularity of Thomas Otway's plays *The Orphan* and *Venice Preserv'd*.

Rambler 77 appeared on 11 December 1750, only weeks after several performances of *The Orphan* (18–19 October) and *Venice Preserv'd* (24, 25, 27 October) were given at the Drury-Lane Theater (managed by Johnson's friend David Garrick). Both tragedies were performed several times earlier in the year as well—as was Otway's ribald comedy *Friendship in*

Fashion.[10] The *Orphan* and *Venice* feature obscene or lewd material, though the bawdy scenes in *Venice* were customarily expurgated during the eighteenth century. Significantly, Johnson's concern in *Rambler* 77 is not with run-of-the-mill writers of libertine literature, but with highly successful, perhaps even canonical, authors—as Otway was by 1750—whose alluring portrayals of vice work to undermine civilized society. "It has been the settled purpose of some writers, whose powers and acquisitions place them high in the ranks of literature, to set fashion on the side of wickedness," Johnson observes, "to recommend debauchery, and lewdness, by associating them with qualities most likely to dazzle the discernment, and attract the affections; and to show innocence and goodness with such attendant weaknesses as necessarily expose them to contempt and derision." Johnson here might be alluding to *Venice Preserv'd*, but his comments are particularly relevant to the *Orphan*, which centered not on the intrigues of the court but on domestic life in rural Bohemia. Polydore, one of the lead characters, is a roguish figure—witness his exposition of amoral sexuality at the end of act 1 and his willingness to cuckold his brother—but his plainspokenness and boldness command admiration, and he is not without moralistic impulses.[11] Indeed, Polydore can be aptly described as a prototype for the amiable yet vice-laden characters on display in the novels discussed in *Rambler* 4.

More importantly, the allusive attacks on Otway in *Rambler* 77 conform to opinions expressed in Johnson's "Life of Otway" (1779). Take for instance Johnson's reluctance to acknowledge the enduring popularity of the *Orphan*. "This is one of the few plays that keep possession of the stage," Johnson states, "and has pleased for almost a century through all the vicissitudes of dramatick fashion." Given Johnson's well-known faith in the common reader and his equally famous pronouncements on the unerring judgment of posterity, one might expect to find in the "Life of Otway" a closely reasoned justification for the high value assigned to the *Orphan* by generations of theatergoers. Yet Johnson seems more interested in excusing, rather than in ratifying, what he sees as the public's ill-considered fondness for the play:

> Of this play nothing new can easily by said. It is a domestick tragedy drawn from middle life. Its whole power is upon the affections, for it is not written with much comprehension of thought or elegance of expression. But if the heart is interested, many other beauties may be wanting, yet not missed.[12]

Johnson's observations on *Venice Preserv'd* are equally hedged:

> By comparing this with his *Orphan* it will appear that his images were by time become stronger, and his language more energetick. The striking pas-

sages are in every mouth; and the publick seems to judge rightly of the faults and excellencies of this play, that it is the work of a man not attentive to decency nor zealous for virtue; but of one who conceived forcibly and drew originally by consulting nature in his own breast.[13]

Here, Johnson acknowledges that the fame of *Venice Preserv'd*, and of Otway's work in general, is essentially well deserved. On the other hand, in Johnson's view Otway's licentiousness—both in his writings and, as is implied here, in his personal life as well—debars him from the front rank of poets and dramatists.[14]

Scarcely less significant are the similarities between the private conduct of the profane author allusively discussed in *Rambler* 77 and events in Otway's life as related in Johnson's biography. Those writers who committed themselves to making allies out of fashion and amorality "naturally found intimates among the corrupt, the thoughtless, and the intemperate," Johnson states in the *Rambler*.

[They] passed their lives amidst the levities of sportive idleness, or the warm professions of drunken friendship; and fed their hopes with the promises of wretches, whom their precepts had taught to scoff at truth. But when fools had laughed away their sprightliness, and the langours of excess could no longer be relieved, they saw their protectors hourly drop away, and wondered and stormed to find themselves abandoned. Whether their companions persisted in wickedness or returned to virtue, they were left equally without assistance; for debauchery is selfish and negligent, and from virtue the virtuous only can expect regard.

In the *Lives*, Johnson describes Otway's sybaritic lifestyle in remarkably similar terms:

Otway is said to have been at this time [late 1670s] a favourite companion of the dissolute wits. But, as he who desires no virtue in his companion has no virtue in himself, those whom Otway frequented had no purpose of doing more for him than to pay his reckoning. They desired only to drink and laugh; their fondness was without benevolence, and their familiarity without friendship. Men of wit, says one of Otway's biographers, received at that time no favour from the Great but to share their riots; "from which they were dismissed again to their own narrow circumstances. Thus they languished in poverty without the support of innocence."[15]

Of interest here is that Johnson quotes from the anonymous prefatory essay to the 1712 collected edition of Otway's works, which he may have read at some point before composing *Rambler* 77.[16] It is even possible that some of the numerous quotations from Otway's works in Johnson's *Dictionary*, which was still being compiled when *Rambler* 77 was written, were drawn from this 1712 edition or later reprintings of it.[17]

One other similarity between the *Rambler* essay and the "Life" is worth mentioning. In *Rambler* 77 Johnson asserts that profane writers are fit subjects for legal prosecution:

> What were their motives, or what their excuses, is below the dignity of reason to examine. If having extinguished in themselves the distinction of right and wrong, they were insensible of the mischief which they promoted, they deserved to be hunted down by the general compact, as no longer partaking of social nature; if influenced by the corruption of patrons, or readers, they sacrificed their own convictions to vanity or interest, they were to be abhorred with more acrimony than he that murders for pay; since they committed greater crimes without greater temptations.[18]

In the *Lives*, the bitter fruits of Otway's dissolution are set forth in similar terms. "Having been compelled by necessities to contract debts, and hunted, as is supposed, by the terriers of the law," Johnson writes, Otway "retired to a publick house on Tower-hill, where he is said to have died of want."[19] Of course, the circumstances here are not identical—*Rambler* 77 refers to legal prosecution for obscenity; in the "Life" Johnson refers to Otway's attempt to avoid debtor's prison—but, as Brian Corman has pointed out in his analysis of the "Life of Otway," Johnson's loathing of Otway's dissipated habits left him strikingly unsympathetic to Otway's personal trials.[20] "Unsympathetic," in fact, aptly sets Johnson's "Life" apart from the harshly condemnatory *Rambler* 77. The allusive idiom of the *Rambler* series allowed Johnson to express deeply held views that would not have been appropriate in the prefatory material to the *Works of the English Poets*, which was retailed as a definitive collection of England's most distinguished poets.

Rambler 139 is very much rooted in contemporary circumstance, even though its subject, John Milton's tragedy *Samson Agonistes*, first appeared in 1671. If "there is any writer whose genius can embellish impropriety, and whose authority can make error venerable," Johnson says before offering readers a depreciative analysis of Milton's dramatic poem, "his works are the proper objects of critical inquisition." *Rambler* 139's historical orientation is stated clearly enough here, but the specific contemporary circumstance that prompted Johnson to write the essay in the first place is briefly alluded to a few sentences later. "The tragedy *Samson Agonistes* has been celebrated as the second work of the great author of *Paradise Lost*," Johnson observes, "and opposed with all the confidence of triumph to the dramatick performances of other nations."[21] It is not Milton's failings per se that prompted Johnson to write *Rambler* 139, we are given to understand here, but the recent pronouncements of critics, who have lavished what Johnson sees as indiscriminate praise on one of Milton's less worthy productions. The critical work in question is almost certainly the 1750 edition of *Paradise Lost*, superintended by a former Lichfield Grammar schoolmate of Johnson's, Thomas Newton.

In his prefatory "Life of Milton," Newton avers that *Samson Agonistes* "is written in the very spirit of the Ancients, and equals, if not exceeds, any of the most perfect tragedies, which were exhibited on the Athenian stage, when Greece was in its Glory." It is possible that Johnson perused Newton's volume itself, or he may have read the review of *Paradise Lost* in the January 1750 issue of the *Monthly Review*, which reproduced the controversial passage quoted here. Whatever the case, *Rambler* 139 is as much a rebuke to an incautious contemporary critic as it is an unvarnished assessment of *Samson Agonistes*.[22]

In sharp contrast to *Rambler* 139, *Rambler* 154 addresses not a canonical work but a revolutionary one—the recently published English translation of Jean-Jacques Rousseau's *The Discourse on the Arts and Sciences*. The *Discourse*, Rousseau's first book, was originally given as a paper at the Academy of Dijon in 1750. The academy awarded Rousseau top honors for his discussion of the proposition: whether the arts and sciences had tended toward the improvement of morals.[23] Rousseau in the *Discourse* argues that civilization has yielded nothing but vice, despair, and criminality. Whether "we turn over the annals of the world, or supply the defects of uncertain chronicles by philosophical searches, we shall not find that the origin of human knowledge answers, in any degree, the ideas we form of it," Rousseau states; "astronomy was begot by superstition, eloquence sprung from ambition, hatred, flattery, and falshood; geometry is a child of avarice, physics rose from vain curiosity; and all, even morality itself, are effects of human pride."[24]

Rousseau goes on to contend that the maturation of professional letters and the attendant evolution of scholarly and aesthetic standards have worked to demean genius. The promising author, if "he has the misfortune to be born among a people" who value learning, inevitably "must lower his genius to the level of the age, and rather apply to mean things which will raise admiration in his own days, than attempt at sublime works which will only shine long after his decease." To lend credibility to his thesis, Rousseau invokes a lately celebrated iconoclast: "Tell us, thou celebrated *Voltaire*, how many nervous energick sentiments thou hast been forced to sacrifice to our false delicacy, and at what expence of noble ideas thou hast complied with the present spirit of gallantry so productive of mean ones?" Rousseau concludes with an exhortation on the superiority of self-revelation to traditional forms of learning. "O virtue! thou sublime science of simple souls!," Rousseau exclaims, "need we be at such pains to discover thee? Are not they principles engraven on every heart? to learn thy precepts, we need only turn our eyes inward on ourselves, and hearken to the voice of conscience commanding silence to our passions." It is worth noting that Rousseau tempers his argument in the final paragraphs, as he acknowledges that the intellectually gifted can make good use of traditional studies. "If any one must be permitted the study of arts and sciences, it should be only those who find strength enough of soul within them," Rousseau observes.[25]

The first English-language edition of Rousseau's *Discourse*, translated by the bookseller William Bowyer (1699–1777), was published on 23 July 1751 and favorably reviewed some five weeks later in the August 1751 issue of the *Monthly*.[26] Though brief objections to Rousseau's main argument are offered, the reviewer ultimately endorses Rousseau's volume. The review's opening sentence calls attention to the *Discourse*'s burgeoning fame. "This piece has been published sometime, in the language in which it was deliver'd, and hath attracted a large share of the public attention." While it is true that Rousseau's arguments "have more of sophistry than demonstration in them," the reviewer observes, it must also be acknowledged that the author "is a compleat master of the declamatory art." Indeed, it was Rousseau's rhetorical prowess—exclusive of his ideas—that impressed the Dijon panel. On awarding him the prize, the reviewer relates, the judges at Dijon told Rousseau

> that he did not so much owe this precedence, in their opinion, to his hypothesis, and the arguments he brought to support it, as to his superior art and skill in handling the subject, above that of his competitors: so that, in fact, they looked upon himself and his fine talents as an example that ought to weigh much against the principles he had employed them to defend.[27]

Johnson must have bristled at what was in his view Rousseau's profoundly dishonest characterization of the relation between the flowering of genius and formal study.[28] Doubtless a personal element entered the picture as well: by the light of Rousseau's thesis, Johnson's *Dictionary* (1755) might easily be dismissed as a useless if not a pernicious enterprise. The credibility given to Rousseau by the Dijon Academy—an institution supposedly devoted to advancing scholarly inquiry—and the *Monthly Review*, a self-professed arbiter of literary taste, must have been even more unsettling. The dates of the review (29 August 1751) and that of *Rambler* 154 (7 September 1751) are close enough to suggest coincidence, but it is worth recalling that *Rambler* essays were routinely "written in haste as the moment pressed," as Boswell tells us, "without even being read over by him before they were printed." The printer of the *Monthly* was William Strahan, who at the time also held the contract to print Johnson's *Dictionary* and who served as an intermediary of sorts between Johnson and his sponsoring booksellers. Johnson "must have been in almost daily contact" with his printer at least from the early months of 1750 until the *Dictionary* was ready for publication, observes J. A. Cochrane in his biography of Strahan, so it is not at all hard to imagine Johnson glancing at the August 1751 issue of the *Monthly* as it was being readied for publication. The *Monthly*, like most contemporary periodicals, was normally published on the first day of the month following the date given on the title page, so the August 1751 issue probably appeared on 1 September, or a day or so afterward.[29]

The rhetorical strategy of number 154 is very much typical of the *Rambler* series. Johnson begins with a commonplace—in this case the indispensability of traditional scholarship to worthwhile literary achievement—which is followed by an analysis of its validity. The essay finishes with a vigorous affirmation of the essential soundness of the commonplace.[30] Those who wish to "become eminent" in the world of letters must first "search books" and then "contemplate nature," Johnson declares. A self-evident piece of wisdom, Johnson suggests, yet authors nowadays increasingly ignore plainly sound advice in the hopes of discovering shortcuts to celebrity:

> The mental disease of the present generation, is impatience of study, contempt of the great masters of ancient wisdom, and a disposition to rely wholly upon unassisted genius and natural sagacity. The wits of these happy days have discovered a way to fame, which the dull caution of our laborious ancestors durst never attempt; they cut the knots of sophistry which it was formerly the business of years to untie, solve difficulties by sudden irradiations of intelligence, and comprehend long processes of argument by immediate intuition.[31]

The "unassisted genius" concept is really nothing more than an apologia for sloth and vainglory, Johnson goes on to argue, and the empty pretensions of those who think of themselves as endowed with "natural sagacity" is soon unmasked when put to any serious test. "The laurels which superficial acuteness gains in triumphs over ignorance unsupported by vivacity, are observed by Locke to be lost whenever real learning and rational diligence appear against her," Johnson observes. The "sallies of gaiety are soon repressed by calm confidence, and the artifices of subtilty are readily detected by those who having carefully studied the question, are not easily confounded or surprised."[32] The rebuke to Rousseau here is obvious enough, but also worth noting is the scorn Johnson heaps on the Dijon Academy for its poor judgment.

A pair of later essays—*Adventurer*s 85 (August 1753) and 137 (February

1754)—can also be read as reactions to the publication of subsequent editions of the *Discourse*. What prompted Johnson to resume his attack on Rousseau's ideas is a matter for speculation. The *Discourse* may have stirred up a great deal of controversy in France, but it did not arouse particularly high levels of sustained public interest in England.[33] No critical discussion of the *Discourse* or its themes appears in the *Gentleman's Magazine* for 1752–53; nor does one find references to the work, or notices of treatises designed to refute or extend Rousseau's thesis, in the *Monthly Review* during the same period. Even so, the *Discourse* evidently attracted enough reader interest to justify subsequent editions. The "Books Published" section of the April 1752 issue of the *Gentleman's Magazine*, for instance, gives notice to a new edition of Rousseau's volume, translated into English by Richard Wynne; this listing is repeated in the February 1753 number of the *Gentleman's*. A "fourth edition" of Bowyer's 1751 translation, carrying a Dublin imprint, appeared in 1752.[34] The literary marketplace's endorsement of Rousseau's ideas, Johnson appears to have thought, was just the sort of subject that the *Adventurer*, a twice-weekly essay serial patterned on the *Rambler*, was meant to consider.[35]

For readers of *Rambler* 154 there is nothing substantively new in *Adventurer* 85. We begin as we do in the earlier essay with a commonplace (taken from Bacon's essay, "Of Studies"): "[R]eading makes a full man, conversation a ready man, and writing an exact man."[36] The recent ascendancy of a theory that disparages traditional learning is mentioned—

> An opinion has of late been, I know not how, propagated among us, that libraries are filled only with useless lumber; that men of parts stand in need of no assistance; and that to spend life in poring upon books, is only to imbibe prejudices, to obstruct and embarrass the powers of nature, to cultivate memory at the expence of judgement, and to bury reason under a chaos of indigested learning.[37]

—followed by assertions that such popularity is unwarranted. Familiar material is placed in evidence. How is it that previous generations, "equally participating of the bounties of nature with ourselves," have written nothing worthy of our attentions, Johnson wonders. And what does such a theory suggest about the wisdom of its proponents—Rousseau in particular? When "an author declares, that he has been able to learn nothing from the writings of his predecessors," Johnson states,

> and such a declaration has been lately made, nothing but a degree of arrogance unpardonable in the greatest human understanding, can hinder him from perceiving, that he is raising prejudices against his own performance; for with what hopes of success can he attempt that, in which greater abili-

ties have hitherto miscarried? or with what peculiar force does he suppose himself invigorated, that difficulties hitherto invincible should give way before him?[38]

As *Adventurer* 85 develops, Johnson continues to raise doubts about Rousseau's character and judgment. "It will, I believe, be found invariably true, that learning was never decried by any learned man," Johnson declares, "and what credit can be given to those, who venture to condemn that which they do not know?" Shrillness of this kind almost certainly reflects a belief that Rousseau's ideas on natural genius had acquired a measure of legitimacy and had continued to gain authority.[39]

Of special interest to Johnson is that Rousseau's ideas demean the humbler but most widely beneficent of authorial occupations, such as translating, compiling, and news writing. As Johnson almost certainly knew from his own wide experiences in the book trade, such occupations were attracting authors in great numbers, many of them equipped with solid but undistinguished literary abilities. Rousseau's theories—particularly the closing paragraphs of the *Discourse*, where Rousseau admits that the sciences are useful only to the brightest of scholars and that ordinary people are better served by ignorance—would encourage aspiring authors to reject worthy but unglamorous employments in favor of consulting their consciences, their imaginative muses or, more likely, their sense of self-importance, with the understanding that unleashing the genius inside is a more reliable path to fame and fortune. In response, Johnson offers a rigorous apologia for scholarly diligence, emphasizing the lofty social and moral purposes of authorship, and—somewhat unusual for Johnson—downplaying the role of genius in the discovery and transmission of knowledge. Very few of us have the ability to make even modest additions to the stock of human knowledge, Johnson declares. Rather,

> the greatest part of mankind must owe all their knowledge, and all must owe far the larger part of it, to the information of others. To understand the works of celebrated authors, to comprehend their systems, and retain their reasonings, is a task more than equal to common intellects; and he is by no means to be accounted useless or idle, who has stored his mind with acquired knowledge, and can detail it occasionally to others who have less leisure or weaker abilities.[40]

Johnson's remarks here amount to a spirited denunciation of Rousseau's claim that traditional scholarly and aesthetic standards undermine what Rousseau insists is our intrinsic sense of goodwill. In *Adventurer* 85 Johnson not only seeks to expose Rousseau's reasoning as meretricious, but he also strives to affirm the humane uses of even the most basic of authorial tasks.

Appearing in February 1754, *Adventurer* 137 ostensibly reflects on the worthiness of the entire *Adventurer* series, which was scheduled to end after the publication of the 140th number. The scope of the essay, however, quickly broadens to encompass a topic of much greater contemporary significance. "As I shall soon cease to write Adventurers, I could not forbear lately to consider what has been the consequence of my labours," Johnson states. "That I have intended well, I have the attestation of my own heart; but good intentions may be frustrated, when they are executed without suitable skill, or directed to an end unattainable in itself." There is perhaps a formulaic element at work here—the *Rambler* had closed on a similarly introspective note, as would the *Idler* series in 1760—but we can also read the preceding sentence as the opening statement of a rebuttal to Rousseau's *Discourse on the Arts and Sciences.* What Johnson sets out to do, in other words, is to evaluate rigorously the proposition that literature obstructs the social and ethical progress of humanity. "Some there are, who leave writers very little room for self congratulation," Johnson observes in what can be read as an allusion to Rousseau's *Discourse,*

> some who affirm, that books have no influence upon the public, that no age was ever made better by its authors, and that to call upon mankind to correct their manners, is, like Xerxes, to scourge the wind or shackle the torrent. This opinion they pretend to support by unfailing experience. The world is full of fraud and corruption, rapine and malignity; interest is the ruling motive of mankind, and every one is endeavouring to increase his own stores of happiness and perpetual accumulation, without reflecting upon the numbers whom his superfluity condemns to want. . . .[41]

Much of the essay is given over to a consideration of the merits of the position set forth here. True enough, Johnson admits, not even the most celebrated works of morality have managed to alter the general prevalence of "corruption, malevolence, and rapine." Making matters worse is the scarcity of readers receptive to literature's preceptorial ends. "The book that is read most, is read by few, compared with those that read it not," Johnson states, "and of those few, the greater part peruse it with dispositions that very little favour their own improvement."[42]

The allowances granted to the Rousseauistic perspective, however, ultimately give occasion for Johnson to emphasize the exalted standing of professional letters in society. "Books of morality are daily written, yet its influence is still little in the world; so the ground is annually ploughed, and yet multitudes are in want of bread," Johnson observes.

> But, surely, neither the labours of the moralist nor of the husbandman are vain; let them for a while neglect their tasks, and their usefulness will be

known; the wickedness that is now frequent would become universal, the bread that is now scarce would wholly fail.[43]

As for the frivolous motives of most readers: books "have always a secret influence on the understanding; we cannot at pleasure obliterate ideas," Johnson declares.

[H]e that reads books of science, though without any fixed desire of improvement, will grow more knowing; he that entertains himself with moral or religious treatises, will imperceptibly advance in goodness; the ideas which are often offered to the mind will at last find a lucky moment when it is disposed to receive them.[44]

Of significance here is that Johnson takes a position at the opposite extreme from Rousseau's. Far from being hopelessly ineffectual at advancing the human condition, Johnson argues, literature has done more good than we can ever determine.

Much like *Rambler*s 77 and 139, Johnson in *Adventurer* 92 attempts to shed new light on a historically significant literary work by allusively evaluating a recently published edition. "Dubius," Johnson's fictional correspondent, offers readers "such observations as have risen to my mind in the consideration of Virgil's pastorals, without any enquiry how far my sentiments deviate from established rules or common opinions." Interestingly enough, the critical survey of Virgil's *Eclogues* that follows is based on the recently published translation by Johnson's friend Joseph Warton—Warton's *Works of Virgil in Latin and English* was published on 25 January 1753; *Adventurer* 92 appeared on 22 September 1753—thus suggesting that a collateral objective of *Adventurer* 92 is to generate public interest in Warton's recent edition. Indeed, in what ultimately amounts to a depreciative survey of Virgil's *Eclogues*—"if we except the first and the tenth, they seem liable either wholly or in part to considerable objections"—Johnson quotes from Warton's translation only when discussing the two best pastoral poems. Thus, Warton's work appears strictly in the context of appreciative commentary; Johnson's blunt criticisms of the remaining eight pastorals, meanwhile, gives the essay the feel of a rigorous and impartial reconsideration of Virgil's poetry.[45]

The handful of essays considered here illuminates Johnson's keen interest in the contemporary literary world—a fascinating, if rather neglected, aspect of Johnson's critical writings. More specifically, the contemporary aspect of these essays should draw greater scholarly attention to the more substantial body of Johnson's published criticism of living writers: the forty-seven reviews Johnson wrote between 1742 and 1764.

Appendix:
The Canon of Johnson's
Literary Magazine Reviews

In his survey of Johnson's reviewing in the *Literary Magazine*, Donald Eddy avers that Johnson did not write the notice of Richard Lovett's *The Subtil Medium Proved* or that of Hoadly and Wilson's *Observations on a Series of Electrical Experiments*. Curiously, Eddy offers no reason for disagreeing with Donald Greene, who initially made what remains a convincing case for Johnson's authorship in his essay, "Johnson's Contributions to the *Literary Magazine*," and J. D. Fleeman, who accepts Greene's attributions in the *New Cambridge Bibliography of English Literature* (vol. 2, 1971). The weight of scholarly opinion falls on the side of accepting these notices as Johnson's, so they are treated as such here. One other piece previously accepted as Johnson's but rejected by Eddy deserves consideration. In his 1956 essay Greene claims that the notice of Bourchier Cleeve's *A Scheme for Preventing a Further Increase of the National Debt* is unquestionably Johnson's, an attribution accepted by J. D. Fleeman. Eddy concedes that Johnson "may have written" the piece, though he refuses to include it in his list of Johnson's reviews on the grounds that "all the extracts used in the review are verbatim quotations and do not show any Johnsonian abridgements." The reviewer's reliance on direct quotation scarcely amounts to a creditable case against Johnson's authorship, if only because many of Johnson's known reviews carry verbatim quotations—as Eddy himself admits elsewhere in his volume.[1] More significantly, Eddy makes no attempt to reject the evidence—the parallels of style; the denunciation of excise commissioners—that led Greene to attribute the review to Johnson in the first place. Also relevant is this anecdote, related by Hester Lynch Piozzi, which demonstrates that Johnson had more than a superficial interest in the national debt:

> [Johnson] shewed me a calculation which I could scarce be made to understand, so vast was the plan of it, and so very intricate were the figures: no other indeed than the national debt . . . [which] would, if converted into silver, serve to make a meridian of that metal, I forgot how broad, for the globe of the whole earth, the real *globe*.[2]

The accumulation of external and internal evidence along with the source of attribution argue for accepting the Cleeve notice as authentic.

Eddy rejects four other reviews that Greene attributes to Johnson: *A Letter from Joseph Ames to John Booth* (*Literary Magazine*, i.77–78); Peter Whalley, ed., *The Works of Ben Jonson* (*Literary Magazine*, i.169–71); John Free, *A Sermon Preached at St. John's on the 29th of May, 1756* (*Literary Magazine*, i.186); *An Account of the Conferences Held, and Treaties Made, between Major-General Sir William Johnson, and the Chief Sachems and Warriors of the Mohawks* (*Literary Magazine*, i.191–93). Each of these reviews comprises nothing more than an extremely brief critical commentary attached to a verbatim extract from the text at hand, thus bringing to mind the pieces attributed to Johnson in the *Gentleman's Magazine* and suggesting also that anyone else on the *Literary Magazine* staff might have written them. Greene's case essentially rests on the fact that they appear in the *Literary Magazine* during Johnson's tenure, that they can be said vaguely to match Johnson's known opinions and writing style, and that nothing present in the reviews themselves rules out Johnson's authorship. I agree with Eddy that there is nothing distinctively Johnsonian about any of these pieces, and I would say further that more than a mere hunch that Johnson wrote these pieces is needed before we include them in Johnson's canon of book reviews.

I do believe that one of the tentative pieces, the review of the *Account of Conferences Held*, should be removed from consideration. Here is the entire critical portion:

> A Book with such words on the first page might easily frighten a reader from turning to the second. And indeed these conferences are more important than entertaining; they however enable us to form some conceptions of the manners of the wild nations. The Preface exhibits an account of the five nations, extracted from *Colden*, and a character of Sir *Wm Johnson*, which may properly interest the curiosity of the Reader. The Vocabulary is so useful to those who compare *French* with *English* accounts, that we should injure our readers by neglecting to insert it.[3]

There is nothing here to tell us positively that Johnson did not write this review, but it must also be said that from stylistic and intellectual points of view at least, the passage is inferior to any of the other reviews known to have come from Johnson's pen. To begin with, I find it hard to believe that Johnson wrote the concluding sentence, given his well-known antipathy toward French imperialism and Gallic expressions. Indeed, it is something of a surprise that Johnson, if we are to assume for a moment that he wrote the review, does not take the opportunity in the review to decry colonial expansion—as he does with considerable intensity in the review of Evans's *Map* and in his inaugural *Literary Magazine* essay, the "Introduction to the Political State of Great Britain." What is more, the phrase "wild nations" seems particularly unJohnsonian, all the more so when we recall that in Johnson's other pieces in the *Literary Magazine* on North American affairs, such as the "Political State" and the "Observations on the Present State of Affairs," Johnson refers repeatedly to the native North Americans as "Indians" and never as members of "wild nations."

Eddy makes a rather halfhearted case for the authenticity of the review of William Whitehead's *Elegies, with an Ode to the Tiber*. While the critical opinions of the brief review can be said vaguely to conform to Johnson's, as Eddy points out, the laudatory temperament of the piece conflicts with Johnson's known views of Whitehead's poetry and with Johnson's generally reserved critical language as a reviewer in the *Literary Magazine*.[4] Put another way, there simply is not enough evidence to justify including the piece in the canon, and there is good reason to doubt its authenticity.

One other work ought to be removed from Eddy's list of Johnson's book reviews, though there is no questioning Johnson's authorship of the piece. The composition entitled "The History of Minorca" contains no critical commentary, nor are prospective book buyers provided with the standard bibliographical data found in period book reviews.[5] In fact, the one bit of descriptive data present is unusual for a review and grossly inaccurate besides. Johnson cites a publication year of 1740, even though the first edition appeared in 1752; Johnson quotes from a later edition, published in 1756. The abridgment is perhaps best understood as news writing rather than reviewing, as Johnson himself suggests in his introductory remarks:

> At this time, when the eyes of Europe are turned upon the expedition of the French against PORT-MAHON, the public will naturally require some account of the island of MINORCA, which we shall extract from the history written in the form of letters, by Mr. Armstrong, in 1740 [*sic*].[6]

Johnson's intent, clearly, is to publicize information on a location that promises to dominate the headlines in the coming months rather than to give notice to a recently published work.

Notes

Abbreviations used in the notes section:

CR   *Critical Review*, 1756–1817.
GM   *Gentleman's Magazine*, 1731–1914.
LM   *Literary Magazine*, 1756–58.
MR   *Monthly Review*, 1749–1845.
UV   *Universal Visiter*, 1756.
Yale *The Yale Edition of the Works of Samuel Johnson*, edited by
      J. H. Middendorf, 13 volumes to date (New Haven: Yale
      University Press, 1958–).

INTRODUCTION

1. For the development of book reviewing, see James G. Basker, *Tobias Smollett: Critic and Journalist* (Newark: University of Delaware Press, 1988); Frank Donoghue, *The Fame Machine: Book Reviewing and Eighteenth-Century Literary Careers* (Stanford, Calif.: Stanford University Press, 1996); Donoghue, "Colonizing Readers: Review Criticism and the Formation of a Reading Public," in *The Consumption of Culture: Image, Object, Text*, ed. Ann Bermingham and John Brewer (London: Routledge, 1995), pp. 54–74; Antonia Forster, "From 'Tasters to the Public' to 'Beadles of Parnassus': Reviewers, Authors and the Reading Public, 1749–1774" (diss. University of Melbourne, 1986); idem, *Index to Book Reviews in England: 1749–1774* (Carbondale: Southern Illinois University Press, 1990); idem, *Index to Book Reviews in England: 1775–1800* (London: British Library, 1997); Richard Taylor, *Goldsmith as Journalist* (Rutherford, N.J.: Fairleigh Dickinson University Press, 1993). Also see E. A. Bloom, "'Labours of the Learned': Neoclassic Book Reviewing Aims and Techniques," *Studies in Philology* 54 (1957): 538–63; Walter Graham, *English Literary Periodicals* (New York: Thomas Nelson & Sons, 1930); Derek Roper, *Reviewing before the Edinburgh, 1788–1802* (London: Methuen, 1978); and Robert D. Spector, *English Literary Periodicals and the Climate of Opinion during the Seven Years' War* (The Hague: Mouton, 1966).

2. The only previous attempts at exploring systematically Johnson's work as a reviewer are Donald Eddy's slim volume, *Samuel Johnson: Book Reviewer in the Literary Magazine* (New York: Garland, 1979), and the fifth chapter of E. A. Bloom's *Samuel Johnson in Grub Street* (Providence, R.I.: Brown University Press, 1957). Eddy's study is chiefly of value for its bibliographical survey of the books Johnson reviewed. Bloom's commentary works adequately only as an introduction.

3. Book reviewing "was a task for which he [Johnson] had no more fondness than for

any of his Grub Street activities," observes E. A. Bloom. "Only on infrequent occasion, when he felt a strong conviction about a subject, did he attempt to make his reviews any more than the customary hack pieces of the day" (*Samuel Johnson in Grub Street*, p. 177). Also see Shirley White Johnston, "The Unfurious Critic: Samuel Johnson's Attitude toward His Contemporaries," *Modern Philology* 77 (1979): 18–25.

4.   See W. P. Courtney and D. N. Smith, *A Bibliography of Samuel Johnson*, with R. W. Chapman and Allen T. Hazen, *Johnsonian Bibliography: A Supplement to Courtney* (New Castle, Del.: Oak Knoll Books, 1984), pp. 2, 156.

5.   *Yale*, 3:14–15, 7:71.

6.   See, for instance, *Rambler*s 3, 93, and 176.

7.   "Johnson's abstention from judicial criticism of contemporaries," writes Shirley White Johnston, "remains nearly absolute" ("Unfurious Critic," p. 22).

CHAPTER 1. SAMUEL JOHNSON AND THE MID-EIGHTEENTH-CENTURY LITERARY WORLD

1.   Courtney and Smith, *Bibliography of Samuel Johnson*, p. 2.

2.   For the state of professional letters in the mid-eighteenth century, see O M Brack Jr., ed., *Writers, Books, and Trade: An Eighteenth-Century English Miscellany for William B. Todd* (New York: AMS, 1994); John Brewer, *The Pleasures of the Imagination: English Culture in the Eighteenth Century* (New York: Farrar Straus Giroux, 1998), pp. 125–200; R. W. Chapman, "Authors and Booksellers," in *Johnson's England*, ed. A. S. Turberville (Oxford: Oxford University Press, 1933), 2:310–30; A. S. Collins, *Authorship in the Days of Johnson* (London: R. Holden & Sons, 1927); John Feather, *A History of British Publishing* (London: Routledge, 1988); Alvin Kernan, *Printing Technology, Samuel Johnson, and Letters* (Princeton: Princeton University Press, 1987); James Raven, *Judging New Wealth: Popular Publishing and Responses to Commerce in England, 1750–1800* (Oxford: Oxford University Press, 1992); Isabel Rivers, ed., *Books and Their Readers* (Leicester, U.K.: Leicester University Press, 1982); Donald Thomas, *A Long Time Burning: The History of Literary Censorship in England* (London: Routledge & Kegan Paul, 1969).

3.   See Basker, *Tobias Smollett*, chapters 1 and 2; Donoghue, *Fame Machine*, chapters 1 and 2; Kernan, *Printing Technology;* Raven, *Judging New Wealth.*

4.   Clavell, *A Catalogue of Books*, ed. D. F. Foxon (Farnborough, U.K.: Gregg Press, 1965); Thomas, *Long Time Burning*, pp. 22–33; also see Philip Pinkus, *Grub Street Stripped Bare* (Hamden, Conn.: Archon Books, 1968); Leslie Shepard, *The History of Street Literature: The Story of Broadside Ballads, Chapbooks, Proclamations, News-sheets, Election bills, Tracts, Pamphlets, Cocks, Catchpennies and other Ephemera* (Newton Abbot, U.K.: David & Charles, 1973).

5.   Alexander Pope, *The Dunciad*, ed. James Sutherland, 3d ed. (London: Methuen, 1965); also see Maynard Mack, *Alexander Pope: A Life* (New Haven: Yale University Press, 1985), pp. 457ff.; David Foxon and James McLaverty, *Pope and the Early-Eighteenth-Century Book Trade* (Oxford: Clarendon Press, 1991), p. 108. *The Dunciad* was advertised on 18 May 1728; Johnson "was entered a Commoner of Pembroke College" on 31 October 1728: see James Boswell, *Boswell's Life of Johnson, Together with Boswell's Journey of a Tour to the Hebrides and Johnson's Diary of a Journey into North Wales,* ed. G. B. Hill, rev. L. F. Powell, 2d ed., 6 vols. (Oxford: Clarendon Press, 1934–64), 1:58 and n. 2.

6.   *The Memoirs of Grub-Street* (London, 1737), 1:ii–iv, 58. Alvin Sullivan, ed., *British Literary Magazines: The Augustan Age and the Age of Johnson, 1698–1788* (Westport, Conn.: Greenwood Press, 1983), pp. 144–49. In its early years the *Grub Street Journal*

enjoyed a circulation of about two thousand, though its readership was effectively far larger, thanks to the regular reprinting of excerpts from each issue in the *GM*. For a useful but somewhat dated book-length treatment of the *Grub Street Journal*, see James T. Hillhouse, *The Grub-Street Journal* (Durham, N.C.: Duke University Press, 1928).

7. The "Advertisement" is prefixed to the first bound volume of the Bodleian Library's copy of the *Monthly*, Ralph Griffiths's own annotated set.

8. See Basker, *Tobias Smollett*, chapters 8 and 10; Donoghue, *Fame Machine*, chapter 1; Donoghue, "Colonizing Readers"; Forster, *Index to Book Reviews, 1749–1774*, pp. 3–17; Forster, "Reviewers, Authors and the Reading Public, 1749–1774"; Jan Fergus and Ruth Portner, "Provincial Subscribers," in Brack, *Writers, Books, and Trade*, pp. 157–76; Betty Rizzo, "Bonnell Thornton, Reviewer: Evolution of a Technique," in Brack, *Writers, Books and Trade*, pp. 335–54. For a listing of the many review journals that began publishing during the 1750s, see *NCBEL*, columns 1298ff.

9. For Johnson's early years as a writer, see Thomas Kaminski, *The Early Career of Samuel Johnson* (Oxford: Oxford University Press, 1987); J. L. Clifford, *Young Sam Johnson* (London: Heinemann, 1955); for a survey of Johnson's career from the late 1740s until the early 1750s, see J. L. Clifford, *Dictionary Johnson* (London: Heinemann, 1979); and Lawrence Lipking, *Samuel Johnson: The Life of an Author* (Cambridge: Harvard University Press, 1998).

10. In a pioneering essay published some years ago, Professor James F. Woodruff called attention to the latent contemporaneous context of the *Rambler* papers (and, by implication, in the *Adventurer* and the *Idler* papers). Curiously, however, Woodruff focuses on current political and social events, while contemporaneous literary issues go largely ignored. See "Johnson's *Rambler* in its Contemporary Context," *Bulletin of Research in the Humanities* 35 (1982): 27–64.

11. Johnson wrote a total of 321 *Rambler*, *Adventurer*, and *Idler* essays. The following are either solely, or in some significant way, concerned with issues of authorship, which includes discussions of literary criticism: *Rambler*: 1–4, 14, 16, 21, 23, 25–27, 36–37, 56, 60, 77, 82–83, 86, 88–94, 106, 117, 121, 122, 125, 136–37, 139–40, 143–46, 152, 154, 156, 158, 163, 168–69, 173, 176–77, 180, 184, 193, 207–8 (total: 54 out of 201). *Adventurer*: 58, 85, 92, 95, 99, 115, 137–38 (8 out of 29). *Idler*: 1–3, 7, 30, 36, 55, 59–61, 63, 65, 66, 68–70, 77, 84–85, 90–91, 94, 97, 102 (24 out of 91).

12. See Basker, *Tobias Smollett*, chapters 1 and 2.

13. For context, see ibid., chapter 1; Alexandre Beljame, *Men of Letters and the English Public in the Eighteenth Century, 1660–1744: Dryden, Addison, Pope* (London: Kegan Paul, 1948); Hillhouse, *Grub-Street Journal;* Charles Kerby-Miller's prefatory essay in *The Memoirs of the Extraordinary Life, Works, and Discoveries of Martin Scriblerus*, ed. Charles Kerby-Miller (Oxford: Oxford University Press, 1988); Pat Rogers, *Grub Street: Studies in a Subculture* (London: Methuen, 1972); Clarence Tracy, *The Artificial Bastard: A Biography of Richard Savage* (Cambridge: Harvard University Press, 1953), chapter 6.

14. For additional context, see Paul Fussell, *The Rhetorical World of Augustan Humanism: Ethics and Imagery from Swift to Burke* (Oxford: Oxford University Press, 1965), pp. 5–12. Also see Paul K. Alkon, *Samuel Johnson and the Moral Discipline* (Evanston, Ill.: Northwestern University Press, 1967); W. J. Bate, *From Classic to Romantic: Premises of Taste in Eighteenth-Century England* (Cambridge: Harvard University Press, 1946).

15. For further context, see Carey McIntosh, *The Choice of Life: Samuel Johnson and the World of Fiction* (New Haven: Yale University Press, 1973), chapter 1.

16. See J. F. Bartolomeo, *A New Species of Criticism: Eighteenth-Century Discourse on the Novel* (Newark: University of Delaware Press, 1994), chapter 2; J. C. Beasley, *Novels of the 1740s* (Athens: University of Georgia Press, 1982); idem, *A Check List of Prose Fiction Published in England, 1740–49* (Charlottesville: University Press of Virginia, 1972);

J. Paul Hunter, *Before Novels: The Cultural Contexts of Eighteenth-Century Fiction* (New York: W. W. Norton, 1990); James Raven, *British Fiction, 1750–1770: A Chronological Checklist of Prose Fiction Printed in Britain and Ireland* (Newark: University of Delaware Press, 1987); William A. Speck, *Society and Literature in England, 1700–1760* (Dublin: Gill & Macmillan, 1983).

17. *Yale*, 3:21.

18. *Yale*, 5:11; for the standing of journalism see Michael Harris, *London Newspapers in the Age of Walpole: A Study of the Origins of the Modern English Press* (Cranbury, N.J.: Associated University Presses, 1987); idem, "Journalism as a Profession or Trade in the Eighteenth Century," in *Author/Publisher Relations during the Eighteenth and Nineteenth Centuries*, ed. R. Myers and M. Harris (Oxford: Oxford Polytechnic Press, 1983), pp. 37–62; also see R. L. Haig, *The Daily Gazetteer: A Study in the Eighteenth-Century English Newspaper* (Carbondale: Southern Illinois University Press, 1960); C. John Sommerville, *The News Revolution in England: Cultural Dynamics of Daily Information* (Oxford: Oxford University Press, 1996), chapters 12 and 13.

19. *Yale*, 5:12.

20. Johnson argues for the importance of journalism in several other pieces. See, for instance, Johnson's "Letter to Mr. Urban" (*GM*, 9:3–5), and his prefatory essay to the *Universal Chronicle*, "Of The Duty of a Journalist," in A. T. Hazen, *Samuel Johnson's Prefaces and Dedications* (New Haven: Yale University Press, 1937), pp. 211–12. For Johnson's standing as a pioneer of high journalistic standards, see Donald Greene, "Samuel Johnson, Journalist," in *Newsletters to Newspapers: Eighteenth Century Journalism*, ed. D. H. Bond (Morgantown, WV: University of West Virginia School of Journalism, 1977), pp. 87–99; also see Bloom, *Samuel Johnson in Grub Street;* Robert DeMaria, *Samuel Johnson and the Life of Reading* (Baltimore: Johns Hopkins University Press, 1997).

21. *Yale*, 2:457; cf. the first number of the *Covent-Garden Journal* (4 January 1752): "The World, it is certain, never more abounded with Authors, than at present," observes Henry Fielding: see *The Covent-Garden Journal*, ed. Bertrand Goldgar (Oxford: Oxford University Press, 1988), p. 14.

22. *Yale,* 2:457–59.

23. *Yale,* 2:459–61; for additional instances of Johnson's emphasis on the crucial importance to aspiring authors of scholarly diligence and patience see *Rambler*s 25, 137, 169, 208.

24. The short-lived *Universal Visiter* was undertaken by Johnson's friend Christopher Smart in early 1756 (see Clifford, *Dictionary Johnson*, pp. 163–64). The full scope of Johnson's contributions has yet to be firmly established, though a useful list can be found in. Courtney and Smith, *Bibliography of Samuel Johnson*, pp. 74–75.

25. *UV*, pp. 159–66.

26. *UV*, pp. 161–62; cf. *Adventurer* 115 (*Yale*, 2:457), and Johnson's passing criticism of avocational authors in *Idler* 2 (*Yale,* 2:7).

27. *UV*, pp. 159–60.

28. *Yale*, 2:264–66.

29. *Yale*, 2:291–92.

30. See Percy G. Adams, *Travel Literature and the Evolution of the Novel* (Lexington: University of Kentucky Press, 1983), pp. 57–80; Charles L. Batten, *Pleasurable Instruction: Form and Convention in Eighteenth-Century Travel Literature* (Berkeley: University of California Press, 1978); Thomas Curley, *Johnson and the Age of Travel* (Athens: University of Georgia Press, 1976), pp. 14–17; for anecdotal evidence of the popularity of travel narratives and natural histories, see *CR*, 1:389; 7:505; for the cultural impact of the archaeological discoveries at Herculaneum in the early eighteenth century, see Turberville, *Johnson's England*, 2:22–25; also see *MR*, 3:393–96; *GM*, 24:261, 577. It is possible that

Johnson here writes with John George Keyssler's *Travels through Germany* (written in 1743; translated into English in 1756) and Patrick Browne's *Natural History of Jamaica* specifically in mind, though clearly he means to make a much broader point about the contemporary marketplace. Both of these titles were reviewed in the *Literary Magazine* in 1756. The first of Keyssler's four volumes contained a description of the Medicean Venus: see *Travels through Germany, Bohemia, Hungary, Switzerland, Italy, and Lorrain* (London, 1756), 1:434–36. Of this first volume Johnson wrote: "[P]erhaps in the opinion of most readers the only objection to his performance is, that he has visited only those countries which every man visits, and therefore has only seen what every man sees." Browne's *Natural History*, Johnson observes, "has described many products of *Jamaica* which are equally to be found in other parts, perhaps in every part of the known world" (*LM*, 1:176, 240). Johnson may have been moved to refer to Herculaneum by the publication in 1759 of the 300-page "large folio," *A Description of the Antique Paintings Discovered at Herculaneum, and Parts Adjacent* (see *MR*, 20:370–71).

31. See Martin Battestin, *Henry Fielding: A Life* (London: Routledge, 1989), pp. 440, 450–52, 532–533; Foxon and McLaverty, *Pope and the Early-Eighteenth-Century Book Trade*, pp. 52–63.

32. See Leopold Damrosch, "Johnson's Manner of Proceeding in the *Rambler*," *English Literary History* 40 (1973): 70–98.

33. *Yale*, 3:9–14.

34. See Terry Belanger, "Publishers and Writers in Eighteenth-Century England," in Rivers, *Books and Their Readers*, pp. 5–25; Brewer, *Pleasures of the Imagination*, chapter 3; Mark Rose, *Authors and Owners: The Invention of Copyright* (Cambridge: Harvard University Press, 1993), pp. 25–41.

35. *Yale*, 3:14.

36. See the initial advertisement of the *Monthly Review* (the copy quoted here is bound following the table of contents of volume 1 of the copy of the *Monthly* in the Bodleian Library): "When the abuse of title-pages is obviously come to such a pass, that few readers care to take in a book, any more than a servant, without a recommendation; to acquaint the public that a summary review of the productions of the press, as they occur to notice, was perhaps never more necessary than now, would be superfluous and vain. The cure then for this general complaint is evidently, and only, to be found in a periodical work, whose sole object should be to give a compendious account of those productions of the press, as they come out, that are worth notice; an account, in short, which should, in virtue of its candour, and justness of distinction, obtain authority enough for its representations to be serviceable to such as would choose to have some idea of a book before they lay out their money or time on it."

37. Preface to *A Dictionary of the English Language, Abstracted from the Folio Edition* (London, 1756). Five thousand copies of this edition were sold between 1756 and 1786—making it nearly as popular as the folio: see J. H. Sledd and G. J. Kolb, *Dr. Johnson's Dictionary* (Chicago: University of Chicago Press, 1955), pp. 107–14. Also see Brewer, *Pleasures of the Imagination*, chapters 3 and 4.

38. *Yale*, 5:13–14.

39. *Yale*, 5:15; see Johnson's "Life of Savage," in *The Lives of the Poets*, ed. G. B. Hill (Oxford: Oxford University Press, 1905), 2:379.

40. *Yale*, 5:16–17.

41. See Woodruff, "Johnson's *Rambler* in Its Contemporary Context," pp. 61–64.

42. In his introduction to the *Yale Shakespeare*, Arthur Sherbo points out that great progress had already been made on the Shakespeare edition by the spring of 1758, and had Johnson "proceeded with the same momentum as before, he would certainly have dispatched the work before his mother's death" in early 1759 (*Yale*, 7:xxii–xxiv).

43. The first "Weekly Correspondent" essay totals 650 words, the latter two total 520 words each. By comparison, the *Rambler* essays average 1,200–1,400 words per essay, the *Idler* papers some 900–1,000 words per essay.

44. All quotations from the *Public Ledger* are taken from E. L. McAdam, "New Essays by Dr. Johnson," *Review of English Studies* 18 (1942): 197–207. The *Public Ledger* was published daily; for further discussion see D. N. Smith, "The Newspaper," in Turberville, *Johnson's England*, 2:349–50; for commentary on the "Chinese Letters," see *The Collected Works of Oliver Goldsmith*, ed. Arthur Friedman (Oxford: Oxford University Press, 1966), 2:ix–xii.

45. McAdam, "New Essays by Dr. Johnson," pp. 198–99; for similar commentary on the indifference and hostility of readers see *Rambler* 1 (paragraphs 8 through 10), *Rambler* 2 (final paragraph); *Rambler* 3 (paragraphs 2 and 3); *Rambler* 146 (paragraphs 4 through 8); *Adventurer* 137 (paragraphs 11 through 15); *Adventurer* 138 (paragraph 14). For Johnson's views on the advantages of anonymity, see *Rambler* 56 (final paragraph) and *Idler* 2 (paragraph 12).

46. For references to professional writing as a "hazardous" activity, see *Rambler*s 1, 3, 21, 93, 144, 176; *Idler* 2; "Reflections on the Present State of Literature, " *UV*, pp. 159–66; Johnson's defense of the *Gentleman's Magazine*'s right to abridge *Trapp's Sermons* (57:555–58); "Account of the Harleian Library" (*GM*, 12:636–39).

47. *Yale*, 3:86–91.

48. Philip Gaskell, *A New Introduction to Bibliography* (Oxford: Oxford University Press, 1972), pp. 160–62.

49. *Yale*, 3:90–91, and note 3. See Mack, *Alexander Pope: A Life*, pp. 660–62; William K. Wimsatt, *The Portraits of Alexander Pope* (New Haven: Yale University Press 1965), pp. xiv–xix; for the growing popularity of celebrity portraits during the middle third of the century see David Piper, *The Image of the Poet: British Poets and Their Portraits* (Oxford: Oxford University Press, 1982), pp. 53–58; the allusion to Pope is perhaps even more timely than it may first appear: Pope's literary executor William Warburton had recently published editions of the *Essay on Criticism* (November 1749) and the *Dunciad* (January 1750): see R. H. Griffith, *Alexander Pope: A Bibliography* (Austin: University of Texas Press, 1927), pp. 513–17.

50. *Yale*, 2:171–74; cf. the "Life of Thomson" (*Lives of the Poets*, 3:283).

51. *Yale*, 2:173; Gaskell, *New Introduction to Bibliography*, p. 177; Foxon and McLaverty, *Pope and the Early-Eighteenth-Century Book Trade*, p. 117. Also see Patricia Hernlund, "Three Bankruptcies in the London Book Trade, 1746–61," in Brack, *Writers, Books, and Trade*, pp. 77–122; for a brief consideration of the status of copyright at midcentury see Belanger, "Publishers and Writers in Eighteenth-Century England," pp. 5–6; Chapman, "Authors and Booksellers," 2:317–23; Rose, *Authors and Owners*, chapter 5, particularly pp. 71–78; for Johnson and the Shakespeare edition, see *Letters of Samuel Johnson*, ed. Bruce Redford, 5 vols. (Princeton: Princeton University Press, 1994), 1:135; Clifford, *Dictionary Johnson*, pp. 168–69.

52. *Yale*, 2:172–73.

53. *LM*, 1:176.

54. See Curley, *Johnson and the Age of Travel*, pp. 37–39; also see Tobias Smollett's review of Browne's *Jamaica* (June 1756): "Such is the progress of philosophy in these days of literature, that we do not despair of seeing a folio . . . written on the natural history of the *Isle of Dogs* near *Greenwich*, or *Duck-Island* in St. *James's Park*" (*CR*, 1:389).

55. Sledd and Kolb, *Dr. Johnson's Dictionary*, pp. 107–14.

56. Clifford, *Dictionary Johnson*, pp. 133–36.

57. *Yale*, 2:174; also see *Yale*, 3:497; 3:89–91; "Reflections on the Present State of Literature," *UV*, p. 163; Septimus Rivington, *The Publishing Family of Rivingtons* (Lon-

don: Rivingtons, 1919), p. 66; J. D. Fleeman, "Johnson's Shakespeare (1765): The Progress of a Subscription," in Brack, *Writers, Books, and the Trade*, pp. 355–66.

58. See Johnson's "Life of Cowley": "The true Genius is a mind of large general powers, accidentally determined to some particular direction" (*Lives of the Poets*, 1:2); *Yale*, 2:172; *Rambler* 23 (*Yale*, 3:126); Johnson's "Life of Blackmore": to the author "must always be assigned the plan of the work, the distribution of its parts, the choice of topicks, the train of argument" (*Lives of the Poets*, 2:243); also see Johnson's "Life of Pope" (*Lives of the Poets*, 3:220).

59. *Letters of Samuel Johnson*, ed. Redford, 1:96.

60. See Jacob Leed, "Patronage in the *Rambler*," *Studies in Burke and His Time* 14 (1972): 5–21; idem, "Johnson and Chesterfield," *Studies in Burke and His Time* 12 (1970): 1677–90. Also see Kernan, *Printing Technology*. Johnson's rejection of Chesterfield, Kernan argues, "became, as a result of the way Johnson played it and Boswell reported it, not just, as it could have been in other hands, another dreary quarrel between a haughty peer and a truculent hack, but a great event in the history of letters and of print, the scene in which not just Samuel Johnson but *the author*, after centuries of subservience to the aristocracy, declares his democratic independence of patronage" (p. 20).

61. Boswell, *Boswell's Life of Johnson*, 1:183; Samuel Johnson, *The Plan of a Dictionary of the English Language* (London, 1747); for additional context, see Sledd and Kolb, *Dr. Johnson's Dictionary*, pp. 85–104.

62. See Boswell, *Boswell's Life of Johnson,* 1:256–66. Johnson's letter to Chesterfield was not published until 1790: see Courtney and Smith, *Bibliography of Samuel Johnson*, pp. 171–72.

63. *Yale*, 4:358; O M Brack Jr. and Gae Holladay, "Johnson as Patron," in *Greene Centennial Studies*, ed. P. Korshin (Charlottesville: University Press of Virginia, 1984), pp. 172–99.

64. Dustin Griffin, *Literary Patronage in England, 1650–1800* (Cambridge: Cambridge University Press, 1996), pp. 221–27, and note 14. Also see Michael Foss, *The Age of Patronage: The Arts in England, 1660–1750* (Ithaca: Cornell University Press, 1971); Paul Korshin, "Types of Eighteenth-Century Literary Patronage," *Eighteenth-Century Studies* (1973–74): 453–73. Though pioneering studies, the Foss volume and Korshin article have been superseded by Griffin's research.

65. Griffin, *Literary Patronage in England,* pp. 221–27; Kaminski, *Early Career of Samuel Johnson*, p. 196; Boswell, *Boswell's Life of Johnson*, 1:320, 373–74, and notes; 3:309–10; 5:35; for Birch's career, see Edward Ruhe, "Thomas Birch, Samuel Johnson, and Elizabeth Carter: An Episode of 1738–39," *PMLA* 73 (1958): 491–500; *Dictionary of National Biography*, 2:530–32.

66. Griffin, *Literary Patronage in England,* pp. 221–27; Boswell, *Boswell's Life of Johnson*, 2:1–2; also see Hazen, *Samuel Johnson's Prefaces and Dedications,* pp. xxi–xxii, and W. A. Speck, "Politicians, Peers, and Publication by Subscription," in Rivers, *Books and Their Readers*, pp. 47–68.

67. For a full discussion of the contemporaneous element in the *Rambler* see Woodruff, "Johnson's *Rambler* in its Contemporary Context," 27–64.

68. Griffin, *Literary Patronage in England,* pp. 1–43.

69. Johnson, *Lives of the Poets*, 2:336, 369, 382–84, 391–92.

70. *Letters of Samuel Johnson*, ed. Redford, 1:213–14.

71. Boswell, *Boswell's Life of Johnson*, 5:59; also see *Rambler* 21 and *Rambler* 104 (*Yale*, 3:119; 4:193–94).

72. *GM*, 9:3–4. In this essay Johnson alludes to the pro-Walpole ministry *Daily Gazetteer* and the opposition weekly paper, *Common Sense*, excerpts from which were regularly published in the *Gentleman's Magazine*.

73. *Yale,* 3:141–42.

74. See Johnson's "Life of Addison" and "Life of Prior" (*Lives of the Poets,* 2:79–158, 180–211). Cf. Collins, *Authorship in the Days of Johnson:* patronage "was at its highest, most serviceable, and most honourable in the reign of Queen Anne, in the days of Somers and Halifax, Harley and St. John. Those men and their friends held it a duty and a privilege to help learning and foster genius from the wealth of the State or their own pockets" (p. 214).

75. *Yale,* 3:147–51.

76. *Yale,* 4:116–19.

77. "When upon some slight encouragement I first visited your Lordship I was overpowered like the rest of Mankind by the enchantment of your address, and could not forbear to wish . . . that I might obtain that regard for which I saw the world contending, but I found my attendance so little encouraged, that neither pride nor modesty would suffer me to continue it" (*Letters of Samuel Johnson,* ed. Redford, 1:95). For additional context, see Sledd and Kolb, *Dr. Johnson's Dictionary,* pp. 95–100.

78. *Yale,* 4:119–20.

79. *Yale,* 5:101–2.

80. For *Rambler*s 21 and 104, see *Yale* 3:119, 4:193–94.

81. *Yale,* 5:102–4; for Johnson's commentary on the advantages of publishing anonymously see *Rambler* 56, *Idler* 2 (*Yale,* 2:8–9, 3:304); "Weekly Correspondent," *Public Ledger,* 2 December 1760, rptd. in McAdam, "New Essays By Dr. Johnson," pp. 197–207; also see Boswell, *Boswell's Life of Johnson,* 3:43–44.

82. *Yale,* 5:102–6.

83. For Johnson as the subject of reviews, see Helen Louise McGuffie, *Samuel Johnson in the British Press, 1749–1784: A Chronological Checklist* (New York: Garland, 1976). The term "critic" and "reviewer" had become synonymous by the mid-1750s, as Johnson's prefatory essay to the *Literary Magazine* demonstrates (*LM,* 1:iv); also see Forster, *Index to Book Reviews: 1749–1774,* pp. 5–6. For analysis of Johnson's broad critical views, see Jean Hagstrum, *Samuel Johnson's Literary Criticism* (Minneapolis: University of Minnesota Press, 1952); W. R. Keast, "The Theoretical Foundations of Samuel Johnson's Literary Criticism," in *Critics and Criticism: Ancient and Modern,* ed. R. S. Crane (Chicago: University of Chicago Press, 1952), pp. 389–407; for Johnson and the primacy of popular judgment, see Clarence Tracy, "Johnson and the Common Reader," *Dalhousie Review* 57 (1977–78): 405–23; Keast, "Theoretical Foundations," pp. 400–403; Kernan, *Printing Technology,* pp. 229–32.

83. See, for instance, Johnson's defense of the *Gentleman's Magazine*'s right to abridge *Trapp's Sermons* (1739: *GM,* 57:556) and *Rambler*s 93 and 176 (*Yale,* 4:133–34; *Yale,* 5:165).

85. For the *Monthly*'s statement of purpose, see the advertisement prefixed to its first bound volume (discussed below). Also see the "Preface" to the Bodleian Library's copy of the *Critical*'s first bound volume. "Animated by the public favour, the *Critical Reviewers* will double their endeavours to fulfil effectually the purposes for which they engaged in this undertaking: they promise that neither prayers nor threats shall induce them to part with their integrity and independence; that they shall thankfully receive all kinds of assistance or correction; and that their view shall be solely directed to the entertainment and information of mankind."

86. *UV,* p. 164; Forster, *Index to Book Reviews: 1749–1774,* pp. 8–9.

87. For Johnson's contributions to the *Chronicle,* see the *New Cambridge Bibliography of English Literature,* column 1141; Boswell, *Boswell's Life of Johnson,* 2:103; also see Bloom, *Samuel Johnson in Grub Street,* pp. 136–40; Clifford, *Dictionary Johnson,* p. 181; Hazen, *Samuel Johnson's Prefaces and Dedications,* pp. 131–32; Smith, "The Newspaper," 2:345–49.

88. *London Chronicle*, 1:1.

89. Cf. Boswell, *Boswell's Life of Johnson:* the "authours of the Monthly Review were enemies to the Church," Johnson is reported to have told King George III; Boswell also reports Johnson as having said that the writers for the *Monthly* "'are Christians with as little christianity as may be; they are for pulling down all establishments'"(2:40; 3:32). Also Donoghue, *Fame Machine*, chapter 1.

90. *London Chronicle*, 1:1.

91. Between early spring 1756 and early summer 1757 Johnson earned his living chiefly as senior reviewer and literary editor of the *Literary Magazine*. See J. D. Fleeman, "The Revenue of a Writer: Samuel Johnson's Literary Earnings," in *Studies in the Book Trade: In Honour of Graham Pollard,* ed. R. W. Hunt, I. G. Philip, and R. J. Roberts (Oxford: Oxford Bibliographical Society, 1975), pp. 216–24.

92. Boswell, *Boswell's Life of Johnson*, 5:274, and note. Also see 3:44, and note.

93. Prefixed to the first bound volume (May–October 1749) of the Bodleian Library's copy of the *Monthly Review*, which was the annotated set of Ralph Griffiths, founder and first editor of the *Monthly*.

94. *MR*, 1:238; Lewis M. Knapp, "Griffiths's 'Monthly Review' as Printed by Strahan," *Notes and Queries* 103 (1958): 216–17; also see Forster, *Index to Book Reviews in England: 1749–1774*, pp. 3–4; James A. Cochrane, *Dr. Johnson's Printer: The Life of William Strahan* (London: Routledge, 1964), pp. 22–29, 103, 145; Clifford, *Young Sam Johnson*, p. 281; Allen Reddick, *The Making of Johnson's Dictionary, 1747–1773* (Cambridge: Cambridge University Press, 1990), pp. 57–59.

95. *Yale*, 3:15–19.

96. *Yale*, 3:15–16.

97. See *Ramblers* 1, 2, 3, 106, 146, and Johnson's first "Weekly Correspondent" essay in the *Public Ledger*, rptd in McAdam, "New Essays by Dr. Johnson," pp. 197–207.

98. *Yale*, 4:122.

CHAPTER 2. JOHNSON AS A REVIEWER OF HISTORICAL, LITERARY, AND PHILOSOPHICAL TITLES IN THE *LITERARY MAGAZINE*

1. *Yale,* 1:56; Boswell, *Boswell's Life of Johnson*, 1:284–85, and note; Clifford, *Dictionary Johnson*, pp. 165–67.

2. *Letters of Samuel Johnson*, ed. Redford, 1:101.

3. Bloom, *Samuel Johnson in Grub Street*, p. 177; Brack and Holladay, "Johnson as Patron," p. 179.

4. For context see Walter Graham, *The Beginnings of English Literary Periodicals* (New York: Octagon, 1972), chapter 1.

5. *LM*, 1:iv.

6. See *MR*, 8:392, 12:386.

7. Clifford, *Dictionary Johnson*, pp. 165–87; Eddy, *Samuel Johnson: Book Reviewer*, pp. 2–15; Sullivan, *British Literary Magazines,* pp. 198–200.

8. See Forster, *Index to Book Reviews 1749–1774*, pp. 9–10.

9. Donald Greene, "Johnson's Contributions to the *Literary Magazine*," *Review of English Studies* 7 (1956): 390–92; Basker, *Tobias Smollett*, p. 169. Johnson's political essays in the *Literary Magazine* are fully considered in Donald Greene, *The Politics of Samuel Johnson* (Athens: University of Georgia Press, 1990), pp. 154–73. Also see the tenth volume of the *Yale* edition, which reprints the two essays noted here and other similar works. In a letter to Charlotte Lennox (30 July 1756) Johnson remarks that the *LM*'s circulation

was one-seventh that of the *GM*'s; during 1746 an average of 3,000 copies of the *GM* were printed each month; by 1797 that figure had risen to 4,550: see *Letters of Samuel Johnson*, ed. Redford, 1:137; Sullivan, *British Literary Magazines*, p. 138; Forster, *Book Reviews: 1775–1800*, p. xxxiii, and note 51. The failure of the *Literary Magazine* can be said to reflect the long odds of success in the review/general interest periodical market at midcentury. Of six literary journals that got underway in 1756, only the *Critical Review* survived beyond 1758 (*New Cambridge Bibliography of English Literature*, columns 1300–02).

10. "To the Public" (*LM*, 1:iv).

11. Also see Brack and Holladay, "Johnson as Patron."

12. Also see Johnson's "Letter to Mr. Urban," *GM*, 9:3–4 (1739).

13. For fuller discussion of Johnson and popular judgment, see Tracy, "Johnson and the Common Reader"; Keast, "Theoretical Foundations," pp. 400–403; Kernan, *Printing Technology*, pp. 229–32.

14. *Yale*, 2:265.

15. At the time of his death Johnson owned numerous issues of the *Monthly* and *Critical:* see Donald Greene, *Samuel Johnson's Library: An Annotated Guide* (Victoria, B.C.: University of Victoria Press, 1975), pp. 51, 85. Of the forty titles reviewed by Johnson in the *Literary Magazine*, twenty were reviewed first by either the *Monthly* or the *Critical*. Johnson reviews four titles—Murphy's *Gray's-Inn Journal*; Robert Keith's *Catalogue of Scottish Bishops*; and the political periodicals the *Test* and the *Con-test*—that are not reviewed in either of the two leading review journals.

16. Johnson, *Johnsonian Miscellanies*, ed. G. B. Hill (London: Constable & Co., 1966), 2:225.

17. Pat Rogers, *Samuel Johnson* (Oxford: Oxford University Press, 1993), p. 6; M. J. Quinlan, *Samuel Johnson: A Layman's Religion* (Madison: University of Wisconsin Press, 1964); *MR*, 14:253–56, 273, 367; for the popularity of religious and philosophical works in Johnson's day see Thomas R. Preston, "Biblical Criticism, Literature, and the Eighteenth-Century Reader," in Rivers, *Books and Their Readers*, pp. 97–126; John Vladimir Price, "The Reading of Philosophical Literature," in Rivers, *Books and Their Readers*, pp. 165–96.

18. Also see Johnson's prefatory note to Charlotte Lennox's *Shakespeare Illustrated* (1753): "Of all the novels and romances that wit or idleness, vanity or indigence, have pushed into the world," Johnson observes, "there are few, of which the end cannot be conjectured from the beginning; or where the authors have done more, than to transpose the incidents of other tales, or strip the circumstances from one event for the decoration of another" (*Yale*, 7:48; also see Johnson, *Johnsonian Miscellanies*, 1:290).

19. Speck, *Society and Literature in England, 1700–1760*, p. 198; Raven, *British Fiction, 1750–1770*, pp. 9–10.

20. *MR*, 13:399; 14:361.

21. Johnson's departure from the *Literary Magazine* was marked by a decline in literary matters and a greater emphasis on politics/current events. Thus, the *Literary Magazine* moved even further away from whatever resemblance it bore to the two leading review journals (Basker, *Tobias Smollett*, p. 169).

22. *CR*, 18:458–62; *Yale*, 4:305; Boswell, *Boswell's Life of Johnson*, 2:48, 84, 233; also see *Letters of Samuel Johnson*, ed. Redford, 2:9, 14. For a considered view of Johnson's outlook on poetry, see Lipking, *Samuel Johnson*, pp. 86–102.

23. Curley, *Johnson and the Age of Travel;* Adams, *Travel Literature and the Evolution of the Novel*, pp. 57–80; also see Batten, *Pleasurable Instruction*.

24. See Donoghue, *Fame Machine;* Forster, *Index to Book Reviews, 1749–1774*, pp. 3–17; Forster "Tasters to the Public"; also see Basker, *Tobias Smollett;* Graham, *English Literary Periodicals*, pp. 196–226.

25. For a systematic discussion of this issue, see Johnston, "Unfurious Critic."

26. The major portion of Eddy's final chapter surveys Johnson's great talent at abstracting, editing, and revising the material extracted from books under review (Eddy, *Samuel Johnson: Book Reviewer*, pp. 83–94).

27. For related commentary, see Brack and Holladay, "Johnson as Patron," pp. 178–99.

28. *Yale*, 4:131.

29. *Letters of Samuel Johnson*, ed. Redford, 1:132; Clifford, *Dictionary Johnson*, pp. 162–70; Fleeman, "Johnson's Earnings"; also see O M Brack Jr., "Samuel Johnson Edits for the Booksellers: Sir Thomas Browne's 'Christian Morals' (1756) and 'The English Works of Roger Ascham' (1761)," *Library Chronicle of the University of Texas* 21 (1991): 12–39. D. D. Eddy believes that Johnson, apart from whatever wages he earned as editor, also held a financial stake in the *LM* (Eddy, *Samuel Johnson: Book Reviewer*, p. 8).

30. Boswell, *Boswell's Life of Johnson*, 3:137; Lipking, *Samuel Johnson*, p. 144; also see O M Brack Jr., "Johnson's *Life of Admiral Blake* and the Development of a Biographical Technique," *Modern Philology* 85 (1988): 523–31. Johnson believed, and his career proved, that "excellence can be achieved by a hired writer who gains satisfaction and a sense of personal integrity, not by some expression of self, but by performing an assigned task well," as Brack points out (p. 524).

31. For the identity of reviewers in the *Monthly*, see Benjamin Nangle, *The Monthly Review, 1rst ser. 1749–1789, Indexes of Contributors and Articles* (Oxford: Oxford University Press, 1934). Though Nangle's *Index* offers comprehensive coverage of the contributors of main articles in the *Monthly*, the authorship of many of the *Monthly Catalogue* notices—briefer pieces appended to the end of each month's issue—remain unknown. The *Critical Review* also carried a *Monthly Catalogue* section beginning with its fifth issue; some of the contributors to this section remain unknown. For the identity of the reviewers in the *Critical*, see Derek Roper, "Smollett's 'Four Gentlemen': The First Contributors to the *CR*," *Review of English Studies* 10 (1959): 38–44.

32. Clifford, *Young Sam Johnson*, p. 186; Kaminski, *Early Career of Samuel Johnson*, pp. 36–40; Ruhe, "Thomas Birch, Samuel Johnson, and Elizabeth Carter," pp. 491–500; also see *Yale*, 6:62–63.

33. Ruhe, "Thomas Birch, Samuel Johnson, and Elizabeth Carter," p. 499.

34. See *Letters of Samuel Johnson*, ed. Redford, 1:36–37, 44, 65, 76–77, 101–2; 5:115, 124, 133, 135. For commentary on Johnson's epistolary style, see Tom Keymer, "'Letters About Nothing': Johnson and Epistolary Writing," in *The Cambridge Companion to Samuel Johnson*, ed. Greg Clingham (Cambridge: Cambridge University Press, 1997), pp. 224–39.

35. *LM*, 1:30.

36. *LM*, 1:30; Johnson cites Birch's *History* in the "Life of Cowley" (*Lives of the Poets*, 1:11–12); Johnson here refers to John Ward (1679–1758), author of *The Lives of the Professors of Gresham College* (London, 1740).

37. *Dictionary of National Biography*, 14:164–65, 988–90; Graham, *Beginnings of English Literary Periodicals*, pp. 5–6.

38. Lewis Knapp, "Smollett and Johnson, Never Cater-Cousins?" *Modern Philology* 66 (1968): 152–54.

39. *CR*, 1:42.

40. *MR*, 14:417–25.

41. For further context see Lawrence Lipking, *The Ordering of the Arts in Eighteenth-Century England* (Princeton: Princeton University Press, 1970), pp. 362–69; Eric Rothstein, *Restoration and Eighteenth-Century Poetry, 1660–1780* (Boston: Routledge & Kegan Paul, 1981), chapter 4.

42. Harry M. Solomon, *The Rise of Robert Dodsley* (Carbondale: Southern Illinois University Press, 1996), pp. 49–50, 149–51; also see David Fairer, "The Writing and Printing of Joseph Warton's *Essay on Pope*," *Studies in Bibliography* 30 (1977): 211–19.

43.   Joseph Warton, *An Essay on the Writings and Genius of Pope* (London, 1756), pp. iii–xi.

44.   *Letters of Samuel Johnson*, ed. Redford, 1:67–68; 77–78; 90–91; Clifford, *Dictionary Johnson*, p. 111; Arthur Sherbo, "Dr. Johnson and Joseph Warton's Virgil," *Johnsonian Newsletter* 18, no. 4 (1958): 12. Johnson's friendship with Joseph Warton evidently cooled after 1756, not because of any single incident but because, as Hugh Reid has pointed out, "Johnson's personality and strongly held, and even more strongly expressed[,] opinions, began to pall on" Joseph Warton and his brother Thomas. See "'The Want of a Closer Union . . .': The Friendship of Samuel Johnson and Joseph Warton," *Age of Johnson: A Scholarly Annual* 9 (1998): 133–43.

45.   *Letters of Samuel Johnson*, ed. Redford, 1:133–34; apparently, Johnson had known of or at least suspected Warton's authorship for at least one week prior to the date of this letter: see Solomon, *Rise of Robert Dodsley*, p. 150.

46.   Bloom, *Samuel Johnson in Grub Street*, pp. 191–92; Eddy, *Samuel Johnson: Book Reviewer*, p. 89; Brack and Holladay, "Johnson as Patron," p. 181.

47.   Johnson, *Lives of the Poets*, 3:216–18; 247–52. Several scholars have interpreted Johnson's emphatic defense of Pope's standing in the "Life" as a rebuttal to Warton's *Essay on the Writings and Genius of Pope*. See Hagstrum, *Samuel Johnson's Literary Criticism*, pp. 133–37; F. W. Hilles, "The Making of the Life of Pope," in *New Light on Dr. Johnson: Essays on the Occasion of his 250th Birthday*, ed. F. W. Hilles (New Haven: Yale University Press, 1959), pp. 257–84; Eddy, *Samuel Johnson: Book Reviewer*, p. 90.

48.   Hagstrum, *Samuel Johnson's Literary Criticism*, pp. 132–36.

49.   Johnson, *Lives of the Poets*, 3:239–40.

50.   Ibid., 3:251–52.

51.   Boswell, *Boswell's Life of Johnson*, 2:167; also see 1:448.

52.   *LM*, 1:36.

53.   Warton, *Essay on the Writings and Genius of Pope*, p. 42.

54.   Ibid., p. 11.

55.   See Lipking, *Samuel Johnson*, pp. 97–102.

56.   *LM*, 1:35.

57.   Warton, *Essay on the Writings and Genius of Pope*, pp. 203–4.

58.   Boswell reports that Johnson intended to write a "History of Criticism, as it relates judging authors, from Aristotle to the present age. An account of the rise and improvements of that art; of the different opinions of authors, ancient and modern" (*Boswell's Life of Johnson*, 4:381 and note 1).

59.   *LM*, 1:37.

60.   *LM*, 1:38.

61.   *LM*, 1:38.

62.   Johnson and Smollett both reviewed the following nine titles: Birch, *History of the Royal Society;* Borlase, *Observations on the Isle of Scilly;* Home, *Experiments on Bleaching;* Warton, *Essay on the Writings and Genius of Pope;* Lucas, *Essay on Waters;* Browne, *Natural History of Jamaica; Philosophical Transactions*, vol. 49; Bever, *The Cadet;* and Mallet, *Conduct of the Ministry.*

63.   Basker, *Tobias Smollett*, chapter 4.

64.   The University of Georgia Press's edition of Smollett's reviews, edited by O M Brack Jr., is forthcoming.

65.   The other Scottish reviewers were John Armstrong and Patrick Murdock; see Basker, *Tobias Smollett*, chapter 4.

66.   *CR*, 1:227; for Smollett's authorship of this review and others by him mentioned in this chapter, see Basker, *Tobias Smollett*, chapter 4 and the appendices.

67.   *CR*, 1:228.

68. *Dictionary of National Biography*, 20:885–88.

69. *CR*, 1:231.

70. *CR*, 1:231–33; Alexander Pope, *Pastoral Poems and An Essay on Criticism*, ed. E. Audra and A. Williams (London: Methuen, 1961), p. 315, and note; Warton, *Essay on the Writings and Genius of Pope*, pp. 174–75; *Dictionary of National Biography*, 1:566–67. Cf. Johnson's commentary on the Petronius reference: "Pope has mentioned *Petronius* among the great names of criticism, as the remarker justly observes without any critical merit. It is to be suspected, that *Pope* had never read his book, and mentioned him on the credit of two or three sentences which he had often seen quoted, imagining that where there was so much there must necessarily be more. Young men in haste to be renowned too frequently talk of books which they have scarcely seen" (*LM*, 1:37).

71. *CR*, 1:228.

72. *CR*, 1:240.

73. *CR*, 1:234–35, 238–39; Basker, *Tobias Smollett*, pp. 92–97.

74. *MR*, 14:528.

75. *MR*, 14:534–36.

76. Thomas Percy and Robert Anderson, *The Correspondence of Thomas Percy and Robert Anderson*, ed. W. E. K. Anderson (New Haven: Yale University Press, 1988), pp. 92–93; also see p. 60.

77. Whether Johnson and Grainger knew each other at this time remains merely a possibility (Clifford, *Dictionary Johnson*, pp. 154–56; Boswell, *Boswell's Life of Johnson*, 1:48 n. 2; Percy and Anderson, *Correspondence*, p. 76); interestingly, Grainger at one point in the review praises Johnson's poetic talents: "There is certainly more distress in Banks's Q. Mary, than in Johnson's Irene; but will any one presume to say, that Banks is as good a poet as Johnson?" (*MR*, 14:534).

78. Jenyns's second letter is "little more than a paraphrase of Pope's epistles, or yet less than a paraphrase, a mere translation of poetry into prose" (*LM*, 2:252).

79. *Yale*, 4:393–401.

80. *LM*, 1:35; *MR*, 14:539.

81. *LM*, 1:38; *MR*, 14:545.

82. *LM*, 1:36; *MR*, 14:551.

83. *LM*, 1:36–37; *MR*, 14:553–54.

84. *LM*, 1:37; *MR*, 15:52.

85. Johnson's defense of Pope's simile here is repeated and enlarged upon in the "Life of Pope" (*Lives of the Poets*, 3:229–30).

86. *LM*, 1:37; *MR*, 15:54.

87. *MR*, 15:77–78.

88. *Dictionary of National Biography*, 8:1153; 9:417.

89. *LM*, 1:39.

90. *Yale*, 2:217; *Lives of the Poets*, 1:79.

91. *LM*, 1:39–41.

92. *LM*, 1:140; *Yale* 7:51. The Shakespeare "Proposals" appeared in April, the review in May. Hampton's translation was published in March (Eddy, *Samuel Johnson: Book Reviewer*, p. 40).

93. Brack, "Samuel Johnson Edits for the Booksellers."

94. James Hampton, *The General History of Polybius. In Five Books. Translated from the Greek* (London, 1756), p. xx.

95. Ibid., pp. xvii–xx.

96. Cf. the *Plan of the Dictionary* (1747): "We are taught by the great Roman orator, that every man should propose to himself the highest degree of excellence, but that he may stop with honour at the second or third: though therefore my performance should fall below

the excellence of other dictionaries, I may obtain, at least, the praise of having endeavoured well" (p. 33). Also see *Boswell's Life of Johnson:* "There are two things which I am confident I can do very well," Johnson is reported to have told Joshua Reynolds; "one is an introduction to any literary work, stating what it is to contain, and how it should be executed in the most perfect manner; the other is a conclusion, shewing from various causes why the execution has not been equal to what the authour promised to himself and to the publick" (1:292).

97. Hampton, *General History of Polybius,* p. 2.

98. Johnson quotes from pages 278–83 of Hampton's volume.

99. *LM,* 1:39–42. Johnson repeats his condemnation of Roman expansionism in a later installment of the Blackwell review (1:239).

100. *LM,* 1:39–41.

101. *MR,* 15:658.

102. *MR,* 14:342; Folard's edition of Polybius appeared between 1727 and 1730 (*Encyclopaedia Britannica,* 11th ed., s.v. "Folard, Jean Charles").

103. Hampton, *General History of Polybius,* p. vii.

104. *MR,* 14:343–44.

105. *MR,* 14:351.

106. *MR,* 15:669.

107. *MR,* 14:334.

108. Thomas Francklin (1721–84), authored sixty-four reviews for the *Critical.* The authorship of reviews in the *Critical* published during 1756—other than those by Smollett—and biographical information on the reviewers are taken from Roper, "Smollett's 'Four Gentlemen'."

109. For the 15 May publication date of the *LM,* see Eddy, *Samuel Johnson: Booker Reviewer,* p. 40; the *Critical*—like most monthly magazines of the eighteenth century—normally appeared at the beginning of the month following that given on the title page, so this number almost certainly appeared no earlier than 1 June 1756 (see Basker, *Tobias Smollett,* p. 46).

110. Precisely when Johnson and Francklin met is not known, though they were certainly on friendly terms by the mid-1770s. Perhaps the two were introduced to each other at David Garrick's wedding (London, 22 June 1749), which Reverend Francklin presided over: see Boswell, *Boswell's Life of Johnson,* 3:83, 3:483, 4:34, 4:479; and G. W. Stone and G. M. Kahrl, *David Garrick: A Critical Biography* (Carbondale: Southern Illinois University Press, 1979), p. 408. Francklin would later dedicate his translation of Lucian's *Demonax* to Johnson: "To Dr. Samuel Johnson, the Demonax of the present age; this piece is inscribed, by a sincere admirer of his truly respectable character": *The Works of Lucian, from the Greek* (London, 1780), 2:63.

111. *CR,* 1:293, 296.

112. *CR,* 1:303.

113. *Dictionary of National Biography,* 2:609–11; Eddy, *Samuel Johnson: Book Reviewer,* pp. 41–42.

114. See Boswell, *Boswell's Life of Johnson,* 1:311; Greene, *Politics of Samuel Johnson,* pp. 173, 241–42; Bloom, *Samuel Johnson in Grub Street,* p. 193.

115. John A. Vance, "Johnson's Historical Reviews," in *Fresh Reflections on Samuel Johnson: Essays in Criticism,* ed. Prem Nath (Troy, N.Y.: Whitson, 1987), pp. 63–84.

116. *LM,* 1:240.

117. Vance, "Johnson's Historical Reviews," p. 75.

118. Boswell, *Boswell's Life of Johnson,* 1:284–85.

119. *LM* 1:41–2, 239–40.

120. *LM,* 1:42; Bloom, *Samuel Johnson in Grub Street,* p. 193. In his 1786 biography

of Johnson, Joseph Towers (1737–99) avers that "Blackwell's style, was, indeed, in some respects, liable to just exceptions; but it seems sufficiently evident, that the high sentiments of liberty, which are displayed in Blackwell's book, was a principal cause of the extreme severity with which Johnson treated him." *The Early Biographies of Samuel Johnson*, ed. O M Brack Jr. and R. E. Kelly (Iowa City: University of Iowa Press, 1974), pp. 215–16; also see O M Brack Jr. and R. E. Kelley, *Samuel Johnson's Early Biographers* (Iowa City: University of Iowa Press, 1971), pp. 58–74.

121. Johnson, *Lives of the Poets*, 3:411–12; also see Johnson's "Life of Milton" (*Lives of the Poets*, 1:157); Greene, *Politics of Samuel Johnson*, pp. 173, 240–48; and Greene's introduction to *Yale* 10, esp. xviii–xxxv.

122. *Yale*, 2:217.

123. *CR*, 1:67.

124. *CR*, 1:67. For a discussion of the debates surrounding the English language in Johnson's day, see Albert C. Baugh and Thomas Cable, *A History of the English Language*, 4th ed. (London: Routledge, 1993), pp. 248–89; Leonard A. Sterling, *The Doctrine of Correctness in English Usage, 1700–1800* (New York: Russell and Russell, 1962). For additional context see Basker, *Tobias Smollett*, pp. 19–22, 75–84; Basker, "Minim and the 'Great Cham': Smollett and Johnson on the Prospect of an English Academy," in *Johnson and His Age*, ed. James Engell (Cambridge: Harvard University Press, 1984), pp. 137–61; Allen Walker Read, "Suggestions for an Academy in England in the Latter Half of the Eighteenth Century," *Modern Philology* 36 (1938–39): 145–56.

125. For context see Basker, *Tobias Smollett*, pp. 74–84.

126. *MR*, 14:237.

127. *MR*, 14:230. The commentary here essentially echoes Rose's review of Blackwell's first volume: the *Memoirs* reflect a "thorough acquaintance with the genius and policy of antient Rome," Rose observes, though Blackwell "is far from being happy in his stile and manner of writing" (*MR*, 8:420–21).

128. See *UV*, pp. 159–66; *Yale*, 2:456–61.

129. Thomas Blackwell, *Memoirs of the Court of Augustus* (Edinburgh, 1755), 2:vi–vii.

130. *LM*, 1:41.

131. *LM*, 1:41–2.

132. *LM*, 1:239–40.

133. *LM*, 1:42.

134. *LM*, 1:239.

135. *LM*, 2:303–4 (misnumbered 305–6).

136. Isaac Newton, *Four Letters from Sir Isaac Newton to Doctor Bentley: Containing Some Arguments in Proof of a Diety* (London, 1756). The letters are reprinted in *The Correspondence of Isaac Newton*, ed. H. W. Turnbull, J. F. Scott, A. Rupert Hall, and Laura Trilling (Cambridge: Cambridge University Press, 1959–77), 3:233–56; also see Turnbull's introduction, 1:xviii–xx.

137. A. Rupert Hall, *Isaac Newton: Adventurer in Thought* (Oxford: Blackwell, 1992), p. 248; also see L. T. More, *Isaac Newton: A Biography* (New York: Dover, 1962), pp. 374–78.

138. For publication dates see Eddy, *Samuel Johnson: Book Reviewer*, p. 43.

139. *LM*, 1:89.

140. For a discussion of Johnson's rhetorical strategy in the *Rambler* see Damrosch, "Johnson's Manner of Proceeding in the *Rambler*"; Stephen Lynn, "Johnson's *Rambler* and Eighteenth-Century Rhetoric," *Eighteenth-Century Studies* 19 (1986): 461–79.

141. *LM*, 1:90–91.

142. Newton, *Four Letters*, pp. 33–35.

143. Bloom, *Samuel Johnson in Grub Street*, p. 187.

144. *MR*, 14:590; also see *CR*, 1:388.

145. Boswell, *Boswell's Life of Johnson*, 1:125 n. 4.

146. For full discussion of Johnson's work as a scholarly editor of the *Christian Morals*, see Brack, "Johnson Edits for the Booksellers," pp. 12–39.

147. *MR*, 14:448.

148. *LM*, 1:141; Johnson, *Lives of the Poets*, 1:20 ("The most heterogeneous ideas are yoked by violence together").

149. *LM*, 1:140–41.

150. *Dictionary of National Biography*, 10:1216.

151. "After the Union [of Scottish and English parliaments in 1707]," writes J. C. D. Clark in *Samuel Johnson: Literature, Religion and English Cultural Politics from the Restoration to Romanticism* (Cambridge: Cambridge University Press, 1994), "antiquarianism in Scotland lost little of its profoundly politicized orientation towards questions of modern Scottish national identity; it was a present-mindedness compelled by a 'post-Union national identity crisis'" (p. 59).

152. Bloom, *Samuel Johnson in Grub Street*, pp. 189–90; Clark, *Samuel Johnson*, pp. 6–10, 133. Interestingly, Clark takes no notice of Johnson's review.

153. *GM*, 12:128–31; also see *Boswell's Life of Johnson*, in which Johnson is reported to have described King William as a "'scoundrel'" (5:255); also see Johnson's biographies of Prior and Addison, in which Johnson writes depreciatively of eulogistic poetry directed at King William (*Lives of the Poets*, 2:85, 185).

154. Eddy, *Samuel Johnson: Book Reviewer*, p. 50.

155. *LM*, 1:172.

156. "Sir, the life of a parson, of a conscientious clergyman, is not easy," Johnson remarked to Oliver Edwards in 1778. "I have always considered a clergyman as the father of a larger family than he is able to maintain. I would rather have Chancery suits upon my hands than the cure of souls" (Boswell, *Boswell's Life of Johnson*, 3:304; also see 1:320).

157. Quinlan, *Samuel Johnson*, pp. 150ff.; *Yale*, 14:117ff.; *Yale*, 15:4–5.

158. For Johnson's outlook on the moral and social purposes of biography, see Robert Folkenflik, *Samuel Johnson, Biographer* (Ithaca: Cornell University Press, 1978), chapter 2.

159. *Dictionary of National Biography*, 3:791–92; 11:883–86; 17:252–54; Boswell, *Boswell's Life of Johnson*, 4:286; 5:356–57; also see Clark, *Samuel Johnson*, pp. 133, 135. Johnson refers briefly to the abolition of the episcopacy in the *Journey to the Western Islands of Scotland* (*Yale*, 9:17).

160. *Dictionary of National Biography*, 3:689, 15:311–12; Charles Parkin, *An Impartial Account of the Invasion under William Duke of Normandy* (London, 1756). For the publication date of the *Account*, see Eddy, *Samuel Johnson: Book Reviewer*, p. 53.

161. *MR*, 14:582.

162. Sir Henry Spelman (1564–1641). Parkin refers to assertions found in Spelman's *Iceni*, which was published posthumously by Bishop Edmund Gibson in *The English Works of Sir Henry Spelman, Kt., Together with His Posthumous Works, Relating to the Laws and Antiquities of England*. The first edition was published in 1695, the second in 1727.

163. *LM*, 1:186–88.

164. Batten, *Pleasurable Instruction*, pp. 82–84.

165. *MR*, 15:369–85; *CR*, 1:490–508.

166. *Yale*, 2:298.

167. "I have been reading 'Twiss's Travels in Spain,' which are just come out." Johnson remarked to Boswell in April 1775. "They are as good as those of Keyssler or Blainville; nay, as Addison's, if you except the learning" (*Boswell's Life of Johnson*, 2:346).

168. *LM*, 1:240–41; the biographical extract is taken from pp. vi–xiii of Keyssler's

Travels through Germany. For Johnson's views on biography, also see Folkenflik, *Samuel Johnson, Biographer,* chapter 2.

169. *LM,* 1:241–42.

170. *LM,* 1:242.

171. *MR,* 14:561–73, 15:97–106, 209–16.

172. The title page of the *Memoirs* carries a date of 1756, but the work was actually published on 8 November 1755 (Eddy, *Samuel Johnson: Book Reviewer,* pp. 56–58).

173. Clifford, *Dictionary Johnson,* p. 90.

174. *LM,* 1:282.

175. *LM,* 1:282.

176. *Encyclopaedia Britannica,* 15th ed.

177. Cf. Johnson's review of the duchess of Marlborough's *Memoirs* (1742), which is discussed at length in chapter 5. The "parent of all memoirs is the ambition of being distinguished from the herd of mankind, and the fear of either infamy or oblivion, passions which cannot but have some degree of influence, and which may at least affect the writer's choice of facts, though they may not prevail upon him to advance known falsehoods" (*GM,* 12:128); for similar commentary, see *Rambler* 60 (1750) and *Idler* 84 (1759).

178. *Yale,* 2:263. In Johnson's day the term "biography" and "autobiography" were synonymous. *Idler* 84 examines what modern readers understand as autobiography.

179. See Elizabeth Harrison, *Miscellanies on Moral and Religious Subjects, in Prose and Verse.* (London, 1756), pp. iii, xii.

180. For a discussion of the marketing of subscription books, see Roy M. Wiles, *Serial Publication in England before 1750* (Cambridge: Cambridge University Press, 1957), chapters 5, 6, and 7.

181. *Dictionary of National Biography,* 17:338–39, 20:978–81.

182. *LM,* 1:282; cf. Johnson's "Life of Watts": "His lines are commonly smooth and easy, and his thoughts always religiously pure; but who is there that, to so much piety and innocence, does not wish for a greater measure of spriteliness and vigour? He is at least one of the few poets with whom youth and ignorance may be safely pleased; and happy will be that reader whose mind is disposed by his verses or his prose to imitate him in all but his non-conformity, to copy his benevolence to man, and his reverence to God" (*Lives of the Poets,* 3:311). Watts was included in the *Lives* at Johnson's request (*Lives of the Poets,* 3:302).

183. *LM,* 1:282.

184. *LM,* 1:282.

185. *LM,* 1:282–88.

186. *MR,* 15:537; the reviewer here refers to Harrison's "Author to the Reader," p. iii of the *Miscellanies.*

187. *Dictionary of National Biography,* 10:769–70.

188. Soame Jenyns, *A Free Inquiry into the Nature and Origin of Evil* (London, 1757).

189. Eddy, *Samuel Johnson: Book Reviewer,* p. 93; *Yale,* 4:133; Richard B. Schwartz, *Samuel Johnson and the Problem of Evil* (Madison: University of Wisconsin Press, 1975), pp. 22–37; also see W. J. Bate, *Samuel Johnson* (London: Chatto & Windus, 1978), p. 375.

190. *LM,* 2:171; cf. Jenyns's opening statements (*Free Inquiry* [1757], pp. 1–2): "I imagin'd it might not be unentertaining either to you [Jenyns's unnamed correspondent], or myself, to put together my sentiments on these important topics ["metaphysical, moral, political, and religious subjects"], and communicate them to you from time to time as the absence of business, or of more agreeable amusements may afford me opportunity. This I propose to do under the general title of an Inquiry into the Nature, and Origin of Evil; *an Inquiry, which will comprehend them all, and which, I think, has never been attended to with that diligence it deserves, nor with that success, which might have been hoped for from that little that has been bestow'd upon it* [emphasis added]."

191. Eddy, *Samuel Johnson: Book Reviewer*, p. 76.
192. *LM,* 2:171.
193. *LM,* 2:299 (misnumbered 301).
194. *LM,* 2:300 (misnumbered 302). As Harry Solomon has pointed out, in the lead sentence here Johnson alludes to Robert Dodsley's "amused toleration of Jenyns's manifest inadequacies" (*Rise of Robert Dodsley*, p. 171).
195. *Yale,* 4:133.
196. *MR,* 16:304, 316; *CR,* 3:448.
197. Soame Jenyns, *A Free Inquiry into the Nature and Origin of Evil*, 4th ed. (London, 1761), pp. ii–xxx.
198. Clifford, *Dictionary Johnson*, p. 171; Eddy, *Samuel Johnson: Book Reviewer*, p. 15; *Yale,* 10:128; Donald Greene believes that Johnson was fired specifically on account of his political views. See Greene, "Samuel Johnson, Journalist," pp. 87–99; also see Greene, *Politics of Samuel Johnson,* p. 269.

CHAPTER 3. JOHNSON AS A REVIEWER OF JOURNALISTIC PUBLICATIONS, FUGITIVE PIECES, AND BOOKS ON PUBLIC AFFAIRS IN THE LITERARY MAGAZINE

1. Greene, "Samuel Johnson, Journalist"; Bloom, *Samuel Johnson in Grub Street;* DeMaria, *Samuel Johnson and the Life of Reading*.
2. In this chapter pamphlets are defined as publications of fewer than one hundred pages.
3. Hazen, *Samuel Johnson's Prefaces and Dedications*, pp. 54–59.
4. Greene, *Politics of Samuel Johnson,* p. 142.
5. In the eight numbers of the *Gray's-Inn Journal* (17 November 1753), Murphy had plagiarized Johnson's *Miscellaneous Observations on Macbeth*. See Bonnie Ferrero, "Samuel Johnson and Arthur Murphy," *English Language Notes* 18 (March 1991): 18–24; idem, "Johnson, Murphy, and Macbeth," *Review of English Studies* 42 (1991): 228–32.
6. Boswell, *Boswell's Life of Johnson*, 1:356; Clifford, *Dictionary Johnson*, p. 126; *Dictionary of National Biography*, 13:1231–34; Eddy, *Samuel Johnson: Book Reviewer*, pp. 2–3. Murphy's apology appeared initially in the "True Intelligence" section of the 22 June 1754 issue; Murphy removed the apology when he prepared the two-volume 1756 octavo edition for the press (see Arthur Murphy, *The Gray's-Inn Journal* [London, 1756], 2:225–331), though it does appear in an earlier quarto edition of *The Gray's-Inn Journal* (London, 1753–54), p. 233: "[B]e it known that in the last Week I received an eastern Story of *Morad* and his Son *Abouzaid*, which the Person, who sent it, told me he had translated from the *French*. As I was very much entertained with this oriental Tale, I published it last Saturday, and then learned too late, that that very same Piece was translated into French from a Paper, justly in great Repute, published here three or four years since." Murphy substituted a commentary on *King Lear* for the plagiarized piece when compiling the 1756 octavo edition (2:219–24).
7. Sullivan, *British Literary Magazines*, pp. 140–44; Eddy, *Samuel Johnson: Book Reviewer*, pp. 38–39; Murphy, *Gray's-Inn Journal* (1756).
8. *LM,* 1:32.
9. *LM,* 1:32.
10. Eddy, *Samuel Johnson: Book Reviewer*, pp. 23–24.
11. *LM,* 1:461.
12. Hazen, *Samuel Johnson's Prefaces and Dedications*, p. 212.

13. *Dictionary of National Biography*, 4:479. Cleeve's second pamphlet, *His Majesty's Royal Bounty: or, A Scheme for Keeping in His Majesty's Service Such a Number of Seamen, that, upon the Breaking Out of a War, . . . May Be Ready to Embark on Board Such of His Majesty's Ships as Shall Be Required* (London, 1756), also totals sixteen pages. A third edition of the *Scheme for Preventing a Further Increase of the National Debt* appeared in 1757.

14. See W. A. Speck, *Stability and Strife: England, 1714–1760* (Cambridge: Harvard University Press, 1977), pp. 252ff.; Basil Williams, *The Whig Supremacy: 1714–1760,* rev. C. H. Stuart (Oxford: Oxford University Press, 1962), pp. 334–38; also see Alice Clare Carter, *The English Public Debt in the Eighteenth Century* (London: Historical Association, 1968); P. G. M. Dickson, *The Financial Revolution in England: A Study in the Development of Public Credit in England, 1688–1756* (London: Macmillan, 1967), chapter 10.

15. *MR*, 14:455; for a discussion of the implausibility of Cleeve's scheme, see *Dictionary of National Biography*, 4:479.

16. *LM*, 1:188–89.

17. *Yale*, 10:126–50. Also see Greene, *Politics of Samuel Johnson,* pp. 162ff.

18. For Johnson's views on the policies of the Newcastle Ministry, see Greene, *Politics of Samuel Johnson,* pp. 154ff.

19. *LM*, 1:189.

20. For the bibliographical history of Evans's volume see Eddy, *Samuel Johnson: Book Reviewer,* pp. 59–62.

21. Johnson's review of Evans's *Map* is reprinted, with explanatory notes and an introduction by Donald Greene, in *Yale,* 10:197–212.

22. *Yale*, 10:197–200; *LM*, 1:294.

23. *MR*, 14:30.

24. *MR*, 14:37.

25. The passage, quoted in both the *Monthly* and the *Literary Magazine,* is reproduced in *Yale,* 10:206–7.

26. *Yale*, 10:210–11. For Johnson's views on colonialism, see Greene's introduction to the *Yale* volume, and Johnson's essay "An Introduction to the Political State of Great Britain," in *Yale,* 10:126–50.

27. Johnson's reviews are printed, along with explanatory notes and an introduction, in *Yale,* 10.

28. Dudley Pope, *At Twelve Mr. Byng Was Shot* (Philadelphia: J. B. Lippincott, 1962), pp. 13, 291–92.

29. *LM*, 1:299–300.

30. *LM*, 1:309.

31. *MR*, 15:420–22; *CR*, 2:285.

32. *LM*, 1:161.

33. Johnson's review is printed, along with explanatory notes and an introduction, in *Yale,* 10.

34. *LM*, 1:344.

35. *LM*, 1:348 [misnumbered 339].

36. *MR*, 15:527–32.

37. Johnson's review is printed, along with explanatory notes and an introduction, in *Yale,* 10.

38. *LM*, 1:348. Johnson's harsh criticism here may be said to foreshadow his dismissive summary of Mallet's career in the *Lives of the Poets* (3:410).

39. *LM*, 1:351.

40. D. Pope, *At Twelve Mr. Byng Was Shot,* chapters 14 through 21.

41. *MR*, 15:524–27; *CR*, 2:376.

42. *Yale*, 10:216.

43. *MR*, 16:360–61.

44. For greater context, see the entries for Bower and Douglas in the *Dictionary of National Biography* (2:956–59; 5:1242–43).

45. *LM*, 1:133.

46. *MR*, 15:91–92; *CR*, 1:558.

47. *MR*, 15:190–92; *CR*, 1:560.

48. *MR*, 16:50–74; *CR*, 3:41–57.

49. *LM*, 1:449.

50. Extracts from the first edition of the *Journal* had been given in the November 1756 issue of the *LM* (Eddy, *Samuel Johnson: Book Reviewer*, pp. 65–66).

51. See *Dictionary of National Biography*, 8:1196–99.

52. Jonas Hanway, *A Journal of Eight Days Journey from Portsmouth to Kingston upon Thames, in Sixty-Four Letters, to Which is Added an Essay on Tea in Thirty-two Letters* (London, 1757), 1:22–24, 211–25; 2:155–78, 221–22, 223–55, 270–88.

53. *LM*, 2:167 (misnumbered 166).

54. For an overview of the Hanway incident, see Clifford, *Dictionary Johnson*, pp. 184–86. The governors of the Foundling Hospital contemplated suing Johnson and the *Literary Magazine*, but decided not to do so chiefly out of fear that a lawsuit—irrespective of its outcome—would yield nothing more than further bad publicity at a historical moment when any sort of blight on the hospital's public image threatened its survival. For further discussion, see Ruth McClure, "Johnson's Criticism of the Foundling Hospital," *Review of English Studies* 27 (1976): 17–26.

55. *LM*, 2:162 (misnumbered 161); Boswell, *Boswell's Life of Johnson*, 1:313; Bloom, *Samuel Johnson in Grub Street*, pp. 199–200; Eddy, *Samuel Johnson: Book Reviewer*, pp. 11–15, 92; Robert DeMaria, *The Life of Samuel Johnson: A Critical Biography* (Oxford: Blackwell, 1993), pp. 186–87.

56. *LM*, 2:162 (misnumbered 161).

57. *LM*, 2:163.

58. For a thorough discussion of the controversy during the eighteenth century in regard to luxury, see John Sekora, *Luxury: The Concept in Western Thought, Eden to Smollett* (Baltimore: Johns Hopkins University Press, 1977), chapters 2 and 3.

59. *LM*, 2:162–63; Hanway, *Journal of Eight Days Journey,* 2:20–24.

60. *LM*, 2:164; cf. Hanway, *Journal of Eight Days Journey,* 2:142–48.

61. There were three debates related to the taxing of spirituous liquors: see B. B. Hoover, *Samuel Johnson's Parliamentary Reporting* (Berkeley: University of California Press, 1953), pp. 118–20; Kaminski, *Early Career of Samuel Johnson*, p. 141.

62. *LM*, 2:166; for Hanway's exoneration of the East India company in regard to the evils of tea drinking, see *Journal of Eight Days Journey,* 2:179–82. The economic and political views expressed in the Hanway review are consistent with Johnson's broader outlook on these subjects: see Greene, *Politics of Samuel Johnson,* pp. 284–85; John H. Middendorf, "Johnson on Wealth and Commerce," in *Johnson, Boswell, and Their Circle,* ed. Mary Lascelles (Oxford: Oxford University Press, 1965), pp. 47–64.

63. *LM*, 2:166–67.

64. *LM*, 2:167; cf. Hanway, *Journal of Eight Days Journey,* 2:189.

65. *LM*, 2:254–55; also see Eddy, *Samuel Johnson: Book Reviewer*, p. 78.

66. *CR,* 4:2.

67. *CR,* 4:7.

68. See Ralph Wardle, *Oliver Goldsmith* (Lawrence: University Press of Kansas, 1957), pp. 75ff.

69. Goldsmith, *Collected Works*, ed. Friedman, 1:76–77.

70. Ibid., 1:79–80; Wardle, *Oliver Goldsmith*, pp. 72–80, 189 and notes. Goldsmith "attracted plenty of patients," writes Wardle in discussing Goldsmith's brief stint as a physician in 1756, but "he received few fees. People who could afford medical care were not disposed to call in an unprepossessing Irishman with a thick brogue" (p. 72).

CHAPTER 4. JOHNSON AS A REVIEWER OF WORKS IN THE PHYSICAL, PRACTICAL, AND NATURAL SCIENCES IN THE *LITERARY MAGAZINE*

1. For Johnson's interest in scientific works and works related to the practical arts, see Middendorf, "Johnson on Wealth and Commerce"; Richard B. Schwartz, *Samuel Johnson and the New Science* (Madison: University of Wisconsin Press, 1971). Johnson was for many years a dues-paying member of the Society for the Encouragement of Arts, Manufactures, and Commerce: see J. L. Abbott, "Dr. Johnson and the Society," in *The Virtuoso Tribe of Arts and Sciences: Studies in the Eighteenth-Century Work and Membership of the London Society of Arts*, ed. D. G. C. Allan and J. L. Abbott (Athens: University of Georgia Press, 1992), pp. 7–17; also see Clifford, *Dictionary Johnson*, pp. 226–28; Boswell, *Boswell's Life of Johnson*, 2:139–40 n. 1.
2. *Yale*, 2:434.
3. *Yale*, 3:49–50; for similar commentary, see *Ramblers* 83 and 137.
4. See Schwartz, *Samuel Johnson and the New Science*, chapters 1 and 2. Johnson offers two definitions of "Projector" in the *Dictionary*. The first is tersely neutral ("One who forms schemes or designs"), the second depreciatory ("One who forms wild impracticable schemes").
5. *Yale*, 2:298, 300.
6. *Alumni Cantabrigienses: Part One*, comp. J. Venn and J. A. Venn (Cambridge: Cambridge University Press, 1927), 4:389. Stephen White, *Collateral Bee-Boxes; or, A New, Easy, and Advantageous Method of Managing Bees* (London, 1756), p. xii.
7. Greene, "Johnson's Contributions to the *Literary Magazine*."
8. International Bee Research Association, *British Bee Books: A Bibliography, 1500–1976* (London: International Bee Research Association, 1979), pp. 68–100; Henry Malcolm Fraser, *The History of Beekeeping in England* (London: Bee Research Association, 1958), chapters 5 and 6; also see E. F. Phillips, *Beekeeping* (New York: Macmillan, 1955); *Encyclopaedia Britannica*, 15th ed., s.v. "Beekeeping."
9. For White's contribution to apiculture, see Fraser, *History of Beekeeping*, pp. 56–57, 62, 69, 70, 74. For an overview of the prominence of agricultural innovation at midcentury, see C. S. Orwin, "Agriculture and Rural Life," in Turberville, *Johnson's England*, 1:261–99. Johnson was a fairly prolific commentator on issues related to agricultural economics: see *Yale*, 10:116–25, 301–12; and Kaminski, *Early Career of Samuel Johnson*, pp. 151–53. Also see Johnson's parliamentary debates on agricultural topics (Hoover, *Samuel Johnson's Parliamentary Reporting*, pp. 208–9), and Johnson's essays on the wool trade, *GM*, 11:170 (1741); 12:83–89 (1742).
10. Eddy, *Samuel Johnson: Book Reviewer*, p. 87; for the *Sully* review, see *LM*, 1:281–82.
11. *LM*, 1:27–28.
12. *LM*, 1:27–28; White, *Collateral Bee-Boxes*, pp. i–xii; 59–62.
13. *LM*, 1:28.
14. *MR*, 14:450.
15. Francis Home, *Experiments on Bleaching* (Edinburgh: Kincaid and Donaldson, 1756); the "Advertisement," which appears in front of the text, is not paginated.
16. *CR*, 1:106–7.

17. *CR,* 1:114. For Smollett's attitude toward Scotticisms, see Basker, *Tobias Smollett,* pp. 82–84.

18. For a biographical sketch of Home, see the *Dictionary of National Biography,* 9:1122–23; for Boerhaave, Homberg, and Stahl, see the relevant entries in *Encyclopaedia Britannica,* 11th ed.

19. For additional context, see Basker, *Tobias Smollett,* pp. 83–85.

20. *MR,* 14:428–29.

21. *LM,* 1:136–41.

22. *LM,* 1:140; also see Home, *Experiments on Bleaching,* p. 297.

23. *LM,* 1:136; cf. *Idler* 70: "They that content themselves with general ideas may rest in general terms; but those whose studies or employments force them upon closer inspection, must have names for particular parts, and words by which they may express various modes of combination, such as none but themselves have occasion to consider" (*Yale,* 2:219).

24. *Dictionary of National Biography,* 8:917–19; also see D. G. C. Allen and R. E. Schofield, *Stephen Hales: Scientist and Philanthropist* (London: Scolar Press, 1980).

25. Stephen Hales, *An Account of a Useful Discovery* (London, 1756).

26. Schofield, *Stephen Hales,* p. 91.

27. *MR,* 14:446.

28. *LM,* 1:143; also see Hales, *Account of a Useful Discovery,* pp. 3–5.

29. Cf. *Rambler* 106: "Some writers apply themselves to studies boundless and inexhaustible, as experiments in natural philosophy. These are always lost in successive compilations, as new advances are made, and former observations become more familiar" (*Yale,* 4:203).

30. *LM,* 1:143.

31. *LM,* 1:143–44.

32. Charles Lucas's objectives are set forth in his preface to *An Essay on Waters* (London, 1756), 1:xv–xviii).

33. G. S. Rousseau, "Bramble and the Sulpher Controversy," *Journal of the History of Ideas* 28 (1967): 577–89.

34. Lucas, *Essay on Waters,* 1:viii.

35. Also see Lucas's *An Appeal to the Commons and Citizens of London . . . by the Last Free Citizen of Dublin* (London, 1756).

36. Lucas, *Essay on Waters,* 1:xviii.

37. Basker, *Tobias Smollett,* pp. 118ff.; Lewis Knapp, *Tobias Smollett: Doctor of Men and Manners* (Princeton: Princeton University Press, 1949), chapter 7.

38. Tobias Smollett, *An Essay on the External Use of Water in a Letter to Dr. ****, with Particular Remarks upon the Present Method of Using the Mineral Waters at Bath in Somersetshire, and a Plan for Rendering Them More Safe, Agreeable, and Efficacious* (London, 1752). For Lucas's commentary on the Bath spas see *Essay on Waters,* 3:259–83, 333–41. For a full consideration of Smollett and Lucas, see G. S. Rousseau, "Bramble and the Sulpher Controversy"; also see Knapp, *Tobias Smollett,* pp. 146–50.

39. *CR,* 1:344–45.

40. Smollett, *Essay on the External Use of Water,* pp. 34–38.

41. Ibid., pp. 39–40.

42. *CR,* 1:321–22.

43. In Smollett's review of Lucas's *Essay on Waters* the initials "*Sh*——" only are given to identify the other author, but the remarks quoted here conform to events in Shebbeare's life between 1740–55: see *Dictionary of National Biography,* 18:1–4. For additional context see James R. Foster, "Smollett's Pamphleteering Foe Shebbeare," *Publication of the Modern Language Association* 57 (1942): 1058–1100; for the earlier review of Shebbeare see *CR,* 1:88–90.

44. *CR,* 1:169–70; Alexander Leighton (1568–1649), religious controversialist, im-

prisoned and tortured in 1630 for his seditious writings; John Lilburne (1614–57), whipped, pilloried, and imprisoned in 1638 for printing and distributing unlicensed books; William Prynne (1600–1669), religious and political controversialist, imprisoned, pilloried, and tortured for his writings, 1633–34 (*Dictionary of National Biography*, 11:880–81, 11:1122–23, 16:432–33).

45. *CR*, 1:344; for Lucas's address to Chesterfield, see *Essay on Waters*, 3:ccix–ccxvii.

46. *CR*, 1:323.

47. *CR*, 1:322.

48. *CR*, 1:341.

49. See *Letters of Samuel Johnson*, ed. Redford, 1:136, and note 1.

50. *LM*, 1:167.

51. Boswell, *Boswell's Life of Johnson*, 1:311; also see Sir Tanfield Leman's review of the *Appeal* in the *Monthly*'s January 1756 issue (14:76–78): here, Lucas is portrayed as a deluded and pompous controversialist.

52. *LM*, 1:167.

53. Lucas, *Essay on Waters*, 1:xxv–xxvii; also see Sledd and Kolb, *Dr. Johnson's Dictionary*, p. 33.

54. *LM*, 1:167.

55. *LM*, 1:167.

56. Bloom, *Samuel Johnson in Grub Street*, p. 198.

57. *LM*, 1:168.

58. *LM*, 1:229. For Johnson's remarkably thorough grasp of the practice of medicine, see John Wiltshire, *Samuel Johnson in the Medical World* (Cambridge: Cambridge University Press, 1991), chapter 2.

59. *MR*, 15:205–8.

60. Dorothy Stimson, *Scientists and Amateurs: A History of the Royal Society* (New York: Henry Schuman, 1948), pp. 65–69; also see Graham, *English Literary Periodicals*, pp. 25–29; idem, *Beginnings of English Periodicals*, pp. 5–8.

61. *LM*, 1:193.

62. For a broader discussion of Johnson and physico-theology, see Schwartz, *Samuel Johnson and the New Science*, pp. 127ff.

63. *Philosophical Transactions. Vol. XLIX. Part I. For the Year* 1755 (London, 1756).

64. *Dictionary of National Biography*, 16:179–80.

65. Boswell, *Boswell's Life of Johnson*, 1:284, and notes 2–4; also see *Dictionary of National Biography*, 13:76–78.

66. *LM*, 1:193.

67. See Wiltshire, *Samuel Johnson in the Medical World*, chapter 3; DeMaria, *Life of Samuel Johnson*, chapter 1.

68. *LM*, 1:197.

69. *CR*, 1:528–29, 2:13–35, 126–35; *MR*, 15:271–81, 361–81.

70. See G. S. Rousseau, "Science Books and Their Readers in the Eighteenth Century," in Rivers, *Books and Their Readers*, pp. 197–255; Larry Stewart, *The Rise of Public Science* (Cambridge: Cambridge University Press, 1992), chapters 8–12; Schwartz, *Samuel Johnson and the New Science,* chapter 1; Herbert W. Meyer, *A History of Electricity and Magnetism* (Cambridge: MIT Press, 1971), chapter 2; though an older work, the following offers a reliable, comprehensive survey of the pioneers of electricity: P. F. Mottelay, comp., *Bibliographical History of Electricity and Magnetism* (London: Griffin & Co., 1922). For a contemporary account of electrical experimentation, see Joseph Priestley, *The History and Present State of Electricity, with Original Experiments*, 2 vols. (London, 1755; reprint, New York: Johnson Reprint Corporation, 1966). For a biographical note on Lovett, see *Dictionary of National Biography*, 12:78.

71. William K. Wimsatt, "Johnson on Electricity," *Review of English Studies* 23 (1947): 257–60; Schwartz, *Samuel Johnson and the New Science,* pp. 14–24, chapter 2.

72. *LM,* 1:232.

73. Richard Lovett, *The Subtil Medium Prov'd* (London, 1756), "To the Reader."

74. Also see G. S. Rousseau, "Science Books and Their Readers"; Schwartz, *Samuel Johnson and the New Science,* chapter 2.

75. *LM,* 1:232; Johnson quotes the entire introductory essay of Lovett's *Subtil Medium Prov'd,* pp. 1–8.

76. *LM,* 1:233; Lovett, *Subtil Medium Prov'd,* p. 4.

77. For a detailed survey of electrical experimentation in the first half of the century, see J. L. Heilbron, *Elements of Early Modern Physics* (Berkeley: University of California Press, 1982), chapter 3; also see Meyer, *History of Electricity and Magnetism,* chapter 2.

78. Lovett, *Sir Isaac Newton's Aether Realized . . . in Answer to the* ANIMADVERSION *made by the* MONTHLY REVIEW (London, 1758), p. 3; also see Roger Lonsdale, "William Bewley and *The MR:* A Problem of Attribution," *Papers of the Bibliographical Society of America* 55 (1961): 309–18. Lonsdale suggests that John Berkenhout may have written at least some of the reviews attributed by B. C. Nangle to Bewley that were published between 1755–67.

79. *MR,* 15:561–62.

80. *Dictionary of National Biography,* 9:910; 21:553–55.

81. Courtney and Smith, *Bibliography of Samuel Johnson,* p. 74; Heilbron, *Elements of Early Modern Physics,* pp. 202–3; Mottelay, *Bibliographical History of Electricity and Magnetism,* pp. 183–85; Boswell, *Boswell's Life of Johnson,* 1:317.

82. *LM,* 1:234. Wilson published an *Essay Towards an Explication of the Phaenomena of Electricity* in 1746; his *Treatise on Electricity* first appeared in 1750 (second edition, 1752). Hoadly published *Three Lectures on the Organs of Respiration* in 1740.

83. For a thumbnail sketch of Franklin's pioneering work, see Meyer, *History of Electricity and Magnetism,* pp. 22–27.

84. Dr. Hoadly and Mr. Wilson, *Observations of a Series of Electrical Experiments* (London, 1756).

85. *LM,* 1:235.

86. *MR,* 15:466–69.

87. *LM,* 1:237.

88. See J. A. Houlding, *Fit for Service: The Training of the British Army, 1715–1795* (Oxford: Clarendon, 1981), pp. 205–6 and note 107.

89. Samuel Bever, *The Cadet: A Military Treatise* (London, 1756), pp. iv–v. William Augustus, duke of Cumberland (1721–65), son of King George II; military commander best known for his victory over Jacobite forces at the Battle of Culloden, 1745 (*Dictionary of National Biography,* 21:337–48).

90. Houlding, *Fit for Service.* For the publication date of the 1756 edition of Bever's volume, see Eddy, *Samuel Johnson: Book Reviewer,* p. 67.

91. See Johnson's "Remarks on the Militia Bill" and his "Observations on the Russian and Hessian Treaties" (*LM,* 1:57–63; 119–21; rptd, with an excellent introduction by Donald Greene, in *Yale,* 10:151–83). Also see Greene, *Politics of Samuel Johnson,* pp. 154–83. Johnson also composed a number of "Parliamentary Debates" related to the raising and funding of armed forces (see Hoover, *Samuel Johnson's Parliamentary Reporting,* pp. 207–18).

92. For context see *Fit for Service,* chapters 1 through 4.

93. William Johnston (fl. 1748–74), was one of the proprietors of *Rasselas* (1759) (*Yale,* 16:xix, xiv, 251).

94. *MR,* 15:402–7; *CR,* 2:244–51.

95. Bever, *Cadet,* pp. viii–ix.

96. Houlding, *Fit for Service*, p. 206.

97. For the "Speech," see *Yale*, 10:264ff.; also see Greene, *Politics of Samuel Johnson*, pp. 175–76. Johnson may have despised large standing armies, and in particular he did not shy from criticizing the ineptitude of Britain's armed forces, but he clearly sympathized with the stress soldiers suffered during military campaigns; equally clear is his admiration for the courage and loyalty of combat-tested soldiers and sailors. Indeed, Johnson equipped himself for militia duty, though of course he was never called to active duty. For context, see Brian Hanley, "The Prevailing Moral Tone of Samuel Johnson's Military Commentary," *New Rambler* 12 (1996–97): 39–45.

98. See Boswell, *Boswell's Life of Johnson*, 3:360–62; 4:319; Brack and Kelly, *Early Biographies of Samuel Johnson*, p. 86.

99. *LM*, 1:343.

100. *Dictionary of National Biography*, 17:426–27; the *Natural History* was published on 5 May (Eddy, *Samuel Johnson: Book Reviewer*, p. 42).

101. Adams, *Travel Literature and the Evolution of the Novel*; Curley, *Johnson and the Age of Travel*, pp. 37–39; Batten, *Pleasurable Instruction*; James A. Williamson, "Exploration and Discovery," in Turberville, *Johnson's England*, 1:88–124; *MR*, 15:146.

102. *CR*, 1:361–64.

103. Alexander Russell, *The Natural History of Aleppo, and Parts Adjacent* (London, 1756), pp. v–vi.

104. *CR*, 1:361–62.

105. *LM*, 1:80.

106. *LM*, 1:80–84; also see Eddy, *Samuel Johnson: Book Reviewer*, p. 43.

107. For Birch's literary career, see Ruhe, "Thomas Birch, Samuel Johnson, and Elizabeth Carter," pp. 491–500.

108. *Dictionary of National Biography*, 2:860–61, 12:368.

109. William Borlase, *Observations on the Ancient and Present State of the Islands of Scilly and Their Importance to the Trade of Great-Britain* (Oxford, 1756), p. 1.

110. Borlase contributed a number of articles to the Royal Society's journal, the *Philosophical Transactions*, one of which was developed into the *Observations on the Ancient and Present State of the Islands of Scilly.* "An Account of the Great Alterations which the Islands of Sylley Have Undergone since the Time of the Antients, Who Mention Them, as to their Number, Extent, and Position," *Philosophical Transactions Vol XLVIII. Part 1. for the Year 1753*, pp. 55–66. A letter from Borlase to Lyttleton on the Scilley Islands appears on pp. 67–69.

111. *CR*, 1:65.

112. *CR*, 1:57.

113. *MR*, 14:448–50; *CR*, 1:57–65.

114. Eddy, *Samuel Johnson: Book Reviewer*, p. 44.

115. *LM*, 1:91–97.

116. "Elegant; neat; laboured; finished" (Johnson's *Dictionary* [1755]).

117. *LM*, 1:95.

118. *LM*, 1:91–97.

119. Cf. *Idler* 97 (*Yale*, 2:300).

120. For a discussion of luxury as a social and political issue during the eighteenth century, see Sekora, *Luxury*, chapters 2 and 3. Sekora notes that, for the period between 1721 and 1771, the "British Museum and London School of Economics possess[ed] more than 460 books and pamphlets in English that discuss luxury; for the whole century the number would nearly double." Sekora also points out that "the controversy over luxury probably reached its highest pitch in British History in the years 1765–1763" (*Luxury*, p. 66).

121. *LM*, 2:163.

122. *LM,* 1:96–97.

123. There are nearly two-dozen listings under "Subordination" in the Hill and Powell edition of *Boswell's Life of Johnson,* see 6:375. Also see Greene, *Politics of Samuel Johnson,* pp. 177–78.

124. Patrick Browne, *The Civil and Natural History of Jamaica* (London, 1756), p. 490; for Browne's biography, see *Dictionary of National Biography,* 3:53.

125. *CR,* 1:391.

126. *CR,* 1:391–92; Sir Hans Sloane (1660–1753), author of *A Voyage to the Islands of Madera, Barbadoes, Nieves, St. Christopher's, and Jamaica, with the Natural History of the last,* 2 vols. (London, 1707–25). For further information on Sloane, see *Dictionary of National Biography,* 18:379.

127. *CR,* 1:409.

128. *MR,* 15:344.

129. *LM,* 1:176.

130. *LM,* 1:176.

131. *LM,* 1:176.

132. See Eddy, *Samuel Johnson: Book Reviewer,* p. 53.

CHAPTER 5. JOHNSON AS AN OCCASIONAL REVIEWER IN THE
GENTLEMAN'S MAGAZINE AND THE *CRITICAL REVIEW*

1. A full listing of the reviews attributed to Johnson can be found in the *New Cambridge Bibliography of English Literature,* columns 1139–40; for the attribution of these pieces, see: Donald Greene, "Was Johnson Theatrical Critic of the *Gentleman's Magazine?*" *Review of English Studies* 3 (1952): 158–61; Gwin Kolb, "More Attributions to Dr. Johnson," *Studies in English Literature* 3 (1962): 77–95; Arthur Sherbo, "Samuel Johnson and the *Gentleman's Magazine,* 1750–1755," in *Johnsonian Studies,* ed. Magdi Wahba (Cairo: Oxford University Press, 1962), pp. 133–59.

2. J. L. Abbott, *John Hawkesworth: Eighteenth-Century Man of Letters* (Madison: University of Wisconsin Press, 1982), pp. 86–109; idem, "The Making of the Johnsonian Canon," in *Johnson after Two Hundred Years,* ed. Paul Korshin (Philadelphia: University of Pennsylvania Press, 1986), pp. 127–39; also see Donald Eddy, "John Hawkesworth, Book Reviewer in the *Gentleman's Magazine,*" *Philological Quarterly* 43 (1964): 223–38.

3. Clifford, *Dictionary Johnson,* p. 57.

4. In his forthcoming edition of Johnson's shorter prose writings, Professor O M Brack Jr. identifies only the Marlborough, Lennox, and Tytler pieces as authentic.

5. Cf. *An Account of the Conduct of the Dowager Duchess of Marlborough, From Her First Coming to Court, to the Year 1710* (London, 1742). After "my dismission from queen ANNE's service," the duchess states in explaining the genesis of her memoirs, "I perceived how industriously malice was employed, in inventing calumnies to load me with, I drew up an account of my conduct in the several offices I had filled under HER MAJESTY." Sarah Churchill (1660–1744) was renowned for her arrogance, pettiness, and querulousness; the *Account* was actually written by Nathaniel Hooke, who was paid five thousand pounds sterling for his work (*Dictionary of National Biography,* 4:316–39). For an overview of the publication circumstances and reception of the *Account,* see Battestin, *Henry Fielding,* pp. 343–45.

6. For any given month, the *Gentleman's Magazine* normally appeared within the first week of the following month, e.g., the March 1742 number probably was published no later than 7 April 1742: see Carlson, *First Magazine,* p. 61 and note 4. The Marlborough

essay was published anonymously, though Johnson later claimed it as his: see *Boswell's Life of Johnson*, 1:19.

7. *GM,* 12:128–31.

8. Johnson's outlook on historiography is treated fully in John A. Vance, *Samuel Johnson and the Sense of History* (Athens: University of Georgia Press, 1984); also see Vance, "Johnson's Historical Reviews"; Greene, *Politics of Samuel Johnson,* p. 147.

9. *GM,* 12:128; also see Boswell, *Boswell's Life of Johnson,* 1:19.

10. See the appendix for an analysis of Johnson's moral essays that allusively comment on contemporaneously published titles.

11. Clifford, *Dictionary Johnson,* pp. 41; Johnson, *A Dictionary of the English Language,* ed. Anne McDermott, CD-ROM (Cambridge: Cambridge University Press, 1996); Chapman and Hazen's supplement to Courtney (included as part of Courtney and Smith's *Bibliography of Samuel Johnson* published by Oak Knoll Books), p. 136. The *Female Quixote* review is attributed to Johnson by G. B. Hill and, later, by Arthur Sherbo (Courtney and Smith, *Bibliography of Samuel Johnson,* p. 38; Sherbo, "Samuel Johnson and the *Gentleman's Magazine,*" p. 140); the review is listed as authentic in the *New Cambridge Bibliography of English Literature* (column 1139). Duncan Isles denies the authenticity of the piece, though he gives no reason whatsoever for disagreeing with Hill and Sherbo: see "The Lennox Connection," *Harvard Library Bulletin* 18 (1970): 317–44 (for the authenticity comment, see p. 343 n. 40). Isles also rejects the claim that Johnson authored the penultimate chapter of the *Female Quixote* (p. 341 n. 31), an assertion seconded by Pat Rogers in *The Johnson Encyclopedia* (Westport, Conn.: Greenwood Press, 1996), p. 230.

12. See Brack and Holladay, "Johnson as Patron," pp. 178–99; for Johnson's views on the difficulties aspiring authors face in gaining a reputation, see *Rambler*s 1–3, 16, 146; Johnson, "Reflections on the Present State of Literature" (*UV,* pp. 159–66); also see Johnson's "Weekly Correspondent" essay, *Public Ledger,* 2 December 1760, rptd. in McAdam, "New Essays by Dr. Johnson."

13. *GM,* 22:146.

14. See *Rambler*s 1–3, 16, 106, and 146.

15. Fielding, *Covent-Garden Journal,* pp. 158–61. For Johnson's opinion of *Don Quixote,* see the "Life of Butler" (*Lives of the Poets,* 1:209).

16. Fielding, *Covent-Garden Journal,* pp. xxix–xxx and note 2, pp. 158–59 n. 3; Battestin, *Henry Fielding,* pp. 542–43; Clifford, *Dictionary Johnson,* pp. 90–92. For the publication date of the *GM,* see Carlson, *First Magazine,* p. 61 and note 4. For a detailed discussion of Johnson's and Richardson's involvement in the composition, revision, and printing of the *Female Quixote,* see Isles, "The Lennox Collection"; Eric C. Walker, "Charlotte Lennox and the Collier Sisters: Two New Johnson Letters," *Studies in Philology* 95 (1998): 320–32.

17. The first issue of the *Covent-Garden Journal* appeared on 4 January 1752 (Fielding, *Covent-Garden Journal,* p. xxvii); for commentary on its evidently modest circulation see Sullivan, *British Literary Magazines,* p. 66 and Fielding, *Covent-Garden Journal,* pp. xlv–xlvi.

18. *MR,* 6:250.

19. *MR,* 6:262.

20. Johnson acknowledged the authorship of this review (Boswell, *Boswell's Life of Johnson,* 1:21).

21. Jayne Elizabeth Lewis, "Mary Stuart's 'Fatal Box': Sentimental History and the Revival of the Casket Letters Controversy," *Age of Johnson: A Scholarly Annual* 7 (1996): 427–73.

22. Ibid., p. 446.

23. Ibid., p. 429.

24. Ibid., p. 435.

25. Ibid., p. 448.

26. *Dictionary of National Biography,* 19:1382; Boswell, *Boswell's Life of Johnson,* 5:40, 387–96; Brack and Kelley, *Early Biographies of Samuel Johnson,* p. 88; Bloom, *Samuel Johnson in Grub Street,* p. 183; and Vance, "Johnson's Historical Reviews," p. 76. For a thorough exploration of Johnson and Jacobitism, see Clark, *Samuel Johnson;* Greene, *Politics of Samuel Johnson,* pp. xxix–xlii. Also see *The Age of Johnson: A Scholarly Annual* 7 (1996) and 8 (1997); and Robert Folkenflik, "Johnson's Politics," in Clingham, *Cambridge Companion to Samuel Johnson,* pp. 102–13.

27. For a brief discussion of Johnson's involvement with the *British Magazine,* see *Yale,* 10:279; also see Basker, *Tobias Smollett,* p. 193.

28. *GM,* 30:453.

29. William Tytler, *An Historical and Critical Enquiry into the Evidence Produced by the Earls of Murray and Morton, against Mary Queen of Scots* (Edinburgh, 1760), p. viii.

30. *MR,* 23:40; *CR,* 9:432. For a brief discussion of the review section of the *British Magazine* and its relation to the *Critical,* see Basker, *Tobias Smollett,* pp. 193–98.

31. *British Magazine,* 1:378.

32. *MR,* 23:39; *CR,* 9:432.

33. *GM,* 30:456.

34. *GM,* 30:456–58.

35. Cf. *Boswell's Life of Johnson:* "[T]he Monthly was done with the most care," Johnson is reported to have told King George III during their famous meeting in 1767, "the Critical upon the best principles" (2:40). Years later when recalling the conversation, Johnson put the matter this way: "The Critical Reviewers, I believe, often review without reading the books through; but lay hold of a topick, and write chiefly from their own minds. The Monthly Reviewers are duller men, and are glad to read the books through" (3:32).

36. Johnson acknowledged authoring the *Telemachus* and *Traveller* reviews; G. B. Hill's attribution of the *Sugar-Cane* review has never been challenged (see Boswell, *Boswell's Life of Johnson,* 1:22, 481–82, and note 4). For the attribution of the *Oroonoko* review to Johnson, see John Wendell Dodds, *Thomas Southerne: Dramatist* (New Haven: Yale University Press, 1933; reprint, Hamden, Conn.: Archon Books, 1970), p. 152 and note 61; also see Brack and Holladay, "Johnson as Patron," p. 182, and note 23; Abbott, *John Hawkesworth,* pp. 78–81.

37. Clifford, *Dictionary Johnson,* p. 223; Boswell, *Boswell's Life of Johnson,* 1:348; Knapp, *Tobias Smollett,* p. 247; Knapp, "Smollett and Johnson."

38. Sullivan, *British Literary Magazines,* p. 74; Claude E. Jones, "Contributors to the *CR,* 1756–1785," *Modern Language Notes* 61 (1946): 433–41; John Nichols, *Literary Anecdotes of the Eighteenth Century* (London: J. Nichols, Son, and Bentley, 1812), 3:398; Cochrane, *Dr. Johnson's Printer,* p. 121; Clifford, *Young Sam Johnson,* pp. 180, 246; and Basker, *Tobias Smollett,* p. 33.

39. The *Monthly* probably did not review Hawkesworth's adaptation, because the play itself was not new. Notice of *Oroonoko* is also given in the *Gentleman's Magazine* for December 1759 (29:588). The brief commentary essentially amounts to a précis of Hawkesworth's preface, and was perhaps written by Hawkesworth himself.

40. For a detailed analysis of the evolution of the narrative from its origins as a novel to its production in 1759, see Dodds, *Thomas Southerne,* pp. 129ff.

41. Abbott, *John Hawkesworth,* pp. 79–81.

42. See Boswell, *Boswell's Life of Johnson,* 1:190, and note 5; and Clifford, *Dictionary Johnson,* pp. 31–32. Also see the "Life of Swift" (1781): "An account of Dr. Swift has been already collected, with great diligence and acuteness, by Dr. Hawkesworth [in 1755], according to a scheme which I laid before him in the intimacy of our friendship. I cannot,

therefore, be expected to say much of a life concerning which I had long since communicated my thoughts to a man capable of dignifying his narration with so much elegance of language and force of sentiment" (*Lives of the Poets*, 3:1).

43. *The Letters of David Garrick*, ed. D. M. Little and G. M. Kahrl (London, 1963), 1:306–7 and note 4; also see Abbott, *John Hawkesworth*, pp. 78–85. For *Edgar and Emmeline*, see G. W. Stone, ed., *The London Stage, Part 4: 1747–1776* (Carbondale: Southern Illinois University Press, 1962), 2:808; Clifford, *Dictionary Johnson*, p. 245; *GM*, 29:186.

44. See Stone, *London Stage*, 2:759.

45. Thomas Southerne, *Oroonoko: a Tragedy* (London, 1759); Southerne's play (staged in 1695) is itself an adaptation of Aphra Behn's novel *Oroonoko* (1688).

46. *CR*, 8:480–81.

47. *CR*, 8:480–82; also see Southerne, *Oroonoko*, prologue and p. v.

48. *CR*, 8:482.

49. *CR*, 8:482.

50. *CR*, 8:486.

51. See Courtney and Smith, *Bibliography of Samuel Johnson*, p. 102; *Letters of David Garrick*, ed. Little and Kahrl, 1:386, 2:471, 475, and notes.

52. Leslie A. Chilton, introduction to *The Adventures of Telemachus, the Son of Ulysses*, by Tobias Smollett, ed. O M Brack Jr. (Athens: University of Georgia Press, 1997), p. xxii; also see note 16.

53. *MR*, 28:109.

54. Philip Gaskell, *A Bibliography of the Foulis Press*, 2d ed. (London: St. Paul's Bibliographies, 1986), p. 293.

55. *Letters of Samuel Johnson*, ed. Redford, 2:214; 3:9; for Johnson and Graham, see Boswell, *Boswell's Life of Johnson*, 5:97; for Graham and Garrick, see Courtney and Smith, *Bibliography of Samuel Johnson*, p. 102.

56. *CR*, 15:314; cf. the prologue to *Telemachus, A Mask* (London, 1763), spoken by "Mentor": "For 'tis my task / (A task superior to all mortal toil) / This day to save the pure untainted heart / Of young Telemachus, his royal charge, / From foul pollution, and the desperate woes / That follow Virtue's loss" (p. 3).

57. *CR*, 15:314–15.

58. *CR*, 15:318.

59. James Grainger, *The Sugar-Cane: A Poem in Four Books* (London, 1764); *Dictionary of National Biography*, 8:368–69; Ralph Straus, *Robert Dodsley: Poet, Publisher and Playwright* (London: John Lane, 1910), pp. 103–36; also see Percy and Anderson, *Correspondence*, pp. 66–69.

60. *MR*, 31:106.

61. *MR*, 31:106.

62. *MR*, 31:106, 118.

63. Johnson had known Grainger at least since 1756 (Boswell, *Boswell's Life of Johnson*, 1:48 and note 2; also see Percy and Anderson, *Correspondence*, pp. 67, 76).

64. Johnson visited Percy between 25 June and 18 August 1764, during which time they cowrote the *London Chronicle* review of the *Sugar-Cane* (Percy and Anderson, *Correspondence*, p. 76 and note 25; also see p. 26 n. 4).

65. Boswell, *Boswell's Life of Johnson*, 2:454; Hazen, *Samuel Johnson's Prefaces and Dedications*, pp. 168–71; Bloom, *Samuel Johnson in Grub Street*, p. 204; also see Boswell, *Boswell's Life of Johnson*, 1:481–82, and note.

66. *CR*, 18:270 (misnumbered 170).

67. Camoëns (1524–80), Portuguese poet and playwright, and Garcilaso (1501–36), Spanish poet, were both soldiers as well. Camoëns lost an eye in the service against the Moors, while Garcilaso was killed in battle fighting for King Charles V. See the *Oxford*

Companion to English Literature, 5th ed. (Oxford: Oxford University Press, 1985), pp. 162–63, 379.

68. *CR,* 18:271.

69. *CR,* 18:272.

70. *CR,* 18:273.

71. Boswell, *Boswell's Life of Johnson,* 5:274 n. 3; Wardle, *Oliver Goldsmith,* p. 100.

72. See Boswell, *Boswell's Life of Johnson,* 2:216, 236, 253–54, 257.

73. Goldsmith, *Collected Works,* ed. Friedman, 5:101; Johnson, *Lives of the Poets,* 2:49.

74. See *The Poems of Samuel Johnson,* ed. D. N. Smith and E. L. McAdam (Oxford: Oxford University Press, 1974), pp. 177, 438–39; Courtney and Smith, *Bibliography of Samuel Johnson,* p. 113.

75. *The Traveller* was published on 19 December 1759 (Wardle, *Oliver Goldsmith,* pp. 156–60).

76. *CR,* 18:458–62; Wardle, *Oliver Goldsmith,* pp. 158–60; Clifford, *Dictionary Johnson,* p. 246; also see Lipking, *Ordering of the Arts in Eighteenth-Century England,* pp. 362–69; Rothstein, *Restoration and Eighteenth-Century Poetry,* chapter 4.

77. See Boswell, *Boswell's Life of Johnson,* 2:5.

78. *MR,* 32:47–55; *GM,* 34:594; also see Wardle, *Oliver Goldsmith,* p. 160; and Boswell, *Boswell's Life of Johnson,* 2:478.

79. Gibbon joined the club in 1774 (Boswell, *Boswell's Life of Johnson,* 1:481, note 3).

80. See Forster, "From 'Tasters to the Public,'" chapter 3 (pp. 162–224).

81. Boswell, *Boswell's Life of Johnson,* 4:127; *Letters of Samuel Johnson,* ed. Redford, 1:179; *Yale,* 16:xlv–xlix.

82. Johnson, *Johnsonian Miscellanies,* 1:345.

83. McGuffie, *Samuel Johnson and the British Press,* pp. 26ff.

CHAPTER 6. BOOK REVIEWING IN THE MORAL ESSAYS: JOHNSON'S COMMENTARY ON RECENTLY PUBLISHED BOOKS IN THE *RAMBLER, ADVENTURER,* AND *IDLER*

1. See *Yale,* 3:19 n. 1. The *Yale* editors incorrectly claim that it was Arthur Murphy who originally made the connection between recent novels and *Rambler* 4; in fact it was Alexander Chalmers who first stated that *Rambler* 4 means to comment on *Tom Jones* and *Roderick Random.* See *The Works of Samuel Johnson, LL.D. A New Edition in Twelve Volumes. With an Essay on His Life and Genius, by Arthur Murphy,* ed. Alexander Chalmers (London: J. Johnson, J. Nichols and Son, R. Baldwin, et al., 1806), 4:26.

2. *Yale,* 2:201–2; The publication of the *Continuation* is noted in the July 1759 issue of the *Gentleman's Magazine* under its monthly "Books Published" section (29:338); the *MR* and the *CR* each reviewed the work in their July issues, which came out during the first week of August (*CR,* 8:54–64; *MR,* 21:21–34).

3. Woodruff, "Johnson's *Rambler* in its Contemporary Context," pp. 53–54.

4. For the publication date of West's poem, see Straus, *Robert Dodsley,* p. 342.

5. *Yale,* 4:284–85.

6. Johnson, *Lives of the Poets,* 3:332.

7. See Johnson's commentary on *Samson Agonistes* in the "Life of Milton" and *Rambler* 139; Johnson's "Dissertation on the Epitaphs Written by Pope" (*UV,* pp. 207–19) is appended to his "Life of Pope"; Johnson's approval of Isaac Watts's poetry in his *Literary*

Magazine review of Elizabeth Harrison's *Moral Miscellanies* (1756) is repeated in the "Life of Watts."

8. *Yale*, 4:40–42.

9. *Yale*, 4:44.

10. Stone, *London Stage, Part 4: 1747–1776*, 1:213–16.

11. See *The Orphan*, I.362–77, III.408–29, in *The Works of Thomas Otway: Plays, Poems, and Love-Letters*, ed. J. C. Gosh (Oxford: Oxford University Press, 1932), 2:19, 45–46.

12. Johnson, *Lives of the Poets*, 1:245.

13. Ibid., 1:246.

14. Cf. Warton, *Essay on the Writings and Genius of Pope*, which suggests that Otway's poetry is on equal footing with Alexander Pope's (pp. iii–xi).

15. *Yale*, 4:42–43; Johnson, *Lives of the Poets*, 1:243.

16. *The Works of Mr. Thomas Otway*, 2 vols. (London, 1712); the prefatory "Some Account of the Life and Writings of *Mr.* Thomas Otway" is not paginated.

17. *Venice Preserv'd*, for instance, is quoted in the *Dictionary* (1755) definition of "Brigantine"; quotations from the *Orphan* appear in the definitions of "Fortune" and "Ward"; for reprintings of the 1712 edition, see Otway, *Works*, ed. Gosh, 1:81–82.

18. *Yale*, 4:44.

19. Johnson, *Lives of the Poets*, , 1:247.

20. Brian Corman, "Johnson and Profane Authors: The Lives of Otway and Congreve," in Korshin, *Johnson after Two Hundred Years*, pp. 225–44.

21. *Yale*, 4:370–71.

22. "The Life of Milton," in *Paradise Lost*, ed. Thomas Newton, 2d ed. (London, 1750), 1:lxii; also see Clifford, *Young Sam Johnson*, pp. 30, 56; *MR*, 2:207.

23. The prize—a gold medal worth 300 livres (equal to 330 francs, ca. 1900)—was awarded in July 1750. For a full discussion of the *Discourse*—its origins, its reception in France—see Maurice Cranston, *Jean-Jacques: The Early Life and Work of Jean-Jacques Rousseau, 1712–1754* (London: Penguin Books, 1983), chapter 13.

24. Jean-Jacques Rousseau, *The Discourse . . . on Whether the Re-establishment of Arts and Sciences Has Contributed to the Refining of Manners* (London, 1751), p. 32.

25. Ibid., pp. 39–41, 56–59.

26. *Dictionary of National Biography*, 6:83–84; Keith Maslen and John Lancaster, eds., *The Bowyer Ledgers* (London: The Bibliographical Society, 1991), p. 282, item 3696.

27. *MR*, 5:237; the reviewer here paraphrases Bowyer's preface: see J. J. Rousseau, *Discourse* (1751), pp. iii–iv.

28. That the fruition of genius depends on formal study is a major thematic element in Johnson's critical writings, particularly in the *Lives of the Poets*. See, for instance, the "Life of Butler": "Imagination is useless without knowledge: nature gives in vain the power of combination, unless study and observation supply materials to be combined," and the "Life of Rochester": "In all his works there is sprightliness and vigour, and every where may be found tokens of a mind which study might have carried to excellence" (*Lives of the Poets*, 1:212, 226). Also see *Rambler* 25: genius "is like fire in flint, only to be produced by collision with a proper subject" (*Yale*, 3:139); for further analysis, see Hagstrum, *Samuel Johnson's Literary Criticism*, pp. 3–20.

29. Boswell, *Boswell's Life of Johnson*, 1:203 and note 6, and 3:42; Cochrane, *Dr. Johnson's Printer*, pp. 22–29, 103, 145; Clifford, *Young Sam Johnson*, p. 281. The date given here for the *MR* is taken from the head of the "Monthly Catalogue" section. For Johnson's opinion of Rousseau as expressed in private conversation, see Boswell, *Boswell's Life of Johnson*, 2:11–12, 74. For a comparative analysis of Rousseau and Johnson, see Mark Temmer, *Samuel Johnson and Three Infidels: Rousseau, Voltaire, Diderot* (Athens:

University of Georgia Press, 1988). Surprisingly, *Rambler* 154 and its companions, *Adventurers* 85 and 137, are not considered in Temmer's study. Also see Richard B. Sewall, "Dr. Johnson, Rousseau, and Reform," in *The Age of Johnson: Essays Presented to C. B. Tinker*, ed. F. W. Hilles (New Haven: Yale University Press, 1949), pp. 307–17. In his comparative evaluation of Rousseau and Johnson as social reformers Sewall offhandedly notes that a connection between *Rambler* 154 and the *Discourse* might exist, though no analysis is offered (p. 314).

30. For a discussion of Johnson's rhetorical strategy in the *Rambler* see Damrosch, "Johnson's Manner of Proceeding in the *Rambler*"; and Lynn, "Johnson's *Rambler* and Eighteenth-Century Rhetoric."

31. *Yale*, 5:55.

32. *Yale*, 5:56.

33. For the reception of the *Discourse* in France, see Cranston, *Jean-Jacques*, chapter 13.

34. *GM*, 22:195; 23:103.

35. For a consideration of Johnson's involvement in the *Adventurer*, see Clifford, *Dictionary Johnson*, pp. 109–16.

36. *Yale*, 2:411–12, and note 1. Rousseau's *Discourse* evidently meant to attack "everything" that Bacon "stood for," observes Maurice Cranston. "The Baconian dream of improving man's life on earth by creating material abundance, Rousseau condemns as a culpable craving for luxury; and luxury, he says, is not a simple evil but one which has always been recognized by the wisest men as an especially corrupting evil" (Cranston, *Jean-Jacques*, pp. 231–32).

37. *Yale*, 2:412.

38. *Yale*, 2:413.

39. *Yale*, 2:412.

40. *Yale*, 2:413.

41. *Yale*, 2:488.

42. *Yale*, 2:488–90.

43. *Yale*, 2:489.

44. *Yale*, 2:491.

45. *Yale*, 2:417–24; Straus, *Robert Dodsley*, p. 346.

Appendix

1. Eddy, *Samuel Johnson: Book Reviewer*, pp. 84–87, 102 and note; Greene, "Johnson's Contributions to the *Literary Magazine*," pp. 384–88; *New Cambridge Bibliography of English Literature*, column 1141.

2. Hester Lynch Piozzi, *Anecdotes of the Late Samuel Johnson, LL.D., during the Last Twenty Years of His Life*, ed. Arthur Sherbo (London: Oxford University Press, 1974), pp. 86–87.

3. *LM*, 1:191.

4. *LM*, 2:31; Boswell, *Boswell's Life of Johnson*, 1:402.

5. Forster, *Index to Book Reviews in England: 1749–1774*, p. 4.

6. *LM*, 1:11.

Bibliography

Abbott, John L. "Dr. Johnson and the Society." In *The Virtuoso Tribe of Arts and Sciences: Studies in the Eighteenth-Century Work and Membership of the London Society of Arts,* ed. D. G. C. Allan and J. L. Abbott. Athens: University of Georgia Press, 1992.

———. *John Hawkesworth: Eighteenth-Century Man of Letters.* Madison: University of Wisconsin Press, 1982.

———. "The Making of the Johnsonian Canon." In *Johnson after Two Hundred Years,* ed. Paul Korshin. Philadelphia: University of Pennsylvania Press, 1986.

Adams, Percy G. *Travel Literature and the Evolution of the Novel.* Lexington: University Press of Kentucky, 1983.

Alkon, Paul K. *Samuel Johnson and the Moral Discipline.* Evanston, Ill.: Northwestern University Press, 1967.

Allen, D. G. C., and R. E. Schofield. *Stephen Hales: Scientist and Philanthropist.* London: Scolar Press, 1980.

Alumni Cantabrigienses. Compiled by John Venn and J. A. Venn. Part 1. Vol. 4. Cambridge: Cambridge University Press, 1927.

Bartolomeo, Joseph E. *A New Species of Criticism: Eighteenth-Century Discourse on the Novel.* Newark: University of Delaware Press, 1994.

Basker, James. "Minim and the 'Great Cham': Smollett and Johnson on the Prospect of an English Academy." In *Johnson and His Age,* ed. James Engell. Cambridge: Harvard University Press, 1984.

———. *Tobias Smollett: Critic and Journalist.* Newark: University of Delaware Press, 1988.

Bate, Walter Jackson. *The Achievement of Samuel Johnson.* Oxford: Oxford University Press, 1955.

———. *From Classic to Romantic: Premises of Taste in Eighteenth-Century England.* Cambridge: Harvard University Press, 1946.

———. *Samuel Johnson.* London: Chatto & Windus, 1978.

Batten, Charles L. *Pleasurable Instruction: Form and Convention in Eighteenth-Century Travel Literature.* Berkeley: University of California Press, 1978.

Battestin, Martin. *Henry Fielding: A Life.* London: Routledge, 1989.

Baugh, Albert C., and Thomas Cable. *A History of the English Language.* 4th ed. London: Routledge, 1993.

Beasley, Jerry C. *A Check List of Prose Fiction Published in England, 1740–49.* Charlottesville: University Press of Virginia, 1972.

———. *Novels of the 1740s.* Athens: University of Georgia Press, 1982.

Beljame, Alexandre. *Men of Letters and the English Public in the Eighteenth Century, 1660–1744: Dryden, Addison, Pope.* London: Kegan Paul, 1948.

Bever, Samuel. *The Cadet: A Military Treatise.* London, 1756.

Birch, Thomas. *The History of the Royal Society of London.* 2 vols. London, 1756.

Blackwell, Thomas. *Memoirs of the Court of Augustus.* 3 vols. Edinburgh, 1753–63.

Bloom, Edward A. "'As a Fly Stings to a Stately Horse': Johnson under Satiric Attack," *Modern Language Studies* 9 (1979): 137–49.

———. "'Labours of the Learned': Neoclassic Book Reviewing Aims and Techniques." *Studies in Philology* 54 (1957): 538–63.

———. *Samuel Johnson in Grub Street.* Providence, R.I.: Brown University Press, 1957.

Bond, Richmond, ed. *Studies in the Early English Periodical.* Chapel Hill, N.C.: University of North Carolina Press, 1957.

Borlase, William. *Observations on the Ancient and Present State of the Islands of Scilly and Their Importance to the Trade of Great-Britain.* Oxford, 1756.

Boswell, James. *Boswell's Life of Johnson, Together with Boswell's Journal of a Tour to the Hebrides and Johnson's Diary of a Journey into North Wales.* Ed. G. B. Hill; rev. L. F. Powell. 2d ed. 6 vols. Oxford: Clarendon Press, 1934–64.

The Bowyer Ledgers. Ed. Keith Maslen and John Lancaster. London: The Bibliographical Society, 1991.

Brack, O M, Jr. "Johnson's *Life of Admiral Blake* and the Development of a Biographical Technique." *Modern Philology* 85 (1988): 523–31.

———. "Samuel Johnson Edits for the Booksellers: Sir Thomas Browne's 'Christian Morals' (1756) and 'The English Works of Roger Ascham' (1761)." *Library Chronicle of the University of Texas* 21 (1991): 12–39.

———. *Writers, Books, and Trade: An Eighteenth-Century English Miscellany for William B. Todd.* New York: AMS Press, 1994.

Brack, O M, Jr., and Gae Holladay. "Johnson as Patron." In *Greene Centennial Studies: Essays Presented to Donald Greene in the Centennial Year of the University of Southern California,* ed. Paul Korshin. Charlottesville: University Press of Virginia, 1984.

Brack, O M, Jr., and Robert E. Kelley. *Samuel Johnson's Early Biographers.* Iowa City: University of Iowa Press, 1971.

Brack, O M, Jr., and Robert E. Kelly, eds. *The Early Biographies of Samuel Johnson.* Iowa City: University of Iowa Press, 1974.

Brewer, John. *The Pleasures of the Imagination: English Culture in the Eighteenth Century.* New York: Farrar, Straus, Giroux, 1997.

The British Magazine (1760–67).

Browne, Patrick. *The Civil and Natural History of Jamaica. In Three Parts.* London, 1756.

Carlson, C. Lennart. *The First Magazine: A History of the Gentleman's Magazine.* Providence, R.I.: Brown University Press, 1938.

Carter, Alice Clare. *The English Public Debt in the Eighteenth Century.* London: Historical Association, 1968.

Clark, J. C. D. *Samuel Johnson: Literature, Religion, and English Cultural Politics from the Restoration to Romanticism.* Cambridge: Cambridge University Press, 1994.

Clavell, Robert. *A Catalogue of Books Printed in England Since the Dreadful Fire of London in 1666 to the End of Michaelmas Term, 1695.* Ed. D. F. Foxon. Farnborough, U.K.: Gregg Press, 1965.

Clifford, James L. *Dictionary Johnson.* London: Heinemann, 1979.

———. *Young Sam Johnson.* London: Heinemann, 1955.

Clifford, James L., and Donald J. Greene. *Samuel Johnson: A Survey and Bibliography of Critical Studies.* Minneapolis: University of Minnesota Press, 1970.

Clingham, Greg, ed. *The Cambridge Companion to Samuel Johnson.* Cambridge: Cambridge University Press, 1997.

Cochrane, James A. *Dr. Johnson's Printer: The Life of William Strahan.* London: Routledge, 1964.

Collins, A. S. *Authorship in the Days of Johnson.* London: R. Holden & Sons, 1927.

Corman, Brian. "Johnson and Profane Authors: the Lives of Otway and Congreve." In *Johnson after Two Hundred Years,* ed. Paul Korshin. Philadelphia: University of Pennsylvania Press, 1986.

Courtney, W. P., and D. N. Smith. *A Bibliography of Samuel Johnson,* with R. W. Chapman and Allen T. Hazen, *Johnsonian Bibliography: A Supplement to Courtney.* New Castle, Del.: Oak Knoll Books, 1984.

Cranston, Maurice. *Jean-Jacques: The Early Life and Work of Jean-Jacques Rousseau, 1712–1754.* London: Penguin Books, 1983.

The Critical Review: or, Annals of Literature (1756–1817).

Curley, Thomas. *Johnson and the Age of Travel.* Athens: University of Georgia Press, 1976.

Damrosch, Leopold. "Johnson's Manner of Proceeding in the *Rambler.*" *English Literary History* 40 (1973): 70–98.

DeMaria, Robert. *The Life of Samuel Johnson: A Critical Biography.* Oxford: Blackwell, 1993.

———. *Samuel Johnson and the Life of Reading.* Baltimore: Johns Hopkins University Press, 1997.

Dickson, P. G. M. *The Financial Revolution in England: A Study in the Development of Public Credit.* London: Macmillan, 1967.

Dodds, John Wendell. *Thomas Southerne: Dramatist.* Hamden, Conn.: Archon Books, 1970.

Donoghue, Frank. "Colonizing Readers: Review Criticism and the Formation of a Reading Public." In *The Consumption of Culture: Image, Object, Text,* ed. Ann Bermingham and John Brewer. London: Routledge, 1995.

———. *The Fame Machine: Book Reviewing and Eighteenth-Century Literary Careers.* Stanford, Calif.: Stanford University Press, 1996.

Eddy, Donald D. "John Hawkesworth, Book Reviewer in the *Gentleman's Magazine.*" *Philological Quarterly* 43 (1964): 223–38.

———. *Samuel Johnson: Book Reviewer in the Literary Magazine: or, Universal Review, 1756–1758.* New York: Garland, 1979.

Evans, Lewis. *Geographical, Historical, Political, Philosophical, and Mechanical Essays. The First, Containing an Analysis of a General Map of the Middle British Colonies in America.* 2d ed. Philadelphia, 1755.

Fairer, David. "The Writing and Printing of Joseph Warton's *Essay on Pope.*" *Studies in Bibliography* 30 (1977): 211–19.

Feather, John. *A History of British Publishing.* London: Routledge, 1988.

Ferrero, Bonnie. "Johnson, Murphy, and Macbeth." *Review of English Studies* 42 (1991): 228–32.

———. "Samuel Johnson and Arthur Murphy." *English Language Notes* 18 (March 1991): 18–24.

Fielding, Henry. *The Covent-Garden Journal.* Ed. Bertrand Goldgar. Oxford: Oxford University Press, 1988.

———. *The History of Tom Jones, a Foundling.* Ed. Fredson Bowers. Oxford: Oxford University Press, 1974.

Fleeman, John David. "The Revenue of a Writer: Samuel Johnson's Literary Earnings." In *Studies in the Book Trade: In Honour of Graham Pollard,* edited by R. W. Hunt, I. G. Philip, and R. J. Roberts. Oxford: The Oxford Bibliographical Society, 1975.

Folkenflik, Robert. *Samuel Johnson, Biographer.* Ithaca: Cornell University Press, 1978.

Forster, Antonia. "From 'Tasters to the Public' to 'Beadles of Parnassus': Reviewers, Authors and the Reading Public, 1749–1774." Diss., University of Melbourne, 1986.

———. *Index to Book Reviews in England: 1749–1774.* Carbondale: Southern Illinois University Press, 1990.

———. *Index to Book Reviews in England: 1775–1800.* London: British Library, 1997.

Foss, Michael. *The Age of Patronage: The Arts in England, 1660–1750.* Ithaca: Cornell University Press, 1971.

Foster, James R. "Smollett's Pamphleteering Foe Shebbeare." *Publication of the Modern Language Association,* 57 (1942): 1058–1100.

Foxon, David, and James McLaverty. *Pope and the Early-Eighteenth-Century Book Trade.* Oxford: Clarendon Press, 1991.

Francklin, Thomas. *The Works of Lucian, from the Greek.* 2 vols. London, 1780.

Fraser, Henry Malcolm. *History of Beekeeping in Britain.* London: Bee Research Association, 1958.

Fussell, Paul. *The Rhetorical World of Augustan Humanism: Ethics and Imagery from Swift to Burke.* Oxford: Oxford University Press, 1965.

Garrick, David. *The Letters of David Garrick.* Ed. D. M. Little and G. M. Kahrl. 3 vols. London: Oxford University Press, 1963.

Gaskell, Philip. *A Bibliography of the Foulis Press.* 2d ed. London: St. Paul's Bibliographies, 1986.

———. *A New Introduction to Bibliography.* Oxford: Oxford University Press, 1972.

The Gentleman's Magazine, and Historical Chronicle.

Goldsmith, Oliver. *The Collected Works of Oliver Goldsmith.* Ed. Arthur Friedman. 5 vols. Oxford: Oxford University Press, 1966.

Graham, George. *Telemachus, a Mask.* London, 1763.

Graham, Walter. *The Beginnings of English Literary Periodicals: A Study of Periodical Literature, 1665–1715.* New York: Octagon, 1972.

———. *English Literary Periodicals.* New York: Thomas Nelson & Sons, 1930.

Grainger, James. *The Sugar-Cane: A Poem in Four Books.* London, 1764.

Greene, Donald J. "Johnson's Contributions to the *Literary Magazine.*" *Review of English Studies* 7 (1956): 367–92.

———. *Johnson's Library: An Annotated Guide.* Victoria, B.C.: University of Victoria Press, 1975.

———. *The Politics of Samuel Johnson.* Athens: University of Georgia Press, 1990.

———. "Samuel Johnson, Journalist." In *Newsletters to Newspapers: Eighteenth-Century Journalism,* ed. D. H. Bond. Morgantown: University of West Virginia School of Journalism, 1977.

————. "Was Johnson Theatrical Critic of the *Gentleman's Magazine?*" *Review of English Studies* 3 (1952): 158–61.

Greene, Donald J., and J. A. Vance. *A Bibliography of Johnsonian Studies, 1970–1985.* Victoria, B.C.: University of Victoria Press, 1987.

Griffin, Dustin. *Literary Patronage in England, 1650–1800.* Cambridge: Cambridge University Press, 1996.

Griffith, R. H. *Alexander Pope: a Bibliography.* Austin: University of Texas Press, 1927.

Hagstrum, Jean. *Samuel Johnson's Literary Criticism.* Minneapolis: University of Minnesota Press, 1952.

Haig, Robert L. *The Gazeteer: A Study in the Eighteenth-Century English Newspaper.* Carbondale: Southern Illinois University Press, 1960.

Hales, Stephen. *An Account of a Useful Discovery to Distil Double the Usual Quantity of Sea-water.* London, 1756.

Hall, A. Rupert. *Isaac Newton: Adventurer in Thought.* Oxford: Blackwell, 1992.

Hampton, James. *The General History of Polybius. In Five Books. Translated from the Greek.* London, 1756.

Hanley, Brian. "The Prevailing Moral Tone of Samuel Johnson's Military Commentary." *New Rambler* 12 (1996–97): 39–45.

Hanway, Jonas. *A Journal of Eight Days Journey from Portsmouth to Kingston upon Thames, in Sixty-Four Letters, to Which is Added an Essay on Tea, in Thirty-two Letters.* 2 vols. London, 1757.

Harris, Michael. "Journalism as a Profession or Trade in the Eighteenth Century." In *Author/Publisher Relations during the Eighteenth and Nineteenth Centuries,* ed. R. Myers and M. Harris. Oxford: Oxford Polytechnic Press, 1983.

————. *London Newspapers in the Age of Walpole: A Study of the Origins of the Modern English Press.* Cranbury, N.J.: Associated University Presses, 1987.

Harrison, Elizabeth. *Miscellanies on Moral and Religious Subjects, in Prose and Verse.* London, 1756.

Hazen, Allen T. *Samuel Johnson's Prefaces and Dedications.* New Haven: Yale University Press, 1937.

Heilbron, J. L. *Elements of Early Modern Physics.* Berkeley: University of California Press, 1982.

Hilles, F. W. "The Making of the Life of Pope." In *New Light on Dr. Johnson: Essays on the Occasion of his 250th Birthday,* ed. F. W. Hilles. New Haven: Yale University Press, 1959.

Hillhouse, James T. *The Grub-Street Journal.* Durham, N.C.: Duke University Press, 1928.

Home, Francis. *Experiments on Bleaching.* Edinburgh, 1756.

Hooke, Nathaniel. *An Account of the Conduct of the Dowager Duchess of Marlborough, from Her First Coming to Court, to the Year 1710.* London, 1742.

Hoover, Benjamin B. *Samuel Johnson's Parliamentary Reporting.* Berkeley: University of California Press, 1953.

Houlding, J. A. *Fit for Service: The Training of the British Army, 1715–1795.* Oxford: Clarendon, 1981.

Hunter, J. Paul. *Before Novels: The Cultural Contexts of Eighteenth-Century Fiction.* New York: W. W. Norton, 1990.

International Bee Research Association. *British Bee Books: A Bibliography, 1500–1976.* London: International Bee Research Association, 1979.

Isles, Duncan. "The Lennox Collection." *Harvard Library Bulletin* 18 (1970): 317–44.

Jenyns, Soame. *A Free Inquiry into the Nature and Origin of Evil.* London, 1757.

———. *A Free Inquiry into the Nature and Origin of Evil.* 4th ed. London, 1761.

Johnson, Samuel. *A Dictionary of the English Language.* 2 vols. London, 1755.

———. *A Dictionary of the English Language, Abstracted from the Folio Edition.* 2 vols. London, 1756.

———. *A Dictionary of the English Language.* CD-ROM. Ed. Anne McDermott. Cambridge: Cambridge University Press, 1996.

———. *Johnsonian Miscellanies.* Ed. G. B. Hill. 2 vols. London: Constable & Co., 1966.

———. *The Letters of Samuel Johnson.* Ed. Bruce Redford. 5 vols. Princeton: Princeton University Press, 1994.

———. *Lives of the English Poets.* Ed. G. B. Hill. 3 vols. Oxford: Oxford University Press, 1905.

———. *The Plan of a Dictionary of the English Language.* London, 1747.

———. *The Works of Samuel Johnson, LL.D. With an Essay on His Life and Genius, by Arthur Murphy, Esq.* 12 vols. London, 1792.

———. *The Works of Samuel Johnson, LL.D. With an Essay on His Life and Genius, by Arthur Murphy, Esq.* Ed. Alexander Chalmers. 12 vols. London: J. Johnson, J. Nichols and Son, R. Baldwin, et al., 1806.

———. *The Works of Samuel Johnson, LL.D.* Ed. Francis P. Walesby. 9 vols. Oxford: Talboys and Wheeler, 1825.

———. *The Yale Edition of the Works of Samuel Johnson.* Ed. John H. Middendorf et al. 13 vols. to date. New Haven, 1958–.

Johnston, Shirley White. "The Unfurious Critic: Samuel Johnson's Attitude toward His Contemporaries." *Modern Philology* 77 (1979): 18–25.

Jones, Claude E. "Contributors to the *Critical Review,* 1756–1785." *Modern Language Notes* 61 (1946): 433–41.

Kaminski, Thomas. *The Early Career of Samuel Johnson.* Oxford: Oxford University Press, 1987.

Keast, W. R. "The Theoretical Foundations of Johnson's Criticism." In *Critics and Criticism: Ancient and Modern*, ed. R. S. Crane. Chicago: University of Chicago Press, 1952.

Keith, Robert. *A Large New Catalogue of the Bishops of the Several Sees within the Kingdom of Scotland, Down to the Year 1688.* Edinburgh, 1755.

Kerby-Miller, Charles, ed. *Memoirs of the Extraordinary Life, Works, and Discoveries of Martinus Scriblerus.* Oxford: Oxford University Press, 1988.

Kernan, Alvin. *Printing Technology, Samuel Johnson, and Letters.* Princeton: Princeton University Press, 1987.

Keyssler, John George. *Travels through Germany, Bohemia, Hungary, Switzerland, Italy, and Lorrain.* 4 vols. London, 1756.

Knapp, Lewis M. "Griffiths's 'Monthly Review' as Printed by Strahan." *Notes and Queries* 103 (1958): 216–17.

———. "Smollett and Johnson, Never Cater-Cousins?" *Modern Philology* 66 (1968): 152–54.

———. *Tobias Smollett: Doctor of Men and Manners.* Princeton: Princeton University Press, 1949.

Kolb, Gwin. "More Attributions to Dr. Johnson." *Studies in English Literature* 3 (1962): 77–95.

Korshin, Paul. "Types of Eighteenth-Century Literary Patronage." *Eighteenth-Century Studies* 7 (1974): 453–73.

———, ed. *Johnson after Two Hundred Years.* Philadelphia: University of Pennsylvania Press, 1986.

Leed, Jacob. "Johnson and Chesterfield." *Studies in Burke and His Time* 12 (1970): 1677–90.

———. "Patronage in the *Rambler.*" *Studies in Burke and His Time* 14 (1972): 5–21.

Lennox, Charlotte, trans. *Memoirs of Maximilian De Bethune, Duke of Sully, Prime Minister to Henry to Henry the Great.* 3 vols. London, 1756.

Lewis, Jayne Elizabeth. "Mary Stuart's 'Fatal Box': Sentimental History and the Revival of the Casket Letters Controversy." *The Age of Johnson: A Scholarly Annual* 7 (1996): 427–73.

Lipking, Lawrence. *The Ordering of the Arts in Eighteenth-Century England.* Princeton: Princeton University Press, 1970.

———. *Samuel Johnson: The Life of an Author.* Cambridge: Harvard University Press, 1998.

The Literary Magazine: or, Universal Review.

The London Chronicle: or, Universal Evening Post.

Lonsdale, Roger. "William Bewley and *The Monthly Review:* A Problem of Attribution." *Papers of the Bibliographical Society of America* 55 (1961): 309–18.

Lovett, Richard. *Sir Isaac Newton's Aether Realized in Answer to the ANIMADVERSION made by the MONTHLY REVIEW.* London, 1758.

———. *The Subtil Medium Prov'd.* London, 1756.

Lucas, Charles. *An Appeal to the Commons and Citizens of London.* London, 1756.

———. *An Essay on Waters.* 3 vols. London, 1756.

Lynn, Stephen. "Johnson's *Rambler* and Eighteenth-Century Rhetoric." *Eighteenth-Century Studies* 19 (1986): 461–79.

Mack, Maynard. *Alexander Pope: A Life.* New Haven: Yale University Press, 1985.

McAdam, E. L. "New Essays by Dr. Johnson." *Review of English Studies* 18 (1942): 197–207.

McClure, Ruth. "Johnson's Criticism of the Foundling Hospital." *Review of English Studies* 27 (1976): 17–26.

McGuffie, Helen Louise. *Samuel Johnson in the British Press, 1749–1784: A Chronological Checklist.* New York: Garland, 1976.

McIntosh, Carey. *The Choice of Life: Samuel Johnson and the World of Fiction.* New Haven: Yale University Press, 1973.

The Memoirs of Grub-Street. 2 vols. London, 1737.

Meyer, Herbert W. *A History of Electricity and Magnetism.* Cambridge: MIT Press, 1971.

Middendorf, John H. "Johnson on Wealth and Commerce." In *Johnson, Boswell, and Their Circle,* ed. Mary Lascelles. Oxford: Oxford University Press, 1965.

The Monthly Review (1749–1845).

More, Lewis Trenchard. *Isaac Newton: A Biography.* New York: Dover, 1962.

Mottelay, Paul F. *Bibliographical History of Electricity and Magnetism.* London: Griffin & Co., 1922.

Murphy, Arthur. *The Gray's-Inn Journal*. London, 1754.

―――. *The Gray's-Inn Journal*. 2 vols. London, 1756.

Nangle, Benjamin. *The Monthly Review, 1rst ser. 1749–1789, Indexes of Contributors and Articles*. Oxford: Oxford University Press, 1934.

The New Cambridge Bibliography of English Literature. Vol. 2. Cambridge: Cambridge University Press, 1971.

Newton, Isaac. *The Correspondence of Isaac Newton*. Ed. H. W. Turnbull, J. F. Scott, A. Rupert Hall, and Laura Trilling. 7 vols. Cambridge: Cambridge University Press, 1959–77.

―――. *Four Letters from Sir Isaac Newton to Doctor Bentley: Containing Some Arguments in Proof of a Diety*. London, 1756.

Newton, Thomas. "The Life of Milton." In *Paradise Lost. A Poem, in Twelve Books. The Author John Milton,* ed. Thomas Newton, 1:i–lxxxv. 2d ed. 2 vols. London, 1750.

Otway, Thomas. *The Works of Mr. Thomas Otway*. 2 vols. London, 1712.

―――. *The Works of Thomas Otway: Plays, Poems, and Love-Letters*. Ed. J. C. Gosh. 2 vols. Oxford: Oxford University Press, 1932.

The Oxford Companion to English Literature. 5th ed. Oxford: Oxford University Press, 1985.

Parkin, Charles. *An Impartial Account of the Invasion under William Duke of Normandy, and the Consequences of It*. London, 1756.

Percy, Thomas, and Robert Anderson. *The Correspondence of Thomas Percy and Robert Anderson*. Ed. W. E. K. Anderson. New Haven: Yale University Press, 1988.

Phillips, E. F. *Beekeeping: A Discussion of the Life of the Honeybee and of the Production of Honey*. New York: Macmillan, 1955.

Philosophical Transactions. Vol. 49. London, 1756.

Pinkus, Philip. *Grub St. Stripped Bare*. Hamden, Conn.: Archon Books, 1968.

Piozzi, Hester Lynch. *Anecdotes of the Late Samuel Johnson, LL.D., during the Last Twenty Years of His Life*. Ed. Arthur Sherbo. London: Oxford University Press, 1974.

Piper, David. *The Image of the Poet: British Poets and Their Portraits*. Oxford: Oxford University Press, 1982.*

Polybius. *The Histories*. Trans. R. W. Paton. 6 vols. London: Heinemann, 1954.

Pope, Alexander. *The Dunciad*. Ed. James Sutherland. 3d ed. London: Methuen, 1965.

―――. *Pastoral Poems and An Essay on Criticism*. Ed. E. Audra and A. Williams. London: Methuen, 1961.

Pope, Dudley. *At Twelve Mr. Byng Was Shot*. Philadelphia: J. B. Lippincott, 1962.

Preston, Thomas R. "Biblical Criticism, Literature, and the Eighteenth-Century Reader." In *Books and Their Readers in Eighteenth-Century England,* ed. Isabel Rivers. Leicester, U.K.: Leicester University Press, 1982.

Price, John Valdimir. "The Reading of Philosophical Literature." In *Books and Their Readers in Eighteenth-Century England,* ed. Isabel Rivers. Leicester, U.K.: Leicester University Press, 1982.

Priestley, Joseph. *The History and Present State of Electricity*. 2 vols. London, 1755. Reprint, New York: Johnson Reprint Corporation, 1966.

The Public Advertiser.

Purver, Margery. *The Royal Society: Concept and Creation*. Cambridge: MIT Press, 1967.

Quinlan, Maurice J. *Samuel Johnson: A Layman's Religion*. Madison: University of Wisconsin Press, 1964.

Ralph, James. *The Case of Authors by Profession or Trade*. London, 1758.

Raven, James. *British Fiction, 1750–1770: A Chronological Check-List of Prose Fiction Printed in Britain and Ireland*. Newark: University of Delaware Press, 1987.

———. *Judging New Wealth: Popular Publishing and Responses to Commerce in England, 1750–1800*. Oxford: Oxford University Press, 1992.

Read, Allen Walker. "Suggestions for an Academy in England in the Latter Half of the Eighteenth Century." *Modern Philology* 36 (1938–39): 145–56.

Reddick, Allen. *The Making of Johnson's Dictionary, 1747–1773*. Cambridge: Cambridge University Press, 1990.

Rivers, Isabel, ed. *Books and Their Readers in Eighteenth-Century England*. Leicester, U.K.: Leicester University Press, 1982.

Rogers, Pat. *Grub Street: Studies in a Subculture*. London: Methuen, 1972.

———. *Samuel Johnson*. Oxford, 1993.

———, ed. *The Johnson Encyclopedia*. Westport, Conn.: Greenwood Press, 1996.

Roper, Derek. *Reviewing before the Edinburgh, 1788–1802*. London: Methuen, 1978.

———. "Smollett's 'Four Gentlemen': The First Contributors to the *Critical Review*." *Review of English Studies* 10 (1959): 38–44.

Rose, Mark. *Authors and Owners: The Invention of Copyright*. Cambridge: Harvard University Press, 1993.

Rothstein, Eric. *Restoration and Eighteenth-Century Poetry, 1660–1780*. London: Routledge, 1981.

Rousseau, G. S. "Bramble and the Sulpher Controversy." *Journal of the History of Ideas* 28 (1967): 577–89.

———. "Science Books and Their Readers in the Eighteenth Century." In *Books and Their Readers in Eighteenth-Century England,* ed. Isabel Rivers. Leicester, U.K.: Leicester University Press, 1982.

Rousseau, Jean-Jacques. *The Discourse Which Carried the Praemium at the Academy of Dijon, in 1750. On this Question, Propos'd by the Said Academy, Whether the Reestablishment of Arts and Sciences Has Contributed to the Refining of Manners*. Trans. William Bowyer. London, 1751.

———. *A Discourse on Whether the Re-establishment of Arts and Sciences Has Contributed to Purify Our Morals*. Trans. Richard Wynne. London, 1752.

———. *The Discourse on Whether the Re-establishment of Arts and Sciences Has Contributed to the Refining of Manners*. 4th ed. Dublin, 1752.

Ruhe, Edward. "Thomas Birch, Samuel Johnson, and Elizabeth Carter." *PMLA* 78 (1958): 491–500.

Russell, Alexander. *The Natural History of Aleppo, and Parts Adjacent*. London, 1756.

Schwartz, Richard B. *Samuel Johnson and the New Science*. Madison: University of Wisconsin Press, 1971.

Sekora, John. *Luxury: The Concept in Western Thought, Eden to Smollett*. Baltimore: Johns Hopkins University Press, 1977.

———. *Samuel Johnson and the Problem of Evil*. Madison: University of Wisconsin Press, 1975.

Sewall, Richard B. "Dr. Johnson, Rousseau, and Reform." In *The Age of Johnson: Essays Presented to C. B. Tinker,* ed. F. W. Hilles, 307–17. New Haven: Yale University Press, 1949.

Shepard, Leslie. *The History of Street Literature: The Story of Broadside Ballads, Chapbooks, Proclamations, News-sheets, Election bills, Tracts, Pamphlets, Cocks, Catchpennies, and Other Ephemera.* Newton Abbot, U.K.: David & Charles, 1973.

Sherbo, Arthur. "Dr. Johnson and Joseph Warton's Virgil." *Johnsonian Newsletter* 18, no. 4 (1958): 12.

———. "Samuel Johnson and the *Gentleman's Magazine*, 1750–1755." In *Johnsonian Studies,* ed. Magdi Wahba. Cairo: Oxford University Press, 1962.

Sledd, J. H., and G. Kolb. *Dr. Johnson's Dictionary.* Chicago: University of Chicago Press, 1955.

Smollett, Tobias. *An Essay on the External Use of Water in a Letter to Dr. ****, with Particular Remarks upon the present Method of using the Mineral Waters at Bath in Somersetshire, and a Plan for Rendering Them More Safe, Agreeable, and Efficacious.* London, 1752.

Solomon, Harry M. *The Rise of Robert Dodsley: Creating the New Age of Print.* Carbondale: Southern Illinois University Press, 1996.

Sommerville, C. John. *The News Revolution in England: Cultural Dynamics of Daily Information.* Oxford: Oxford University Press, 1996.

Southerne, Thomas. *Oroonoko: A Tragedy.* London, 1759.

Speck, William A. *Society and Literature in England, 1700–1760.* Dublin: Gill & Macmillan, 1983.

———. *Stability and Strife: England, 1714–1760.* Cambridge: Harvard University Press, 1977.

Spector, Robert D. *English Literary Periodicals and the Climate of Opinion during the Seven Years' War.* The Hague: Mouton, 1966.

Sterling, Leonard A. *The Doctrine of Correctness in English Usage, 1700–1800.* New York: Russell and Russell, 1962.

Stewart, Larry. *The Rise of Public Science: Rhetoric, Technology, and Natural Philosophy in Newtonian Britain, 1660–1750.* Cambridge: Cambridge University Press, 1992.

Stimson, Dorothy. *Scientists and Amateurs: A History of the Royal Society.* New York: Henry Schuman, 1948.

Stone, George Winchester, and George M. Kahrl. *David Garrick: A Critical Biography.* Carbondale: Southern Illinios University Press, 1979.

Stone, George Winchester, ed. *The London Stage, Part 4: 1747–1776.* 3 vols. Carbondale: Southern Illinois University Press, 1962.

Straus, Ralph. *Robert Dodsley: Poet, Publisher, and Playwright.* London: John Lane, 1910.

Sullivan, Alvin, ed. *British Literary Magazines: The Augustan Age and the Age of Johnson.* Westport, Conn.: Greenwood Press, 1983.

Taylor, Richard. *Goldsmith as Journalist.* Rutherford, N.J.: Fairleigh Dickinson University Press, 1993.

Temmer, Mark. *Samuel Johnson and Three Infidels: Rousseau, Voltaire, Diderot.* Athens: University of Georgia Press, 1988.

Thomas, Donald. *A Long Time Burning: The History of Literary Censorship in England.* London: Routledge & Kegan Paul, 1969.

Tracy, Clarence. *The Artificial Bastard: A Biography of Richard Savage*. Cambridge: Harvard University Press, 1953.

———. "Johnson and the Common Reader." *Dalhousie Review* 57 (1977–78): 405–23.

Trapp, Joseph. *The Nature, Folly, Sin, and Danger, of Being Righteous Over-much*. London, 1739.

Turberville, A. S. *Johnson's England: An Account of the Life and Manners of His Age*. 2 vols. Oxford: Oxford University Press, 1933.

Tytler, William. *An Historical and Critical Enquiry into the Evidence Produced by the Earls of Murray and Morton, against Mary Queen of Scots*. Edinburgh, 1760.

The Universal Visiter, a Memorialist. For the Year 1756.

Vance, John A. "Johnson's Historical Reviews." In *Fresh Reflections on Samuel Johnson: Essays in Criticism*, ed. Prem Nath. Troy, N.Y.: Whitson Publishing, 1987.

———. *Samuel Johnson and the Sense of History*. Athens: University of Georgia Press, 1984.

Walker, Eric C. "Charlotte Lennox and the Collier Sisters: Two New Johnson Letters." *Studies in Philology* 95 (1998): 320–32.

Wardle, Ralph M. *Oliver Goldsmith*. Lawrence: University Press of Kansas, 1957.

Warton, Joseph. *An Essay on the Writings and Genius of Pope*. London, 1756.

White, Stephen. *Collateral Bee-Boxes; or, A New, Easy, and Advantageous Method of Managing Bees*. London, 1756.

———. *Collateral Bee-Boxes; or, A New, Easy, and Advantageous Method of Managing Bees*. 2d ed. London, 1759.

Wiles, Roy M. *Serial Publication in England before 1750*. Cambridge: Cambridge University Press, 1957.

Williams, Basil. *The Whig Supremacy: 1714–1760*. Rev. C. H. Stuart. Oxford: Clarendon, 1962.

Wiltshire, John. *Samuel Johnson in the Medical World: The Doctor and the Patient*. Cambridge: Cambridge University Press, 1991.

Wimsatt, William K. "Johnson on Electricity." *Review of English Studies* 23 (1947): 257–60.

———. *The Portraits of Alexander Pope*. New Haven: Yale University Press, 1965.

Woodruff, James F. "Johnson's *Rambler* in Its Contemporary Context." *Bulletin of Research in the Humanities* 35 (1982): 27–64.

Index